WTO and the Greater China

Nijhoff International Trade Law Series

VOLUME 8

The titles published in this series are listed at brill.nl/nint

WTO and the Greater China

Economic Integration and Dispute Resolution

By

Chien-Huei Wu

MARTINUS
NIJHOFF
PUBLISHERS

LEIDEN · BOSTON
2012

Library of Congress Cataloging-in-Publication Data

Wu, Chien-Huei.
WTO and the greater China : economic integration and dispute resolution / by Chien-Huei Wu.
p. cm. -- (Nijhoff international trade law series ; vol. 8)
Originally presented as the author's thesis (Ph. D.)--European University Institute, Florence, 2009, with title: The WTO memberships of China, Taiwan, Hong Kong, China and Macau, China : their contribution to judicial settlement of trade disputes.
Includes bibliographical references and index.
ISBN 978-90-04-20898-8 (hardback)
1. World Trade Organization. 2. Foreign trade regulation. 3. Dispute resolution (Law)--China. 4. China--Foreign economic relations--Taiwan. 5. China--Foreign economic relations--China--Hong Kong. 6. China--Foreign economic relations--China--Macau (Special Administrative Region) I. Title.

K4610.W83 2012
382'.920951--dc23

2012007322

This publication has been typeset in the multilingual "Brill" typeface. With over 5,100 characters covering Latin, IPA, Greek, and Cyrillic, this typeface is especially suitable for use in the humanities. For more information, please see www.brill.nl/brill-typeface.

ISSN 1877-7392
ISBN 978 90 04 20898 8 (hardback)
ISBN 978 90 04 20899 5 (e-book)

This book is printed on acid-free paper.

To my parents, my son and daughter and my wife.

CONTENTS

ACKNOWLEDGEMENT

Looking back from the vantage point of today, it seems that I have travelled a long way from Taipei to Florence, and then back to Taipei, from the first sentence of my doctoral thesis, the original form of this work to this acknowledgement. This journey in space and time has not always been pleasant. For much of the time, indeed, pressure outweighed pleasure. I am in debt to many for this work coming into existence.

I must express my immense gratitude to Professor Petersmann, gratitude which can never be overstated. He has always been ready to help me during the past few years. Without his guidance, this work would not have been possible. I also want to express my gratitude to Professor Cremona, who opened the door to the world of EU external relations, kindly offering me suggestions regarding my work in this aspect. I would also want to thank Professor Hsu and Lo for their guidance in the early stage of my legal research. I would also like to thank Ingeborg van der Laan from Martinus Nijhoff for her help during the publishing process and Emma Chang for her excellent editing job. Part of this work has been previously published in *Global Jurist*, *NTU Law Review*, *Contemporary Asia Arbitration*, and *European Yearbook of International Economic Law*. I am grateful to their generous permission for reprint.

This work tries to account the latest development and has thus undergone substantial revision, given that so much has been changed since I submitted my final draft for the thesis defence in European University Institute in 2009. The peculiar setting of the four Members of the Greater China in the WTO has much to explore. I hope this work would shed some light on this subject matter and offer the reader a better understanding of its complexities. Expecting the first book is just like expecting the first baby, even though it is only at the beginning of a long academic journey seemingly without end. Looking ahead, the words of Tennyson again come into my mind: to strive, to seek, to find, and not to yield.

Chien-Huei Wu
Taipei, 28 February 2012.

LIST OF ACRONYMS AND ABBREVIATIONS

ADA	Agreement on Implementation of Article VI of the General Agreement on Tariffs and Trade 1994 (Anti-Dumping Agreement)
ATCA	Agreement on Trade in Civil Aircraft
ATC	Agreement on Textile and Clothing
ASCM	Agreement on Subsidies and Countervailing Measures
ASG	Agreement on Safeguards
ARATS	Association for Relations across the Taiwan Straits (China)
BOFT	Bureau of Foreign Trade (Taiwan)
CAA	Civil Aviation Agency
CCP	Chinese Communist Party
CEPA	Closer Economic Partnership Arrangement
CFA	Court of Final Appeal (Hong Kong Special Administrative Region; Macau Special Administrative Region)
CFI	Court of First Instance
CPC	Central Product Classification of United Nations
CRTA	Committee on Regional Trade Agreements
DPP	Democratic Progress Party
DSB	Dispute Settlement Body (WTO)
DSU	Understanding on Rules and Procedures Governing the Settlement of Disputes
ECFA	Economic Cooperation Framework Agreement
ECHR	The Convention on the Protection of Human Rights and Fundamental Freedoms, or European Convention on Human Rights
ECJ	Court of Justice of the European Union
ECtHR	European Court of Human Rights
EU	European Union
FSC	Financial Supervision Committee
FTA	Free Trade Agreement
GATS	General Agreement on Trade in Services
GATT	General Agreement on Tariffs and Trade
GATT 1994	General Agreement on Tariffs and Trade 1994
GPA	Agreement on Government Procurement
HKBL	Hong Kong Basic Law
HKGCC	Hong Kong General Chamber of Commerce
HKSAR	Hong Kong Special Administrative Region

ICCPR	International Covenant on Civil and Political Rights
ITA	Information Technology Agreement
KMT	Kuomintang or the Nationalist Party
MABL	Macau Basic Law
MAC	Mainland Affairs Council (Taiwan)
MASAR	Macau Special Administrative Region
MOE	Ministry of Education
MOEA	Ministry of Economic Affairs (Taiwan)
MOF	Ministry of Finance (Taiwan)
MOFCOM	Ministry of Foreign Commerce (China)
MOFTEC	Ministry of Foreign Trade and Economic Cooperation (China)
MOI	Ministry of Interior
MOTC	Ministry of Transportation and Communications (Taiwan)
MRAs	Mutual Recognition Arrangements
NPC	National People's Congress
NPCSC	National People's Congress Standing Committee
OCMFA	Office of the Commissioner of the Ministry of Foreign Affairs
PNTR	Permanent Normal Trade Relation
PSI	Agreement on Pre-shipment Inspection
SAR	Special Administrative Region
SARS	Severe Acute Respiratory Syndrome
SEF	Straits Exchange Foundation (Taiwan)
SETC	State Economic and Trade Commission (China)
SPC	Supreme People's Court (China)
SPP	Supreme People's Procuratorate (China)
SPS Agreement	Agreement on Sanitary and Phytosanitary Measures
SSR	Second Supplementary Report
TAA	Taipei Airline Association
TPKM	Separate Customs Territory of Taiwan, Penghu, Kinmen and Matsu
TRIMs	Agreement on Trade-Related Investments Measures
TRIPS	Agreement on Trade-Related Aspects of Intellectual Property Rights
URAA	Uruguay Round Agreement Act
USITC	International Trade Commission of the United States
USTR	United States Trade Representative
VCLT	Vienna Convention on the Law of Treaties
WTO	World Trade Organisation
YCTPA	Yunlin County Towelling Producers' Technology Development Association

TABLE OF LEGISLATION

GATT/WTO Agreements and Documents

Agreement on Customs Valuation

Agreement on Government Procurement

Agreement on Implementation of Article VI of the General Agreement on Tariffs and Trade 1994

Agreement on Import Licensing Procedures

Agreement on Pre-shipment Inspection

Agreement on Safeguards

Agreement on Subsidies and Countervailing Measures

Agreement on Trade-Related Aspects of Intellectual Property Rights

Agreement on Trade-Related Investments Measures

Appellate Body's Working Procedures for Appellate Review

General Agreement on Tariffs and Trade 1994

General Agreement on Tariffs and Trade

General Agreement on Trade in Services

Protocol for the Accession of Portugal to the General Agreement on Tariffs and Trade

Protocol on the Accession of the People's Republic of China to the WTO

Report of the Working Party on the Accession of People's Republic of China

Report of the Working Party on the Accession of Taiwan, Penghu, Kinmen and Matsu

Understanding on Rules and Procedures Governing the Settlement of Disputes

Vienna Convention on the Law of Treaties

WTO Agreement

UN Declarations, Resolutions and Other Int'l Legal Instruments

Basic Principles on the Independence of Judiciary

Beijing Statement of Principles on the Independence of Judiciary in the LAWSAIA Region

Draft Bangalore Principles of Judicial Conduct

Draft Universal Declaration on the Independence of Judiciary

European Charter on the Statute for Judges and Explanatory Memorandum

European Convention on Human Rights

Joint Declaration of the Government of the United Kingdom of Great Britain and Northern Ireland and the Government of the People's Republic of China on the Question of Hong Kong

Principles and Guidelines on the Right to Fair Trial and Legal Assistance in Africa

Recommendation No. R(94) 12 of the Committee of Ministers to Member States on the Independence, Efficacy and Role of Judges

Universal Declaration of Human Rights

Bilateral Agreements in the Greater China

China-Hong Kong Closer Economic Partnership Arrangement

Regulation on Anti-Dumping and Countervailing Duties (China)

Regulation on Import Relief (Taiwan)

Regulation on Several Problems in the Trial of Trade-Related Administrative Litigation Cases (China)

Regulation on the Examination and Recognition of Chinese Diplomas (Taiwan)

Regulation on the Permission of Trade between Taiwan and China (Taiwan)

Regulations on the Application of Law in the Trial of Anti-Dumping Administrative Litigation Cases (China)

Statute Governing Relations between People of the Taiwan Area and Mainland Area (Taiwan)

Statute on Commercial Arbitration (Taiwan)

Statute on the Relations of Hong Kong and Macau (Taiwan)

Third Five-Year Court Reform Programme (China)

Trade Act of 1974 (United States)

TABLE OF CASES

GATT/WTO Disputes

European Court of Human Rights Cases

National Court Cases

CHAPTER ONE

INTRODUCTION

The constitutional feature of the World Trade Organisation (the WTO) – that it does not limit its membership to sovereign states – allows Taiwan, albeit as a separate customs territory, to accede to it and thus creates an unusual legal landscape in the international trading system, where both Taiwan and China enjoy full membership.[1] This peculiarity is further intensified when China's two separate-customs-territory Members – Hong Kong, China and Macau, China – are added to the picture. The interactions among the four WTO Members of China, Taiwan, Hong Kong, China and Macau, China (the Greater China)[2] are unique.

As Hong Kong and Macau became Contracting Parties to the General Agreement on Tariffs and Trade (GATT[3] or the Agreement) through the sponsorship of the United Kingdom (the UK) in 1986 and of Portugal in 1991 respectively and participated in and accepted the result of the Uruguay Round negotiations, they are among the founding Members of the WTO when this new organisation came into

[1] John H. Jackson observes that Taiwan crafted its application for GATT (and then the WTO) membership as a separate customs territory so that it would not offend China. He also mentions that Hong Kong, through the sponsorship of the United Kingdom, became a Contracting Party to GATT, and transcribed into being a subscribing Member of the WTO. However, it seems that Jackson fails to differentiate the accession procedures employed by these two Members. The rules governing their accession procedures differ. *See* J H Jackson, *Sovereignty, the WTO, and Changing Fundamentals of International Law* (Cambridge University Press, Cambridge 2006) 109. Jackson is also among those scholars who refer to the WTO Agreement as 'the WTO Constitution'. He emphasises on the institutional features of the WTO and the distribution of powers between the WTO and its Members. *See* J H Jackson, *The World Trade Organization: Constitution and Jurisprudence* (Royal Institute of International Affairs, London 1998) 47–51.

[2] In this work, China refers to 'People's Republic of China'. In peculiar cases, 'People's Republic of China' may be drawn in contrast to 'Republic of China', which is the official title of Taiwan. Taiwan's official nomenclature in the WTO is 'Separate Customs Territory of Taiwan, Penghu, Kinmen, and Matsu', abbreviated as 'Chinese Taipei'. When stressing Taiwan's WTO membership, this work will use this nomenclature or the abbreviation 'Chinese Taipei' but will use mostly Taiwan for convenience and better comprehension. As the terms 'Hong Kong, China' and 'Macau, China' are the official titles within the WTO, this work will employ these official nomenclatures when referring their status and activities in this organisation. When focusing their status of special administrative regions of China, this work will refer to them as the Hong Kong Special Administrative Region 'the HKSAR' and Macau Special Administrative Region 'the MASAR'. Otherwise, Hong Kong and Macau will mostly used for convenience. This work addresses to China, Taiwan, Hong Kong and Macau as 'the Greater China' without subscribing to the 'One China' policy or 'One China' principle. The term 'the Greater China' is used merely for the sake of convenience and the purpose of avoiding wordiness.

[3] To avoid confusion, the term GATT generally refers to GATT 1947; hence the 1994 agreement will be noted as the GATT 1994.

being in 1995. China and Taiwan acceded to the WTO at the Doha Ministerial Conference, where China's accession process was finalised on 10 November 2001 and Taiwan's one day later. Consequently, China became the 143rd Member of the WTO on 11 December 2001, while Taiwan, as a separate customs territory became the 144th Member on 1 January 2002.[4]

In view of this unique legal landscape within the WTO, this work thus aims to examine the integration of the Greater China at different fora: multilaterally; bilaterally or domestically. It also locates the subject matter in a broader context where the role of judges in external trade will be explored. It will use the interactions between these four WTO Members as an example to illustrate how dispute resolution mechanisms at different fora contribute to judicial settlement in trade disputes. Given the unusual complexities of these four Members in the WTO, this introductory chapter aims to offer some background knowledge on this issue. This introductory chapter will not only cover legal issues, but will also include some policy aspects. It will be comprised of three sections: the legal bases for these four Members' acquiring their memberships, Hong Kong's and Macau's accession processes to the GATT and China's and Taiwan's accessions to the WTO; and the main impacts of China's and Taiwan's memberships. This introductory chapter will end with a roadmap of this work, outlining the overall structure and main contents of each chapter.

I. Different Roads to Geneva: Legal Bases and Accession History

Hong Kong and Macau, as separate customs territories were sponsored by the UK and Portugal and became Contracting Parties to the GATT. With the certification of China, Hong Kong and Macau were able to sign the Marrakesh Agreement Establishing the World Trade Organisation and thus became founding Members of the WTO. China and Taiwan acceded to the WTO at the Doha Ministerial Conference in 2001. As GATT is the predecessor of the WTO, their accession procedures are nearly identical; it is thus logical to examine firstly the legal basis as well as the accession processes for Hong Kong and Macau to become Contracting Parties to the GATT and then explain how they became WTO Members. Therefore, I will firstly discuss the case of Hong Kong and Macau and then that of Taiwan and China. Based on this arrangement, the following will discuss the different legal bases for the accession procedures provided within the GATT and the WTO Agreement and then examine the accession processes of Hong Kong and Macau

[4] For background knowledge on China's accession to the WTO and its relationship to the Chinese Taipei's accession and to Hong Kong, China and Macau, China, *see* WTO, 'China's accession to the WTO and its relationship to the Chinese Taipei's accession and to Hong Kong, China and Macau, China' <http://www.wto.org/english/thewto_e/acc_e/chinabknot_feb01.doc> accessed 1 September 2011.

to GATT as well as to the WTO. This section will then follow by examining the accession history of Taiwan and China to the WTO.

A. *Hong Kong and Macau*

1. *Legal Basis of the Accession of Hong Kong and Macau to the GATT*

Apart from the twenty-three founding Contracting Parties, the GATT provided two procedures for nations and separate customs territories to become Contacting Parties to the Agreement. The common approach was governed by Article XXXIII of the GATT, which prescribed that a government or a government acting on behalf of separate customs territory could accede to the Agreement by a two-thirds majority vote 'on terms to be agreed between such government and the CONTRACTING PARTIES.'[5] No specific guidelines or criteria had been laid down concerning the 'terms to be agreed.' According to Jackson, the willingness to negotiate tariff concessions with the existing Contracting Parties, known as 'negotiating the ticket of admission', was essential to obtain enough votes to accede to the Agreement.[6]

Article XXVI:5 of the GATT provided a second path to becoming a Contacting Party to the Agreement was through the sponsorship of a parent country. Sub-paragraphs 5(a) and 5(c) of this Article prescribed:

> (a) Each government accepting this Agreement does so in respect of its metropolitan territory and of the other territories for which it has international responsibility, except such separate customs territories as it shall notify to the Executive Secretary to the CONTRACTING PARTIES at the time of its own acceptance.
>
> (c) If any of the customs territories, in respect of which a contracting party has accepted this Agreement, possesses or acquires full autonomy in the conduct of its external commercial relations and of the other matters provided for in this Agreement, such territory shall, upon sponsorship through a declaration by the responsible contracting party establishing the above-mentioned fact, be deemed to be a contracting party

This sponsorship procedure was primarily used by countries that became independent in the early 1960s. These newly independent countries had formerly been ruled by Contracting Parties to the GATT; the Agreement was therefore applicable to them through their parent countries.[7] The advantage of this sponsorship

---

[5] GATT, Art. XXXIII.

[6] J H Jackson, *The World Trading System: Law and Policy of International Economic Relations* (The MIT Press, Cambridge, Massachusetts 1989) 45. This accession process will be discussed in detail when analysing China and Taiwan's accession history.

[7] J H Jackson, et al., *Legal Problems of International Economic Relation: Case, Materials and Texts on the National and International Regulation of Transnational Economic Regulations* (4th edn West Group, St. Paul, Minn. 2002) 321.

approach was that these newly independent countries were not required to negotiate tariff concessions to obtain their tickets of admission. It was generally assumed that, after these colonies claimed independence and became GATT Contracting Parties through the sponsorship of their parent countries, the commitments as contained in the schedules of their parent countries originally negotiated on behalf of these colonies by their parent countries would continue to be applicable to them. However, these schedules tended to be very brief and often do not cover most of the tariff commitments; in some cases, there were no tariff schedules at all.[8] Importantly, this procedure was not limited to countries; separate customs territories that satisfied the requirement of 'possessing or acquiring full autonomy in the conduct of its external commercial relations and of the other matters provided for in this Agreement' could also accede to GATT through this sponsorship procedure.

Some elements of sub-paragraphs 5(a) and 5(c) of Article XXVI need further clarification. The first point relates to those territories for which a GATT Contracting Party has international responsibility. Paragraph 1 of the Provisional Application Protocol made it clear that the application of the Agreement had been limited to the metropolitan territories of Belgium, France, the Netherlands and the UK.[9] Paragraph 2 nonetheless provided that, the aforementioned countries could extend the provisional application of the Agreement to other territories with a notice to the Secretary-General of the United Nations.[10] In other words, the Agreement might be applicable to territories other than metropolitan ones, after the aforementioned countries notified their intent to include these territories.

The second issue relates to the criterion of 'full autonomy in the conduct of its external commercial relations and the other matters provided for in this Agreement', which was set in place to ensure that the customs territory in question had the right *de jure* and/or *de facto* to act on its own behalf and to fulfil

[8] Ibid 232–233.

[9] The GATT was essentially expected to be applied provisionally to the Contracting Parties, with the main objective to relax the government-mandated trade protections. When the GATT was being negotiated, another wider project, the International Trade Organisation (ITO), was also being formulated. The ITO was expected to serve as the institution responsible to administer the Havana Charter. Before concluding the ITO negotiation, the GATT participating governments decided to temporary apply the GATT by virtue of the Protocol of Provisional Application. The entry into force of the GATT on 1 January 1948 was thus meant to be provisional, pending on the conclusion of negotiation and the entry into force of the Havana Charter. Article XXIV of the GATT regulated the relationship between the GATT and the Havana Charter. However, due to the unwillingness of the Congress of the United States (the US) to ratify it on 6 December 1950, the Havana Charter never came into force. The provisional application of the GATT lasted until its transformation into the WTO. *See* P C Mavroidis, *The General Agreement on Tariffs and Trade: A Commentary* (Oxford University Press, Oxford 2005) 1–5.

[10] GATT, *Guide to GATT Law and Practice: Analytical Index* (6th edn WTO, Geneva 1995) 917.

its obligations.[11] Such information enabled the GATT Contracting Parties to judge on the legal autonomy of the separate customs territory concerned. Since 1963, the application for accession under Article XXVI:5(c), especially those made by the newly independent states, had been dealt by a certified Executive Secretary (Director General) to ensure that the conditions had been fully fulfilled. During the GATT era, four customs territories for which a parent country was responsible for their international responsibility were considered to have autonomy over their external commercial relations and other matters provided under the Agreement. Hong Kong and Macau were two of them.[12]

2. *The Accession Process of Hong Kong to the GATT and WTO*

Before Hong Kong joined the GATT as an independent entity, Hong Kong's participation in the GATT was governed by a declaration of the UK concerning the application of the Agreement to Hong Kong on 28 June 1948.[13] Hong Kong was sponsored by the UK in 1986 through Article XXVI:5(c) of the GATT and thus, as a separate customs territory, became a GATT Contracting Party. Being a signatory to and agreeing to be bound by the WTO Agreement, Hong Kong became one of its founding Members.[14]

Regarding Hong Kong's status as a separate customs territory within the WTO after China resumed its sovereignty in 1997, a communication circulated by Hong Kong on the eve before the handover to the WTO Secretariat and subsequently to the Members best clarifies the question at issue.[15] In this communication, some important historical events have been highlighted. It firstly notes that the Director General of the GATT circulated a communication issued by the UK on 24 April 1986 (document L/5986). In that 1986 communication, the UK declared that Hong Kong, being a separate customs territory, possessed full autonomy to conduct its external commercial relations and other matters listed in the GATT. The UK further stated that Hong Kong, according to Article XXVI:5(c) of the GATT and in accordance with the wishes of Hong Kong, should be deemed as a GATT

[11] Ibid 919.

[12] The other two were Lesotho and Liechtenstein, *see* GATT, *Status of Lesotho – De Facto Application of the GATT* (28 October 1966) L/2701; GATT, *Admission of Liechtenstein as a Contracting Party – Certification by the Director-General* (5 April 1994) L/7440.

[13] Mavroidis (n 9) 258.

[14] Although Hong Kong and Macau acceded to the GATT under the category of the separate customs territory just like Taiwan, the legal bases of their applications differ in that they were sponsored by the United Kingdom and Portugal. The precedents of Hong Kong and Macau also explain why China insisted that it should accede to the GATT before Taiwan. Only after China become a GATT Contracting Party can Taiwan join the GATT through China's sponsorship under Article XXVI:5(c) of the GATT.

[15] WTO, *Communication from Hong Kong* (3 June 1997) WT/L/218.

Contracting Party. Following the certification process, the Director-General then certified that since Hong Kong had met with the conditions of Article XXVI:5(c) of the GATT, it would become a GATT Contracting Party on 23 April 1986.[16]

At the same time, the Director General also circulated a communication issued by China (document L/5987), stating that Hong Kong would become a Special Administrative Region (SAR) when China resumed its sovereignty over Hong Kong and would retain its status as a separate customs territory, with the power to continue to decide on its economic and trade policies, and to maintain and develop its economic, trade and other businesses under the name of 'Hong Kong, China.' This communication also referred to the *Joint Declaration of the Government of the United Kingdom of Great Britain and Northern Ireland and the Government of the People's Republic of China on the Question of Hong Kong* (the *Sino-British Joint Declaration*) which in Section VI of Annex I specifically provided that the Hong Kong Special Administrative Region (the HKSAR) would be able to participate in relevant international organisations and international trade agreements, such as the GATT.[17]

Consequently, when the WTO came into force on 1 January 1995, Hong Kong, being a Contracting Party to the GATT and a full participant in the Uruguay Round, became an original member of the WTO as Hong Kong assumed all of the corresponding rights and obligations through formally accepting the Final Act Embodying the Results of the Uruguay Round of Multilateral Trade Negotiations. Finally, when China resumed its exercise of sovereignty over Hong Kong on 1 July 1997, Hong Kong began using the name 'Hong Kong, China'.[18]

3. *The Accession History of Macau to the GATT and WTO*

When Portugal acceded to the GATT, the protocol also identified Portugal's acceptance in respect of all its separate customs territories.[19] The GATT was thus applicable to Macau. In 1991, Macau was sponsored by Portugal through Article XXVI:5(c) of the GATT and, as a separate customs territory, became a GATT Contracting Party. Macau signed and approved the WTO Agreement and thus became one of the founding Members of the WTO.

In parallel to Hong Kong, on the eve before China resumed its sovereignty over Macau, Macau circulated a communication to the WTO Secretariat and

---

[16] Ibid 1.

[17] Ibid.

[18] Ibid 1–2.

[19] Portugal's Accession Protocol, in paragraph 11 provides, "Portugal accepting this Protocol, pursuant to sub-paragraph (b) of paragraph 10 does in respect of all Portugal's separate customs territories." *Protocol for the Accession of Portugal to the General Agreement on Tariffs and Trade* (1962) GATT BISD 11S/20, 24.

Members outlining key legal instruments and events relating to its membership.[20] In the communication distributed by Macau, similar information was presented. It referred to Portugal's communication on 14 January 1991 (document L/6806), where it is stated that Macau is a separate customs territory with full autonomy in its external commercial relations and other matters listed in the Agreement. Portugal's communication was circulated by the Director General's certification that Macau had become a Contracting Party to the GATT from 11 January 1991 since Macau had fulfilled with the requirements prescribed by Article XXVI:5(c) of the Agreement.[21] Simultaneously, China circulated a communication (document L/6807) to the Director General of the GATT where China stated that Macau would also become a SAR of China from the date that China resumed its sovereignty. Macau "would maintain the current social and economic systems and retain its economic and trade policies, on its own, using the name of 'Macau, China', maintain and develop relations, and conclude and implement agreements, with all States, regions and relevant international organisations in the economic, trade and other fields."[22] As a result, Macau became a GATT Contracting Party on 11 January 1991 and subsequently became a founding member of the WTO. As foreseen, Macau started to participate in the WTO under the name of 'Macau, China' after the hand-over on 20 December 1999.[23]

B. *Taiwan and China*

1. *From GATT to WTO: Legal Bases for the Accession of China and Taiwan*

Rules governing the accession procedures have not been significantly changed when the WTO came into being. The important feature – that of allowing customs territories to accede has been carried over. The parent country sponsorship option was, however, not reproduced in the WTO Agreement. The 'terms to be agreed' criterion remains to be the key assessing element for new Members to accede to this organisation. Similar to its predecessor, the WTO Agreement provides few hints on the interpretation of the 'terms to be agreed.' As a result, the GATT practices on the accession negotiations have great influence in shaping those in the WTO.[24] Following the GATT practices, the WTO, after receiving an application for accession, will establish a Working Party with the mandate to examine the accession processes, to conduct multilateral negotiations, and to draft an accession

[20] WTO, *Communication from Macau* (8 November 1999) WT/L/333.
[21] Ibid 1.
[22] Ibid.
[23] Ibid.
[24] Jackson, et al. (n 7) 234.

protocol. The accession decision will be finalised by the Ministerial Conference. Although the WTO Agreement provides a two-third majority voting mechanism, this is rarely used.[25]

Article XXXIII of the GATT and Article XII of the WTO Agreement govern the accession procedures. Article XXXIII of the GATT provides:

> A government not party to this Agreement, or a government acting on behalf of separate customs territory possessing full autonomy in the conduct of its external commercial relations and of the other matters provided for in this Agreement, may accede to this Agreement, on its own behalf or on behalf of that territory, on terms to be agreed between such government and the CONTRACTING PARTIES. Decisions of the CONTRACTING PARTIES under this paragraph shall be taken by a two-thirds majority.

Paragraph 1 of Article XII of the WTO Agreement reads as followed:

> Any State or separate customs territory possessing full autonomy in the conduct of its external commercial relations and of the other matters provided for in this Agreement and the Multilateral Trade Agreements may accede to this Agreement, on terms to be agreed between it and the WTO. Such accession shall apply to this Agreement and the Multilateral Trade Agreements annexed thereto.

These two articles put forward three key elements for the accession procedures: the subject eligible for WTO membership; the criterion of 'terms to be agreed' and the final accession decision. The term 'a government' defines the scope of the subjects eligible for the WTO accession. According to Jackson, the drafters of the GATT defined a GATT Contracting Party as 'a government' and not as 'a nation' or 'a state' in order to allow a government with less than complete sovereignty to join or participate in the GATT.[26] Among the twenty-three original GATT Contracting Parties, Ceylon (Sri Lanka), Burma (Myanmar), and Southern Rhodesia (Zimbabwe) were then not independent states. They were admitted to participate in the negotiation processes as the UK had clarified that they possessed 'full autonomy in the conduct of their external commercial relations and of the other matters provided for in the Agreement'.[27] It follows that apart from states, a separate customs territory 'possessing full autonomy in the conduct of its external commercial relations and of the other matters provided for' within the GATT or the WTO Agreement can also accede to the GATT or to the WTO.

---

[25] Jackson, et al. (n 7) 232.

[26] WTO, *Guide to GATT Law and Practice: Analytical Index* (n 10) 1017. *See* also the following discussion on Taiwan's accession.

[27] GATT, *Second Session of the Preparatory Committee of the United Nations Conference on Trade and Employment – Report of the Ad Hoc Sub-Committee of the Tariff Agreement Committee on Paragraph 3 of Article XXIV* (15 September 1947) E/PC/T198 <http://www.wto.org/gatt_docs/English/SULPDF/92290253.pdf> accessed 1 September 2011.

Regarding the conditions for accession, the criterion of the 'terms to be agreed between it and the WTO' ('terms to be agreed between such government and the CONTRACTING PARTIES') are not entirely clear. The WTO's *Secretariat's Technical Note on the Accession Process* (hereinafter 'the *Technical Note*')[28] offers some guidance on the WTO accession. The negotiation processes fall into two main categories: multilateral negotiations on rules to be applied between the acceding Member and existing WTO Members (notably, the Protocol on the Accession of People's Republic of China to the WTO, hereinafter 'China's Accession Protocol')[29] and bilateral (plurilateral) negotiations on market access.[30] After an application for accession is submitted, the WTO will establish a Working Party to conduct the multilateral negotiations. The Working Party will embody the market access commitments in bilateral negotiations into its Working Party Report on the applicant's accession and prepare a draft accession protocol. The final accession decision will need to be approved at the WTO Ministerial Conference.

When China and Taiwan applied for GATT memberships, and subsequently WTO memberships, some political concerns, especially the so-called 'One China' policy, had been raised. Thus, in order to resolve the political controversies, Taiwan chose to submit its application as a separate customs territory. This was partly because of the political reality. The following will be devoted to the accession process of China and Taiwan; emphasis will be placed upon multilateral and bilateral negotiations.

2. *China's Accession History to the GATT and WTO*

It took China fifteen years to accede to the WTO. China's accession is widely regarded as the most significant event in the WTO to date.[31] The reason why China is so unique remains contested and unsettled. As argued by Alexandroff and others, there were continuous concerns among some existing Members which feared that their domestic markets would be swamped by China's large and potentially enormous productive capacity. Besides, China's non-market economy characterised by its state intervention and huge amount of trade volume contributed by

[28] WTO, *Technical Note on the Accession process* (1 November 2000) WT/ACC/7/Rev.2. The technical note also refers to a set of procedures covered in WT/ACC/1, 4, 5, 8 and 9, which are drawn by the WTO Secretariat in consultation with Members.

[29] WTO, *The Accession of the People's Republic of China – Decision of 10 November 2001* (23 November 2001) WT/L/432.

[30] Ibid 3.

[31] *See, e.g.*, J H Jackson, 'The Impacts of China's Accession to the WTO' in D Z Cass, et al. (eds), *China and the World Trading System: Entering the New Millennium* (Cambridge University Press, Cambridge; New York 2003) 19. Jackson regards China's accession as the most significant activity in WTO's 'seven-year life'. For an overview of the accession process, *see* R Bhala, 'Enter the Dragon: An Essay on China's WTO Accession Saga' (2000) 15 American University International Law Review 1469.

state-owned enterprises deepened their worries, as the experiences of the GATT in integrating non-market economy, such as Poland proved to be mostly unpleasant. Moreover, the accession of China might exemplify the weakness of the governance and regulatory capacity in the existing world trading system.[32]

Although Republic of China[33]was one of the twenty three founding GATT Contracting Parties, after the Chinese civil war between the Chinese Communist Party (the CCP) and the Nationalist Party (Kuomintang, the KMT) between 1945 to 1949, the defeated Nationalist Party retreating to Taiwan notified the GATT that Republic of China would be withdrawing from the GATT system. In 1965, the Taiwanese government requested for an observer status in the GATT and such a request was granted. Nonetheless, the observer status was subsequently removed in 1971, following the United Nations General Assembly Resolution 2758 (XXVI) claiming that it would recognise the People's Republic of China as the only legitimate government of China. As the Chairman, Carlos Besa declared that GATT would follow decisions of the United Nations on essential political matters. In light of the aforementioned Resolution, he invited Taiwan's representative to withdraw. The Chairman then enquired whether there was a wish to take vote on this issue. Since no request had been made, he then declared that a consensus had been reached to remove Taiwan's observer status; some delegations had subsequently stated that they did not agree with this consensus.[34]

In 1986, nearly thirty years after Taiwan's withdrawal from the GATT, the People's Republic of China notified the GATT Secretariat of its wish to resume its status as a GATT Contracting Party[35] and its willingness to renegotiate on the terms of its membership. A GATT Working Party was established in 1987 and was turned into a WTO Working Party when the WTO was established in 1995. There have been several decisive events that have affected the pace and the course of this negotiation. Prior to the Tiananmen massacre, there were considerable measurable progress but since this massacre, negotiation was blocked for almost two and a half years. Although China had participated in the Uruguay Round negotiations, it failed to become one of the original Members of the WTO because its negotiation had not been concluded at that stage. At the Singapore Ministerial Conference, China failed make a deal with the United States (the US) which prevented it from

---

[32] A S Alexandroff, et al. (eds), *China and the Long March to Global Trade: The Accession of China to the World Trade Organization* (Routledge, London; New York 2002) 231–32.

[33] When the GATT was negotiated and concluded, the People's Republic of China has not yet been established.

[34] GATT, *Contracting Parties – Twenty-seventh Session – Summary Record of the First Meeting – Held at the Palais des Nations, Geneva, on Tuesday, 16 November 1971* (19 November 1971) SR.27/1, 1–4.

[35] It is also recalled in the preamble of China's Accession Protocol that China was an original Contracting Party to the GATT 1947.

successfully acceding to the WTO at this meeting. However, the bombing of Chinese Embassy in Belgrade in May 1999 brought about political change in the US and made it possible for the US and China to make a deal.[36]

Among the bilateral negotiations on market access, the Sino-EU and Sino-US bilateral agreements are of utmost importance in terms of the degree of liberalisation. The Sino-US agreement on China's accession to WTO was bundled to the US' conferral of Permanent Normal Trade Relation status (the PNTR status) on China.[37] It was not until November 1999 and May 2000 when China finally made deals with the European Union (the EU) and the US and paved its way to Geneva. These two bilateral agreements are briefly noted below.

When testifying before the House of Representatives, the former United States Trade Representative Ambassador Barshefsky claimed the bilateral WTO accession agreement between the US and China to be comprehensive and fully enforceable. These commitments would be included into China's Working Party Report and constitute a part of China's legal obligations under the WTO. Chinese market would be immediately open to the US enterprises.[38] The bilateral agreement is dealt with all agricultural products, industrial goods and services sectors; compromise was reached on some unresolved key issues such as the import surge mechanism, anti-dumping and telecommunications. The highlights of the Sino-US bilateral agreement include trading rights, distribution services, tariffs, non-tariff barriers, information technology products, chemicals, wood and paper products, autos, domestic support and export subsidies in agricultural products, sanitary and phytosanitary standard, specific service areas, like banking, insurance, security, telecommunication and the audiovisual services. The Sin-EU bilateral

---

[36] J L Gertler, 'Negotiating China's Protocol of Accession' in A S Alexandroff, et al. (eds), *China and the Long March to Global Trade : the Accession of China to the World Trade Organization* (Routledge, London, New York 2002) (n 32) 23. *See* also G Yang and J Cheng, 'The Process of China's Accession to the WTO' (2001) 4 Journal of International Economic Law 297.

[37] The Normal Trade Relation is a concept in the US trade law, which is similar to the Most-Favoured-Nation Treatment. Under the US Trade Act of 1974, the Normal Trade Relation status can be conditionally granted to non-market economies. Since the principle of Most-Favoured-Nation Treatment is one of the core WTO principles, it would be applied between the US and China. Therefore, the US could not review annually whether to grant the Normal Trade Relation status. For further discussion on PNTR in relations to China's accession, *see* A S Alexandroff, 'Concluding China's Accession to the WTO: The U.S. Congress and Permanent Most Favored Nation Status for China' (1998) 3 UCLA International Law & Foreign Affairs 23. *See* also S A Rhode and J H Jackson, 'United States law and China's WTO accession process' (1999) 2 Journal of International Economic Law 497; C Tiefer, 'Sino 301: How Congress can effectively review relations with China after WTO accession' (2001) 34 Cornell International Law Journal 55.

[38] United States Congress House, *US-China Bilateral Trade Agreement and the Accession of China to the WTO: Hearing before the Committee on Ways and Means, House of Representatives, One Hundred Sixth Congress, Second Session, 16 February 2000* (US GPO, Washington 2001) 39–45.

agreement also touches upon non-market economy dumping methodology, textiles and state-owned and state-invested companies.[39]

With regard to the Sino-EU bilateral agreement, similar concerns were also noted.[40] The agreement is divided into different sectors: industrial goods, trade in services and agriculture. It also covers horizontal issues. Similar emphasis was placed on sensitive sectors such as agricultural products, motor vehicles, telecommunication, insurance and distribution services. The Sino-EU bilateral agreement also addresses non-discrimination and transparency requirements, rules on export restriction and state monopoly.[41]

The negotiation between China and the EU was closely linked to that between China and the US. As Algieri points out, whereas the Sino-US agreement had already been concluded during the Sino-EU bilateral negotiation, the results of the Sino-EU negotiation would eventually affect the ongoing US congressional debates on granting PNTR status to China.[42] In fact, when the Sino-US agreement was signed in November 1999, many topics that were also important to the EU had been clarified. While the EU surely wished to obtain more concessions from China, China would not readily agree with its demand; otherwise, China would have created itself obstacle for obtaining the PNTR status.

3. *Taiwan's Accession History to the GATT and WTO*

As provided by Article XXXIII of the GATT and Article XII of WTO Agreement, 'any state or separate customs territory' can apply for the accession. Instead of using its official name (Republic of China), Taiwan chose to accede to GATT and, subsequently, the WTO under the name of 'Separate Customs Territory of Taiwan, Penghu, Kinmen and Matsu' (TPKM). It aimed to avoid the political difficulty known as the 'One China' policy. However, Taiwan's application under the category of the separate customs territory is governed by Article XXXIII, not by

---

[39] *See* White House National Economic Council, *Summary of the US-China Bilateral WTO Agreement* (15 November 1999), reprinted in 16 International Trade Reporter (BNA) 1888 (17 November 1999) <http://www.uschina.org/public/991115a.html> accessed 1 September 2011.

[40] 'The Sino-EU Agreement on China's Accession to the WTO: Results of the Bilateral Negotiations' <http://trade.ec.europa.eu/doclib/docs/2003/april/tradoc_111851.pdf> accessed 1 September 2011; *see* also, 'Highlights of the EU-China agreement on WTO' <http://trade.ec.europa.eu/doclib/docs/2003/september/tradoc_113818.pdf> accessed 1 September 2011.

[41] The automobile trade is a main target of complaints against China in the WTO Dispute Settlement Mechanism. The Panel found against China and the findings are mostly upheld by the Appellate Body. See Panel Report on *China – Measures Affecting the Imports of Automobile Parts* (WT/DS339/AB/R, WT/DS340/AB/R, WT/DS342/AB/R, adopted 12 January 2009, upheld (WT/DS339/R) as modified by Appellate Body Report, WT/DS339/AB/R, WT/DS340/AB/R, WT/DS342/AB/R.

[42] F Algieri, 'EU Economic Relations with China: An Institutionalist Perspective' in R L Edmonds (ed), *China and Europe since 1978: A European Perspective* (Cambridge University Press, Cambridge 2002) 75.

Article XXVI:5(c) as claimed by China. This indicates Taiwan possesses effective autonomy and independence in its external relations so that it can act on its own behalf.[43]

This application was immediately objected by China. In a letter to the Director General, China's Representative argued that the application was 'utterly illegal'[44] and should thus be ignored. China contested that the application would be *de jure* invalid without its confirmation. According to China, Taiwan was one of its local governments sharing similar status to Hong Kong, China and Macau, China. In China's view, its confirmation about Taiwan being a separate customs territory of China was indispensable for the application to be valid. This controversy remained the focus of debates as to whether the GATT should establish a Working Party to examine Taiwan accession. Even at the final stage of Taiwan's accession process, China tried to change Taiwan's official name into 'China's Separate Customs Territory of Taiwan, Penghu, Kinmen, and Matsu' but this was objected to by the US.

On 29 September 1992, the Chairman of the General Council, Mr. B. K. Zutshi, made an important statement concerning the accession of Chinese Taipei. He stated that he had carried out extensive consultations on the subject of establishing a Working Party to examine the potential accession of the Separate Customs Territory of Taiwan, Penghu, Kinmen, and Matsu. He found that, "all Contracting Parties had acknowledged the view that there was only one China, as expressed in the United Nations General Assembly Resolution 2758 of 25 October 1971."[45] Based on this acknowledgement, the chairman further noted that many Contracting Parties, therefore, had agreed with the view of China that Chinese Taipei, as a separate customs territory, should not accede to the GATT before China itself. However, some Contracting Parties did not share this view. Nevertheless, there was a great desire to establish a Working Party for Chinese Taipei.[46]

The Chairman then concluded that there was a consensus among the GATT Contracting Parties on (1) continuing the work of the Working Party on China's status as a Contracting Party (2) establishing a Working Party for Chinese Taipei, and (3) enforcing the sequence of these separate accession applications. With regard to the sequence of these two applications, he concluded:

---

[43] P L Hsieh, 'Facing China: Taiwan's Status as a Separate Customs Territory in the World Trade Organization' (2005) 39 Journal of World Trade 1195, 1199–1200.

[44] 'China takes early Action to Block Taiwan's GATT membership application' (1990) 7 *International Trade Reporter* (BNA) No.4 (24 Jan. 1990) 131, citing S Chan, 'Taiwan's Application to the GATT: A New Urgency with the Conclusion of the Uruguay Round' (1994) 2 Indiana Journal of Global Legal Studies 275, 275. For this historical controversy, *see* also Y Qin, 'GATT Membership for Taiwan: An Analysis in International Law' (1992) 7 New York University Journal of International Law and Politics 1059.

[45] GATT, *Minutes of Meeting – Held in the Centre William Rappard on 4–5 November 1992* (27 October 1992) C/M/259 3.

[46] Ibid.

> "[T]he Council should give full consideration to all views expressed, in particular that the Council should examine the report of the Working Party on China and adopt the Protocol for the PRC's accession before examining the report and adopting the Protocol for Chinese Taipei, while noting that the working party reports should be examined independently."[47]

It was therefore agreed by the GATT Contracting Parties that, albeit with the understanding that the examination of China's Working Party Report and the adoption of that set of accession protocol should take precedence over those of Taiwan, these two accession applications should be dealt independently. A compromise regarding Taiwan's status had been reached; a Working Party to examine Taiwan's application was then finally established at the meeting of 29 September 1992.

As China and Taiwan eventually acceded to the WTO in 2001, the sequence controversy lost its relevance. Nonetheless, other elements put forward by this Chairman's statement is still of great importance, as they may help to clarify the legal effect of the 'One China' policy within the WTO, in light of the potential argument that since Taiwan is a province of China it has no competence to make a complaint against China, its own central government.[48] The first paragraph of the Working Party Report on the Accession of the Separate Customs Territory of Taiwan, Penghu, Kinmen and Matsu refers to the 29 September-1 October 1992 meeting minutes (document C/M/259). However, the context of the Working Party Report makes it clear that the reference is only meant to indicate the intent of the General Council to establish a Working Party to examine Taiwan's accession application as a separate customs territory under Article XXXIII of the GATT. In this introductory paragraph, there is no reference to the Chairman's statement, particularly on the acknowledgement of the United Nations Resolution and the priority of China's accession. Further, paragraph 224 of Taiwan's Working Party Report, which lists all paragraphs thereof containing legal commitments and is incorporated into Taiwan's Accession Protocol and thus becomes part of Taiwan's WTO obligations, does not refer to paragraph 1. Therefore, this introductory paragraph referring to the meeting minutes of 29 September-1 October 1992 does not constitute a legal commitment binding on Taiwan.

Moreover, the Chairman's statement reads, "all Contracting Parties had acknowledged the view that there was only one China, as expressed in the United

---

[47] Ibid 4 (*emphasis added*).

[48] It is argued the WTO is more politicised than GATT. The accessions of China and Taiwan contribute to this politicisation process. The recent dispute concerning the title of Taiwan's mission in the WTO correspondence directory, also known as the blue book, and China's blocking Taiwan from acceding to the Government Procurement Agreement are cited as the evidences for this argument. *See* A Reich, 'The Threat of the Politicization of the WTO' (2005) 26 University of Pennsylvania Journal of International Economic Law 779, 807–808.

Nations General Assembly Resolution 2758 of 25 October 1971."[49] The verb 'acknowledge' neither imposes obligations nor confers any rights. In addition, although Taiwan did accede to the WTO a day after China, it should nevertheless be noted that conflicting views remain on many issues, even on the approach to give priority to China's accession.

From Taiwan's perspective, its accession to WTO is vital to its economy and diplomatic importance. Although most of the negotiation processes had been finished by 1999,[50] the above-mentioned concerns expressed by the Chairman prevented Taiwan from finalising its accession package. It was not until China's accession had been accepted that Taiwan was also admitted, on the very next day, to the WTO. Apart from this 'political' aspect of Taiwan's accession, some Contracting Parties were concerned about Taiwan's potential claim of being a developing country. As a result, to ease the accession procedure, Taiwan declared that it would not 'claim any right granted under WTO Agreements to developing country Members or to a Member in the process of transforming its economy from a centrally-planned into a market, free-enterprise economy.'[51]

II. The Four Members of the Greater China in the WTO

A. *WTO Membership as an Impulse to China's Legal Reform*

According to Bhattasali, there are two major approaches circling the 'China in the WTO' debates. The first emphasises on the legal rights and obligations under the WTO law and thus underlines the importance to ensure that China meets with its legal commitments and enjoys its legal rights. The second strives to see how China's membership may serve as a key component in restructuring the Chinese economy. China's WTO membership may act as a vehicle to further China's economical and political reforms, given that China's policy-makers also perceive China's WTO accession as a means to fulfil its external and internal strategic goals. Externally, the WTO membership is aimed to facilitate the peaceful emergence of China as a great trading nation and to avoid trade tensions commonly associated with the emergence of new major trading powers. Internally, China aims to, by virtue of the WTO membership, accelerate the process of domestic reform, to

[49] GATT, *Minutes of Meeting – Held in the Centre William Rappard on 4–5 November 1992* (27 October 1992) C/M/259 3.

[50] The Taiwan-US agreement was signed on 20 February 1998 while the Taiwan-EU agreement was signed on 23 July 1998.

[51] WTO, *Report of the Working party on the Accession of the Separate Customs Territory of Taiwan, Penghu, Kinmen and Matsu (hereinafter TPKM Working Party Report)* (5 October 2001) WT/ACC/TPKM/18, para. 8.

lock in the progress of economic liberalisation and make the economic reform irreversible with the disciplines of WTO rules.[52] The WTO Agreement and China's Accession Protocol can thus guide China on these reforms.

Different from other WTO accession protocols, China's Accession Protocol is not a standardised document and it presents itself as a unique document in the WTO treaty structure. Covering a wide range of subjects, China's Accession Protocol prescribes a set of special rules applicable solely between China and other WTO Members. Among these rules, the obligation to provide an independent and impartial judicial review appears most unusual. Under Section 2(D) of the accession protocol, China shall establish, or designate, and maintain impartial and independent tribunals to promptly review all administrative actions relating to the implementation of laws, regulations, judicial decisions and administrative rulings on any general application referred within Article X:1 of GATT 1994, Article VI of General Agreement on Trade in Services (GATS) and all relevant provisions within the trade-related aspects of intellectual property rights (TRIPS) Agreement. These review procedures should also provide an opportunity to appeal the administrative decisions to a judicial body. Such arrangement indicates other WTO Members' concerns on China's capacity and willingness to implement its legal obligations.

The inclusion of domestic judicial review is an instrument to ensure China's faithful implementation of its WTO obligations, which pre-supposes that an independent and impartial judicial review would strengthen the protection of the rights and interests of China's trading partners. While this presupposition may well sustain, what remains unclear is whether and how China could fulfil its judicial review obligation. Besides, one has to further explore how the WTO panel/Appellate Body should review this case should a compliant regarding China's failure to implement this obligation is brought before the WTO Dispute Settlement Mechanism.

During China's first Trade Policy Review, China's faithful implementation of this independent and impartial judicial review was questioned. During that Trade Policy Review, the US voiced its concerns with respect to the role played by the Chinese Communist Party during the proceedings and decisions of China's Supreme People's Court (the SPC) and the lower courts. The Chinese government replied as follows:

> According to the Constitution, the Organic Law of the People's Courts of the People's Republic of China and the Judges Law of the People's Republic of China, the people's

[52] D Bhattasali, et al., 'Impacts and Policy Implications of WTO Accession for China' in D Bhattasali, et al. (eds), *China and the WTO: Accession, Policy Reform, and Poverty Reduction Strategies* (World Bank, Washington, D.C. 2004) 1.

> courts exercise judicial power independently and are not subject to interference by any administration, public organization or individual. When exercising this power, the people's courts shall strictly abide by the Constitution, the Organic Law of the People's Courts of the People's Republic of China and other substantial and procedural laws related to the specific cases.[53]

However, this reply did not fully answer the question. Although China's reply indicated that Chinese's courts are not subject to the interference of 'any administration, public organisation or individual', it was not clear whether the Chinese Communist Party would fall into these three categories. In addition, Chinese government did not mention the requirements for Chinese courts to be responsible to the National People's Congress (the NPC) and did not clarify the relationship the relationship between Chinese Communist Party and the NPC.

Notwithstanding the other Members' concerns as mentioned, China does see its accession to the WTO as a vehicle to enhance its domestic reform. According to Halverson, China's accession "acts not just as a lever to force reform, but it also serves to lock in economic reform and make it irrevocable."[54] Although China joined the WTO with the main objective of enhancing its economic development,[55] the extensive rule-of-law obligations and commitments set out in China's Accession Protocol, especially the obligation to establish an independent and impartial judicial review, not only affect the development of China's trade regimes, but also have overwhelming impacts on its on-going legal reform. Halverson furhter notes, "[f]or China, continuing economic development and prosperity depend upon a continued growth and evolution of Chinese constitutionalism, rule of law, and, in particular, an independent judicial review."[56] The WTO membership thus acts as an instrument for China to perform its legal reform.

---

[53] WTO, *Trade Policy Review Body – 19 and 21 April 2006 – Trade Policy Review – People's Republic of China – Minutes of Meeting – Addendum* (11 September 2006) WT/TPR/M/161/Add.2, 14.

[54] K Halverson, 'China's WTO Accession: Economic, Legal and Political Implications' (2004) 27 Boston College International and Comparative Law Review 319, 334.

[55] China's accession to the WTO was a state-led, leadership-driven and top-down political process. While the reformists fought for the accession, the conservatives remained reluctant. Reformists aimed to join the WTO with the balancing of the costs and benefits of the WTO membership. It was expected that the WTO accession would give China a considerable comparative advantage in the global market. It would force state-owned enterprises to operate in a more efficient manner when faced with foreign competitions and may also help to fight against corruption, or even to elevate China's political status in the international scene. It is argued that three factors – elite politics, bureaucratic politics and foreign pressure – contributed to the shaping of China's accession policy. *See* H Feng, *The Politics of China's Accession to the World Trade Organization* (Routledge, London, New York 2006).

[56] M U Killion, 'China's Amended Constitution: Quest for Liberty and Independent Judicial Review' (2005) 4 Washington University Global Studies Law Review 43, 48. However, some literature has also argued that the judicial independence and the protection offered by the judiciary are still very limited due to the interference, caseloads, and high withdrawal rates. *See* V M Hung, 'China's WTO Commitment on Independent Judicial Review: Impact on Legal and Political Reform' (2004) 52 American Journal of Contemporary Law 77, 82–89.

China's Accession Protocol is thus cited as an example to justify Petersmann's arguments of domestic constitutional function of WTO rules which emphasises how WTO rules may control domestic law or policy making. According to Petersmann, the WTO law should not be interpreted in purely economic terms and that legal and political objectives are no less important than trade liberalisation. WTO law shares major features of constitutionalism: it not only employs formal constitutional techniques but also includes various substantive constitutional principles.[57] WTO law can be conceived as a part of the multilevel constitutional framework that shapes the form of multilevel trade governance. Based on multilevel constitutional framework, Petersmann thus argues that China's accession to the WTO contributes to its establishment of an open market and of rule of law by virtue of these international obligations relating to private rights to trade, intellectual property rights protection, access to judicial review.[58]

B. *Taiwan's Return to the International Trading System*

As an island poor in natural resources, external trade has always played an indispensable role in Taiwan's economic development. However, Taiwan had been excluded from the international trading system since its observer status in the GATT was removed in 1971. Taiwan has been anxious to re-join the international trading system for various reasons. In the first place, economic interests are certainly of great importance. Since its withdrawal from the United Nations, Taiwan maintains diplomatic relations with only very limited countries, which effectively prevents Taiwan from concluding bilateral agreements regarding National Treatment, Most-Favoured-Nation treatment or market access. Taiwan thus turns to the multilateral framework under the GATT/WTO. If Taiwan had been a Contracting Party to GATT, the GATT rules would apply to trade activities between Taiwan and its trading partners and recourses under the disputes settlement mechanism would be available. The multilateral framework thus provides

[57] E U Petersmann, 'Multilevel Trade Governance in the WTO Requires Multilevel Constitutionalism' in C Joerges and E U Petersmann (eds), *Constitutionalism, Multilevel Trade Governance and Social Regulation* (Hart Publishing, Oxford and Portland, Oregon 2006) 5–58. Petersmann argues that WTO law uses the formal techniques of (1) the distinction of long term constitutional rules and post-constitutional decision making; (2) the legal primacy of the WTO agreement over conflicting provisions in the Multilateral Trade Agreements annexed the WTO Agreement; and (3) the protection of freedom of trade, Most-Favoured-Nation Treatment, National Treatment, private property rights and rule of law subject to broad exceptions to protect public interests. He also argues that four substantive principles have been included in WTO law: separation of powers; rule of international law; respect of universal human rights; and the concern of social justice.

[58] E U Petersmann, *Dispute Prevention, Dispute Settlement and Justice in International Economic Law* (forthcoming).

an opportunity for Taiwan to safeguard its trade interests. For these economic reasons, accession to the GATT and the WTO appears very appealing and seems to be the only solution. The constitutional feature of the WTO concerning the eligibility of being a WTO Member has enabled Taiwan to find a way to re-enter into the international trading system.

In addition to economic concerns, Taiwan's accession to the WTO has also political and diplomatic implications. As Charnovitz points out, Taiwan sees its WTO membership as an opportunity to return to the international plane because of its nearly universal membership and its ever-widening domains, such as human rights and environment issues.[59] Although the mandate of the WTO Agreement concerns mainly economic aspects, the WTO nevertheless provides Taiwan with an opportunity to posture itself in the international scene.

C. *Cross-Taiwan-Strait Trade Relations*

The changing political economy corresponds with the evolution of Taiwan's trade policy toward China. In 2000, Taiwan experienced a historic political change. The long-ruling KMT lost the presidential election and became the opposition party while the Democratic Progress Party (the DPP) became the ruling party. During the KMT government, the former President Lee Teng-Huei had a dominated role in Taiwan's trade policy toward China.[60] Due to the fear of the potential hollowing-out Taiwan's industries to China, he thus proposed a 'No Haste, Be Patient' policy and maintained various restrictions on trade and investment with China. In addition, in order to reduce Taiwan's economic dependence on China, he also proposed to diverse Taiwan's export to Southeast Asian countries in the so-called 'Go South' policy.[61]

Under the DPP government, this 'No Haste, Be Patient' regulatory policy was mostly upheld with slightly modifications. Although the DPP claimed its China policy as 'Positive Openness with Effective Management', restrictions on trade and investment activities had nevertheless persisted. There thus existed an imbalance between the political dialogue and the economic exchange between Taiwan and China. It was normally referred to as 'political chill/economic zeal', which highlighted the contradiction between economic interdependence and political hostility.

[59] *See, e.g.*, S Charnovitz, 'Taiwan's WTO Membership and its International Implication' (2006) 1 Asian Journal of WTO and International Health Law and Policy 401, 401–402.

[60] It is also President Lee Teng-Huei who, in an interview with Deutsche Welle radio station on 7 July 1999, defines the relation between Taiwan and China as 'a special relationship between State and State'.

[61] On Taiwan's 'Go South' policy, *see* S-Y Peng, 'Economic Relations between Taiwan and Southeast Asia: A Review of Taiwan's 'Go South' Policy' (1998) 16 Wisconsin International Law Journal 639.

This situation thus got some WTO Members concerned. When pursuing its WTO membership, Taiwan had hoped that the WTO memberships of Taiwan and China would help to normalise the cross-Taiwan-strait trade relations. As both Taiwan and China opted not to take non-application approaches toward each other, it was believed that trade relations between Taiwan and China could channel more smoothly through the WTO. Nevertheless, even after Taiwan's accession to the WTO in 2002, Taiwan's external trade with China was still subject to many restrictions and had not been fully liberalised. Types of restrictions ranged from the implementation of the market access commitments and the infringement of Most-Favoured-Nation Treatment and/or National Treatment to various restrictions on outbound investments toward China.

Concerns had been strongly voiced by many other Members, as illustrated in Taiwan's first Trade Policy Review conducted on 20 and 22 June 2006. Many WTO Members spoke out on their concerns regarding the cross-Taiwan-strait trade relations.[62] Taiwan's representative claimed that the cross-strait relations has been 'special and complex', 'unique and complicated', and 'not a simple trade issue'. In response to Taiwan's assertions, the Chinese representative commented that Taiwan could not excuse itself from running counter to the fundamental principles of non-discrimination and Taiwan should realise that this argument would be difficult to justify, especially given that four years had passed, and various restrictions persisted.[63]

The commencement of the Ma government in 2008 marked a new era for the economic integration between Taiwan and China since restrictive measures against China have been largely lifted. Among these liberalisation measures, the inking of the Economic Cooperation Framework Agreement (the ECFA) between Taiwan and China is an unprecedented step and it has attracted much attention. Given its nature of framework agreement, the ECFA thus instructs the Parties to further negotiate on trade in goods, trade in services and establishing a suitable dispute settlement mechanism.

D. *Trade Policy of Hong Kong and Macau and Economic Integration Into China*

In terms of the economic developments in Hong Kong and Macau, three events are of great significance: the GATT/WTO memberships; the handover to China;

[62] Apart from China, which had indicated Taiwan has violated many WTO rules, notably the non-discriminatory principle, Switzerland, Japan, EC, and other Members had also questioned about Taiwan's restrictions on the cross-strait trade. The discussant of the Trade Policy Review also expressed similar concerns on this issue; *see* WTO, *Trade Policy Review – Separate Customs Territory of Taiwan, Penghu, Kinmen and Matsu* (22 September 2006) WT/TPR/M/165, paras. 33–35, 47, 53, 65.

[63] Ibid para. 138.

and the signing of the Closer Economic Partnership Arrangements CEPAs with China. Prior to its formal accession to the GATT, Hong Kong had already participated in GATT activities. The Hong Kong Office in the Mission of the UK had sought recourse under Article XXIII:2 of GATT and requested for the establishment of a panel by the GATT Contracting Parties.

In *Norway – Restrictions on Imports of Certain Textile Products* (*Norway – Textiles*), the UK acting on behalf of Hong Kong requested a panel to be established and the panel found Norway's Article XIV action was not consistent with Article XIII of GATT so it should either be immediately terminated or be brought in accordance with the provisions of Article XIII.[64] Additionally, in the Panel report on *EEC – Quantitative Restriction on Certain Products from Hong Kong* (*EEC – Import Restrictions*), after the UK brought a complaint against the EEC on behalf of Hong Kong, France was found to infringe its obligations assumed in Article XI of the GATT and to *prima facie* nullify and impair the benefits of Hong Kong accruing therefrom.[65]

Compared to Hong Kong, Macau's experiences in participating in the GATT prior to its accession were much more limited. Since its accession to the GATT and subsequently to the WTO, Macau has not been as active as Hong Kong. This was partly because the UK had constantly helped Hong Kong to develop its capacity in becoming a participant of the international trading system with an aim to ensuring its market economy and political autonomy would be sufficient even after the handover to China, since the resumption of its sovereignty over Hong Kong was inevitable. In contrast, Macau was not able to benefit from help from Portugal.

Hong Kong and Macau experienced a significant constitutional change when they were returned to China and the Hong Kong Basic Law (the HKBL) and the Macau Basic Law (the MABL) became their mini-constitutions. As certified by China, these two Special Administrative Regions (the SARs) of China are qualified as separate customs territories 'possessing full autonomy in the conduct of its external commercial relations and of the other matters provided for the WTO Agreement.' Their WTO memberships would thus remain unchanged and would still be able to participate in the international trading system.

---

[64] GATT Panel Report, *Norway – Restrictions on Imports of Certain Textile Products* (*Norway – Textiles*), L/4959, adopted 18 June 1980, BISD 27S/119, paras. 16–8.

[65] GATT Panel Report, *EEC – Quantitative Restrictions Against Imports of Certain Products from Hong Kong* (*EEC – Import Restrictions*), L/5511, adopted 12 July 1983, BISD 30S/129, para. 34.

[65] WTO, *Turkey – Restrictions on Imports of Textile and Clothing Products – Request for Consultations by Hong Kong* (15 February 1996) WT/DS29/1. As the date of this submission was 15 February 1996, Hong Kong's official name within the WTO was still 'Hong Kong', not 'Hong Kong, China'. Yet, when it intervened as a third party in the complaint brought by India, its official name had become 'Hong Kong, China'.

After the WTO came into being, Hong Kong used to file one complaint. In *Turkey – Restrictions on Imports of Textile and Clothing Products*,[66] Hong Kong requested for a consultation on Turkey's quantitative restrictions on imports of textile and clothing products. This consultation request addressed the same issue as the famous *Turkey – Restrictions on Imports of Textile and Clothing Products* (*Turkey – Textiles*),[67] complained by India because of the customs union agreement between European Community and Turkey. There although Hong Kong, China did not request for the establishment of a panel, it intervened as a third party in the complaint brought about against Turkey by India. Overall, Hong Kong's participation in the WTO has been very active, which is evident through its hosting of 2005 Hong Kong Ministerial Conference.

Trade policies of Hong Kong and Macau have some important and distinctive characteristics. In the Hong Kong government report during its first Trade Policy Review after the handover, Hong Kong's import and export system had been characterised as '(a) zero tariffs; (b) minimum controls; and (c) no subsidies or assistance to export.'[68] With regard to its role as intermediary to China, while some argue that the role will be terminated with the full opening of China's economy and the emergence of rival hubs such as Shanghai and Shenzhen; others argue that Hong Kong is still comparatively more competitive, especially in the area of financing and profession services.[69] In respect of Macau, it is characterised by its free-port status and zero-tariff policy, as mandated by Article 110 of the Macau Basic Law. Macau's economy also relies much on services trade, where the gambling service plays a pivotal role.

However, the Asian financial crisis exploded immediately after the handover. These two economies, especially Hong Kong, experienced a great set back in their economic development. The gradual recovery was challenged again when the Severe Acute Respiratory Syndrome (the SARS) broke out. The situation in Macau was no better. Stagnating development and a growing crime rate had long plagued Macau. Against this background, some efforts were required to boost the economic development of these two SARs. The Closer Economic Partnership Arrangements (the CEPAs) between China and Hong Kong (and subsequently between China and Macau) are designed to meet this need.

---

[66] Ibid.

[67] Appellate Body Report, *Turkey – Restrictions on Imports of Textile and Clothing Products*, WT/DS34/AB/R, adopted 19 November 1999, DSR 1999:VI, 2345.

[68] WTO, *Trade Policy Review Report – Hong Kong, China by Government* (11 November 1998) WT/TPR/G/52, para. 46.

[69] Y-W Sung, 'The Evolving Role of Hong Kong as China's Middleman' in L S Ho and R Ash (eds), *China, Hong Kong and the World Economy: Studies on Globalization* (Palgrave Macmillan, New York 2006) 152–169.

The CEPAs may thus be read in a broader context. This arrangement of closer economic partnership was proposed with the aim to resolve the legitimacy crisis of Hong Kong. Its judicial autonomy had been undermined, since a judgment given by the Court of Final Appeal on the right to abode was 'overruled' by the NPCSC.[70] Citizens of Hong Kong gradually lost their patience with the long-awaited suffrage election. Resentment towards the Chief Executive surged as economy depression and higher unemployment rate continued to soar. The CEPA thus serves as a means not only to boost the economic development in Hong Kong but also to prevent the 'One China, Two Systems' policy from collapsing.

As Sung points out, the China-Hong Kong CEPA is unique in various ways. First, it is the first 'Free Trade Agreement' signed by two Members of the WTO, whom happened to be of the same country. It is also peculiar in terms of rights and obligations undertaken by the two Parties: while China offers so much 'concessions,' Hong Kong offers almost nothing. The two parties draw a sharp contrast from each other in their sizes, openness, and economic developments: Hong Kong is small, highly developed and very open, and China is large, less developed, and relatively closed.[71] As the China-Hong Kong CEPA provides Hong Kong preferential market access in some services areas, it is believed that Hong Kong will benefit much from China's opening of its services trade. With regard to Macau, as the gambling industry is the drive of its economy, with the signing of the China-Macau CEPA, tourists from China is believed to have contributed greatly to the recovery of Macau's economy.

An interesting question is why China bothers to sign a 'Free Trade Agreement' with Hong Kong (and Macau) as they are already free ports with zero-tariff policy. It is not difficult to understand that Hong Kong wishes to take advantage of the 'open-up' of China and to contribute to Hong Kong's economic growth as Hong Kong's economic policy has long emphasised on its role as an 'intermediary' of China. Hong Kong also wanted to relocate its services industries in China before China compiles with its commitments in respect to fully liberalising its services trade to all WTO Members.[72]

From an economic viewpoint, it may be argued that China will gain hardly any benefits from entering into a Free Trade Agreement with Hong Kong. However, a deeper analysis can overrule this supposition. From a intra-national context, this

---

[70] *See* further, *infra* Chapter VIII, text to (n 43) *et seq.*

[71] Y-W Sung, *The Emergence of Greater China: The Economic Integration of Mainland China, Taiwan and Hong Kong* (Palgrave Macmillan, New York 2005) 199–200.

[72] As for the case of Macau, zero-tariffs for trade in goods seem not very beneficial to Macau since its economy relies much on its services trades, in particular gambling services. Chinese visitors and the tourism services are of great significance to the Macau's economy and this limits the scope of the CEPA's main text and its annexes. This exposes one of the weaknesses of translating the experiences of China-Hong Kong CEPA to the China-Macau CEPA.

arrangement of a closer economic partnership was precisely proposed with the objective to resolve Hong Kong's legitimacy crisis. China has a significant interest in preventing the 'One Country, Two Systems' policy from collapsing. The implication of the CEPAs in the international economic context is equally important. According to Article 4 of the CEPAs, specific provisions in China's Accession Protocol and its Working Party Report will not be applicable between these Contracting Parties. The legal text reads as follows:

> The two sides recognize that through over 20 years of reform and opening up, the market economy system of the Mainland has been continuously improving, and the mode of production and operation of Mainland enterprises is in line with the requirements of a market economy. The two sides agree that Articles 15 and 16 of the 'Protocol on the Accession of the People's Republic of China to the WTO' and paragraph 242 of the 'Report of the Working Party on the Accession of China' will not be applicable to trade between the Mainland and Hong Kong (Macau).[73]

Section 15 of China's Accession Protocol governs the method in determining price comparability in anti-subsidy and anti-dumping investigations. In the anti-dumping procedures, Members are entitled to adopt 'a methodology that is not based on a strict comparison with domestic prices or costs in China.' Other methodologies may also be employed in identifying and measuring subsidy benefit in anti-subsidy proceedings taking the 'prevailing terms and conditions in China' into account and thus establishing appropriate benchmarks. Section 16 lays down a transitional product-specific safeguard measure to which Members may opt to adopt, to prevent and to provide remedy for market disruptions. Paragraph 242 of China's Working Party Report deals with the potential market disruption arising from the import of Chinese textile products with the expiry of the Agreement on Textile and Clothing (the ATC), as China's textile export amounts to a significant market share.

In the CEPA, Hong Kong explicitly recognises China as a market economy. Even though this practice only has a symbolic significance, it paves a way for China to negotiate with its other trading partners on the issue of its market economy status. Additionally, the non-application of Section 15 and 16 of China's Accession Protocol and paragraph 242 of the Working Part Report helps China to negotiate with its trading partners by copying the same provisions, and consequently reduces the impacts of these 'WTO-plus' obligations as set out in China's Working Party Report and its Accession Protocol.[74]

---

[73] CEPA, Art. 4.

[74] This approach has proven to be very successful. According to the Trade Policy Review Report conducted in 2006, China has included the recognition of its market economy status into every regional and bilateral free trade agreements, and economic partnership agreements. *See* WTO, *Trade Policy Review – Report by the Secretariat – People's Republic of China* (28 February 2006) WT/TPR/S/161, para. 46, *et seq*. *See* also WTO, *Trade Policy Review – Report by the Secretariat – China – Revision*

III. The Structure of the Work

The existence of the four Members of the Greater China in the WTO illustrates the struggles with the international trading system between the power-oriented and rule-based approaches. The sponsorships allowing Hong Kong and Macau to be deemed as Contracting Parties to the GATT illustrate the influence of parent countries upon territories subject to their international responsibility. Prior to China's accession to the WTO, the memberships of Hong Kong, China and Macau, China in the WTO appeared to be ironic: the central government was not a member while the regional governments were. This 'imbalance' between central authority and special administrative regions strengthen China's determination to join to the WTO.

Those who esteem highly on national sovereignty and resist China's WTO accession tend to link the two memberships of Hong Kong, China and Macau, China with past imperialism. The WTO memberships of Hong Kong, China and Macau, China are thus perceived as an arrangement by the UK and Portugal to prevent these two special administrative regions from being fully integrated into China. This perception from the logic of power politics upon the WTO system remains influential. At the same time, China's Accession Protocol can is as a milestone for the constitutionalisation of the WTO, since it covers various 'rule of law' obligations. China's and Taiwan's accessions also indicate the ambition of the WTO to become a real 'world trade organisation' with universal membership.

Although the designation of defining the Contracting Parties as 'governments' and allowing separate customs territories to accede to the GATT was mainly out of functional and realistic needs of territories to participate in the international trade regime during their process of seeking independence, this constitutional feature of the GATT/WTO system turns out to be a good example of the transformation of the world trading system. If one perceives the WTO not only as a mechanism to meet the needs of Hong Kong and Macau to participate in the world trading system but also as a safeguard for their economical and political autonomy and as venue for Taiwan to pursue international trade diplomacy, such functional approach may gradually evolve and point to a different direction. One will then

(12 August 2008) WT/TPR/S/199/rev.1, para. 53, *et seq.* So far, A Framework Agreement on Comprehensive Economic Cooperation between China and ASEAN, Chile-China FTA, China – Pakistan Preferential Trade Agreement, China-Australia Trade and Economic Framework Agreement (aiming to establish an FTA), China-New Zealand Trade and Economic Cooperation Framework Agreement, China and the Southern African Customs Union (SACU) Joint Declaration (with the aim to establishing a FTA), China – Gulf Cooperation Council Framework Agreement on Economic, Trade, Investment and Technology Cooperation, as well as the accompanying talks and negotiations have recognised China as a market economy. Before commencing the FTA negotiations, Iceland and Switzerland have also recognised China as a market economy.

see the diversity of this world trading system where China exercises its sovereignty but its two SARs possess full autonomy in the conduct of its external commercial relation and where Taiwan, a state unrecognised by most countries can pursue its international trade diplomacy. One will also appreciate the contribution of the WTO to economic integration of the Greater China.

China's resumption of its sovereignty over Hong Kong and Macau and the signings of the two CEPAs between China and Hong Kong and Macau have illustrated a new practice in this world trading system. The merging of Hong Kong and Macau's market economy with China's socialist economy presents an interesting story. It does not only test the compatibility of a market economy with a non-market economy, but also points out the crucial element that are often neglected in the international trading system: the difficulty in identifying one economy as a purely planned economy and thus being treated as non-market economy. As the two CEPAs had been notified the WTO Committee on Regional Trade Agreement in accordance with the procedures laid down in Article XXIV:7, it is safe to say that these CEPAs are international agreements, except in their names. These two CEPAs thus also provide good materials for exploring the possibility of a 'Free Trade Agreement' between two WTO memberships of the same country.

The ECFA between Taiwan and China is also an interesting story: the economic integration between two potentially antagonistic entities. In addition to the WTO Dispute Settlement Mechanism and domestic courts, the bilateral ECFA also provides a forum for Taiwan and China to resolve potential trade disputes and divergences. The inking of the ECFA also illustrates how the WTO framework under its rules on free trade agreements facilitates and regulates the process of economic integration between Taiwan and China.

The legacy of power politics may well linger on in this world trading system. This is clearly illustrated in Taiwan's quest to become a WTO member; for example, the WTO Chairman's statement on the sequence of the accession between China and Taiwan; China's failed effort in changing Taiwan's official name in the GATT/WTO; and Taiwan's struggle in acceding to the GPA. In addition, the influence of power politics is also apparent in Taiwan's restrictions imposed against China due to political concerns. Such legacy clearly indicates the necessity for further constitutionalisation in the international trade arena; in this constitutionalisation process, effective judicial review of foreign trade decisions at the multilateral WTO level, the bilateral ECFA and CEPA level and the domestic level.

The aim of this introductory chapter is to offer the readers with an understanding of the background of these four WTO Members so that readers can easily comprehend the complexities of this issue. I hope that by reading this introductory chapter, the readers will be equipped with a basic knowledge of the context in which these four WTO Members is situated and thus be able to appreciate this unique legal landscape. Before this introductory chapter comes to end, it is feasible and beneficial to outline main contents of this work. This work comprises four parts, which I structure as follows.

The first three chapters deal with the introductory background knowledge, the research question, and the employed methodology. The research question chapter aims to present the demand for an effective dispute settlement mechanism in the Greater China at the international WTO level, domestic/national level and the potential regional level. It examines the objective to strengthen domestic judicial review during the Uruguay Round negotiations and constraints for the realisation of this goal. It then discusses why a mechanism to resolve trade disputes among these four memberships is so important, especially in light of the highly politicised cross-strait trade issues. The methodology chapter firstly presents three versions of WTO constitutionalism and examines their contribution to judicial settlement of trade disputes in the Greater China.

The second part of this work also consists of chapters four to six. Chapter IV will examine various provisions under the WTO agreements governing domestic judicial review. Chapter V focuses on China's obligation to provide an independent and impartial judicial review as prescribed within its accession protocol. It will also address the potential challenges within the WTO Dispute Settlement Mechanism to implement this obligation. It will examine global and regional standards of judicial independence and impartiality. Chapter VI will be devoted to the impact of Taiwan's WTO membership upon its judicial branch. Specifically, it will deal with the legitimacy and capacity of Taiwan's domestic courts to intervene and to participate in cross-strait trade issues, especially when national security is at stake.

The third part is also comprised of three chapters: chapters seven to nine. Chapter VII examines the cross-strait trade disputes at the multilateral WTO, bilateral and domestic level. Chapter VIII explores potential trade disputes between China and Hong Kong and Macau and examines whether external trade falls within the exclusive competence of these two SARs. It also analyses the CEPAs concluded between China and its two SARs. Chapter IX then discusses trade disputes between Taiwan and Hong Kong and Macau and argues that a private international law approach may be helpful.

The last part of this work, Chapter X, concludes this work by summarising the main findings and the major arguments of this work and probes the future directions for legal and economic integration of the four WTO Members of the Greater China.

CHAPTER TWO

EFFECTIVE JUDICIAL REVIEW IN EXTERNAL TRADE RELATIONS IN THE GREATER CHINA

I. Closer Economic Interdependence Gives Rise to Trade Disputes

Since China began its open reform in 1978, the economic interdependence in the Greater China has become closer and closer. It has also accelerated since China's and Taiwan's accessions to the WTO. In 2003, for Taiwan the total trade with China exceeded trade with the United States (the US) or Japan, and since then China has become Taiwan's largest trading partner. Since 2003, Taiwan has ranked steadily China's 7th dominating trading partner. For Hong Kong and Macau, China has also long been their largest trading partner. As a consequence of the enormous trade volume and high degree of economic interdependence, trade frictions and trade disputes have surfaced. There are numerous good examples of such frictions, followed by trade remedies measures adopted by China and Taiwan against each other. Currently, both Taiwan and China maintain several trade defence measures against each other.[1] Regarding the WTO Dispute Settlement Mechanism, although China and Taiwan have not officially sought recourse to this intergovernmental forum, Taiwan has constantly participated as a third party in these complaints to which China is a party.[2] With respect the relations between China and Hong Kong and Macau, China has exercised its competence in interpreting the Basic Law of Hong Kong (the HKBL). This may undermine the economic autonomy of these two Special Administrative Regions (the SARs).[3] Private parties also resort to domestic courts in Taiwan and Hong Kong or Macau to seek recognition and enforcement of civil judgments and arbitral awards so as to protect their rights and interests.[4]

As political branches are more susceptible to influences of the interests groups and, they may be 'captured' by protectionism. By contrast, as the judiciary is obliged to act with neutrality and impartiality, effective judicial review is thus

[1] WTO, *Committee on Anti-Dumping Practices-Semi-Annual Report under Article 16.4 of the Agreement – China* (1 October 2010) G/ADP/N/202/CHN 12; *see* also other previous semi-annual reports of Anti-dumping committee. WTO, *Committee on Anti-Dumping Practices-Semi-annual report under article 16.4 of the Agreement-The Separate Customs Territory of Taiwan, Penghu, Kinmen and Matsu-Revision* (25 February 2011) G/ADP/N/209/TPKM/rev.1.

[2] *See infra* Chapter VII.

[3] *See infra* Chapter VIII.

[4] *See infra* Chapter VIIII

proved to essential to safeguard rights and interests of individuals and enterprises under the WTO Agreement.

Under the existing WTO legal system, two levels of judicial review exist: the intergovernmental WTO Dispute Settlement Mechanism and the domestic judicial review. This chapter thus wishes to examine the existing provisions governing these two levels of judicial protection and to illustrate why a further strengthened judicial review is desirable. It will discuss firstly the intergovernmental WTO Dispute Settlement Mechanism and then goes to examine the often-neglected domestic judicial review. It will then examine the constraints of domestic judicial review in foreign trade relations and argue for a strengthened judicial review.

Three arguments are offered to justify this claim: the legitimacy of judicial review international trade decisions; contribution to consistency and coherence of international economic relations; and judicial protection of rights and interests of individual economic actors. This chapter then argues that strengthened judicial protection is of even greater importance for trade dispute resolution in the Greater China to achieve the following goals: rational decision-making; the safeguard of economic autonomy of Hong Kong and Macau; compliance to the WTO rules; the protection of right to trade. Lastly, this chapter points to the role of the WTO Dispute Settlement Mechanism in resolving cross-Taiwan-strait trade disputes and enhancing economic integration.

II. Effective Judicial Review and Implementation of the WTO Agreement

A. *Intergovernmental Dispute Settlement Mechanism in the WTO*

It is not possible and not the aim of this section, to discuss the WTO Dispute Settlement Mechanism in a comprehensive manner. However, it is feasible to provide an overview of this intergovernmental dispute settlement mechanism, as it will facilitate the following analysis of the two-level judicial review in relation to international trade decisions. Compared to its power-oriented predecessor GATT, the WTO Dispute Settlement Mechanism is widely viewed as a rule-based system where 'security and predictability' is to be safeguarded and 'rights and obligations' of Members are to be preserved. This dispute settlement mechanism can be separated into four stages: consultation; panel proceedings; Appellate Body proceedings; and recommendation, implementation, and surveillance. With regard to this dispute settlement mechanism, three quick points should be noted at this stage: compulsory jurisdiction, quasi-automatic adoption of the WTO panel/Appellate Body reports and the establishment of a permanent Appellate Body.

Article 6.1 of the DSU provides that, a panel shall be established no later than the second meeting of the DSB after the request firstly appears on the agenda of the Dispute Settlement Body (the DSB), unless the DSB decides not to establish the panel by consensus. This is generally referred to as 'negative consensus' or 'reverse consensus'. In practice, the requesting Member is unlikely to join the consensus against the establishment of panel. If it is preferable not to establish the panel, the request may be withdrawn. Besides, as the provision reads that a panel shall be established no later than the second meeting of DSB, it suggests that the respondent Member may 'block' the establishment of a panel for once. Consequently, a panel is usually established at the second meeting of the DSB. This differs from some other international dispute resolution practices where agreements of the acceptance of jurisdiction are indispensable.

'Negative consensus' is also applied to the adoption of the WTO panel/Appellate Body reports. These reports should be unconditionally adopted unless the DSB by consensus decides not to adopt them.[5] This practice again differs from the GATT practices, where the responding party could block the adoption of panel reports. The 'negative consensus' makes the WTO panel/Appellate Body reports quasi-automatically adopted, which highly strengthens the efficacy of the WTO Dispute Settlement Mechanism.

Another novel practice of the WTO Dispute Settlement Mechanism is the establishment of a permanent Appellate Body. This standing Appellate Body serves as a safeguard against legally wrong panel reports, which greatly contributes to the consistence and coherence of the WTO jurisprudence. This permanent Appellate Body, compared to *ad hoc* panellists, is equipped with greater experiences and expertise in WTO law and jurisprudence. The establishment of a standing Appellate Body to hear appeals from panels further strengthens the legalised and judicialised character of this dispute settlement mechanism. As observed, the adoption of panel reports by the political consensus of the GATT Council had been much abused in the final period of the Uruguay Round negotiations. The quasi-automatic adoption of panel reports is aimed to correct this defect. Nevertheless, this quasi-automatic adoption necessitates a mechanism to ensure the accuracy of these panel reports; a standing Appellate Body is expected to meet this need.[6]

Before analysing domestic judicial remedies, it is also desirable to note that, as the WTO Dispute Settlement Mechanism remains intergovernmental in nature, Members tend to enact domestic legislation providing opportunities for individual economic actors to petition for referring to this dispute settlement mechanism. The *Section 301 of the Trade Act of 1974* and *Trade Barrier Regulation* of the

---

[5] DSU, Arts. 16.4, 17.14.

[6] E U Petersmann, *The GATT/WTO Dispute Settlement System: International Law, International Organizations, and Dispute Settlement* (Kluwer Law International London, The Hague, Boston 1997) 186.

European Union (the EU) are best examples. These instruments can be thus regarded as an indirect link between the WTO Dispute Settlement Mechanism and domestic judicial remedies. As Shaffer observes, a 'public-private partnership' where private individuals and enterprises work side by side with United States Trade Representative (the USTR) as a partner is visible in the proceedings of WTO Dispute Settlement Mechanism.[7]

B. *The Role of Domestic Courts in the WTO Agreement*

1. *The Trend to Strengthen Domestic Judicial Review*

Prior to the establishment of the WTO, it had already been proposed to strengthen the domestic enforcements of the GATT rules.[8] During the negotiation processes of the Uruguay Round, Switzerland submitted a communication to the Negotiation Group on Dispute Settlement addressing domestic implementation.[9] It presented three models of introducing international trade laws into domestic legal order, namely, to give full effects of the international trade law in the domestic legal order, selectively to have qualified self-executing provisions directly implemented, and to leave it to the member states to decide the way in which international trade laws are enforced. In light of the infeasibility of an over-reaching ambition, Switzerland maintained that the third approached was preferable. However, Switzerland proposed that the following elements concerning domestic procedures should be included:

> Provisions for fair hearing for all parties substantially affected by administrative or judicial action related to international trade. In case of urgent determination, the right to a hearing may be granted upon complaint only.
> Obligation to provide, at least upon complaint, a reasoned decision without undue delay.
> Prompt and effective provisional measures in case of pending irreversible damage.
> Prompt and effective administrative or judicial review of administrative action related to international trade. The scope of judicial review may be limited to issues

[7] G Shaffer, ''Public-Private Partnership' in WTO Dispute Settlement: the US and EU Experience' in Y Taniguchi, et al. (eds), *The WTO in the Twenty-first Century: Dispute Settlement, Negotiations, and Regionalism in Asia* (Cambridge University Press, Cambridge 2007) 153. *See* also G Shaffer, *Defending Interests: Public-Private Partnerships in WTO Litigation* (Brookings Institution Press, Washington, D.C. 2003).

[8] *See, e.g.*, E U Petersmann, 'Strengthening the Domestic Legal Framework of the GATT Multilateral Trade System: Possibilities and Problems of Making GATT Rules Effective in Domestic Legal System' in E U Petersmann and M Hilf (eds), *The New GATT Round of Multilateral Trade Negotiations: Legal and Economic Problems* (Kluwer Law and Taxation Publishers, Deventer 1991).

[9] GATT, *Uruguay Round-Group of Negotiations on Goods-Negotiating Group on Dispute Settlement-Communication from Switzerland* (18 January 1990) MTN.GNG/NG13/W/36, 4.

> of law, excluding questions of fact and discretionary exercise of authority within the law.[10]

This proposal intended to widen the scope of the subject matters that were entitled to the judicial protection. It replaced with the original wording of 'administrative action relating to customs matters' as used in the GATT with more precise and clearer terminology and widened the scope of domestic judicial review. In this proposal, Switzerland argued that Article X:3(b) of the GATT could not be effective if non-tariff measures were not covered. Based on this reasoning, Switzerland proposed that Article X:3(b) should be expressly applied to all areas covered in the Agreement, including non-tariff barriers.[11]

According to Petersmann, Switzerland's proposal aiming to strengthen domestic implementation of international trade rules and to providing effective judicial protection of individuals and enterprises, has been largely adopted in the following negotiation processes and has been included into the Uruguay Round Multilateral Trade Agreements.[12] Such examples can be found in Article X:3(b) of the GATT 1994, Article 13 of the Anti-Dumping Agreement, Article 11 of the Agreement on Customs Valuation, Article 4 of the Agreement on Pre-shipment Inspection, Article 23 of the Agreement on Subsidies and Countervailing Measures, Article VI of the GATS, Article 41 to Article 50 and Article 59 of the TRIPS Agreement, and Article XX:2 of the Government Procurement Agreement.[13]

The trend to strengthen the effectiveness of domestic judicial review is also evidenced by China's Accession Protocol to the WTO, which, in Section 2(D), explicitly prescribes the obligation to provide an independent and impartial judicial review. Besides, China's Accession Protocol lays down more stringent requirement on this judicial review by dictating an 'opportunity for appeal' reviewed by 'judicial body'.[14] Moreover, Members are not required to eliminate the existing procedures, if these procedures provide objective and impartial reviews of administrative actions even though they are not fully or formally independently of the agencies. Nor are Members obliged to institute a new review mechanism which would be inconsistent with their constitutional structure or the nature of their legal systems.[15] Nevertheless, such leeway is not available for China. As China's Accession Protocol makes it clear, those tribunals should be independent of the agency entrusted with administrative enforcement.[16] China cannot escape this obligation

---

[10] Ibid.
[11] Ibid.
[12] Petersmann (n 8) 244.
[13] Ibid 194.
[14] J Y Qin, ''WTO-plus' Obligations and Their Implications for the World Trade Organization Legal System – An Appraisal of the China Accession Protocol' (2003) 37 Journal of World Trade 483, 496.
[15] GATS, Art. VI:2(b).
[16] Qin (n 14) 495–496.

on the ground that such designation would be inconsistent with its constitutional structure or the nature of its legal system.

China's Accession Protocol also lays down several institutional requirements governing the designation of this prompt review. For example, the tribunal shall have no substantial interests of the outcome of the decision;[17] no penalty shall be imposed on the right to appeal;[18] the decision of the appeal should be given to the appellant with reasons provided in writing;[19] and be notified of the right for further appeals.[20] The independence and impartiality of Chinese courts is expected to be enhanced by dictating the tribunals to be independent of administrative agencies. This in turn would strengthen domestic judicial protection in China by virtue of the right to appeal to be reviewed by judicial organs.

2. *Constraints of Domestic Judicial Review and Need to Further Strengthen It*

Notwithstanding the ambition to strengthening domestic judicial review during the Uruguay Round negotiations; the enforcement of WTO rules in domestic courts is still subject to various constraints. Part of theses constraints derive from the nature of the WTO Agreement, which leaves much room for Members to decide the way in which it is implemented. More importantly, political branches deliberately impose stringent constraints upon domestic courts with a view to limit their competence in enforcing the WTO rules.[21] Although various provisions in the WTO agreements regulate domestic judicial review, how to designate this domestic judicial review is still, with limited exceptions, conditional on their national legal systems and their judicial approaches.[22]

As the WTO agreements loosely regulate the form and shape of this domestic judicial review, therefore, domestic courts decide by themselves whether they opt for judicial restraint or judicial activism according to their own perceptions of the separation of powers and checks and balances. Domestic courts act with great caution when dealing with foreign trade relations, compared to domestic affairs. External relations, including external trade relations, have been conventionally

[17] China's Accession Protocol, S. 2(D), para. 1.

[18] China's Accession Protocol, S. 2(D), para. 2.

[19] Ibid.

[20] Ibid.

[21] On the constraints imposed on the implementation of Uruguay Round Agreements, *see, e.g.*, D W Leebron, 'Implementation of the Uruguay Round Results in the United States' in J H Jackson and A O Sykes (eds), *Implementing the Uruguay Round* (Oxford University Press, Oxford 1997) 209–21; P L H Van den Bossche, 'The European Community and the Uruguay Round Agreements' in J H Jackson, Alan O. Sykes (ed), *Implementing the Uruguay Round* (Oxford University Press, Oxford 1997) 93.

[22] The two important exceptions are the 'Independent Entity' as provided in the Agreement on Pre-shipment and the 'challenge procedures' put forward in the Agreement on Government Procurement.

considered the province of legislative and executive branches. The court is not in a good position to intervene.[23] So far, this judicial self-restraint has not been fundamentally changed even after the WTO Agreement aiming at strengthening domestic judicial review entered into force.

A good example illustrating this self-restraint approach is the *Corus Staal BV. v. Department of Commerce*[24] handed down by the Court of Appeal of Federal Circuit. The Court declares that WTO decisions are 'not binding on the United States, much less this court',[25] given that the Uruguay Round Agreements Act explicitly prevents the application of conflicting provisions of the WTO Agreement in the US domestic legal order. According the Court, in order to deal with these conflicts, the Congress has enacted legislation that authorises the USTR, an arm of the Executive branch, in consultation with various Congressional and Executive bodies and agencies to 'determine whether or not to implement WTO reports and determinations and, if so implemented, the extent of implementation'.[26] The Court then concludes that the GATT/WTO agreements do not trump domestic legislation, and that if the US statutory provisions are inconsistent with these GATT/WTO agreements, it is strictly 'a matter for Congress'.[27]

This holding makes it clear that if one aims to refer to domestic courts for the implementation of the WTO rules, various constraints would be encountered with. Political organs, in accepting and ratifying the WTO Agreement, have either removed the jurisdiction of judicial organs and thus prevented the courts from hearing disputes relating to its implementation, or explicitly prescribed domestic implementing acts to being applicable law in adjudicating a case. These practices have substantially undermined the competence of judicial organs in overseeing foreign trade measures. Secondly, the judiciary itself has long embraced the self-restraint approach when foreign trade relations are at stake. Given the external and internal constraints, an effective judicial review in foreign trade measures remains unavailable regardless of the negotiators' efforts in advocating strong domestic judicial review and successful inclusion a number of provisions regulating this subject matter in the Final Act of the Uruguay Round negotiations.

In view of these, one is tempted to propose for a further strengthened judicial protection. However, this proposal should firstly address the court's legitimacy in reviewing external trade measures, and then justify itself both by its enhancement to consistency and coherence between international trade obligations and

[23] T Cottier and M Oesch, 'The Paradox of Judicial Review in International Trade Regulation: Towards a Comprehensive Framework' in T Cottier and P C Mavroidis (eds), *The Role of the Judge in International Trade Regulation* (The University of Michigan Press, Ann Arbor, Mich. 2003) 288–289.

[24] *Corus Staal BV. v. Department of Commerce*, 395 F. 3d 1343. (Fed. Cir. 2005)

[25] *Corus Staal BV. v. Department of Commerce*, 1348.

[26] Ibid.

[27] Ibid.

national legal order and its contribution to protection of rights and interests of individual economic actors under the WTO Agreement. Otherwise, it will not overcome those weaknesses as noted above. Therefore, the following will firstly examine these three issues and explores the contribution of strengthened judicial review to the Greater China.

3. *Legitimacy of Judicial Review International Trade Decisions*

When called upon to review international trade decisions, domestic courts tend to rely upon 'political question' doctrine either to decline to exercise jurisdiction or to defer to decisions of political organs. Domestic courts tend to argue that they are not equipped with expertise in the field of international trade. International trade decisions, involving with the complexity of legal, political, and economic dimensions, are not justiciable in nature and should be thus deferred to political branches. Even if domestic courts do engage into the review process, they adopt deferential standards of review.

This approach is however not flawless. Firstly, the distinction between domestic affairs and external relations has become highly unjustified as decisions of external relations are inevitably implemented, side by side, by domestic measures. Foreign relations and domestic affairs are interrelated and a clear-cut division is not possible. Just as judicial protection, an indispensable element of rule of law should be provided in the field of domestic affairs, it should also be extended to foreign areas, as individual rights in the foreign trade relations are no less prone to arbitrary administrative interference than those in domestic affairs.

One may tend to argue that the judiciary is not a legitimate actor to deal with cases concerning foreign relations, as it is not sensitive and responsive to political needs. However, it is exactly this lack of sensitivity that makes it the best guardian to ensure rational decision-making. A review by a neutral judiciary, which is not involved in the political and economic interests of international relations, and which is thus able to prevent itself from being captured by interest groups and to depoliticise the external trade decisions, contributes to the rationality of foreign trade policy-making.

As has been seen in the economic development of the US, exporting groups and importing groups compete to shape a country's trade policies. High tariffs arise when protectionism prevails. The high tariffs authorised by Smoot-Hawley Act had forced other countries to retaliate by raising their tariffs against the US exports and turned out to be a cause of the Great Depression.[28] Given that political

[28] K W Dam, 'Cordell Hull, the Reciprocal Trade Agreement Act, and the WTO' in E U Petersmann (ed), *Reforming the World Trading System: Legitimacy, Efficiency and Democratic Governance* (Oxford University Press, Oxford 2005) 85.

branches are not always rational decision-makers, such argument based on 'political question' doctrine that calls for respect for the wisdom of politicians and deference to political branches has no merit. Judicial review should therefore act as a vehicle for 'checks and balances' to prevent political branches from abusing their powers. The role of the judiciary is of even greater importance in the field of external trade decisions as a wide discretion is conferred to administrative agencies. Judicial review thus proves to be essential to ensure this discretionary power to be carefully exercised.

Judicial review, by means of substantive and procedural functions can help to preserve liberal trade policies. Being neutral, in the sense of the absence of political influences, interest group pressures, electoral politics and foreign policy concerns, judiciary is able to interpret and apply laws in a principled manner and thus contributes to the consistency and coherence of foreign trade law and policy. With regard to the procedural function, judiciary by imposing more stringent transparency and procedural requirements upon administration helps to unveil and rationalise the executive decision-making in foreign trade relations; it is thus possible to make the opaque foreign trade policy subject to the deliberation by civil society.[29]

One might argue against judicial review of international trade decisions based on accountability. Such argument is related to the argument of lack of democratic legitimacy of judiciary. As judiciary is not elected, and not accountable to the people, courts are not in a position to deal with international trade decisions. As international trade relation has high degree of foreign policy implication, it should be left to political branches whose decisions are to be examined by regular elections. This argument should also be rejected. Accountability should not rely solely upon electoral systems. With its decisions open to the civil society and subject to public comments and deliberation, judiciary is no less accountable to the people.

In sum, courts are legitimate and are under their constitutional obligation to engage in judicial review in foreign trade relations, as they are responsible for ensuring the rational decision-making of political branches. With effective judicial review, consistent and coherent interpretations and applications of foreign trade laws can be carried out and procedural requirements can be faithfully observed. In this way, rationality and reasonableness in the decision-making is enhanced. Judicial review is thus an indispensable instrument for the protection of individual rights as well as 'checks and balances' of state powers.

---

[29] R E Hudec, 'The Role of Judicial Review in Preserving Liberal Trade Policies' in M Hilf and E U Petersmann (eds), *National Constitutions and International Economic Law* (Kluwer Law and Taxation Publishers, Deventer, Boston 1993) 549–551.

4. *Consistency and Coherence in International Economic Relations*

Judicial review of external trade measures in the domestic context which has a stronger constitutional setting seems to be more restrained than that at the international level of the WTO where the constitutional framework dictating 'checks and balances' of powers is much weaker. In other words, domestic courts that are situated in established constitutional structures and equipped with strong law-enforcing powers, are expected to deal with protectionism more rigorously but they do not. This paradoxical imbalance results in incoherence and inconsistency which runs counter to the essential goals of legislation, jurisprudence and doctrines in an increasingly globally integrated trading system.[30]

In order to address this paradoxical imbalance, Cottier and Oesch propose a constitutional approach in pursuit of the consistency and coherence in international trade relations. They argue that consistent and coherent standards of review both on the domestic and global level necessitate an expansion of constitutional thinking to 'bring about reasonable inter-linkages of different layers of governance'.[31] With this constitutional thinking, it helps to 'shape attitudes toward the role of courts in international economic relations and thus of judicial review both at home and regional and global level, reflecting a mutual relationship of domestic and international fora.'[32] According to them, this constitutional thinking will contribute to the consistency and coherence of standards of judicial review at every level, and will address democratic legitimacy of international trade rules in a broader context.[33]

In this vein, judicial review plays a pivotal role in these inter-linkages when consistency and coherence is at stake. The defects of the existing multilevel judicial remedies in this world trading systems lie mainly in domestic courts as they tend to defer to political branches and allow conflicting interpretations and application of the WTO law. Such fragmentation does not only undermine the effectiveness of international trade rules, but it also menaces the legitimacy of domestic courts. Therefore, domestic courts in hearing international trade decisions are responsible for ironing out conflicting interpretations and applications between international trade obligations and national laws. As the international obligations bind all governmental bodies, domestic courts are also obliged to ensure their faithful implementation. Domestic courts thus play an important role in contributing to consistency and coherence of this world trading system.

---

30 Cottier and Oesch, in Cottier, et al. (eds) (n 23) 287–306.
31 Ibid 301.
32 Ibid.
33 Ibid.

5. *Judicial Protection of Rights and Interests of Individual Economic Actors*

Although the world trading system was established in the form of international agreement, governments being the subjects of the Marrakesh Agreement, it does not necessarily mean that individuals have no space in the scene of this world trading system. As the Panel correctly defines the role of the WTO in *United States – Sections 301–310 of the Trade Act of 1974*, holding that:

> The GATT/WTO did *not* create a new legal order the subjects of which comprise both contracting parties or Members and their nationals. However, it would be entirely wrong to consider that the position of individuals is of no relevance to the GATT/WTO legal matrix. Many of the benefits to Members which are meant to flow because of the acceptance of various disciplines under the GATT/WTO depend on the activity of individual economic operators in the national and global market places. The purpose of many of these disciplines, indeed one of the primary objects of the GATT/WTO as a whole, is to produce certain market conditions which would allow this individual activity to flourish.[34]

The aim to provide security and predictability in multilateral trade system is to protect the individual economic operators as 'the lack of security and predictability affects mostly these individual operators',[35] since the 'multilateral trading system is, per force, composed not only of States but also, indeed mostly, of individual economic operators'.[36] In other words, whereas the WTO agreements address rights and obligations of Members, the rights of individuals are thus to be indirectly secured in this 'integrated, more viable and durable multilateral trading system'.[37] As international trade activities are eventually carried out by individual economic actors, including exporters, importers, service suppliers, and intellectual property rights holders, it is the rights and obligations of these individual economic actors in need of protection by a secure and predictable multilateral trading system.

As Charnovitz points out, the WTO agreements give individual economic actors an entitlement to various substantive and procedural rights, ranging from intellectual property rights to 'due process' requirements in national legal systems.[38] In addition, China's Accession Protocol, in Section 5 also provides the right to trade, the right to import and export goods.[39] The availability and scope of the right to

---

34 Panel Report, *United States – Sections 301–310 of the Trade Act of 1974* (hereinafter, *US – Section 301 Trade Act*), WT/DS152/R, adopted 27 January 2000, DSR 2000: II, 815, paras. 7.71–7.72.

35 Ibid para. 7.76.

36 Ibid.

37 Preamble of Marrakesh Agreement Establishing the World Trade Organisation.

38 S Charnovitz, 'The WTO and the rights of the individual' (2001) 36 Intereconomics 98, 98–108, reprinted in *Trade Law and Global Governance* (Cameron May, London 2002) 377–96.

39 China's Accession Protocol, S. 5(1).

trade shall be progressively liberalised, and foreign individuals and enterprises should be treated no less favourably than enterprises and individuals in China. China's Accession Protocol has further evidenced that rights of individuals are not of no relevance to this world trading system.

The rights of these individual economic actors are at the heart of this world trading system, and the domestic courts are in a better position to ensure these rights to be fully protected. China's WTO obligation to establish, or designate, and maintain an independent and impartial judicial review also evidences this need. Domestic courts are a better forum to deal with private trade disputes in light of efficiency, transaction cost, or even the promotion of rule of law. As far as private trade disputes are concerned, domestic courts are by no means the best guardian for the rights and interests of these individual economic actors. Resorting to the intergovernmental WTO Dispute Settlement Mechanism should remain subsidiary. Only when WTO Members fail to provide an effective judicial review, or when domestic courts ignore their international obligations or misinterpret WTO rules should Members refer to the WTO Dispute Settlement Mechanism.[40] With a better protection of rights and interests of individual economic actors in domestic courts, the entire world trading system can be made more effective.[41]

C. *The Formation of Two-Level Judicial Review in WTO Law*

Compared to the considerable amount of literature focusing on the WTO panel/ Appellate Body proceedings, discussions concerning judicial remedies in domestic courts appear to be relatively rare. While the negotiation of improvements and clarifications of the DSU is among the issues of the Doha Agenda[42] and attracts a wide academic attention,[43] judicial review in the domestic level has been continuously put aside due to sovereignty concerns.

Although the negotiators of the Uruguay Round aim to strengthen domestic judicial review, a well-functioning two-level judicial review in the WTO system has yet to be realised. As pointed out by Hilf, there is no institutional linkage between these two levels of judicial protection in the WTO legal system. There is

---

[40] E U Petersmann, 'Multi-level Judicial Trade Governance without Justice? On the Role of Domestic Courts in the WTO Legal and Dispute Settlement System' (2006) EUI Working Paper 2006/44, 19–21 <http://cadmus.iue.it/dspace/bitstream/1814/6432/1/LAW-2006-44.pdf> accessed 1 September 2011.

[41] M Hilf, 'The Role of National Courts in International Trade Relations' in E U Petersmann (ed), *International Trade Law and the GATT/WTO Dispute Settlement System* (Kluwer Law International London, The Hague, Boston 1997) 579.

[42] WTO, *Ministerial Conference-Fourth Session-Doha, 9–14 November 2001-Ministerial Declaration – Adopted on 14 November 2001* (20 December 2001) WT/MIN(01)/DEC/1, para. 30.

[43] *See, e.g.*, contributions to F Ortino and E U Petersmann (eds), *The WTO Dispute Settlement System 1995–2003* (Kluwer Law International London, The Hague, Boston 2004).

no exhaustion of local remedies rule; national courts are not able to refer cases to the WTO Dispute Settlement Body for preliminary ruling or interpretation; and individuals have no access to this dispute settlement mechanism. There is thus an inherent danger of divergent or conflicting interpretations of the WTO rules.[44] It seems that such institutional linkage will not be established in the near future, and such linkage appears undesirable to most WTO Members. However, conflicting interpretations and applications of the WTO rules in domestic legal systems should be redressed in order to prevent this world trading system from fragmenting. It is even so when one takes into account the holding of the US Court of Appeal of Federal Circuit mentioned above. There the Court arrogantly decides the WTO decisions are not binding on the US, much less on that court. In response to this defect, Petersmann thus proposes that Members should enter into additional commitments:

> requiring domestic courts to interpret domestic trade rules (e.g. on customs valuation, antidumping, intellectual property rights) in conformity with the WTO obligations of the country concerned; and
> empowering domestic courts to apply specifically agreed, precise and unconditional WTO rules (as provided for in Article XX of the WTO Agreement on Government Procurement) at the request of private plaintiffs vis-à-vis administrative trade restrictions inconsistent with WTO law.[45]

Hard cases however remain hard, when legislature explicitly derogates the WTO obligations by enacting WTO-inconsistent legislation with clear legislative intention. This constraint imposed on domestic courts would eventually lead disputes to the WTO Dispute Settlement Mechanism. Whereas domestic courts should provide a primary forum for the settlement of trade disputes, particularly with private trade disputes, these disputes would inevitably be referred to the WTO Dispute Settlement Mechanism when domestic courts are unable to 'absorb' or to 'resolve' them.

III. The Contribution of Strengthened Judicial Protection to The Greater China

The above section illustrates the importance of the judiciary in foreign trade relations. This section will further elaborate the particular importance of judicial review, both at the domestic and intergovernmental WTO level, in relation to trade disputes in the Greater China. It will be based on the above-established rationale of why courts should engage in judicial review in foreign trade relations

[44] Hilf, in E U Petersmann (ed) (n 41) 571.
[45] Petersmann (n 40) 21.

more rigorously. However, some special factors related to these four Members should be dealt with separately. Apart from rational decision-making, three arguments are offered: to ensure WTO compliance; to ensure economic autonomy of Hong Kong and Macau; to fully protect the right to trade in China. Finally, this section will point out the significance of the WTO Dispute Settlement Mechanism to the Greater China, especially to China and Taiwan.

A. *Judicial Review in Ensuring Rational Decision-Making*

Cross-Taiwan-strait trade between China and Taiwan has long been highly politicised on both the WTO level and the domestic level. As mentioned in Chapter I, cross-strait relations were referred to as 'special and complex', 'unique and complicated', and 'not a simple trade issue'. Therefore, Taiwan 'had not immediately been able to carry out a comprehensive overhaul of the cross-strait trade and economic regulations'.[46] These statements reflect the political sensitivity of cross-Taiwan-strait trade relations.

The nomenclature of Taiwan in the WTO is another good example. During the course of Taiwan's Trade Policy Review in 2006, the representative of Il Salvador referred to Taiwan as 'Republic of China'. China immediately requested the floor to make a point of order, stating that there was an understanding in the WTO with regard to the nomenclature and titles of officials of Taiwan. That is, Taiwan entered into the WTO as a separate customs territory, not as a state.[47] According to China, Taiwan, being a separate-customs-territory Member should be treated the same as other two separate customs territories in the WTO, namely, Hong Kong, China and Macau, China. This was reflected in of China's early communications to Taiwan, which referred to Taiwan's mission as 'Economic and Trade Office', borrowing similar terminology used by missions of Hong Kong, China and Macau, China.

It would be too naïve to believe that such political obsessions do not exist in the mindset of national judges. Nevertheless, when seeking to make reasoned decision, courts are obliged to justify themselves with appropriate legal basis. This prevents the courts from being unduly influenced by mere irrational political preferences. The neutrality of courts also enables judges to reach decisions in a principled manner, taking into account with various conflicting constitutional rules and principles, laws and regulations. Courts are thus in a better position to balance competing interests and values in an unbiased way.[48] Depoliticisation

---

[46] WTO, *Trade Policy Review – Separate Customs Territory of Taiwan, Penghu, Kinmen and Matsu-Minutes of Meeting* (22 September 2006) WT/TPR/M/165, para. 138.

[47] Ibid para. 94.

[48] It should be carefully noted that competing interests and values here referred to are not limited to trade interests, less to exporter's trade interests. A recently petition to initiate anti-dumping investigation against print paper from China helps to present these conflicting interests. While the

through 'judicial governance' contributes to disentanglement of the complexity of cross-Taiwan-strait trade relation and to public deliberations in this contested and divided area.

B. *Judicial Review in Hong Kong and Macau to Ensure High Degree of Autonomy in Economic Affairs*

Since Hong Kong and Macau were returned to China, they have participated in the WTO under the official name of 'Hong Kong, China' and 'Macau, China'. Their status as separate customs territories and their competence to participate in the WTO are explicitly prescribed in the Hong Kong Basic Law (the HKBL) and Macau Basic Law (the MABL).[49] Nonetheless, these two Basic Laws do not explicitly provide any exclusive competence for these two Special Administrative Regions (the SARs), whereas the two Basic Laws assign national defence and foreign affairs to be part of the exclusive competence of Central Authority.[50] It is also unclear whether these two SARs retain the residual competence. Consequently, whether the economic autonomy of these two SARs can sustain their participation in the WTO is worrying.

Importantly, the NPC and the NPCSC possess the competence to interpret the Basic Laws, the interpretations binding on and to be followed by courts in the SARs. This poses a great threat to economic autonomy in Hong Kong and Macau as the jurisprudential consistency and coherence in these two SARs might be undermined. So far, the Chief-Executive of the HKSAR has requested for interpretation of the HKBL for three times and the Court of Final Appeal (the CFA) on its own initiative has also made the first request for interpretation in 2011. The first three requests for interpretation have been answered and the fourth is still pending. This fourth request relates to the application of state immunity to recognition and enforcement of arbitral awards in the HKSAR and poses great threat to the economic autonomy of the HKSAR.[51]

The practices of interpreting the HKBL may undermine the 'security and predictability' of trade environment when established jurisprudence by the CFA in the HKSAR might be altered. These practices may also lead to the limitation of competence of these two SARs in participating in the world trading system.

---

major domestic paper industry favours anti-dumping duty to protect the 'injured industry', another major publisher argues against this initiate, indicating the economic difficulties which small-size publishers are faced with as well as the potential cultural impacts when the publishing industries become even more withered once the production costs surges as a result of the anti-dumping duties. The issue of 'competing interests and values' will be further elaborated in Chapter III.

[49] HKBL, Art. 116; MABL, Art. 112.

[50] HKBL, Arts. 11, 12; MABL, Arts. 13, 14.

[51] *See infra* Chapter VIII, text to (n 49) *et seq.*

Within this context, courts in these two SARs are of crucial importance in preserving their autonomy in economic affairs even though their situation seems difficult. Put simply, courts are responsible for ensuring that WTO rules are fully respected and implemented in these two SARs and that the competence of these two SARs in participating in the WTO will not be weakened. As Hong Kong and Macau, being a free port and maintaining zero-tariff policy, present themselves as highly free economies, the courts in Hong Kong and Macau should strive to preserve the economic autonomy of these two SARs.[52]

C. *Judicial Review to Ensure WTO Compliance*

China's capacity and willingness to carry out its WTO obligation was repeatedly questioned long before it entered into the WTO. Consequently, a transitional review mechanism with the mandate to monitor China's implementation efforts was established in the WTO. Apart from this transitional review mechanism, some Members also enact national legal instruments to oversee China's implementing efforts and to ensure the conformity with WTO rules.[53] Among various areas, China's implementation of the TRIPS Agreement is a good illustration of why domestic judicial review is so important to ensure WTO compliance and how effective it can be.

Since its accession, China has been forced to strengthen its intellectual property rights protection as this issue is on the spotlight of US-China and EU-China trade. In response to an agreement between Chinese Deputy Premier Wu Yi and the US government at the 15th annual meeting of the US-China Joint Commission on Commerce and Trade, the Supreme People's Court (the SPC) and the People's Supreme Procuratorate (the SPP) jointly issued *An Interpretation on Several Issues of Concrete Application of Laws in Handling Criminal Cases of infringing Intellectual Property* on 22 December 2004.[54] According to some observers, the 2004 *Interpretation* touches upon five main elements:

(1) lower the numerical thresholds determining the criminal status of infringing acts; (2) allow for accomplice liability for importers, exporters, landlords, and others who

---

[52] This competence issue will be further elaborated in Chapter VIII.

[53] For example, the Congress of the US enacted the US-China Relations Act of 2000, which requires the USTR under section 421 to report annually to the Congress on the compliance to China's commitments relating to its accession to the WTO. Both multilateral commitments and any bilateral commitments made to the US are included. The USTR has subsequently prepared an annual report on China's WTO compliance to Congress since 2002. Apart from this, the US-China Economic and Security Review Commission, created in 2000 under the National Defence Authorisation Act of 2001, also reports to the Congress annually. WTO compliance is also of one the highlights of these annual reports.

[54] An English version of this interpretation <http://www.wipo.int/wipolex/en/text.jsp?file_id=199787> accessed 1 September 2011.

> assist infringers; (3) permit goods produced in factories and/or kept in warehouses to be included in sales calculations; (4) authorize using the number of illegally duplicated disks or internet advertising revenue to satisfy the for-profit requirement; and (5) expand the definition of an infringing trademark.[55]

Another *Interpretation* in relation to criminal cases of infringing intellectual property rights was issued on 5 April 2007. This 2007 *Interpretation* widens the scope of 'reproduction and distribution' governed in Article 217 of China's criminal law to include advertising for the sale of copyright-infringing products. It also lowers the thresholds, in terms of illegal copies, redefining 'serious' or 'especially serious' as referred to in Article 217 of China's criminal law. The 2007 *Interpretation* was an effort to prevent the US from bringing a complaint against China on the enforcement and protection intellectual property rights to the WTO.[56] These efforts made by the SPC illustrate their importance in implementing the TRIPS Agreement and protecting intellectual property rights. These efforts reflect the role that other WTO Members expect Chinese courts to play: it is through Chinese courts where minimum standards of protection can be ensured.[57]

Compliance with WTO law through effective judicial review of external trade measures in of equal importance to Taiwan. As indicated in the Secretariat Report during its first Trade Policy Review, Taiwan prohibits inbound cross-Taiwan-strait trade involving some 2,200 tariff lines[58] and cross-Taiwan-strait trade can only be made by indirect shipment through a third port, usually Hong Kong.[59] With regard to cross-strait direct investment, 'little inbound investment has been allowed, and outbound investment, if not prohibited, requires the approval of the relevant Chinese Taipei authorities'.[60] These measures apparently contradict the principle of Most-Favoured-Nation treatment, one of the fundamental non-discriminatory rules of the WTO. Although the transhipment requirement has been lifted by virtue of the ink of direct-transportation agreements,[61] a number of trade restrictive measures against China persist. Faced with these restrictions of cross-Taiwan-strait trade, it is of crucial importance for domestic courts to allow individual

[55] B Qiang, et al., 'China: New Franchising and Direct Selling Regulations' (2006) 40 The International Lawyer: International Legal Developments in Review 2005 547, 556.

[56] *See infra* Chapter IV, text to (n 44) *et seq*; Chapter VII, text to (n 82) *et seq*.

[57] The author has argued elsewhere that, the TRIPS Agreement, given its detailed procedural and substantial prescriptions, has transformed Chinese administrative law. During this process of transformation, Chinese courts play a pivotal role. C-H Wu, 'How Does TRIPS Transform Chinese Administrative Law?' (2008) 8 Global Jurist <http://www.bepress.com/gj/vol8/iss1/art6> accessed 1 September 2011.

[58] WTO, *Trade Policy Review-Report by the Secretariat-Separate Customs Territory of Taiwan, Penghu, Kinmen and Matsu* (16 May 2006) WT/TPR/S/165, 14.

[59] Ibid 40.

[60] Ibid 17.

[61] *See infra* Chapter VII, text to (n 103) *et seq*.

economic actors to challenge these WTO inconsistent laws and regulations and ensure the WTO compliance.[62]

D. *Independent and Impartial Judicial Review to Ensure Full Protection of Right to Trade in China*

China's Accession Protocol includes two atypical obligations: to provide an independent and impartial judicial review and to protect right to trade. These two obligations indicate that WTO Members are subscribed to the idea that with an independent and impartial judicial review in place where individual economic actors can assert the right to trade, China's WTO obligations can be more effectively implemented. Members realise that effective enforcement of China's WTO obligations should not rely solely upon the attitude of Chinese government; individuals should be to allowed to challenge WTO-inconsistent measures in domestic courts.[63]

These two obligations appear even more critical in light of the fact that the judiciary in China is often identified with corruption, lack of independence, and subject to interference and that human rights are rarely respected.[64] China's records in human rights protection are continuously notorious. Economic freedoms and trading rights may be subject to various restrictions and easily infringed. This situation again underlines the importance to these two obligations as embodied in China's Accession Protocol, but their implementation nonetheless remains at the hands of Chinese government. The crucial issue here is thus how to ensure that these two obligations are fully implemented, and how to evaluate whether judicial review in China is independent and impartial and whether right to trade in China is fully protected, or not.

E. *The Importance of WTO Dispute Settlement Mechanism*

With two levels of judicial review presented above, trade disputes would inevitably come to Geneva when they are beyond the capacity of domestic courts. Some examples help to illustrate the significance of the WTO Dispute Settlement Mechanism to the Greater China, especially to China and Taiwan. It is clear that

[62] It should be noted that, WTO compliance is not identical to trade liberalisation, as conflicting values such as public morals, human, animal, or plant life or health and the conservation of exhaustible natural resources, are explicitly referred to in the general exceptions. Security exception is also another example. The hard case presented to Taiwanese courts here is how to balance conflicting interests and competing values especially when national security is at stake.

[63] This issue will be further dealt with in Chapter V.

[64] V M Hung, 'China's WTO Commitment on Independent Judicial Review: Impact on Legal and Political Reform' (2004) 52 American Journal of Comparative Law 77, 82–89.

domestic courts are still governed by constitutional constraints. They are obliged to respect their international obligations; however, they are also obliged to observe their constitutional rules and principles. When one conflicts with the other, it is unfeasible and impractical to refer these disputes to domestic courts. Further, to force China to implement its WTO obligation to provide an independent and impartial judicial review in a meaningful way depends much upon the pressure of other WTO Members and the potential challenges in the WTO Dispute Settlement Mechanism.

With regard to cross-Taiwan-strait trade relations, how China and Taiwan would avail themselves of this WTO Dispute Settlement Mechanism was highly uncertain and much disputed at the point when they acceded to the WTO. Nevertheless, ten years after their accessions, it seems a bit clearer. Even though some argues that being a Member in the WTO does not alter Taiwan's status as a separate custom territory, and not a state,[65] and China should feel secured in terms of 'sovereignty concerns,' it is commonly believed that China is unlikely to lodge a complaint against Taiwan in the WTO. This seems a firm and settled position of China. Some Chinese trade officials and lawyers were worried that Taiwan might jump into the WTO Dispute Settlement Mechanism in order to show that it has a different identity from China. However, Taiwan seems to have taken a cautious approach in dealing cross-Taiwan-strait trade issue in the WTO Dispute Settlement Mechanism. As will be seen in chapter VII, Taiwan has availed this mechanism by joint-consultation and intervention as a third party, which might help both Taiwan and China to get prepared to deal with cross-Taiwan-strait trade disputes in the WTO Dispute Settlement Mechanism.[66]

IV. Short Conclusion

This chapter has illustrated the ever closer economic interdependence in the Greater China and pointed to potential trade disputes. In view of these, this chapter thus argues that strengthened judicial review is desirable and necessary. This chapter firstly presents the constraints for the realisation of effective two-level judicial review under the WTO and clarifies why the judicial review remains ineffective regardless the ambition of negotiators during the Uruguay Round to enhance its effectiveness. In order to overcome these obstacles, this chapter explores the legitimacy of judiciary in intervening in external trade relations; its

---

[65] *See, e.g.*, Q Kong, 'Can the WTO Dispute Settlement Mechanism Resolve the Trade Disputes Between China and Taiwan?' (2002) 5 Journal of International Economic Law 747, 756–757.

[66] The cross-strait issue in the WTO Dispute Settlement Mechanism will be dealt with in Chapter VII.

contribution to consistency and coherence international trade relations and to the protection of rights and interests of individual economic actors. This chapter then argues that a strengthened judicial review is even more compelling for the Greater China for the following reasons: to ensure rational decision-making; to ensure economic autonomy in Hong Kong and Macau; to enhance WTO compliance; and to maintain an independent and impartial judicial review to ensure fuller protection of right to trade in China. This chapter finally articulates the significance of the WTO Dispute Settlement Mechanism for the Greater China, in particular for Taiwan and China. However, how to resolve hard cases remains unanswered. A good example of these hard cases would be the dilemma of courts in Taiwan when they are called upon to balance with Taiwan's WTO obligations and its national security concerns. This answer depends how judges perceive international obligations and constitutional obligations and their role as 'judges' in reconciling these two. This question will be further addressed in Chapter III, and the hard case of Taiwanese courts will be resolved in Chapter VI.

CHAPTER THREE

WTO CONSTITUTIONALISM AND ITS CONTRIBUTION TO JUDICIAL SETTLEMENT OF TRADE DISPUTES IN THE GREATER CHINA

I. Introduction

This chapter deals with the methodological approach of this work and argues that a constitutional approach on the WTO law will contribute to judicial settlement of trade disputes in the Greater China. Whereas it may touch upon current debates related to the WTO in a broad context, special regard is paid to the particularities of these four WTO Members and their interaction within this forum. With respect to the broad context, Section II analyses three versions of WTO constitutionalism focusing on the horizontal distribution of competence between different WTO organs, vertical allocation of competence between Members and the WTO and empowerment of private parties in this world trading system through effective judicial protection.

In applying these approaches to the Greater China, this chapter argues that the right to trade and the obligation to provide an independent and impartial judicial review as set out in China's Accession Protocol, complemented by national constitutions and the two Basic Laws would contribute to the constitutionalisation of external trade relations in the Greater China. It will also illustrate how the WTO Agreement or their WTO memberships may act as a pre-commitment to these four Members. Finally, it also argues that an effective judicial review in foreign trade relations in the Greater China is an essential and indispensible element for legal and economic integration processes.

II. Three Versions of Constitutionalism in the WTO

Constitutionalism in the WTO is one the most contested and divided concepts. Even for those who embrace the same terminology, they may focus on different dimensions and refer to different concepts. By and large, three approaches may be distinguished. The first approach stresses on the WTO as an organisation and underlines the distribution of competence between different organs and the institutional balance of the WTO. The second approach focuses on the allocation of competence between the WTO and its Members and concerns the linkage between the WTO law and domestic legal systems. These two approaches focus on structural aspects of the WTO and pay attention to allocation of powers horizontally between various bodies of the WTO – the governing bodies, Councils, and the Dispute Settlement Mechanism and vertically between the WTO and its Members. The third approach focuses on the role of international economic actors in the world trading system, underlines the rights and interests of private parties under the WTO Agreement and thus advocates for an effective judicial review both through the intergovernmental WTO Dispute Settlement Mechanism and domestic courts.

A. *Institutional Architecture and Distribution of Competence Between WTO Organs*

According to the first approach, the term 'WTO Constitution' is employed in a sense that this constitution defines a particular system of governing rules underpinning architecture of this organisation. A clearly defined institutional architecture is of crucial importance as the WTO is shaping world economics and influencing non-economic goals.[1] Being aware of great impacts of globalisation and the inability of states to deal with it, Jackson argues that international economics in a globalised world needs an appropriate international institution. According to him, the market mechanism cannot function unless there are effective human institutions to provide a sound framework underlying this global economic market. The WTO is one of the appropriate places to deal with this framework. In order to succeed with this task, the WTO should fix several constitutional flaws. Institutionally, the WTO relies too much on consensus-based decision-making and relatively lacks of openness. It should also redress its overemphasis on reciprocity, sovereignty, and the interests of producers. Institutionally, the WTO relies too much on consensus-based decision-making and relatively lacks of openness.[2]

B. *Allocation of Competence Between Members and the WTO*

Cottier proposes his vision of WTO constitutionalism out for the concerns of vertical allocation of powers. He argues that regional and global integration processes will significantly reshape the role and function of national constitutions, as regulatory powers of these regional and global organisations, such as the European Union, Bretton Woods institutions and the WTO have increasingly aggrandised. Because the regulatory measures by regional or global integration laws need to be complemented or implemented by national measures, they might shift and upset the existent balance of traditional constitutional patterns, as the fulfilment of

---

[1] J H Jackson, *The World Trading Organisation: Constitution and Jurisprudence* (Royal Institute of International Affairs, London 1998) 102–103.

[2] J H Jackson, 'Sovereignty, Subsidiarity, and Separation of Powers' in D L M Kennedy and J D Southwick (eds), *The Political Economy of international Trade Law: Essays in Honor of Robert E Hudec* (Cambridge University Press, Cambridge 2002) 28–31.

regional and global obligations may lead to the erosion of the distinction of task national constitutions assign to central and local governments.[3] A broader constitutional concept, extending from national level to regional and global level, is thus proposed in order to fix this problem. Powers and responsibilities should be allocated to the most appropriate level. A domain may also be regulated by different levels at the same time.[4] This demands a framework capable of taking into good account of the balance of power and assigning the powers to the most appropriate level. This framework should also take into consideration horizontal competing interests in different subject matters, notably non-economic concerns. In order to build up with such framework, a constitutional understanding is indispensible.[5]

In terms of the WTO, Cottier argues that the constitutionalism in the WTO is primarily a matter of attitudes and perceptions of existing instruments and their proper role and function. In other words, the most important point in pursuing constitutionalism in the WTO is one's attitudes and perceptions of the WTO Agreement and the role and function of this organisation. These attitudes and perceptions influence firstly interpretations and applications of existing instruments, and subsequently the shape of these instruments. This constitutionalism in the WTO enables existent instruments to include positive standards in various fields. It will finally address the issue of legitimacy of policy goals in the WTO since rule-making and standard-setting in the global level has expanded exponentially. It is thus essential to strike a balance between governments at different levels and to bring producers, consumers, and public good interests into this policy-making process.[6] In a word, Cottier's idea of the WTO constitutionalism aims firstly to deal with the distribution of powers at different levels. This WTO constitutionalism would then addresses conflicting interests and competing values, such as trade and environment or human rights.

C. *Empowerment of Individuals and Judicial Protection of Their Rights and Interests under the WTO Agreement*

The third approach is advocated by Petersmann. Petersmann's constitutional approach on the WTO law comprises several features. To begin with, he argues

[3] T Cottier, 'Reforming the Swiss Federal Constitution: An International Lawyer's Perspective' in M Butler, et al. (eds), *The Making of Modern Switzerland: 1848–1998* (St. Martin's Press, New York 2000) 80–87. On the comment of this 'five-storey' house, *see* R Howse and K Nicolaidis, 'Legitimacy through 'Higher Law'? Why Constitutionalizing the WTO Is a Step Too Far?' in T Cottier and P C Mavroidis (eds), *The Role of the Judge in International Trade Regulation* (The University of Michigan Press, Ann Arbor, Mich. 2003) 320–325.

[4] Ibid 91.

[5] T Cottier, 'Limits to the International Trade: the Constitutional Challenge' (2000) American Society of International Law Proceedings 220, 221.

[6] Ibid 222.

that the WTO Agreement should be read as a constitutional instrument. Based on this understanding, WTO law should not be interpreted in purely economic terms since the legal and political objectives of the WTO are no less important than trade liberalisation. According to him, the WTO Agreement does not only employ formal techniques ('constitutional methods') but also includes various substantive principles (constitutional principles). These constitutional methods and constitutional principles are characteristics of constitutionalism. WTO law can thus be conceived a part of multilevel constitutional framework in multilevel trade governance.[7]

As far as the multilevel governance is concerned, the 'WTO Constitution' complements with national constitutions as national governments, in such globally interdependent world are not capable of allocating the international division of labour, providing basic needs and protecting global public interests. Besides, this 'WTO Constitution' can also help to set up multilevel restraints and to prevent human rights of citizens from being abused by government powers.[8] With this multilevel constitutionalism in place, trade governance can be duly decentralised to appropriate corresponding levels where Most-Favoured-Nation treatment, National Treatment, private property rights, protection of freedom of trade, and rule of law are constitutionally safeguarded. This multilevel constitutionalism will also require national legal order to show due respect to WTO law, particularly dictating stricter compliance to the WTO rules and more effective judicial protection in domestic courts.

III. The Pursuit of WTO Constitutionalism and Its Contribution to Judicial Settlement of Trade Disputes in Greater China

The three versions of constitutionalism in the WTO as noted in the previous section originate from the same observation of this ever globalising/globalised world, where one single state is not able to handle with various complicated trade and trade-related issues. Besides, trade and trade-related measures taken by one state may have great exterritorial impact.[9] They may adversely affect foreign countries, individuals and enterprises. Cooperation between states by contractual agreements appears inefficient and ineffective and thus demands the establishment of an institutionalised organisation to address these issues. However, this institutionalised organisation with great regulatory powers has been continuously

[7] E U Petersmann, 'Multilevel Trade Governance in the WTO Requires Multilevel Constitutionalism' in C Joerges and E U Petersmann (eds), *Constitutionalism, Multilevel Trade Governance and Social Regulation* (Hart Publishing, Oxford; Portland, Oregon 2006) 32–33.

[8] Ibid 35.

[9] An illustrative example is the *US-Shrimps* case.

questioned by its 'legitimacy deficit', in terms of its competence covering wide-ranging areas and the penetrating effect of its regulatory decisions.

An approach focusing on the institutional feature, notably, the horizontal allocation of powers is thus proposed by Jackson to deal with this 'legitimacy deficit'. His 'WTO Constitution' emphasises on institutional aspects of this world trading system. Cottier also takes his departing point from the allocation of powers, but he concerns mainly the vertical one. He emphasises how these global norms come into domestic constitutional legal order, and thus argues that a constitutional understanding is necessary to ensure consistency and coherence between the international legal order and domestic constitutional legal order. Powers and responsibilities can also be allocated to the most appropriate level where competing values and interests can be taken into due account. Petersmann's effort aims to empower individuals to protect themselves against arbitrary protectionist interventions of domestic governments. WTO law can thus serves as weapons to wield against these interventions. According to Petersmann, to allow individuals to challenge WTO-inconsistent domestic measures is the best way to make these WTO rules effective. These WTO rules are not limited to trade concerns. Effective implementation of these WTO rules can also bring about rule of law, protection of human rights and realisation of social justice.[10]

These three approaches reflect some of the fundamental issues when pursuing constitutionalism in the WTO. Within the WTO, this constitutionalism has to define clearly the distribution of competence between different WTO organs and ensure the institutional balance and well-functioning of this organisation. It has also to clarify the relationship between the organisation and its constituencies and to define the mandate or competence of this organisation. These two issues may not bring about so much controversy as they have long been topics of public international law. However, when one pursues WTO constitutionalism further, the WTO Dispute Settlement Mechanism, by virtue of its compulsory jurisdiction, may arouse concerns, as this dispute settlement mechanism has great capacity in ensuring compliance and imposing sanctions and deeply penetrates into domestic legal system. This brings to a related issue: the legal status of WTO Agreement within the domestic legal system and its applicability in the domestic courts. Finally, this WTO constitutionalism has to locate international economic actors in

[10] On the most fierce critic of Petermann's human rights approach to international economic law, *see* P Alston, 'Resisting the Merger and Acquisition of Human Rights by Trade Law: A Reply to Petersmann' (2002) 13 European Journal of International Law 815; R Howse, 'Human Rights in the WTO: Whose Rights, What Humanity? Comment on Petersmann' (2002) 13 European Journal of International Law 651, 655. For further examination and critics of Jackson's and Petersmann's arguments in relation to the constitutionalisation of the WTO, *see* D Z Cass, *The Constitutionalization of the World Trade Organization* (Oxford University Press, Oxford 2005).

this world trading system, to define their rights and interests arising from the WTO Agreement and to provide possible judicial remedies if their rights and interests are infringed.

The decisive point here is one's conception of the role of the judge and the adjudicating process in the WTO. Further, one has to redefine the relationship between law and politics in this world trading system.[11] The WTO Dispute Settlement Mechanism has been widely regarded as the most important achievement during the Uruguay Round negotiations. The strengthened domestic judicial review is also perceived as a major success. The WTO judges, both the Appellate Body members and judges in domestic courts are expected to assume substantial responsibility of judicial trade governance in this world trading system.

'Courts and regional integration' has been extensively explored in literature in relation to European integration.[12] Although these European experiences are unique, it does not necessarily prevent one from appreciating the importance of courts in the course of global economic integration. Meanwhile, the role of judges in international economic adjudication has been attracting more and more attention, and numerous publications are devoted to exploration of the WTO Dispute Settlement Mechanism. As experiences of European integration suggest, with the proliferation of trade and rules, it requires someone to monitor, apply and enforce these rules. Courts have been proved the best guardian of private interests and individual rights.

Judicial review, in particular constitutional review, is claimed to perform four regulatory functions: it operates as a counterweight to majority rule, pacifies the politics, legitimises public policy and protects human rights. These functions are most apparent when courts act as 'positive' legislators. When the effectiveness of resolving constitutional disputes is sustained, it attracts more non-judicial actors to pursue their interests through constitutional review. Judges are thus made responsible to exercising more powers of decision-making. Techniques of constitutional adjudication will become an important mode of argumentation and decision-making in judicial systems, which is partly a logical and normative consequence of direct effect of rights provisions and partly a result of complex dialogues between constitutional judges and the judiciary.[13] With the expansion of

---

[11] Howse & Nicolaidis, in T Cottier and P C Mavroidis (eds) (n 3) 320.

[12] *See, e.g.*, A M Slaughter, et al., *The European Court and National Courts - Doctrine and Jurisprudence: Legal Change in its Social Context* (Hart Publishing, Oxford 1998); M P Maduro, *We the Court. The European Court of Justice and the European Economic Constitution: A Critical Reading of Article 30 of EC Treaty* (Hart Publishing, Oxford; Portland, Oregon 1998). *See* also M L Volcansek, 'Courts and Regionalism' in F Snyder (ed), *Regional and Global Regulation of International Trade* (Hart Publishing, Oxford and Portland, Oregon 2002) 165–180.

[13] A Stone Sweet, *Governing with Judges: Constitutional Politics in Europe* (Oxford University Press, Oxford 2000) 114.

judicial powers and gradual but inevitable infusion into other judicial actors, a form of decentralised judicial governance is thus made possible and available.[14]

In respect of the quasi-judicial governance in the WTO, the WTO judges sit in the centre of these debates presented above and are also the key to resolve them. The attempt to include human rights dimension in the WTO relies upon effective judicial protection. A rights-based approach toward WTO law cannot be sustained if 'rights' are not guaranteed by and resort cannot be had to courts. It is clear that 'rights' referred to in the DSU means the rights of the WTO Members, not rights as understood by human rights law. However, it does not imply that individual rights are absent in WTO law. The world trading system is mainly composed of individual economic actors whose rights are to be ensured in this system. Although these rights, to great extent, are indirectly defined and protected and resort to the WTO Dispute Settlement Mechanism should be sought indirectly through its home countries, these rights nevertheless serve as a good basis for individual actors to claim in the domestic courts.

Truly, these rights are mainly economic rights. It should be nevertheless stressed that a minimum notion focusing on non-discrimination, individual rights (though mainly economic rights) and dispute-settlement mechanisms (particularly courts) will gradually develop into a set of individual constitutional rights protected from any form of power. With the protection of economic rights under dispute-settlement mechanisms, international rule of law can be gradually developed, and sufficient inputs can be thus obtained to 'feed' this global constitutionalism.[15]

On the other hand, the authority of constitutional principles embedded in the WTO agreements will not be fully respected, and the constitutional function of WTO law cannot be effective, if sanctions for the non-compliance are not in place. The Dispute Settlement Mechanism in the WTO is certainly an important device for these sanctions; no less important is domestic judicial review. One might even be tempted to say that all the WTO judges are responsible for the effectiveness of WTO law. However, the crucial question is who the WTO judges are. Why should national judges honour WTO law at the expense of national constitution and legislation? This again is the 'hard case'. It traces back to one's perception of constitutionalism: namely, whether national constitutional order should allow these WTO constitutional principles to flow in to ensure individual rights are better protected both at the WTO and national level. These constitutional principles in WTO law

[14] Ibid 136–139. Stone Sweet argues that such diffusion is not limited to judicial actors, but also to legislative actors. He concludes, in the last sentence of his book, that '[I]n the end, governing with judges also means governing like judges.'

[15] M P Maduro, 'The Constitution of the Global Market' in F Snyder (ed), *Regional and Global Regulation of International Trade* (Hart Publishing, Oxford and Portland, Oregon 2002) 63.

can actually complement national constitutionalism, and help to guarantee individual rights.[16]

Building upon these analyses, the remainder of this section investigates whether a constitutional approach on the WTO law is essential and beneficial for trade dispute resolution in the Greater China. It firstly illustrates the importance of the WTO membership as pre-commitments for these four Members of the Greater China. It then explores the constitutional significance of right to trade as provided in China's Accession Protocol and the importance of national constitutions and the two Basic Laws. Finally, it points to the way to bring about effective judicial review for the resolution of trade disputes in the Greater China.

A. *WTO Obligations as Pre-Commitments*

One major constitutional function of WTO law is to ensure domestic constitutional guarantee of these fundamental market freedoms, non-discrimination treatment and judicial remedies. WTO obligations which Members undertake can be viewed as pre-commitments through hand-tying for the long-term benefits at the expense of short-term benefits. Such pre-commitments are indispensable for a country to lock in the progress of its economic reform and to make the reform irreversible. It is also an essential vehicle for Chinese reformists to counter against domestic political opposition and to resist protectionism. Such pre-commitments might be viewed as 'undemocratic'. However, these undemocratic pre-commitments substantially contribute to the sustainability of Chinese economic reforms and make the gradual legal and political reforms possible. China's pre-commitments to the right to trade and to the continuous economic liberalisation are justified by their out-put legitimacy in terms of the following aspects: greater opportunities of self-development; better protection of properties rights and the gradual-evolving civil and political rights. A free economic market will eventually sustain enough foundation for the development of a stronger civil society.

In respect of Taiwan, cross-Taiwan-strait trade relations have been long captured by protectionism and political interests. This over-politicisation prevents cross-Taiwan-strait trade policies from being reasonably and deliberately debated. Pre-commitments are of great significance here in that they help to maintain consistency and coherence between the Taiwan's international obligations and its national regulatory measures. While Taiwan committed to abide by WTO laws and

---

[16] For a discussion on constitutional nationalism and multilevel constitutionalism, *see* E U Petersmann, 'State Sovereignty, Popular Sovereignty and Individual Sovereignty: From Constitutional Nationalism to Multilevel Constitutionalism in International Economic Law?' in W Shan, et al. (eds), *Redefining Sovereignty in International Economic Law* (Hart Publishing, Oxford and Portland, Oregon 2006) 27–60.

implement its international obligations under the WTO Agreement, it maintained numerous WTO-incompatible trade restrictions against China. This exposes a great inconsistency and incoherence between its international commitments and national decision-making. Therefore, the domestic constitutional function of the WTO in controlling domestic decision-making is thus necessary and indispensable. A constitutional approach toward WTO law focusing on its domestic constitutional function, will help national decision-makers to resist the influence of protectionism and specific political interests, and thus minimise the discrepancy between international commitments and national decision-making.

The understanding of pre-commitments is also of great significance to Hong Kong and Macau. Their status as Contracting Parties to the GATT and subsequently Members of the WTO should be perceived as a contractual understanding between China and UK, as well as between China and Portugal. It is also a mechanism to ensure their economic autonomy through the presence in the international scene. Regarding the economic autonomy of Hong Kong and Macau, in addition to the two aforementioned declarations, two instruments are of constitutional importance. One is China's communications to the GATT concerning the separate customs territory status of Hong Kong and Macau, which possess full autonomy in the conduct of their external commercial relations and of other matters provided for in the Agreement. The other is the recognition, in the two Basic Laws, of the competence of these two SARs to participate, as separate customs territories, in the international organisations as well as international agreements. Although the HKBL and the MABL are national legislation passed by the NPC, their constitutional contractual character should not be neglected. They are not only a contract between China and its two SARs to ensure that the market economic autonomy remains unchanged for fifty years, but they are also a fruit from the contractual agreements of Sino-British Joint Declaration and Sino-Portuguese Joint Declaration. The authority of these two Basic Laws derives not only from Chinese constitution, but also from these two international agreements. These pre-commitments do not only constitutionally control the domestic trade policy-making in Hong Kong and Macau, but they also place a constitutional constraint upon China in relation to the economic autonomy of these two SARs.

B. *Right to Trade, National Constitutions, and Basic Law*

China' accession to the WTO has tremendous importance not only because of economic impact, but also because of its constitutional and legal significance. A minimum notion of constitutionalism may be established on the foundation of non-discrimination, individual rights (albeit economic rights), and dispute settlement mechanisms. These elements are actually explicitly provided in China's Accession Protocol to the WTO. Apart from fundamental non-discrimination principles, including Most-Favoured-Nation treatment and National Treatment,

China's Accession Protocol includes also the obligation to provide the right to trade, defined as the right to import and to export, and an independent and impartial judicial review. These elements will gradually sustain a constitutional approach to WTO law, which ensures not only the commercial interests of the state but also the trading rights of individuals.

Section 5 of the Accession Protocol begins with the recognition of China's right to regulate trade, but prescribes that such regulation should be in accordance with the WTO Agreement. It then dictates that the scope and availability of this right to trade should be progressively liberalised. Three years after China's accession, except for those goods still reserved for state trading listed in Annex 2A, all individuals and enterprises shall have the right to trade in all goods throughout Chinese customs territory.

The right to trade is defined as the right to import and export. Goods imported into China should be accorded with National Treatment. Foreign individuals and enterprises, in respect of the right to trade should also be accorded with treatment no less favourable than Chinese individuals and enterprises. Those goods reserved for state trading should also be phased out according to the schedule in the Annex. The specific schedule was set as follows. Beginning one year after accession, joint-venture enterprises with minority share of foreign-investment would be granted full rights to trade; beginning two years after accession majority share foreign-invested joint ventures would be granted full rights to trade; within three years after accession, all enterprises in China would be granted the right to trade. Foreign-invested enterprises would not be required to establish in a particular form or as a separate entity to engage in importing and exporting activities.[17] Therefore, ten years have passed China's accession; all enterprises in China should be granted to the right to trade, except for those reserved to state trading.

Distribution service is not covered by the right to trade, even though these two elements are of the same importance for foreign individuals and enterprises to engage in economic activities in China. As generally understood, international trade in goods depends much on the domestic trade and distribution sectors. The degree of competition in these domestic distribution sectors has major influence on trade in goods, as distribution service can greatly facilitate trade in goods. The distribution service can be thus regarded as a linkage between trade in goods and trade in services.[18] Detailed commitments in distribution service are identified in China's Working Party Report. Before acceding to the WTO, China generally did not permit foreign companies to distribute products in China, namely, to provide

[17] WTO, *Working Party Report on the Accession of China* (hereinafter, the Working Party Report) (1 October 2001) WT/ACC/CHN/49, para. 83.

[18] J Francois and I Wooton, Market Structure in Services and Market Access in Goods, CEPR Discussion Paper No. 5135, 1, available at SSRN <http://ssrn.com/abstract=784687> accessed 1 September 2011.

wholesaling, retailing, franchising or commission agent services or to provide related services, such as repair and maintenance services. In its accession package, China agreed to phase out these prohibitions over three years, subject to limited exceptions.[19] As previously noted, these restrictions should have been lifted as the phase-out period elapsed.

It is true that the right to trade recognised in China's Accession Protocol is comparatively limited in scope, and that this right to trade has to be further supplemented and materialised by domestic implementations. However, a WTO-consistent interpretation of this right in Chinese domestic legal system can provoke better domestic constitutional guarantee in conformity with its international liberalisation commitments. Such interpretation is of particular importance in Chinese context as most economic activities, prior to its open-up policy, were dominated by state powers. It is thus important to make market freedoms available and fair competition possible so that individuals are able to pursue their own self-developments through their human capacities by exercising positive freedoms (e.g. freedom of profession, property, and trade).[20] Liberal economic rights are no less important than civil and political rights concerns, at least in the case of China. It would be too naïve to argue for political and civil rights when one's property and possession cannot be guaranteed. In this vein, the 2004 Constitutional Amendment that explicitly recognises private properties rights, and lays down the obligation for the State to protect these rights can be seen as a response to China's WTO obligation of the right to trade.

A constitutional approach on the WTO is of the same importance to Taiwan. The closer economic interdependence between Taiwan and China has already been a given fact which will be further strengthened and accelerated. In this context, one has to figure out how to deal with potential trade disputes arising from economic interdependence amidst political antagonism. Private individuals and enterprises are the way out. Namely, private individuals and enterprises should be empowered to engage in their economic activities and where necessary and appropriate, to challenges WTO-inconsistent measures in domestic courts.

It was expected that Taiwan would normalise its trade relations with China since its Taiwan accession to the WTO, as Taiwan and China did not opt for non-application. However, various restrictions on out-bound investments and on market accesses for Chinese products persist even though ten years has passed since Taiwan's accession. The paradoxical dilemma must be broken through. Judicial

[19] The US initiated two requests for consultations under the Dispute Settlement Understanding on 10 April 2007, one of which the right to trade and distribution service are the subject matter. WTO, *China-Measures Affecting Trading Rights and Distribution Services for Certain Publications and Audiovisual Entertainment Products-Request for Consultations by the United States* (16 April 2007) WT/DS363/1.

[20] Petersmann, in Cottier, et al. (eds) (n 3) 56.

enforcement of WTO rules in Taiwanese courts through the challenges of private individuals and enterprises appear to the best way out. Rights and interests of these private economic actors are also in need of judicial protection in Taiwan. This need calls for the normalisation and constitutionalisation of cross-Taiwan-strait trade relations.

The normalisation and constitutionalisation of Taiwan's trade relations with China closely link to the domestic constitutional function of WTO law, in terms of its constitutional control of domestic regulatory measures. Although the extremely unusual reference of right to trade is not existent in Taiwan's accession protocol. Nonetheless, those WTO fundamental principles, in particular non-discrimination principles and various clear and unconditional market access commitments lend good arguments against these arbitrary and unreasonable trade restrictions.

External trade competence of Hong Kong and Macau and their free trade policies have special status in these two SARs. They are both entitled to participate in international organisations and international trade agreements, as guaranteed by their constitutional instruments, the HKBL and MABL.[21] Both Hong Kong and Macau should maintain the status of free port,[22] pursue the policy of free trade and safeguard the free movements of goods, intangible assets, and capitals.[23] External trade competence and free trade policy are not only important for the economic development of these two SARs, but also indispensable for their exercises of legal autonomy. With free trade and close integration into the world economy, fully guaranteed economic rights can thus help to sustain civil and political rights in Hong Kong and Macau.[24]

C. *Judicial Governance in External Trade Relations*

A constitutional approach on the WTO law, especially by empowering individuals to challenge WTO-inconsistent measures in domestic courts, would also contribute to judicial protection in external trade relations in the Greater China. Although judicial practices in Chinese courts are still far from the ideal type of western models, China's WTO obligation to provide an independent and impartial judicial

[21] HKBL, Art. 116; MABL, Art. 112.

[22] HKBL, Art. 114; MABL, Art. 110.

[23] HKBL, Art. 114; MABL, Art. 111.

[24] It is thus fair to say that those who denounce right to trade as non-human rights fail to appreciate the possibility for economic rights to give substantial feedback to political rights. While it is true that without further legal and political reform, Chinese economic reform will not sustain, it is also true that without an open economic market, Chinese legal and political reform finds no foundations.

review is bringing about significant changes to Chinese legal system, in particular in respect of the administrative litigations concerning intellectual property rights.

It is partly because the TRIPS Agreement provides detailed procedural requirements and substantial elements of intellectual property right that lay down a minimum standard by which China has to abide. It is also partly because intellectual property rights are individual rights in nature that lend a good weapon for rights holders to wield their rights and interests. As a great number of intellectual property rights are possessed by foreign individuals and enterprises, their resort to Chinese domestic courts for judicial remedies are actually backed with the support of their own national governments. These challenges in Chinese domestic courts, supported by governments of home countries, force China to faithfully implement its judicial review obligation to protection the right to trade.

The recognition of constitutional significance of China's international obligation of the right to trade and to provide an independent and impartial judicial review would sustain a thin form of constitutionalism where private individuals can seek judicial remedies in defending their trading rights. Admittedly, this thin form of constitutionalism concerns mainly economic rights. Nonetheless, it may gradually evolve with the expansion of judicial powers.

Similarly, a constitutional approach on the WTO law would lend strength for Taiwanese courts in hearing case relating to China trade. In stepping into China trade relations issues, Taiwanese courts may be confronted with the arguments that they are not legitimate and incapable to examine these subject matters. It may be argued to be in no legitimate position to 'encroach' into the domain of presidential power, especially when national security is at stake. This argument links cross-Taiwan-strait trade relations closely to national security, and subsequently excludes the possibility of judicial review in cross-Taiwan-strait trade relations. Cross-Taiwan-strait trade may also be argued to closely relate to, apart from being highly political, strategies of Taiwan's economic developments where various interests are at stake. The constitutional court is not equipped with expertise in this field and is not capable of making the correct decision. Withholding the constitutional significance of Taiwan's WTO obligations, Taiwanese courts will be able to defeat those arbitrary regulatory measures in the name of national security and to pacify the political irrationality of cross-Taiwan-strait trade relations is the key to these cross-strait controversies. Without captured by the ideology of national security, Taiwanese courts will be able to ensure competing interests being taken into due account and being rightly balanced.

Empowerment of individuals through judicial review may also contribute to judicial autonomy of Hong Kong and Macau. As some members of the legislative council and the Executive Chief, if not nominated by Chinese central government, are not directly elected, their willingness and legitimacy to safeguard the economic autonomy in these two SAR are questionable. The Court of Final Appeal (the CFA) in these two SARs turns out to be the best guardian for their economic autonomy as they are distant from political intervention and interference. The CFA, in its famous *Ng Ka Ling*[25] case proved itself the best guardian of legal and economic autonomy in Hong Kong not to be encroached by Chinese Central Authority. Applying the WTO constitutionalism to Hong Kong and Macau emphasises the role of judiciary in adhering to open market and free trade policy which helps to ensure their economic autonomy.

IV. Short Conclusion

This chapter has examined three versions of the WTO constitutionalism focusing on the institutional architecture; distribution of powers between the WTO and its Members; and the empowerment of individuals through effective judicial protection. Based on these analyses, this chapter argues that a constitutional approach is desirable and necessary to resolve trade disputes in the Greater China based on three arguments.

Firstly, this chapter underlines the constitutional significance of the WTO membership as a pre-commitment to these four WTO Members of the Greater China. The WTO accession is a pre-commitment to China for widening and deepening economic and legal reforms and thus for promotion of rule of law in China. The WTO accession is a pre-commitment to Taiwan for the progressive liberalisation of cross-Taiwan strait trade relations in order to enhance economic and legal integration and to contribute to mutual understanding. The WTO memberships of Hong Kong, China and Macau, China are also pre-commitments of these two separate-customs-territory Members to adhere to free trade policies and thus to maintain their economic autonomy. Their WTO memberships are also China's pre-commitments to these two SARs in relation to their legal and economic autonomy to participate in the international trading system.

Secondly, this chapter argues that WTO constitutionalism would complement domestic constitutions. The independent and impartial judicial review and the right to trade prescribed in China's Accession Protocol would sustain a thin form of constitutionalism. With the expansion of judicial power, this thin form may gradually 'thicken'. The pursuit of WTO constitutionalism may also help to normalise and constitutionalise Taiwan's trade relations with China. Further, in recognition of the constitutional significance of WTO membership of Hong Kong and Macau, economy autonomy covering free-port status and free trade policies in the HKBL and the MABL will be upheld.

---

[25] *Ng Ka Ling v. Director of Immigration* [1999] 1 HKLRD 315 (CFA).

Thirdly, this chapter argues that the WTO constitutionalism may contribute to judicial protection of right to trade in China. It also lends some strength to Taiwanese courts in overcoming arguments based on national security. The empowerment of individuals through judicial protection would also enhance judicial autonomy of Hong Kong and Macau and safeguard legal and economic autonomy in these two SARs.

CHAPTER FOUR

DOMESTIC JUDICIAL REVIEW IN WTO AGREEMENTS

I. Introduction

As noted in chapter II, the effort to strengthen domestic review has been reflected in the Final Act of Uruguay Round Agreements. Various provisions governing domestic judicial review can be found in various agreements annexed to the WTO Agreement. These provisions include Article X:3(b) of the GATT 1994, Article 13 of the Anti-Dumping Agreement, Article 11 of the Agreement on Customs Valuation, Article 4 of the Agreement on Pre-shipment Inspection, Article 23 of the Agreement on Subsidies and Countervailing Measures, Article VI of the GATS, Article 41 to Article 50 and Article 59 of the TRIPS Agreement, and Article XX:2 of the Government Procurement Agreement. This chapter will then examine these provisions in detail.

Before examining these provisions each by each, it will be a good starting point to cite the authority governing the rule of interpretation and what the WTO panel/Appellate Body has said on this point. As directed by Article 3.2 of the Understanding on Rules and Procedures Governing the Settlement of Disputes (the DSU), the WTO provisions should be interpreted 'in accordance with customary rules of interpretation of public international law.' The jurisprudence of the WTO panel/Appellate Body has continuously stressed the importance of the fundamental rule of treaty interpretation set out in Article 31(1) of the Vienna Convention on the Law of Treaties (the VCLT). In the very first case of *United States – Standards for Reformulated and Conventional Gasoline* (*US – Gasoline*),[1] the Appellate Body held that, this general rule of interpretation 'has attained the status of a rule of customary or general international law. As such, it forms part of the 'customary rules of interpretation of public international law'[2] which should guide the interpretations of the *General Agreement* and the other 'covered agreements' of the WTO Agreement. The Appellate Body then further adds, in *Japan – Taxes on Alcoholic Beverages* (*Japan – Alcoholic Beverages II*)[3] that 'Article 32 of the VCLT, dealing with

[1] Appellate Body Report, *United States – Standards for Reformulated and Conventional Gasoline* (*US – Gasoline*), WT/DS2/AB/R, adopted 20 May 1996, DSR 1996:I, 3.

[2] Appellate Body report, *US – Gasoline*, 17.

[3] Appellate Body Report, *Japan – Taxes on Alcoholic Beverages* (*Japan – Alcoholic Beverages II*), WT/DS8/AB/R, WT/DS10/AB/R, WT/DS11/AB/R, adopted 1 November 1996, DSR 1996:I, 97.

the role of supplementary means of interpretation, has also attained the same status.'[4] Article 31(1) of the VCLT provides as follows:

> A treaty shall be interpreted in good faith in accordance with the ordinary meaning to be given to the terms of the treaty in their context and in the light of its object and purpose.

As pointed out by the Panel in *United States – Sections 301-310 of the Trade Act of 1974* (*US – Section 301 Trade Act*),[5] elements referred to in this provision, namely, text, context and object-and-purpose correspond to well-established textual, systemic and teleological methodologies of treaty interpretation. These four elements as well should be read in a holistic manner.[6] It is a general *rule* of interpretation rather than general *rules* in the plural by which a sequence of separate tests are to be applied in a hierarchical order.[7] In this vein, interpretation must be based above all upon the text of the treaty. That is, the text is the departure point of this interpretative process. However, 'the provisions of the treaty are to be given their ordinary meaning in their context. The object and purpose of the treaty are also to be taken into account in determining the meaning of its provisions'.[8] Therefore, this chapter will follow this approach: starting from the ordinary meaning of the 'raw' text of provisions governing domestic (judicial) review, and then construing it in its context and in the light of the object and purpose of the treaty. However, it does not mean that all of these four elements as well as good faith are to be employed in interpreting every single provision.

On the other hand, before examining these provisions, it is also worth citing what the Panel holds in *United States – Anti-Dumping Measures on Stainless Steel Plate in Coils and Stainless Steel Sheet and Strip from Korea* (*US – Stainless Steel*).[9] The Panel says, the dispute settlement mechanism is not intended to serve as a mechanism to examine the consistency of a Member's particular decisions or rulings with its own domestic law and practice. This task should be reserved mainly for each Member's judicial system. WTO panels are not in a good position to perform the same function of domestic courts scrutinising the conformity of these decisions or ruling with relevant domestic law and practice. One should caution not to 'effectively convert every claim that an action is inconsistent with domestic

[4] Appellate Body report, *Japan – Alcoholic Beverages II*, 12.

[5] Panel Report, *United States – Sections 301–310 of the Trade Act of 1974* (*US – Section 301 Trade Act*), WT/DS152/R, adopted 27 January 2000, DSR 2000:II, 815.

[6] Panel Report, *US – Section 301 Trade Act*, para. 7.22.

[7] Ibid.

[8] Appellate Body report, *Japan – Alcoholic Beverages II*, 12.

[9] Panel Report, *United States – Anti-Dumping Measures on Stainless Steel Plate in Coils and Stainless Steel Sheet and Strip from Korea* (*US – Stainless Steel*), WT/DS179/R, adopted 1 February 2001, DSR 2001:IV, 1295.

law or practice into a claim under the WTO Agreement'[10] based on Article X:3(b) of the GATT 1994.

The Panel further adds in the 64th footnote that, 'it is for this reason that both Article X:3(b) of GATT 1994 and Article 13 of the Anti-Dumping Agreement require Members to maintain appropriate judicial, arbitral or administrative tribunals or procedures.' The Panel tries to allocate jurisdiction between the two levels of judicial review: the WTO Dispute Settlement Mechanism and the domestic judicial review. Although the Panel attributes the task to 'test the consistency of Member's decisions or rulings with the member's domestic law and practice' to domestic judicial review, however, it does not further elaborate what domestic judicial review should be like. In fact, the WTO panel/Appellate Body has not ever addressed this issue. Nevertheless, as China's Accession Protocol includes more stringent obligation in respect of domestic judicial review, it will be indispensable to examine together with these existent provisions when a complaint in relation to China's obligation to provide an independent and impartial judicial review is brought about into the WTO.

Bearing this in mind, this chapter will thus examine numerous provisions in Uruguay Round Agreements in relation to domestic judicial review. This chapter will arrange as follows: it will start with the GATT 1994 and other agreements annexed to the GATT 1994, except the Agreement on Pre-shipment Inspection, followed by the GATS. It will examine numerous provisions related to domestic judicial authority provided in the TRIPS Agreement and finally those provisions provided in the Agreement on Pre-shipment Inspection and the Agreement on Government Procurement. A short conclusion will then be offered in the end of this chapter.

II. Article X: 3 of GATT 1994 and Annexed Agreements

The legal text of this provision reads:

> (b) Each contracting party shall maintain, or institute as soon as practicable, judicial, arbitral or administrative tribunals or procedures for the purpose, *inter alia,* of the prompt review and correction of administrative action relating to customs matters. Such tribunals or procedures shall be independent of the agencies entrusted with administrative enforcement and their decisions shall be implemented by, and shall govern the practice of, such agencies unless an appeal is lodged with a court or tribunal of superior jurisdiction within the time prescribed for appeals to be lodged by importers; Provided that the central administration of such agency may take steps to obtain a review of the matter in another proceeding if there is good cause to believe that the decision is inconsistent with established principles of law or the actual facts.

[10] Ibid.

This provision in the GATT 1994 in relation to domestic (judicial) review is identical to that provided in the GATT 1947 of which the scope is limited to customs matters. The following will examine those elements included in this provision.

A. *Maintain or Institute As Soon As Practicable Judicial Arbitral or Administrative Tribunals or Procedures*

In implementing this obligation, Members are required to 'maintain, or institute as soon as practicable, judicial, arbitral or administrative tribunals or procedures'. The ordinary meaning of 'maintain' is to 'cause or to enable a condition or state of affairs to continue.'[11] In other words, to 'maintain' means to keep this condition or state of affairs at the same level or rate; to 'institute' means to set in motion or to establish. This provision has to be read together with the subsequent paragraph which prescribes that procedures in force on the date of this agreement, provided they are objective and impartial, do not have be substituted or eliminated. Therefore, to 'maintain' tribunals or procedures means that the level of protection provided by these tribunals or procedures should be kept at the same level and should not be weakened. Besides, the level of protection should be comparable to standards of 'objective and impartial'. If a comparable level of protection was not available upon the signature of this agreement, Members are then required to establish these tribunals or procedures as soon as practicable. However, whether it is practicable depends on the capacity of Members, especially in relation to least developed countries. Thus, it will be then difficult to distinguish between lack of resources and intentional failure to carry out their oblations.

Secondly, these review mechanisms may be judicial, arbitral or administrative in nature. In other words, this 'domestic (judicial) review' has not to be a review by judicial organs provided it is '*independent of the agencies entrusted with administrative enforcement*'. A review by administrative tribunals or procedures within the executive branch or even by arbitral tribunals might be permissible provided these reviewing mechanisms are 'independent' in terms of Article X:3(b). Procedures satisfying the standards of 'objective and impartial' as laid down in the subparagraph (c) are not required to be substituted or eliminated even though they are fully or formally independent of the agencies entrusted with administrative enforcement.

B. *Competence and Jurisdiction of the Prompt Review and Right of Appeal*

The literal meaning of 'prompt' suggests readiness and quickness to act. The Oxford Concise English Dictionary defines it as 'done or acting without delay.'[12]

[11] J Pearsall, et al. (eds), *Concise Oxford English Dictionary* (Oxford University Press, USA 2002) 858.
[12] Ibid 1114.

However, this definition offers little guidance since how ready or quick to act is a relative concept. It depends on the nature of the task and on with what it is compared, which should also be measured in the context of domestic legal system. However, when determining whether a review is prompt enough or not, the nature of 'customs matters' in particular light of the increasing emphasis on trade facilitation in these matters should be taken into due account, as the dynamics of competitive market in international trade may significantly change. 'Prompt' should also be read together with the objective and purpose of this provision to provide effective domestic review. The promptness of this review is an important element to ensure its effectiveness. It would be difficult to imagine a delayed review decision could be an effective one.

This domestic review should be competent to review or to correct administrative actions. To 'review' means to examine the correctness of administrative actions. To 'correct' means to 'put right' to 'make straight' or to 'amend.' It also suggests the substitution of right for wrong. Therefore, a competence to review or to correct means to check the correctness of administrative actions. In case of incorrect decisions, this review mechanism should be competent to substitute the right for the wrong administrative decisions. In this sense, repeal should be included in this correction, as repeal and correction share the same conceptual features of removing the wrongfulness in these administrative actions. However, it is not as clear in relation to the authority to order the administration to make certain decisions. Nevertheless, without such authority, this review mechanism cannot be regarded as effective. The jurisdiction of this review mechanism should be limited to administrative actions relating to customs matters. Therefore, non-tariff measures are not included and resort cannot be had to this review mechanism, which greatly undermines the effectiveness of this review mechanism. With the progressive liberalisation of tariff areas, non-tariff barriers are of even greater importance.[13] This domestic review should also have the authority to have decisions to be implemented by agencies responsible for administrative enforcement. It should also have the authority with regard to how these decisions are implemented.

The legal text also provides that decisions delivered by this review mechanism should be carried out unless they are appealed within the prescribed time constraint. However, to include a right to appeal against these decisions is not compulsory. In other words, a Member is not obliged to make available a right to appeal in these tribunals or procedures.[14] Although these decisions should be implemented by enforcement agencies, another proceedings initiated by central

[13] Efforts to redress this ineffectiveness during negotiation processes of the Uruguay Round were made. The extended scope and its effectiveness will be examined in subsequent sections of this Chapter.

[14] With regard to 'right of appeal', the TRIPS Agreement has strengthened this aspect.

administration against decisions made by the review mechanism may be nevertheless permissible on the ground that there is good cause for this central administration to believe that these decisions delivered by the review mechanism is against the principle of laws or actual facts. That is, central administration may be allowed to re-initiate proceedings against these decisions only when these decisions are believed to be against the principles of law and thus being illegal, or the facts on which the contested decision is based have not been accurately established.

C. *Independence Requirement and Objective and Impartial Procedures in Force*

An institutional/organic requirement of this review mechanism is that it should be 'independent of the agencies' which are in charge of administrative enforcement. Being 'independent' means being 'free from outside control'[15] and 'not subject to another's authority'.[16] It also suggests 'separate'. In this vein, this review mechanism should be free from the control and should not be subject to the authority of administrative enforcement agencies. In this sense, the term 'formally' in subparagraph (c) is relevant in determining independence of this review mechanism. It has to be at least formally separate from agencies entrusted with administrative enforcement. The 'objective and impartial' standard in terms of subparagraph (c) should also be taken into account, as the objective and purpose of this independence requirement is to avoid conflicts of interests and thus ensure the impartiality and objectiveness of this review mechanism. In the end, effective domestic (judicial) review will be materialised. Therefore, whether these tribunals and procedures are independent of agencies entrusted administrative enforcement should also be determined by examining whether there could be potential conflicts of interests between these tribunals or procedures and the administrative enforcement agencies.

In subparagraph (c) of Article X:3, it is nevertheless prescribed that existent procedures in force on the date of this Agreement, which provide objective and impartial review of administrative action, do not have to be substituted or eliminated, even though they are not 'fully or formally independent of the agencies entrusted with administrative enforcement'. Therefore, if a Member believes that procedures in force on the date of this Agreement are objective and impartial, it is not required to substitute or eliminate these existing procedures. The criteria of 'impartial' and 'objective' are of crucial importance.

'Impartial' means 'treating all rivals and disputants equally.'[17] That is, these tribunals or procedures should not privilege any parties to these disputes.

[15] Pearsall (n 11) 720.
[16] Ibid.
[17] Ibid 711.

Equal opportunities to be heard and to defend are thus important in this sense. The 'principle of equality of arms' is also relevant in terms of information and evidence available to these complainants. As the object and purpose of these tribunals and procedures are to strengthen domestic (judicial) review, access to information and evidence is essential for importers effectively to defend their rights and interests through this review mechanism.

The Panel addresses the term 'impartial' in *Argentina – Measures Affecting the Export of Bovine Hides and Import of Finished Leather* (*Argentina – Hides and Leather*).[18] Although it relates to 'impartial administration of laws, regulations, judicial decisions and administrative rulings of general application', how the Panel sees impartiality can nevertheless shed some light here. As this dispute is related to the presence of 'partial and interested representatives of certain industrial associations' in the process of customs administration, it can arguably be transformed into one addressing review procedures in light of 'principle of equality of arms' and '*ex parte* contact.' The Panel emphasises 'the presence of private parties with conflicting commercial interests in the customs process',[19] and the advantage that any interested party may take in this process to 'obtain confidential information to which they have no right'.[20]

Impartial procedures should also enable two parties equally to participate and to be heard. It thus links to the right of information in these review procedures. Parties to these procedures should not be privileged or prejudiced in terms of their access to information and their rights in relation to the protection of confidential information. This is of particular importance in these review procedures as the decisions subject to review are delivered by custom authorities. They may take advantage in their access to information whereas complaining importers may rely upon customs authorities for such information.

The requirements of 'objective' and 'impartial' are closely related. Being 'objective' means not being 'influenced by personal feelings or opinions in considering facts and making decisions.'[21] That is, such tribunals or procedures should not be biased, especially customs-authority biased. In this vein, prohibition of *ex parte* contact is important to avoid undue influence to decision-makers in these tribunals or procedures. In this line, the impartiality contributes to the objectiveness, as the former will prevent decision-makers in this review mechanism from being biased.

Whether these procedures are 'objective and impartial' enough to conform to this subparagraph should be determined by Members. That is, in case of doubts, a

[18] Panel Report, *Argentina – Measures Affecting the Export of Bovine Hides and Import of Finished Leather* (*Argentina – Hides and Leather*), WT/DS155/R and Corr.1, adopted 16 February 2001.

[19] Panel Report, *Argentina – Hides and Leather*, para. 11.99.

[20] Ibid para. 11.100.

[21] Pearsall (n 11) 981.

Member employing these procedures should, upon request provide full information in relation to these procedures so that all Members can decide the conformity with this subparagraph in terms of the impartiality and objectiveness of these procedures. So far, no decision in relation to these procedures has been made. In case of a complaint with regard to subparagraph (b) where the respondent Member affirmatively defends by referring to subparagraph (c), the WTO panel/Appellate Body will face with a dilemma similar to that in *India – Quantitative Restrictions on Imports of Agricultural, Textile and Industrial Products* (*India – Quantitative Restrictions*)[22] and *Turkey – Restrictions on Imports of Textile and Clothing Products* (*Turkey – Textiles*).[23] Should the WTO panel/Appellate Body decide this issue on its own as Members have not decided on this point? Should they respect the institutional balance of the WTO and refrain from stepping into this issue?

III. Article 13 of Anti-Dumping Agreement and Article 23 of Agreement on Subsidies and Countervailing Measures

Article 13 of the Anti-Dumping Agreement (the ADA) and Article 23 of the Agreement on Subsidies and Countervailing Measures (ASCM) include similar provisions regulating judicial review. The legal text of Article 13 of the ADA reads:

> Each Member whose national legislation contains provisions on anti-dumping measures shall maintain judicial, arbitral or administrative tribunals or procedures for the purpose, inter alia, of the prompt review of administrative actions relating to final determinations and reviews of determinations within the meaning of Article 11. Such tribunals or procedures shall be independent of the authorities responsible for the determination or review in question.

As this provision limits its application to a Member 'whose national legislation contains provisions on anti-dumping measures', it is clear that those Members, as in the case of Hong Kong and Macau in this work which do not have anti-dumping legislation, are under no obligation in terms of this provision. Members employing anti-dumping measures in their legislation are obliged to 'maintain' judicial, arbitral and administrative tribunals or procedures. The implementing measures under this obligation are almost identical to Article X:3(b) of the GATT 1994. However, the term 'institute' is not referred to in this provision. It is because whenever a domestic anti-dumping legislation is enacted, this legislation should be immediately equipped with review mechanisms. To 'institute as soon as

[22] Appellate Body Report, *India – Quantitative Restrictions on Imports of Agricultural, Textile and Industrial Products* (*India – Quantitative Restrictions*), WT/DS90/AB/R, adopted 22 September 1999, DSR 1999:IV, 1763.

[23] Appellate Body Report, *Turkey – Restrictions on Imports of Textile and Clothing Products* (*Turkey – Textiles*), WT/DS34/AB/R, adopted 19 November 1999, DSR 1999:VI, 2345.

practicable' is not permissible. Besides, this 'judicial review' is not limited to judicial organs. Administrative or arbitral tribunals or procedures may be permissible provided the independence requirement laid down in this provision has been met.

As noted by Vermulst, the ADA does not either impose an obligation upon Members to establish specialised courts to hear anti-dumping and other similar trade remedy disputes.[24] This is not difficult to understand. Since Members are not required to maintain a prompt review by judiciary, it appears more difficult to impose more stringent obligation to provide review by specialised courts in judiciary. Further, court proceedings in relation to anti-dumping measures in some WTO Members are notoriously time-consuming. However, thus far they have not been challenged under this provision.[25] Sometimes recourse to the WTO Dispute Settlement Mechanism may be more prompt than domestic review. The case of anti-dumping duties against anti-dumping duties on Korean dynamic random memory semiconductors is a good example. While the Panel report on *United States – Anti-Dumping Duty on Dynamic Random Access Memory Semiconductors (DRAMS) of One Megabit or Above from Korea* (*US – DRAMS*)[26] had been adopted on 19 March 1999, proceedings in the court of international trade was still pending. When the court finally laid down its decision on 19 May 1999, the decision of the WTO Panel was however not relied upon.[27] That said, the challenge against the 'promptness' of domestic review has not been reported.

The 'prompt review' of such tribunals or procedures should have jurisdiction on 'administrative actions relating to final determinations and reviews of determinations within the meaning of Article 11'. The 'final determinations' as the raw text suggests, do not include provisional measures. Besides, 'reviews of determinations' should be read in the context of Article 11, where 'reviews of determinations' refer to reviews of the necessity for continued imposition of anti-dumping duties as well as price undertakings. These 'reviews of determinations' identified in Article 11.3 of the ADA also cover the review as to whether the expiry of the duty or price undertakings would be likely to lead to continuation or recurrence of dumping and injury.

Therefore, reviews of determinations cover two categories: to review the necessity to for continued imposition of anti-dumping duties or undertakings, and before the expiry of these anti-dumping duties or undertakings, the review of

[24] E Vermulst, *The WTO Anti-Dumping Agreement: A Commentary* (Oxford University Press, Oxford 2006) 214.

[25] Ibid.

[26] Panel Report, *United States – Anti-Dumping Duty on Dynamic Random Access Memory Semiconductors (DRAMS) of One Megabit or Above from Korea* (*US – DRAMS*), WT/DS99/R, adopted 19 March 1999.

[27] *Hyundai Electronics Co.* v. *United States* (1999), 53 F. Supp. 2d 1334 (Ct. Int'l Trade).

the likeliness of the continuation or recurrence of dumping and injury. In fact, the likeness of the continuation or recurrence of dumping and injury is a factor to determine the necessity for continued imposition of anti-dumping duties or undertakings, as any anti-dumping duty or undertaking shall remain in force as long as and to the extent necessary to counteract dumping that is causing injury.[28] If there is no likeness for the continuation or recurrence of dumping and injuries, the continued imposition of anti-dumping duties and undertakings is thus unjustified. Lastly, this 'prompt review' should be applicable to 'review of determinations' both on the initiative of administrative authorities or upon request are included.

As regards the jurisdiction of the judicial review under the ASCM, Article 23 of the ASCM includes almost identical content to that of the ADA. The 'prompt review' of such tribunals and procedures should have jurisdiction on 'administrative actions relating to final determinations or reviews of determinations within the meaning of Article 21'. The 'final determinations', as the raw text suggests, provisional measures may not be included in this 'prompt review'. Besides, the 'reviews of determinations' should be read in the context of Article 21 of the ASCM where the 'reviews of determinations' include the review of the necessity for continued imposition of countervailing duties as well as undertakings. Similar to anti-dumping measures, the reviews of determinations also cover the review as to whether the expiry of the countervailing duties or undertakings would be likely to lead to continuation or recurrence of subsidisation and injury. Consequently, there are also two categories of reviews of determinations indentified in the ASCM: the review of the necessity for continued imposition of countervailing duties and undertakings, and the review, before the expiry of countervailing duties and undertakings, the likeness of continuation or recurrence of subsidisation and injury. Following the same logic of the ADA, the 'reviews of determinations' both on the initiative of administrative authorities and upon request should be subject to this review mechanism.

Compared to the ADA, the ASCM provides a lenient requirement on the standing of the access to judicial review. As provided, such tribunals or procedures 'shall provide all interested parties who participated in the administrative proceedings and are directly and individually affected by the administrative actions with access to review.' Although the ASCM is mainly analogous to that in the ADA, 'judicial review' provided in the ASCM goes beyond what is contained in ADA.[29] All interested parties who participated in the administrative proceedings and are directly and individually affected by the administrative actions should be

[28] ADA, Art. 11.1.

[29] S Charnovitz, 'The WTO and the rights of the individual' (2001) 36 Intereconomics 98, 98–108, reprinted in *Trade Law and Global Governance* (Cameron May, London 2002) 377–96.

provided with access to review. Two requirements are prescribed in relation to the standing of these interested parties in such tribunals or procedures. One is that these interested parties should have participated in the administrative proceedings. The other is that they have to be directly and individually affected by the administrative actions.

As the countervailing measures involve a wide variety of competing interests, including importers, exporters and consumers, it is important for these interested parties to be properly heard and participate both in the administrative proceedings as well as in the review mechanism. This interpretation can also be supported by reading together with Article 19.2 of the ASCM, which provides that 'procedures should be established which would allow the authorities concerned to take due account of representations made by domestic interested parties whose interests might be adversely affected by the imposition of a countervailing duty'. In the accompanying footnote, it also explicitly provides that consumers and industrial users of the imported product subject to investigation are covered by the term 'domestic interested parties' as defined. Although the note reads 'for the purpose of this paragraph' the legal text of Article 23 makes it clear that these consumers and industrial users of the imported product, if having participated in the administrative proceedings, can also refer to the review mechanism. Different reading would lead to inconsistency and incoherence. It will be also against the object and purpose of Article 19.2 of the ASCM to define 'domestic interested parties' as including consumers and industrial users of the imported product subject to investigation. Further, the aim of Article 23 of the ASCM is to provide *all* interested parties to have access to the review mechanism. To exclude consumers and industrial users of the import product runs counter to the object and purpose of this review mechanism and undermines its effectiveness.

As far as 'all interested parties' is concerned, *Argentina – Hides and Leather* is also relevant here. The Panel firstly notes that an inherent danger of partiality arises whenever a party with a contrary commercial interest but no relevant legal interest, is allowed to participate in an administrative action. The Panel then points out that this danger 'could be remedied by adequate safeguards'.[30] The word 'safeguard' is telling here. Countervailing measures may concern various legal and/or commercial interests. What is important here is to make these interests safeguarded by equal opportunities to participate in administrative proceedings and review mechanisms. Therefore, both legally and commercial affected parties may fall within the scope of 'all interested parties'. However, it would be infeasible and against procedural economy if parties not participating in administrative proceedings could have the standing in the review mechanism. Therefore, it is

[30] Panel Report, *Argentina – Hides and Leather*, para. 11.101.

reasonable to limit the access of this review mechanism to parties having participated in administrative proceedings.

With regard to 'directly and individually affected', the most important criterion in relation to the standing of this review mechanism, a good departure point would be the ordinary meaning of 'directly' and 'individually'. 'Direct' suggests 'without intervening factors or intermediaries.'[31] 'Individual' means the characteristic of a 'single', 'separate' and 'particular person', opposite to a general group.[32] However, these definitions seem to offer little aid in clarifying who is eligible to have resort to this review mechanism. The line cannot be drawn without referring to the objective and purpose of this provision. The aim of this provision is to offer an opportunity for interested parties to have an access to the review mechanism. However, given the limited resources of judicial, arbitral or administrative tribunals or procedures, this access should be made available to those who have sufficient interest in these countervailing measures. Therefore, directly and individually affected should be interpreted in this light. Nevertheless, as noted above, 'domestic interested parties' as defined in the accompanying note include consumers and industrial users of the imported product subject to investigation. It is still not a clear-cut to distinguish whether every single, particular consumer or industrial user is 'directly or individually affected' or not.

IV. Article 11 of Agreement on Customs Valuation and Article 3(5) of Agreement on Import Licensing Procedures

Compared to Article X:3(b) of GATT 1994, the scope of Article 11 of the Agreement on Customs Valuation is limited to the 'determination of customs value', but more stringent requirements are imposed upon the review mechanism. This article should be read together with its accompanying Interpretative Note. As prescribed, Members are obliged to provide a review for the determination of custom value by the judiciary. The initial review may be carried out by an authority within the customs administration or by an independent body. However, as made clear in the Interpretative Note, 'the importer shall have the right in the final instance to appeal to the judiciary'. That is, even if the decision of customs value determination is initially reviewed by an authority within the customs administration or by an independent body, the importers should have the right to refer to the judiciary to make this initial decision reviewed.

However, this article is applicable only to the determination of customs value. As indicated in the Interpretative Note, this article deals only with the 'valuation

[31] Pearsall (n 11) 405.

[32] Ibid 722.

determination made by the customs administration for the goods being valued'. The term 'valuation' here is decisive in contrast to 'custom matters', as employed in Article X:3(b) of the GATT 1994. Valuation means 'an estimation of something's worth'[33] in a specific sum or amount. Therefore, the application of this provision is limited to the estimation and determination of the goods being valued. Other customs matters are not applicable. While this provision imposes more stringent requirement on the review body, having to be judicial authority at the final appeal, the scope of application is narrower. It is understandable that more stringent requirement is imposed in relation to the review body since the value of the goods determines the tariffs to be imposed. Tariff-reduction can arguably be regarded as one of the most important issues in the old GATT system. In order to ensure the benefit of tariff-reduction being effectively realised, it is indispensable to guarantee that the value of goods is not unreasonably raised.

In contrast, paragraph 5(e) of Article 3 of the Agreement on Import Licensing Procedures regulates loosely on the requirement of judicial review. According to this provision, whenever an application for the license is not successful, the reason for this rejection should be given upon request of the applicant. The unsuccessful applicant should be given a right of appeal or review in order to review this decision. However, this provision does not impose any specific requirement on the review mechanism. It only obliges Members to provide the unsuccessful applicant a right to appeal or review 'in accordance with domestic legislation or procedures'. There is no further requirement for these domestic legislation or procedures. Therefore, the review mechanism as put forward in the Agreement on Import Licensing Procedures is much weaker than others.

V. Article VI:2 of the GATS

Provisions governing domestic (judicial) review in the GATS are analogous to those in the GATT 1994. The implementing measures required are also to 'maintain or institute as soon as practicable judicial, arbitral or administrative tribunals or procedures.' Similar to the GATT 1994, the GATS does not oblige Members to provide judicial review. Administrative or arbitral tribunals or procedures may also be permissible. The legal text of this provision reads:

> (a) Each Member shall maintain or institute as soon as practicable judicial, arbitral or administrative tribunals or procedures which provide, at the request of an affected service supplier, for the prompt review of, and where justified, appropriate remedies for, administrative decisions affecting trade in services. Where such procedures are not independent of the agency entrusted with the administrative decision

[33] Ibid 1584.

> concerned, the Member shall ensure that the procedures in fact provide for an objective and impartial review.
>
> (b) The provisions of subparagraph (a) shall not be construed to require a Member to institute such tribunals or procedures where this would be inconsistent with its constitutional structure or the nature of its legal system.

A. *Competence, Jurisdiction, and Authority*

This domestic review should be competent to provide 'prompt review' and where justified, 'appropriate remedies' for the administrative actions affecting trade in services. Therefore, this domestic review should have jurisdiction only on administrative decisions in relation to services trade. The scope of services trade should be read together with the first paragraph, which limits the obligation of reasonable, objective and impartial administration of measures of general application to sectors where specific commitments are undertaken. Therefore, this obligation of domestic review is limited to those sectors in which Members have specifically made commitments. The same term 'prompt' is employed in the GATS. Similar difficulties exist when determining the promptness of this review. However, one has to bear in mind the differences between trade in goods and services trade. Apart from this prompt review of administrative decisions, this review mechanism should have the authority to order appropriate remedies. Whether remedies should be limited to compensation is not clear. However, in light of the object and purpose of an effective domestic review, the local tribunal should have the authority to order administrative agencies to act or not to act in a certain manner.

B. *Independence of the Agency Entrusted with the Administrative Decision Concerned*

Compared to requirements imposed by the ADA, the ASCM, and the Agreement on Customs Valuation, the 'independence' requirement imposed by the GATS on the review mechanism is lenient. The procedures for this review do not have to be 'independent of the agency entrusted the administrative decision concerned'. However, Members are obliged to ensure these procedures provide for an 'objective and impartial' review. The same requirement of being 'objective and impartial' as prescribed in Article X:3(c) of the GATT 1994 is also imposed upon these procedures. Besides, compared to Article X: 3(c) of the GATT 1994, such procedures governed by Article VI:2(a) of the GATS do not have to be the existent procedures 'in force on the date of this Agreement'. That is, even in the case of subsequently instituted procedures that govern this domestic review mechanism, if these procedures are 'objective and impartial', they are not required to be independent of the agency entrusted of the administrative decision at issue.

C. *Inconsistent with its Constitutional Structure or the Nature of Its Legal System*

Another major weakness of this domestic review provided in the GATS is that the following subparagraph (b) explicitly admits the derogation to this obligation. Subparagraph (b) provides that subparagraph (a) shall not be 'construed to require a Member to institute such tribunals or procedures where this would be inconsistent with its constitutional structure or the nature of its legal system'. Therefore, whether 'it would be inconsistent with its constitutional structure or the nature of its legal system' or not is extremely difficult, if not impossible, to determine. It may turn out to be the best 'exit' for Members to escape from their domestic review obligation.

VI. TRIPS Agreement

The enforcement of intellectual property rights laid down in the TRIPS Agreement is generally regarded as one of its major achievements. It prescribes a variety of requirements in relation to domestic remedies. It is not limited to review of administrative actions regarding the determination of intellectual property rights. It also covers various procedural rules governing civil and criminal procedures. The review mechanism provided by the TRIPS Agreement has stepped forward going from controlling governmental measures to private infringing actions against intellectual property rights by individuals and enterprises.

Article 41.1 of the TRIPS Agreement lays down a general framework governing the enforcement procedures, demanding effective actions against intellectual property rights infringements. The following paragraphs regulate fair and equitable procedures, reasoned decisions without undue delay; an opportunity for the parties to be heard in the proceedings, and an opportunity for judicial review of these decisions. Apart from this general regulatory framework, rules governing civil and administrative procedures and remedies, provisional measures, and special requirements on boarder measures are laid down in the following three sections of this enforcement part. Four core elements are provided in these enforcement rules, namely, judicial review; fair and equitable procedures; participation, evidence and right of information; and remedies and provisional measures.

A. *Judicial Review*

Judicial review may be perceived as interlinked with the other three elements. To be sure, fair and equitable procedures requirement is applicable to judicial proceedings. Right to be heard, evidence and right of information, remedies and provisional measures are also part of these judicial proceedings. However, it is justifiable to be dealt with on its own merit, as it is the controlling element of these requirements. Such arrangement is also justified on the ground 'judicial review' of administrative decisions can be arguably distinguished from civil and criminal judicial procedures. The enforcement part of the TRIPS Agreement sets out rules in relation to civil, administrative and criminal procedures that evidence Members' attachment to judicial authorities in ensuring the domestic protection of intellectual property rights. Article 41.4 prescribes that an opportunity for review by judicial authority of final administrative decisions should be made available. Further, right of appeal of the initial judicial decisions, at least in legal aspects should be provided. It is because of the legal tradition of some Members of which the appellate courts can consider only the legal aspects of a disputed case, but not the factual basis.[34] This right of appeal is also subject to the 'jurisdictional provisions concerning the importance of a case.' This is mainly out of concern that Members are not required to allocate their judicial resources on cases of mirror economic importance.[35] A number of subsequent articles impose upon Members the obligation to institutionalise judicial authorities to have the power to order specified measures; a systematic refusal of judicial authorities to exercise this power might constitute nullification or impairment of rights and obligation under the WTO Agreement.[36]

B. *Fair and Equitable Procedures*

Members are required to provide fair and equitable procedures in relation to the enforcement of intellectual property rights, which shall not 'unnecessarily complicated or costly' or entail 'unreasonable time limits' or 'unwarranted delays.' Article 42 provides requirements on civil and administrative procedures and remedies in more detail. Members are obliged to make available to the rights holders civil judicial procedures for the enforcement of intellectual property rights to right holders. 'Make available' is interpreted as rights holder's entitlement to have access to civil judicial proceedings that are effective for the realisation of their rights covered by the agreement.' Rights holders, as defined in the accompanying note 11, include federations and associations having legal standing to assert such rights. In contrast to the term 'owner of a registered trademark' used in Article 16.1, rights holders are interpreted by the Appellate Body as persons who claim to have legal standing to assert rights.[37]

---

[34] C M Correa, *Trade Related Aspects of Intellectual Property Rights: A Commentary* (Oxford University Press, Oxford 2007) 416.

[35] Ibid.

[36] D Gervais, *The TRIPS Agreements: Drafting History and Analysis* (2nd edn Sweet & Maxwell, London 2003) 289.

[37] Appellate Body Report, *US – Section 211 of Omnibus Appropriation Act of 1998* (*US – Section 211 Appropriations Act*) (2 January 2002) WT/DS176/AB/R, para. 217.

A right of defence, as formulated as a right to timely written notice with sufficient detail is explicitly referred to in this article. Moreover, the right to be represented by independent legal counsel should also be made available in these procedures. In addition, parties should have the opportunity to substantiate their claims and to present all relevant evidence. In addition, those rights covered in Article 42, as interpreted by the Appellate Body, are procedural in nature, aiming to guarantee 'an international minimum standard for nationals of other members within the meaning of Article 1.3 of the TRIPS Agreement.'[38]

C. *Right to Be Heard, Evidence, and Right of Information*

The right to be heard, evidence, and the right of information are also provided in the TRIPS Agreement. The right to be heard is to be read in the context of evidence examination. Under the general obligation concerning the enforcement procedures, only the evidence on which parties are offered an opportunity to comment can be taken into account for decisions on the merits of a case.[39] Besides, in respect of provisional measures and the suspension of the release of goods, defendants should be provided with possibility for the review of these boarder measures decisions; right to be heard should be included in this review procedure.[40]

Another similar provision relates to the denial of the access of information; whenever a party to the proceedings voluntarily and without good reasons denies access to or does not provide necessary information, judicial authorities may make preliminary or definitive determinations based on information presented to them. However, opportunities to be heard on the allegations or evidence should also be made available.[41] This denial of access to information should be read together with the first paragraph, which requires that judicial authorities should have the authority to order the opposing party to provide the evidence when 'a party has presented reasonably available evidence sufficient to support its claims and has specified evidence relevant to substantiation of its claims which lies in the control of the opposing party'.[42] Some points should be made clear here. Firstly, starting from Article 43, several subsequent articles begin with '*the judicial authorities shall have the authority*'. As held by the Panel on *India – Patent Protection for Pharmaceutical and Agricultural Chemical Products, Complaint by the European Communities* (*India – Patents* (*EC*)), the phrase 'judicial authorities shall have the authority' suggests a degree of judicial discretion. Regardless of this discretion,

[38] Ibid para. 221.
[39] The TRIPS Agreement, Art. 41(3).
[40] The TRIPS Agreement, Arts. 50(5), 55.
[41] The TRIPS Agreement, Art. 43.
[42] The TRIPS Agreement, Art. 43(1).

judicial authorities are required to act in a certain way when the prescribed conditions are satisfied, rather than merely having the authority to do so.[43]

The Panel, *China – Measures Affecting the Protection and Enforcement of Intellectual Property Rights* (*China – Intellectual Property Rights*)[44] also touches upon this issue. The Panel firstly turns to the dictionary definition of 'authority' and then clarifies that the obligation imposed upon Members is to empower their domestic authorities to 'have authority, but not to 'exercise' authority. The Panel then contrasts the terminology used by other provisions in relation to minimum standards of protection, such as that Members shall provide protection or that certain protection shall be provided. The Panel then reaches the conclusion that the term 'shall have authority' reflects the discretionary power of the judicial authorities in choosing the orders with respect to specific infringements.[45] The obligation, 'judicial authorities shall have the authority', does mean that judicial authorities are required to exercise that authority in a particular way, unless otherwise specified.[46] Moreover, that the judicial authorities 'shall have the authority' to order certain types of remedies does not suggest that the discretionary power of judicial authorities is confined to only these types of remedies. Domestic judicial authorities are free to order other types of remedies.[47]

Besides, with a view to persuade the court to order the opposing party to produce certain evidence, the claiming party has to meet two requirements: to present reasonably sufficient evidence and to specify relevant evidence. That is, the claiming party firstly has to provide evidence that is reasonably available, and this evidence provided should be sufficient to support its claims. Secondly, the claiming party has to specify the evidence lying in the control of the opposing party.

The right of information relates to the disclosure of the identity of third party involved in the production and distribution of the infringing goods or services, as well as of the channels of this distribution.[48] This right of information is of crucial importance to fight against professional infringement. As judicial authorities have the authority to order the infringer to disclose the identity as well as the channels of distribution, sanctions with regard to non-cooperation, such as 'contempt of court' may be applicable to the refusal.[49]

---

[43] Panel Report, *India – Patent Protection for Pharmaceutical and Agricultural Chemical Products, Complaint by the European Communities* (*India – Patents* (*EC*)), WT/DS79/R, adopted 22 September 1998, para. 7.66.

[44] Panel Report, *China – Measures Affecting the Protection and Enforcement of Intellectual Property Rights* (*China – Intellectual Property Rights*), (26 January 2009) WT/DS362/R.

[45] Panel Report, *China – Intellectual Property Rights*, para. 7.236.

[46] Panel Report, *China – Intellectual Property Rights*, para. 7.238.

[47] Panel Report, *China – Intellectual Property Rights*, para. 7.239.

[48] The TRIPS Agreement, Art. 47.

[49] Gervais (n 36) 301.

D. *Remedies and Provisional Measures*

Several remedies are included in the enforcement part of TRIPS Agreement, covering injunctions, damages, and provisional measures. The indemnity of the defendant is also included. With regard to injunction, judicial authorities are authorised to order the infringer to desist from an infringement. It is of particular importance for the prevention from the entry of infringing products into the channels of commerce when procedures of customs clearance are finished.

In case that the infringer engages into infringing activities, knowingly or with reasonable grounds to know, the judicial authorities should be competent to order infringer to pay damages. These damages should be adequate to compensate the damages of the intellectual property rights holders; other expenses, including attorney's fees may also be ordered to be paid. When appropriate, recovery of profits and/or payment of pre-established damages may be also ordered to be paid even if the infringers does not engage into infringing activities, knowingly or with reasonable grounds to know. However, Members' obligation will be fulfilled when courts are conferred the authority to impose the payment of expense. It is not obligatory for the courts to order these expenses to be covered. There is some degree of judicial discretion. The same applies to recovery of profits and/or payment of pre-established damages by the infringer who does not knowingly, or with reasonable grounds to know, engage into infringing activities. Furthermore, 'recovery of profits and/or payment of pre-established damages' may shed some light in interpreting the scope of damages in the first paragraph. In other words, damages referred to in the first paragraph may cover these two. However, it is up to national legislation to determine 'damages adequate to compensate the injury' provided they meet minimum standards of the TRIPS Agreement.

In order to create an effective deterrent to infringement, Article 46 of TRIPS Agreement provides additional remedies. Courts are authorised to order to destroy or dispose in a specified way the infringing goods, and materials and implements predominantly used for the creation of these infringing goods. With regard to the disposal of the infringing products, materials and implements, it is of crucial importance that this disposal should be able to exclude them from the channels of commerce. Article 46 also explicitly provides that when dealing with this disposal, the court should take into account 'the proportionality between the seriousness of the infringement and the remedies ordered as well as the interests of third parties'. The disposal of infringing products is among the subject matters in *China – Intellectual Property Rights*. The US contends that the practices of Chinese customs authorities with regard to the disposal of infringing goods, as required by relevant Chinese regulations, are inconsistent with Article 46. Infringing goods are allowed to enter into the channels of commerce after removing their infringing features; only when these infringing features of these goods cannot be removed will they be destroyed. In the view of the US, these regulations and practices are

WTO-inconsistent.[50] Such claim may be justifiable in light of the last sentence of this article that provides that the mere removal of the unlawfully affixed trademark does not sufficiently permit these infringing products to enter into channels of commerce. Even though this sentence addresses solely to counterfeit trademark goods, the same concerns in relation to entry into channels of commerce exist. The object and purpose of this article is to provide an effective deterrent to infringement and to prevent these infringing products from entering into the channels of commerce in order not to disrupt the market. The priority of permitting the entry into channels of commerce by removing the infringing features stipulated by the alleged Chinese regulation thus runs counter to this object and purpose.

On the other hand, it is also essential to balance the rights and interests of defendant, especially in case of the abuse of enforcement procedures. Consequently, Article 48 provides that a defending party should be adequately compensated for those measures taken upon the requests of the claiming party that has abused the enforcement procedures. Judicial authorities should also be authorised to order expenses to be paid by the applicant. However, liability of public authorities and officials may be exempted if these actions 'are taken or intended in good faith in the course of the administration of that law.'[51]

Lastly, provisional measures are also of great significance in domestic enforcement procedures. The terms 'prompt' and 'effective' are telling in interpreting these provisions in Article 50. These provisional measures aim to prevent the occurrence of infringement and preserving the evidence. These provisional measures are of particular importance for the prevention of the entry of infringing products into channels of commerce. The provisional measures can also be *inaudita altera parte* taken; however, more stringent requirements are imposed in this regard. Although it may not be limited to those cases where the delay is likely to cause irreparable harm or there is demonstrable risk of evidence being destroyed, however, the same characteristics of emergency should apply for those provisional measures *inaudita altera parte* imposed.

In other words, the interests of the defending party should be counterbalanced. The claiming party may be required to present reasonably available evidence to justify the necessity for the adoption of provisional measures. A sufficient degree of certainty that the right of applicant is being infringed or that the infringement is imminent should be demonstrated and substantiated. Besides, the judicial authorities should be authorised to order the applicant to provide 'security or

---

[50] WTO, *China – Measures Affecting the Protection and Enforcement of Intellectual Property Rights – Request for Consultations by the United States* (16 April 2007) WT/DS362/1, 3.
[51] The TRIPS Agreement, Art. 48(2).

equivalent assurance sufficient to protect the defendant and to prevent abuse.'[52] When provisional measures are *inaudita altera parte* taken, a quick notice should be given to defending party, and a review where a right to be heard is provided should be made available upon the request of defendant party. In cases where provisional measures are revoked, where they lapse due to the act or omission of the applicant, or where there is no infringement, judicial authorities should be authorised to order compensation to be paid by the applicant.[53]

VII. Article 4 of Pre-Shipment Inspection Agreement

Agreement on Pre-shipment Inspection (the PSI Agreement) has a special arrangement for their review mechanism. An Independent Entity, as a subsidiary body of the Council for Trade in Goods is established within the WTO. This review procedure provides an opportunity which empowers exporters to directly invoke international trade law in the WTO. It should be composed of an organisation representing exporters and an organisation representing inspection entities.[54] In an agreement concluded with the WTO, The International Chamber of Commerce (representing exporters) and the International Federation of Inspections Agencies (representing pre-shipment inspection entities) agreed jointly to constitute this Independent Entity.[55] Both the exporters and the inspection entities can refer a dispute to this Independent Entity.[56] In case of such referral, an arbitral panel will be established to hear the dispute. The panel will have to rule whether parties to the dispute have complied with the PSI Agreement. The panel should also offer opportunities for both parties to present views in person or in writing.[57] The decision of the panel should be binding on both parties.[58]

As of 1 September 2011, two cases are reported. The parties to these two disputes are the same: the company Alcatel CIT and Société Générale de Surveillance – SGS Holding France. During the proceeding of the first case, the parties settled the dispute satisfactorily. Nevertheless, a dispute between parties arose in the following year and was again referred to the Independent Entity. The Panel thus ruled on the substantial part of this dispute.[59]

---

52 The TRIPS Agreement, Art. 50(3).

53 The TRIPS Agreement, Art. 50(7).

54 The PSI Agreement, Art. 4(a).

55 WTO, *Guide to WTO Law and Practice: Analytical Index* (1st edn WTO, Geneva 2003) 839.

56 The PSI Agreement, Art. 3(c).

57 The PSI Agreement, Art. 3(f).

58 The PSI Agreement, Art. 3(h).

59 WTO, *Agreement on Preshipment Inspection – Independent Entity – Independent Review Procedure (PSI/IE/2005/1) – Decision of the Panel* (2 November 2005) G/PSI/IE/R/1; WTO, *Agreement*

VIII. Article XX of Government Procurement Agreement

The challenge procedures provided in Article XX of the Government Procurement Agreement (the GPA) is unique in terms of comprehensive requirements on their designation and applicable laws. As Arrowsmith notes, the procedural requirements and substantial obligations on judicial remedies in other provisions of the WTO agreements are not as detailed or stringent as those of the GPA. Greater deference is given to Members' domestic legal traditions on review mechanisms in those areas in question.[60] By contrast, the GPA lays down not only general requirements for the challenge procedures that have to be 'non-discriminatory', 'timely', 'transparent' and 'effective', but also other specific requirements such as the standing, jurisdiction and competence.

A. *'Non-Discriminatory', 'Timely', 'Transparent' and 'Effective'*

The general requirements of these challenge procedures are 'non-discriminatory', 'timely', 'transparent' and 'effective'. Non-discrimination has been dealt with in Article III of the GPA. As challenge procedures fall into the scope of 'all laws, regulations, procedures and practices regarding government procurement', requirements laid down Article III are applicable. Non-discrimination should be read both in the sense of Most-Favoured-Nation treatment and National Treatment; products, services, and suppliers of other Parties to the GPA should be accorded 'treatment no less favourable than that accorded to *domestic* products, services and suppliers, and that accorded to products, services and suppliers of *any other Party*'.[61]

The 'timely' requirement, closely related to the 'effective' requirement, is elaborated in Article XX:8 of the GPA stressing the importance of a timely decision with a view to preserving commercial and other interests. As the main objective of the challenge procedures is to correct breaches of the agreement, instead of providing compensation, rapid resolution of complaints is essential. Therefore, effective challenge procedures should include timely resolution and thus make possible the profit-seeking of suppliers.

B. *Standing, Jurisdiction and Competence*

Article XX:2 of the GPA defines the criteria of the standing before the challenge According to this provision, suppliers may refer to these challenge procedures with regard to these procurements in which they have, or have had, an interest.

---

on Preshipment Inspection – Independent Entity - Independent Review Procedure (PSI/IE/2006/1) – Decision of the Panel (14 November 2006) G/PSI/IE/R/2.

[60] S Arrowsmith, *Government Procurement in the WTO* (Kluwer Law International, Dordrecht: The Netherlands 2003) 385.

[61] GPA, Art. III (emphasis added).

Two criteria should be addressed here: 'suppliers' and 'have, or have had, an interest.'

There are conflicting views with regard to the scope of 'suppliers'. It may be arguably confined to those who are seeking to be a party to a government's contract. It may also be interpreted in a broader sense, covering contractors, subcontractors or those operating further down the supply chain of works, supplies, and services. The difference here is whether these subcontractors or other operators down in the supply chain are eligible to refer to these challenge procedures. In light of the object and purpose of Article XX, namely, to provide effective protection to ensure the GPA to be faithfully observed, a broader interpretation is desirable. This can be further justified when conflicts of interests between contractors and subcontractors arise. Subcontractors would have to resort to these challenges procedures independent of their contractors.[62]

The GPA then confines the standing to challenge to those suppliers who 'have, or have had, an interest'. 'Interest' is not defined in the GPA and may include legal interests or commercial interests. Whereas a reasonable limitation of the standing to interested supplier appears justifiable in view of the capacity and resources of these challenge procedures, it would be unacceptable to impose undue constraint upon the standing to make the access to these challenges procedures unreasonably difficult. Arrowsmith thus argues that it would be contrary to Article XX:2 of the GPA, if suppliers required to show that they would definitely or probably have won the contract.[63]

The challenge procedures should have jurisdiction on 'alleged breaches of the Agreement'. Petersmann argues that the term 'alleged breaches of the Agreement' suggests direct applicability of the GPA.[64] However, Arrowsmith takes a moderate view that suppliers can invoke and enforce substantial obligations of the GPA only when these substantial obligations have legal effects in domestic law.[65] If in the domestic legal sphere, the transformation legislation deliberately omits or amend the substantive rules of the GPA, suppliers may be prevented from relying directly to the pertinent provisions thereof. The applicable laws in the challenge procedures may thus be limited to national legislations.

Under the GPA, the competence of the challenge procedures should include at least three aspects: interim measures; an assessment and a possibility for a decision on the justification of the challenge; and the correction of the breach of the agreement or the compensation for the loss or damages suffered. The interim

62 Ibid 391–392.
63 Ibid 393.
64 E U Petersmann, *The GATT/WTO Dispute Settlement System: International Law, International Organisations, and Dispute Settlement* (Kluwer Law International, London: The Hague: Boston 1997) 194.
65 Arrowsmith (n 60) 386.

measures are meant to correct breaches of the agreement and to preserve commercial opportunities. To preserve commercial opportunities is of great importance as the compensation provided in Article XX:7(c) may be limited to 'costs for tender preparation or protest'. These interim measures also aim to ensure that complainant's position in the procurement concerned will not be prejudiced during the processes of challenge procedures. Secondly, Article XX:7(b) of the GPA provides an assessment and a possibility for a decision on the justification of the challenge. This provision means merely that the challenge procedures should have the authority to examine on the merits of the complaints and to determine the existence of the breaches of the GPA. The GPA does not deal with standard of review which will depend on domestic legal traditions in relation to this subject matter. The third competence of these challenge procedures is its competence to correct of the breach of the Agreement or to compensate for the loss or damages suffered. The term 'or' here is ambiguous. It is not entirely clear whether the challenge procedures are required to include both correction and compensation or either may suffice.

C. *A Court or by an Impartial and Independent Review Body*

There are several requirements imposed upon the review body of the challenge procedures. According to Article XX:6, if this review body is not a court, it has to be 'an impartial and independent review body' with no interest in the outcome of the procurement. Drafters of the GPA prefer these challenges reviewed by a court. If the review is not carried out by the court, it is desired that the decision would be subject to judicial review. If it is not the case, various procedural and transparency requirements are imposed. The provision reads as follows:

> (a) participants can be heard before an opinion is given or a decision is reached;
> (b) participants can be represented and accompanied;
> (c) participants shall have access to all proceedings;
> (d) proceedings can take place in public;
> (e) opinions or decisions are given in writing with a statement describing the basis for the opinions or decisions;
> (f) witnesses can be presented;
> (g) documents are disclosed to the review body.

Several elements in this provision need to be further elaborated. Firstly, two specific requirements are imposed with regard to the impartiality and independence of this review body. It has to involve no interest of the outcome of the procurement. This requirement is mainly out of the concerns of conflicts of interests. Besides, the members of this review body should be secure from external influence during the term of appointment. This is also a vehicle to safeguard the independence and impartiality of members of this review body. The GPA further prescribes detailed procedures for this review body, such as the right to be heard, represented and accompanied and to present witnesses and the right to full access to public proceedings and information. It also dictates the review body to deliver its decisions with reason in written. These procedural rules essentially model those governing judicial proceedings.

IX. Short Conclusion

This chapter has examined various provisions of the WTO agreements governing domestic judicial review. It begins with Article X:3(b) of the GATT 1994 and those agreements annexed thereto. These provisions cover Article 13 of the ADA, Article 23 of the ASCM, and Article 11 of the Agreement on Customs Valuation. It then examines Article VI of the GATS and investigates Article 41 to Article 50 and Article 59 of the TRIPS Agreement. Finally, it deals with Article 4 of the PSI Agreement and Article XX:2 of the GPA. The interpretation is based upon the rule of interpretation dictated by Article 3.2 of the DSU. It also follows the practice of the WTO panel/Appellate Body, namely, text, context, object and purpose.

Before concluding this chapter, it is feasible to examine the relationship between these domestic review provisions and other substantive obligations. As the Panel in the *US – Stainless Steel* declares, it is inappropriate for the WTO Dispute Settlement Mechanism to "function as a mechanism to test the consistency of a Member's particular decisions or rulings with the Member's own domestic law and practice; that is a function reserved for each Member's domestic judicial system".[66] The same concerns arise. Is the WTO panel/Appellate Body suited to perform as the final appeal of domestic review?

The relationship between substantive obligation and Article X was firstly touched upon in *European Communities – Regime for the Importation, Sale and Distribution of Bananas III (EC – Bananas III)*.[67] When addressing Article X:3(a), the Appellate Body held, "Article X applies to the *administration* of laws, regulations, decisions and rulings. To the extent that the laws, regulations, decisions and rulings themselves are discriminatory, they can be examined for their consistency with the relevant provisions of the GATT 1994."[68] In *European Communities – Measures Affecting the Importation of Certain Poultry Products (EC – Poultry)*,[69] the Appellate Body refers to the afore-mentioned ruling and briefly discusses the application of Article X. According to the Appellate Body, "Article X relates to

[66] Panel Report, *US – Stainless Steel*, para. 6.50.

[67] Appellate Body Report, *European Communities – Regime for the Importation, Sale and Distribution of Bananas (EC – Bananas III)*, WT/DS27/AB/R, adopted 25 September 1997.

[68] Appellate Body Report, *EC – Bananas III*, para. 200(emphasis original).

[69] Appellate Body Report, *European Communities – Measures Affecting the Importation of Certain Poultry Products (EC – Poultry)*, WT/DS69/AB/R, adopted 23 July 1998.

the *publication* and *administration* of laws, regulations, judicial decisions and administrative rulings of general application, rather than to the *substantive content* of such measures".[70]

Whereas these two cases deal with Article X:3(a) of the GATT 1994, the holding of the Appellate Body applies equally to Article X:3(b) as these two provisions share the same characteristics. Besides, the holding of the Appellate Body refers to Article X, instead of being limited Article X:3(a). Thus, the same distinction between objectiveness and impartiality of this 'prompt review' and the substantive content of the decisions subject to this review can also be drawn.

Borrowing the phrase used by the Panel in *Argentina – Hides and Leather,* Article X:3(b) of the GATT 1994 aims to control the manner in reviewing administrative actions, rather than the substantive decisions of the review mechanisms in question.[71] While there are no persuasive reasons to prevent the WTO panel/ Appellate Body from reviewing the substantive content of decisions delivered by these domestic courts, the drafters of the WTO Agreement do not intend to transform every claim relating to substantive obligation into one based upon Article X:3(b) of GATT 1994 or any other relevant provisions.

[70] Appellate Body Report, *EC – Poultry*, para. 115 (emphasis original).
[71] Panel Report, *Argentina – Hides and Leather*, para. 11.72.

CHAPTER FIVE

JUDGING JUDGES: CHINA'S WTO OBLIGATION TO PROVIDE AN INDEPENDENT AND IMPARTIAL JUDICIAL REVIEW

I. Introduction

China's accession to the WTO has attracted much attention and numerous scholarly works have been devoted to this issue.[1] A less explored subject is China's WTO obligation to provide an independent and impartial judicial review, as embodied in Protocol on the Accession of People's Republic of China to the WTO (hereinafter China's Accession Protocol). Although Chinese judicial reform has been related to its WTO accession, little literature examines whether the progress made so far would be sufficient to pass the scrutiny of the WTO Dispute Settlement Mechanism. This obligation is of great significance both to WTO law and to Chinese legal system.

Regarding the WTO law, this 'independent and impartial judicial review' obligation prescribed in China's Accession Protocol is cited as an example to justify the argument that WTO law should not be interpreted in purely economic terms and that its legal and political objectives are just as important as trade liberalisation. As the WTO Agreement does not only employ formal constitutional techniques, but it also embodies various substantive constitutional principles, WTO law shares major features of constitutionalism and can thus be conceived as a part of the multilevel constitutional framework that governs multilevel trade governance.[2]

[1] According to Bhattasali's observation, two main approaches are employed to look upon China's WTO membership. One is from the perspective of the legal rights and obligations, examining challenges involved in meeting China's legal commitments and in ensuring that China's rights are maintained. The second approach places the emphasis on the trade and policy changes, and explores what efforts to be made with the aim to integrating China's open market into the global economy. In this vein, the major focus is to see how China's WTO membership serves as a key component in the restructuring of the Chinese economy as well as other policy goals, notably, its peaceful emergence as a great trading power. *See* D Bhattasali, et al., 'Impacts and Policy Implications of WTO Accession for China' in D Bhattasali, et al. (eds), *China and the WTO: Accession, Policy Reform, and Poverty Reduction Strategies* (World Bank, Washington, D.C. 2004) 1.

[2] E U Petersmann, 'Multilevel Trade Governance in the WTO Requires Multilevel Constitutionalism' in C Joerges and E U Petersmann (eds), *Constitutionalism, Multilevel Trade Governance and Social Regulation* (Hart Publishing, Oxford and Portland, Oregon 2006) 32–33. Petersmann argues that WTO law uses the formal techniques of (1) the distinction of long term constitutional rules and post-constitutional decision making; (2) the legal primacy of the WTO agreement over conflicting provisions in the Multilateral Trade Agreements annexed the WTO agreement; and (3) protection of

The WTO Agreement is claimed to be 'one of the most revolutionary transformative agreements in the history of international law.'[3]

As for the impact of this obligation on the Chinese legal system, Cao Jianming, the vice-president of the Supreme People's Court (the SPC), delivered a speech on 'China and the rule of law' shortly after China's entry into the WTO. He stated that the accession to the WTO would have a profound impact both on the rule of law and on the judicial reform in China, even though he thought that the existing legal system for administrative procedure and judicial review had already met the requirements of the WTO.[4] This statement seems unconvincing. On the contrary, Chinese judicial system should be reformulated in order to fulfil its WTO obligation.

As is pointed out, China's accession to the WTO constituted an unprecedented opportunity to reform its judicial branch by reshaping the relationships between the courts, the local governments and the Chinese Communist Party (the CCP), since China's accession has put its economic, legal and political system under strict scrutiny. The fact that the aggrieved foreign parties can always, through its own countries resort to the WTO Dispute Settlement Mechanism for legal redress, presents a great pressure for China and forces it to implement meaningful reform to establish an independent and impartial judicial review.[5] In other words, the binding nature of this WTO obligation and the potential non-compliance sanctions compel China to take its independent and impartial judicial review's legal obligation seriously. Effective enforcement is obligatory.

Such concerns are also evidenced in China's first Trade Policy Review conducted in 2006. During the Trade Policy Review, the United States (the US) voiced its concerns with respect to the role of the CCP in the proceedings and the decisions taking place at the SPC and at the lower courts. Chinese government replied with the following answer:

> According to the Constitution, the Organic Law of the People's Courts of the People's Republic of China and the Judges Law of the People's Republic of China, the people's courts exercise judicial power independently and are not subject to interference by any administration, public organisation or individual. When exercising this power, the people's courts shall strictly abide by the Constitution, the Organic Law of the

reedom of trade, Most-Favoured-Nation treatment, National Treatment, private property rights and rule of law subject to broad exceptions to protect public interests. He also argues that four substantive principles are included in WTO law: rule of international law, the respect of universal human rights obligations of WTO members, separation of powers and the concern of social justice.

[3] E U Petersmann, *Dispute Prevention, Dispute Settlement and Justice in International Economic Law* (Forthcoming).

[4] J Cao, 'WTO and the Rule of Law in China' (2002) 16 Temple International and Comparative Law Journal 379, 379. For updated review of the socialist rule of law with Chinese characteristics, *see* J Lee, 'Socialist Rule of Law with Chinese Characteristics' (2007) 43 Issues & Studies 115.

[5] V M Hung, 'China's WTO Commitment on Independent Judicial Review: Impact on Legal and Political Reform' (2004) 52 American Journal of Contemporary Law 77, 120–125.

> People's Courts of the People's Republic of China and other substantial and procedural laws related to the specific cases.[6]

However, this reply does not fully answer the question. It is unclear whether the CCP would fall under the category of administration, public organisations or individuals, which would imply that the courts should not be subject to its interference. In addition, what Chinese government failed to point out were those articles requiring the courts to be responsible to the People's Congress and those articles governing the relationship among courts, the CCP and People's Congress.

Against this background, this chapter aims to examine these efforts so far made in relation to China's 'independent and impartial judicial review' obligation and to ascertain the compatibility with the WTO requirements. However, this chapter will not engage into empirical studies. It covers China's progress on judicial reform only to the extent necessary to examine whether China has satisfied with its WTO obligation on 'an independent and impartial judicial review'. Nor will this chapter touch upon whether the WTO requirement of 'an independent and impartial tribunal' meets the needs of China's developments. Given the binding effect of China's WTO obligation, this chapter will focus on the conformity of Chinese judicial system to this obligation.

Following this introductory Section, Section II will firstly examine China's 'independent and impartial judicial review' obligation based on what has been elaborated in Chapter II, namely the role of domestic courts in the WTO Agreement.[7] Since the existing WTO jurisprudence does not offer a clear answer on what an 'independent and impartial judicial review' should be, Section III draws on global and regional standards for 'judicial independence'[8] in order to clearly define the nature and scope of this obligation. Section IV will review some major efforts made by China in relation to the fulfilment of this obligation and then continue to explore how to interpret this 'independent and impartial judicial review' obligation in answering whether the existing judicial system can pass the scrutiny in the WTO Dispute Settlement Mechanism. This chapter will end with a short concluding remark summarising the major arguments presented and the main findings of this chapter and points to the direction for future reform in Chinese judicial system.

---

[6] WTO, *Trade Policy Review Body – 19 and 21 April 2006 – Trade Policy Review – People's Republic of China – Minutes of Meeting – Addendum* (11 September 2006) WT/TPR/M/161/Add.2, 12.

[7] *See supra* Chapter II, Section II. B, text to (n 21) *et seq* (the role of the domestic courts in the WTO Agreement).

[8] Various approaches are offered to clarify the concept of 'judicial independence'. For an empirical study of this topic, *see, e.g.*, E G Jensen and T C Heller (eds), *Beyond Common Knowledge: Empirical Approaches to the Rule of Law* (Stanford University Press, Stanford 2003). For an interdisciplinary study, *see, e.g.*, S B Burbank and B Friedman (eds), *Judicial Independence at the Crossroads: An Interdisciplinary Approach* (Sage Publications, Thousand Oaks, California; London; New Delhi 2002). *See* also studies on judicial independence in the post-communist countries in A Sajo (ed), *Judicial Integrity* (Martinus Nijhoff Publishers, Leiden 2004).

II. China's Obligation to Provide An Independent and Impartial Judicial Review

A. *China's Accession Protocol to the WTO*

As noted in Chapter II, there was a trend to strengthen the effectiveness of domestic judicial review during the negotiation of the Uruguay Round. This trend is also evidenced in China's WTO Accession Protocol where the obligation to provide an independent and impartial judicial review is explicitly prescribed in Section 2(D). The legal text reads as follows:

> 1. China shall establish, or designate, and maintain tribunals, contact points and procedures for the prompt review of all administrative actions relating to the implementation of laws, regulations, judicial decisions and administrative rulings of general application referred to in Article X:1 of the GATT 1994, Article VI of the GATS and the relevant provisions of the TRIPS Agreement. Such tribunals shall be impartial and independent of the agency entrusted with administrative enforcement and shall not have any substantial interest in the outcome of the matter.
>
> 2. Review procedures shall include the opportunity for appeal, without penalty, by individuals or enterprises affected by any administrative action subject to review. If the initial right of appeal is to an administrative body, there shall in all cases be the opportunity to choose to appeal the decision to a judicial body. Notice of the decision on appeal shall be given to the appellant and the reasons for such decision shall be provided in writing. The appellant shall also be informed of any right to further appeal.

When compared with the existing provisions in the WTO agreements, China's 'independent and impartial judicial review' obligation deserves further exploration in several aspects: the scope of subject matters; the definition of 'general application'; institutional requirements; and independence and impartiality. However, before proceeding to examining these elements, it is worthwhile to explore the objective and purpose of this obligation. Why is an independent and impartial judicial review desirable for WTO Members when negotiating for China's accession?[9] The Working Party Report does not provide clues on it; section III.4 (titled 'Judicial Review') merely reiterates that some members of the Working

[9] It is interesting to note that, for those new member states of the European Union (the EU), the judicial independence was among the highlights of their accession process. However, China's WTO obligation and those new member states' judicial independence requirements apparently derive from different logic, as the objective of the EU and the WTO much differ. However, the scope of independent judicial review is much more wider; civil and political rights are of equal, if not more, importance in the accession process of the European Union, *See, e.g.*, Open Society Institute, *Monitoring the E U Accession Process: Judicial Independence* (Open Society Institute, Budapest ; New York 2001).

Party wished for independent tribunals to be established.[10] The necessity and justification for such independent tribunals have not been fully explained.[11] It is nevertheless clear that members of the Working Party attached great value and importance to independent tribunals, and held of the view that independent tribunals can contribute to the smooth settlement of trade disputes and the protection of rights and interests of individual economic actors under the WTO agreements.

On China's 'independent and impartial judicial review' obligation, a delicate but important point to note is that China is obliged to 'establish, or designate, and maintain tribunals, contact points *and* procedures', while GATT X:3(b) dictates members to 'maintain, or institute as soon as practicable, judicial, arbitral or administrative tribunals *or* procedures.' By comparing these two provisions, it is thus clear that all these three elements (i.e., tribunals, contacts points, and procedures) should be covered in China's implementing measures for this obligation. Although tribunals are usually connected with procedures, however, as GATT X:3(b) refers to tribunals 'or' procedures, it appears that mere procedures that are capable of providing a review mechanism comparable to the prescribed standards should also be accepted as an alternative in meeting this requirement. By contrast, having a tribunal, a 'body' established to settle certain types of dispute, is indispensable to China's implementation measures.[12] Besides, in Article X:3(c) of the GATT 1994, it is nevertheless prescribed that the existing procedures set in place do not have to be substituted or eliminated, if these procedures provide objective and impartial review for administrative actions, even though they are not 'fully or formally independent of the agencies entrusted with administrative enforcement'. Therefore, if a Member believes that the procedures in place are objective and impartial, that Member may not be required to substitute or eliminate these existing procedures. Additionally, a Member is not required to introduce a new review mechanism which would be inconsistent with its constitutional structure or legal system (Article VI:2(b) of GATS). In contrast, the second sentence of the Section

---

[10] WTO, Report of the Working Party on the Accession of People's Republic of China (hereinafter 'China's Working Party Report') (1 October 2001) WT/ACC/CHN/49, paras. 76–77.

[11] The Working Party Report on the Accession of Viet Nam, for example in paragraph 123, 124, 135, has also dealt with this independent and impartial judicial review of administrative actions. However, this obligation is not prescribed in Viet Nam's Accession Protocol. Besides, instead of reformulating an obligation of different duties, Viet Nam was requested to commit that its judicial review would be consistent with the requirements of the WTO agreements. The Working Party Report on the Accession of Viet Nam (27 October 2006) WT/ACC/VNM/48, para. 135.

[12] With regard to the definition of 'tribunals', the Court of Justice of the EU has laid down a variety of case-law to examine who is eligible and obliged to refer to it for preliminary ruling under Article 267 of the Treaty on the Functioning of the European Union (Article 234 of EC Treaty). *See, e.g.*, Vassen v. Beambtenfonds Voor Het Mijnbedris, Case C-61/65 [1966] E.C.R. 261, Dorsch Consult Ingenieurgesellschaft mbH v Bundesbaugesellschaft Berlin mbH, Case C-54/96 [1997] E.C.R. I-04961. The author owes this point to Professor Petersmann.

2(D)(1) of China's Accession Protocol clearly stipulates that tribunals in China should be 'independent of the agency entrusted with administrative enforcement,' so such leeway is not available to China.[13]

In respect of the jurisdiction, some elements are worth noting. As provided in the legal text, these tribunals should have the jurisdiction on 'administrative actions relating to the implementation of laws, regulations, judicial decisions and administrative rulings of general application referred to in Article X:1 of the GATT 1994, Article VI of the GATS and the relevant provisions of the TRIPS Agreement.' The scope of this application has to be further defined to some degree. Nevertheless, what these relevant provisions under the TRIPS Agreement are exactly referred to may be subject to dispute. It may be interpreted as referencing to Articles 41 to 40 and 59 of the TRIPS Agreement. Yet, it is rather unclear in this regard. On the other hand, the Working Party Report may provide some guidance on defining the scope of administrative actions in terms of Section 2(D) of the Accession Protocol. It set out that such should cover 'the implementation of national treatment, conformity assessment, the regulation, control, supply or promotion of a service, including the grant or denial of a licence to provide a service and other matters.'[14] These administrative actions should thus also be subject to the prompt review of independent and impartial tribunals. In another word, the subject matters which Section 2(D) covers are apparently wider that those by the relevant provisions of the WTO Agreements.

Apart from the subject matters, the term 'of general application' is also of great importance. In *United States – Restrictions on Imports of Cotton and Man-made*

---

[13] J Y Qin, ''WTO-plus' Obligations and Their Implications for the World Trade Organisation Legal System – An Appraisal of the China Accession Protocol' (2003) 37 Journal of World Trade 483, 495–496. While it is true that judicial review to administrative measures in relation to trade matters could be regarded as a commonly-required obligation as previously established in the existent WTO agreements. This chapter argues that the obligation to provide an independent and impartial judicial review as embodied in China's Accession Protocol is wider in scope and more stringent in its formulation. This obligation thus constitutes as a 'WTO-plus' obligation. Although Members' doubts about the independence and impartiality of China's courts are unquestionably justifiable, the arrangement to provide detailed obligations in one single country's accession protocol, normally a standardised document without dealing with substantial obligations, is unprecedented, and so far, the only case. By comparing to the accession protocol of Viet Nam, one can easily draw a sharp contrast. While Members might also have doubts about the independence and impartiality of Viet Nam's courts, given that Viet Nam is still a communist country. A similar arrangement does not exist. While in the Working Party Report on the Accession of Viet Nam to the WTO does refer to obligation relating to judicial review to trade measures, such as custom valuation, rule of origin and trade-related intellectual property rights, in particular compulsory licensing and the termination and invalidation of invention patents, the Accession Protocol does not include this obligation. *See* Report of the Working Party on the Accession of Viet Nam, WT/ ACC/VNM/48 (27 October 2006) (n11), paras. 235, 243, 409, 430 and 433. In addition, the Protocol of the Accession of the Socialist Republic of Viet Nam to the World Trade Organisation is actually a standardised document, just as other accession protocols do. WT/L/662 (15 November 2006).

[14] China's Working Party Report, para. 79.

Fibre Underwear (*US – Underwear*), the Panel held, that 'if, for instance, the restraint was addressed to a *specific company* or applied to a *specific shipment*, it would not have qualified as a measure of general application. However, to the extent that the restraint affects an *unidentified* number of economic operators, including domestic and foreign producers, we find it to be a measure of general application'.[15] This view was upheld by the Appellate Body.[16] According to this interpretation, whether a law, a regulation, a judicial decisions or an administrative ruling is 'of general application' depends on whether it can affect an unidentified number of economic operators. Those addressed to individual persons or entities should not be regarded as of general application.

The Accession Protocol also lays down several institutional requirements governing the designation of this 'independent and impartial judicial review'. For example, the right to appeal should be without penalty;[17] the decision of the appeal should be given to the appellant with reasons provided in writing;[18] the right for further appeals should also be informed;[19] and the tribunal should have no substantial interests of the outcome of the decision.[20] An 'opportunity for appeal' reviewed by 'judicial body' if the initial review of the disputed administrative actions is heard by an administrative body. This requirement of review by 'judicial' body does not exist within the WTO agreements. As pointed out, China's Accession Protocol contains more stringent requirements for domestic judicial review, which constitutes as a 'WTO-plus' obligation.[21]

The requirement of 'without penalty' is also absent in Article X:3(b) of the GATT 1994, Article VI of the GATS and the relevant provisions of the TRIPS Agreement. It is nevertheless referred to in the Custom Valuation Agreement. The Interpretive Note in the Custom Valuation Agreement informs that 'without penalty' means that appellant should not be subject to a fine or threat of fine merely because an importer chooses to exercise the right to appeal. A dictionary definition of 'penalty' is a punishment imposed for breach of law, rule or contract, and a 'fine' means a certain sum of money imposed as the penalty for an offence. 'Punishment' and 'offence' are telling here. Therefore, fees to cover the administrative costs should not be regarded as a fine and thus do not fall into the scope of this

[15] Panel Report, *United States – Restrictions on Imports of Cotton and Man-made Fibre Underwear* (*US – Underwear*), WT/DS24/R, adopted 25 February 1997, modified by Appellate Body Report, WT/DS24/AB/R, para. 7.65 (emphasis added).

[16] Appellate Body Report, *United States – Restrictions on Imports of Cotton and Man-made Fibre Underwear* (*US – Underwear*), WT/DS24/AB/R, adopted 25 February 1997, 21.

[17] China's Accession Protocol, S. 2(D)(2).

[18] Ibid.

[19] Ibid.

[20] China's Accession Protocol, S. 2(D)(1).

[21] For the 'WTO-plus' obligations in relation to China's accession to the WTO, *see* Qin (n 13).

penalty. This reading is supported by the Interpretive Note, which provides that payment of normal court costs and lawyers' fees shall not be considered a fine. However, these court costs and lawyers' fees should be limited to the amount necessary to cover the administrative expenses. In terms of the objective and purpose of this provision, these costs and fees should not have the effects of preventing or prohibiting appellants from referring to the review mechanisms as set out for in the aforementioned provisions. Besides, the requirement of giving a reasoned decision given in writing forces review bodies to justify that their decisions have been rationally taken. This also provides a good safeguard to prevent the abuse on discretionary power. Instructions on further appeal helps the Chinese appellants to be better informed on these review mechanisms as most foreign individuals and enterprises find them to be incoherent and confusing.

Above all, the most important element in the designation of Chinese judicial review is contained in the second sentence of Section 2(D)(1) of the China's Accession Protocol. The tribunals should be 'impartial' and 'independent of the agency entrusted with administrative enforcement', and they should not 'have any substantial interest in the outcome of the matter'. These three criteria are actually interlinked. With regard to being 'independent', tribunals are required to be formally and structurally 'independent of the agency entrusted with administrative enforcement'. An ordinary meaning of 'impartial' is to treat all rivals and disputants equally. That is, these tribunals or procedures should not privilege any parties. Equal opportunities to be heard and to defend are thus important in this sense. The 'principle of equality of arms' is also relevant in terms of information and evidence to be made available to complainants. As the objectives of these tribunals are to strengthen domestic judicial review, accessing information and evidence is essential for appellants to effectively defend their rights and interests under this review mechanism. The criterion of impartiality is also closely related to the requirement of 'no substantial interest in the outcome of the matter'. Having no substantial interests in the outcome of the matter, tribunals are prevented from being biased due to personal feelings or opinions when considering facts and/or making decisions. Objective decisions may be easier achieved. Besides, the requirement of 'no substantial interests' is also related to the requirement of being 'independent of the agency entrusted with administrative enforcement'. If tribunals are dependent upon the agencies that entrusted them with the administrative enforcement, they may be influenced by these agencies and have conflicting interests, which eventually may undermine the impartiality of these tribunals.

With regard to the WTO jurisprudence, as previously noted, the Panel had addressed the term 'impartial' in *Argentina – Hides and Leather*. Although it relates to 'impartial administration of laws, regulations, judicial decisions and administrative rulings of general application,' how that Panel interpreted impartiality can nevertheless shed some light in this context here. As *Argentina – Hides and Leather* relates to the presence of 'partial and interested representatives of certain industrial associations' in the process of customs administration, it can arguably be transformed into a review procedure for 'principle of equality of arms' and '*ex parte* contact.' The Panel emphasises 'the presence of private parties with conflicting commercial interests in the customs process.'[22] Furthermore, whether any interested party has taken advantage of this process to 'obtain confidential information to which they have no right'[23] should also be taken into due account.

However, the previous 'textual' analysis of China's obligation to provide 'an independent and impartial judicial review' fails to provide a clear picture of what this obligations actually entails. Are these tribunals obliged to be independent only 'of the agency entrusted with administrative enforcement', and not of the other organs? Such interpretation is apparently unconvincing and against the objective and purpose of this obligation: to strengthen the rights and interests of individual economic actors protected under the domestic judicial system. It is thus essential to refer to the other legal systems when interpreting the nature and scope of this obligation correctly. This reference is also justifiable as the Appellate Body of *United States – Standards for Reformulated and Conventional Gasoline*, clearly held that the WTO agreements should not 'be read in clinical isolation from public international law.'[24]

One may then wonder how the WTO agreements should be read or interpreted. This comes back to the 'general rule of interpretation' and the Appellate Body has to recognise its status within 'a rule of customary or general international law' where it should clarify the existing provisions of the WTO agreements. Article 31(1) of the Vienna Convention on the Law of Treaties (the VCLT) provides, 'a treaty shall be interpreted in good faith in accordance with the ordinary meaning to be given to the terms of the treaty in their context and in the light of its object and purpose.' The crucial point here is thus what constitutes as the context of a treaty. While general principles of public international law may be applicable in this

---

[22] Panel Report, *Argentina – Measures Affecting the Export of Bovine Hides and Import of Finished Leather* (*Argentina – Hides and Leather*), WT/DS155/R and Corr.1, adopted 16 February 2001, para. 11.99.

[23] Ibid para. 11.100.

[24] Appellate Body report, *United States – Standards for Reformulated and Conventional Gasoline* ('*US – Gasoline*'), WT/DS2/AB/R, adopted 29 April 1996, 17. Besides, as the preamble of Vienna Convention on the Law of Treaties (the VCLT) explicitly prescribes that disputes concerning treaties should be settled by 'peaceful means and in conformity with the principles of justice and international law', and Article 31(1) of the Convention provides that a treaty shall be interpreted in good faith in accordance with the ordinary meaning to be given to the terms of the treaty in their context and in the light of its object and purpose', a question deserves further exploration here is the relevance of international human rights obligation in relation to access to justice to the interpretation

context, this again begs the question as to what constitutes as the 'general principles of public international law.'[25]

Nevertheless, if one analyses the wording of the Appellate Body carefully, it reads as followed: 'that direction reflects a measure of recognition that the *General Agreement* is not to be read in clinical isolation from public international law.' In rejecting a clinical isolated reading of the public international law, the Appellate Body presupposes that a 'correct' reading of the General Agreement and the other covered agreements is *not* 'in clinical isolation from the public international law'. When directing the interpreters not to read the General Agreement and the other covered agreement in clinical isolation from the public international law, the Appellate Body actually, albeit implicitly, instructs the interpreters to read the General Agreement and the other covered agreements in light of the public international law.

This position finds its support from other relevant WTO panel/Appellate Body jurisprudence. In *United States – Import Prohibition of Certain Shrimp and Shrimp Products* (*US – Shrimps*),[26] the Appellate Body approached this issue with a positive voice. It firstly recognised the principle of good faith to be both a general principle of law and a general principle of international law; by citing Article 31(3(c) of VLCT[27] the Appellate Body then opines that its task 'is to interpret the language of the chapeau [of Article XX of GATT 1994], seeking additional interpretative guidance, as appropriate, from the general principles of international law'.[28]

Further, the Panel in *EC – Approval and Marketing of Biotech Products* was called upon to deal with the relevance of the Cartagena Protocol on Biodiversity to the WTO agreements, in particular the Agreement on Sanitary and Phytosanitary

---

of China's WTO obligation to provide an independent and impartial judicial review. These international human rights obligations range from Article 8 of Universal Declaration of Human Rights to Article 9 of International Covenant on Civil and Political Rights, and Article 6 of The European Convention on Human Rights, to which China may (and may not) be a Contracting Party or not. Cf. *infra* text to (n 27) *et seq*.

[25] An illustrative example of this is the debate of 'precautionary principle' in *European Communities – Measures Affecting the Approval and Marketing of Biotech Products* (*EC – Approval and Marketing of Biotech Products*), Panel Report, *EC – Approval and Marketing of Biotech Products*, WT/DS291/R, WT/DS292/R, WT/DS293/R, Corr.1 and Add.1, 2, 3, 4, 5, 6, 7, 8 and 9, adopted 21 November 2006.

While the EC argues that precautionary principle as embodied in Cartagena Protocol on Biodiversity is a general principle of international law, the United States takes the opposite position. (paras. 4.523-524; 4.539-544). The Panel finds in favour of the United States, holding that the precautionary principle does not constitute a general principle of international law.

[26] Appellate Body Report, *United States – Import Prohibition of Certain Shrimp and Shrimp Products* (*US – Shrimps*), WT/DS58/AB/R, adopted 6 November 1998, DSR 1998: VII, 2755.

[27] Article 31(3)(c) of VCLT provides that 'there shall be taken into account, together with the context: (c) any relevant rules of international law applicable in the relations between the parties.'

[28] Ibid para. 158.

Measures (the SPS agreement). The Panel again referred to Article 31(3)(c) of the VCLT. The Panel took a cautious approach in exploring the relevance of this protocol. The Panel concluded that, as one of the parties to this dispute, the US, was not a party to the Cartagena Protocol on Biodiversity, this protocol was not a 'rule of international law applicable in the relations between the parties'. The Panel was thus not required to take this protocol into account. Nevertheless, the Panel also noted:

> Requiring that a treaty be interpreted in the light of other rules of international law which bind the States parties to the treaty ensures or enhances the consistency of the rules of international law applicable to these States and thus contributes to avoiding conflicts between the relevant rules.[29]

According to this holding, while the author is fully aware of the counterarguments against the introduction of the European Court of Human Right (the ECtHR) when interpreting China's *WTO* obligation to provide an independent and impartial judicial review,[30] one should never overlook the importance of 'other rules of international law which bind the States parties'.

In addressing to the concept of a 'denial of justice' on the treatment of aliens in customary international law, Francioni, based on a survey of universal and regional human rights instruments and national practices, argues that the individual's right to access justice 'has emerged and is exercised independently or in cooperation with national state of the affected individual.'[31] According to Francioni, the alien's right of access to justice should be satisfied with the requirements for fair and equitable treatment and for effective protection. He writes, 'access to justice is not simply access to courts, but availability to a system of fair and impartial justice the effectiveness and legitimacy of which may be reviewed under the international standard on the treatment of aliens.'[32] The requirements of fair and equitable treatment and of effective protection are reflected in the enforcement part of

[29] Panel report, *EC – Approval and Marketing of Biotech Products*, para. 7.70.

[30] Arguments against this approach may be: most of those international and regional instruments, in the form of soft laws, are not 'relevant rules of international law applicable in the relations between the parties,' since China do not participate in the drafting of those instruments; China is not a party to the ECHR and thus not bound by the jurisprudence of the ECtHR. Therefore, those global and regional instruments and the jurisprudence of the ECtHR is not relevant in interpreting China's WTO obligation to provide an independent and impartial judicial review. Nevertheless, it should be pointed out that even taking the cautious approach adopted by the Panel on *EC – Approval and Marketing of Biotech Products*, those universal/regional declarations, standards and instruments in which China participates should be of great relevance in interpreting its own obligation, even in the realm of WTO law.

[31] F Francioni, 'The Rights of Access to Justice under Customary International Law' in F Francioni (ed), *Access to Justice as a Human Right* (Oxford University Press, Oxford ; New York 2007) 8.

[32] Ibid 11.

the TRIPS Agreement. The Panel on *China – Measures Affecting the Protection and Enforcement of Intellectual Property Rights* (*China-Intellectual Property Rights*)[33] was also called upon to examine whether the criminal penalty imposed by China's Criminal Law and the two *Judicial Interpretations* by the SPC constituted as an effective deterrent for 'wilful trademark counterfeiting or copyright piracy on a commercial scale'. As the objective and purpose of China's obligation to provide an independent and impartial judicial review is mainly to ensure the WTO-consistency of Chinese laws and regulations, it was designed to indirectly protect the rights and interests of foreign individuals and enterprises in China. It is thus clear that the right of access to justice, derived from the treatment of aliens and allowing for the availability of an effective and legitimate, fair and impartial justice system in line with the international standard, is of great relevance in interpreting China's WTO obligation to provide an independent and impartial judicial review.

Apart from the element of 'treatment of aliens' under the customary international law, Francioni also develops a human rights foundation for access to justice. According to him, human rights derived from various multilateral treaties of the United Nations, soft law and customary rules to create 'a system of international obligations binding upon states in their mutual relations, toward international community as a whole, and sometimes, directly upon individuals and private entities.'[34] Human rights obligations then entail a minimum standard of fair treatment and respect for human dignity.[35] Based on his observation on the expansion of the right of access to justice in domestic law and the increase of direct access to international adjudicatory mechanisms, notably the ECtHR, he proclaims an individual's right to access to justice should have a minimum standard of human rights.[36] It is thus clear that the global and regional instruments for judicial independence and impartiality and the jurisprudence of the ECtHR are relevant in interpreting China's WTO obligation to provide 'an independent and impartial judicial review'. On the one hand, they explain and clarify the concept of the right of access to justice; on the other hand, they offer guidance in defining this scope and nature of this right.

As noted above, the two elements of the individual right of access to justice are the 'treatment of aliens' and the 'access to justice as a human right' and they impose international obligations that are binding on all States. The right of access

[33] Panel Report, *China – Measures Affecting the Protection and Enforcement of Intellectual Property Rights* (*China – Intellectual Property Rights*) (26 January 2009) WT/DS362/R, para. 7.396, *et seq.*

[34] Ibid 29.

[35] Francioni (n 31) 30.

[36] Ibid 33–42.

to justice thus constitutes as a part of 'other rules of international law which bind the States parties'. Along this line, the interpretation of China's WTO obligation to provide an independent and impartial judicial review should be construed in the spirit of the individual right of access to justice and in conformity with global and regional instruments on judicial independence and impartiality such as the jurisprudence of the ECtHR.[37]

B. *The Possibility of A Complaint Under the WTO on China's Obligation to Provide An Independent and Impartial Judicial Review*

Before proceeding to discuss the standards for the WTO panel/Appellate Body to take in handling a complaint relating to China's 'independent and impartial judicial review' obligation, it is necessary to clarify whether such a complaint within the WTO is not fictional and thus deserves close examination and in-depth analysis. Firstly, Article X:3(a) of the GATT 1994 has been referred to in some complaints. The WTO panel/Appellate Body have also laid down some criteria for the 'impartiality' and 'objectivity' elements of the administration of laws, regulations and judicial decisions and administrative rulings of general application. Since complaints on the impartiality and objectivity of the administration have been brought about in the WTO and been subject to the review of the WTO panel/ Appellate Body, a complaint on the impartiality and independence of judiciary can easily be formulated based on this pattern.

Secondly, in the WTO jurisprudence, there are also complaints in relation to particular judgments of domestic courts.[38] Although complaints with regard to substantive obligations should be dealt with independently from the claim based

---

[37] Here, it should be also reminded of the distinction between the interpretation of the obligation to provide an independent judicial review as included in China's Accession Protocol and the legal basis for the Panel/Appellate Body to adjudicate the case. While the author argues that this obligation to provide an independent and impartial judicial review should be read in light of public international law, China is under its WTO obligation to provide this independent and impartial judicial review. It is this *WTO* obligation which forms the legal basis of the panel/Appellate Body's ruling and it is limited to this obligation too. Namely, if a complaint on this obligation is brought about in the WTO Dispute Settlement Mechanism, the terms of the reference of the WTO panel/Appellate Body is to examine, in the light of the relevant provisions of the covered agreements (including China's Accession Protocol, notably, the obligation to provide an independent and impartial review) cited by the complaining party.

[38] A closely-related example is the *United States – Section 211 Omnibus Appropriations Act of 1998* (*US – Section 211 Appropriations Act*), where the Appellate Body, in paragraph 202–232, examines precisely 'a conclusion by a court based on Section 211'. In this complaint, the Appellate Body clarifies the comparable civil protection as required by Article 42 of the TRIPS Agreement has been provided by Section 211(a)(2) of the Omnibus Appropriations Act of 1998. WT/DS176/AB/R, adopted 1 February 2002, paras. 203–232.

upon the violation of 'independence' and 'impartiality' of judicial review,[39] a claim based upon the violation of the general independent and impartial obligation of the Chinese courts may come along with the claim upon the violation of a particular obligation or commitment.

Furthermore, the complainants in *China – Measures Affecting Imports of Automobile Parts* (*China – Auto Parts*),[40] referred to obligations and commitments as set out for in the China's Accession Protocol.[41] The complainants in *China – Intellectual Property Rights* also identified two specific judicial interpretations by the SPC in the submission to request for a consultation, and the submission of requested for the establishment of a panel.[42] These jurisprudential developments not only indicate the result of a particular national court judgment is subject to the WTO Panel/ Appellate Body's review, but the WTO panel/Appellate Body can also scrutinise judicial interpretations of the SPC.[43] Given these developments in the WTO Dispute Settlement Mechanism, it is thus reasonable to expect that the

---

[39] The relationship between substantive obligation and Article X was firstly touched upon in *European Communities – Regime for the Importation, Sale and Distribution of Bananas* (*EC – Bananas III*). The Appellate Body, when addressing ArticleX:3(a), the Appellate Body holds in *EC – Bananas III*: 'Article X applies to the *administration* of laws, regulations, decisions and rulings. To the extent that the laws, regulations, decisions and rulings themselves are discriminatory, they can be examined for their consistency with the relevant provisions of the GATT 1994' (emphasis original), WT/DS27/AB/R, adopted 25 September 1997, para. 200. In *European Communities – Measures Affecting the Importation of Certain Poultry Products* (*EC – Poultry*), the Appellate Body refers to the aforementioned ruling, briefly discusses the application of Article X as follows: 'Article X relates to the *publication* and *administration* of laws, regulations, judicial decisions and administrative rulings of general application, rather than to the *substantive content* of such measures' (emphasis original), WT/DS69/AB/R, adopted 23 July 1998, para. 115.

[40] *China – Measures Affecting Imports of Automobile Parts* (*China – Auto Parts*) (18 July 2008) WT/DS339/R, WT/DS340/R, WT/DS342/R.

[41] In EC's submission for the request for the establishment of the Panel, it is submitted that 'China has acted inconsistently with its obligations under the Marrakesh Agreement Establishing the World Trade Organisation, as set out in the Protocol on the Accession of the People's Republic of China to the WTO, in particular Part I paragraph 7.3 of the Protocol of Accession of China, and in paragraph 203 of the Working Party Report on the Accession of China in conjunction with Part I, paragraph 1.2 of the Protocol of Accession of China, and paragraph 342 of the Working Party Report on the Accession of China, (18/09/2006) WT/DS339/8, 3. Obligations and commitments provided in accession protocol and working party report are also referred to in *China – Certain Measures Granting Refunds, Reductions or Exemptions from Taxes and other Payments* (*China – Taxes*), *See* WTO, *China - Certain Measures Granting Refunds, Reductions or Exemptions from Taxes and Other Payments – Request for the Establishment of a Panel by the United States* (13 July 2007) WT/DS358/13; *China – Certain Measures Granting Refunds, Reductions or Exemptions from Taxes and Other Payments – Request for the Establishment of a Panel by Mexico* (13 July 2007) WT/DS359/13.

[42] WTO, *China – Measures Affecting the Protection and Enforcement of Intellectual Property Rights - Request for Consultations by the United States* (16 April 2007) WT/DS362/1, para. 1(2); (21 August 2007) WT/DS/362/7, para. 1(2), 1(3). The Panel on *China – Intellectual Property Rights*, after reviewing the threshold laid down by China's criminal law and the disputed judicial interpretations, finds in favor of China. Panel Report on *China – Intellectual Property Rights* (26 January 2009) WT/DS362/R, para. 7.396, *et seq.*

[43] Judicial interpretation is a peculiar designation in Chinese legal system. It is delivered by Supreme People's Court and enjoys the legal status of Chinese national law. It is aimed to serve as guidance to the lower court and is legal-binding in nature. *See generally*, N Liu, *Opinions of the*

complaint on to the independence and impartiality of the Chinese courts would be soon to come.

Above all, regarding the interpretative approach taken by the WTO panel/ Appellate Body on this obligation,[44] the importance of the Article 31 of VCLT, in particular the 'good faith' element, should be noted. This approach is consistent with the established WTO panel/Appellate Body jurisprudence. The Panel on *China – Auto Parts* partly touched upon this issue. It alluded to a commitment made by China in paragraph 93 of its Working Party Report. By virtue of Section 1.2 of China's Accession Protocol, this commitment which referred to paragraph 342 of China's Working Party Report was incorporated into China's Accession Protocol and constituted an integral part of the WTO Agreement.[45] The Panel then noted that it would 'interpret China's commitment under paragraph 93 of the Working Party Report in accordance with the interpretative rules of the *Vienna Convention* to determine whether China has acted inconsistently with commitments under paragraph 93 of the Working Party Report'.[46]

This interpretative approach is of great relevance to the interpretation of China's WTO obligation to provide an independent and impartial judicial review since this panel relates directly to China's 'WTO-plus' commitment. The interpretative approach taken by the Panel on *China – Auto Parts* basically follows the existing practice of the WTO panel/Appellate Body. This approach supports the argument and the analysis put forward in the chapter: one should interpret China's

Supreme People's Court: Judicial Interpretation in China (Sweet & Maxwell Asia; Sweet & Maxwell, Hong Kong; London 1997). *See* also N Liu, 'An Ignored Source of Chinese Law: the Gazette of the Supreme People's Court' (1989) 5 Connecticut Journal of International Law 271; N Liu, 'Legal Precedents with Chinese Characteristics: Published Cases in the Gazette of Supreme People's Court' (1991) 5 Journal of Chinese Law 107. The issue of judicial interpretation will be further elaborated in Chapter VIII, *see infra* Chapter VIII, text to (n 1) *et seq.*

[44] For different approaches to interpret China's 'WTO-plus' obligation, *see, e.g.*, D Huang, 'Legal Interpretation of Paragraph 242 of the Report of the Working Party on the Accession of China under the World Trade Organization Legal Framework' (2006) 40 Journal of World Trade 137; T W Huang, 'Taiwan's Protocol 16 Special Safeguard and Anti-dumping Enforcement on Imports from China' (2002) 41 Journal of World Trade 371. In interpreting the product-specific safeguard mechanism as embodied in China's Accession Protocol, Dongli Huang argues that this obligation should be read, to the most possible extent, in line with the existent WTO agreements in order to maintain the consistence and coherence of the WTO legal system; by contrast, Thomas Weishing Huang holds the contrary. He argues that, if one equals this product-specific safeguard mechanism to existent safeguard regime, the objective and purpose of this product-specific safeguard mechanism would be much undermined.

[45] Panel Report, *China – Auto Parts*, para. 7.740.

[46] Panel Report, *China – Auto Parts*, para. 7.741. During the Appellate Review, the parties do not dispute the interpretative approach taken by the Panel with respect of paragraph 93 of China's Working Party Report. While the Appellate Body reverses the Panel's finding that the nature of China's measures of imposing a 'charge' or 'duty' on importers of completely knock down and semi knock down kits, as required by Decree 125, is an ordinary customs duty, the Appellate Body does not reject the Panel's interpretative approach. Appellate Body Report, *China – Measures Affecting the Imports of Automobile Parts* (*China – Auto Parts*)(15 December 2008) WT/DS339/AB/R, WT/ DS340/AB/R, WT/DS342/AB/R, paras. 210–252.

WTO obligation to provide an independent and impartial judicial review in accordance with the interpretative rules laid down by the VCLT, particularly Article 31. This approach evinces the relevance of global and regional standards when interpreting this WTO obligation to provide an independent and impartial judicial review.

III. Global and Regional Standards on Independence and Impartiality

A number of global and regional legal instruments have addressed the issue of 'judicial independence'. Apart from the administration of justice aspect – which includes the financial autonomy, sufficient resources, appointment, tenure, and promotion – two elements constitute the core of 'judicial independence' when adjudicating a case: independence and impartiality. In addition to the jurisprudence of the WTO panel/Appellate Body, it is indispensable to further explore these two concepts in the context of public international law. These international legal instruments, albeit mostly soft laws in nature, may contribute to a better understanding of judicial independence and impartiality and thus a better understanding of China's WTO obligation.

As previously noted, these two concepts are interrelated and some jurisprudence tends to examine these two concepts together.[47] However, as most international instruments deal with these two concepts separately, it is thus more feasible to follow this pattern. Besides, independence should be examined from two aspects: institutional independence and individual independence. Institutional independence means that judiciary, as a whole, should be independent from other branches, such as legislatures and executives. Individual independence means that an individual judge, when adjudicating a case, should not be subject to influence and interference both inside and outside the judiciary.

A. *Independence*

1. *Institutional Independence*

The *Basic Principles on the Independence of Judiciary* (hereinafter the UN Principles)[48] of the United Nations offer some guidelines in relation to institutional independence. It is believed that judicial independence enshrined in the

[47] *See, e.g., Findlay v. the United Kingdom* (App no 22107/93) (1997) ECtHR Series 1997-I no 30, para. 73.

[48] Basic Principles on the Independence of Judiciary, adopted by Seventh United Nation Congress on the Prevention and the Treatment of Offenders held in Milan from 26 August to 6 September 1985 and endorsed by General Assembly resolution 40/32 of 29 November 1985 and 40/146 of 13 December 1985.

constitution or by the law helps to guarantee the prevention of judiciary from the interference of other governmental organs and institutions. Legislatures and executives are obliged to respect and observe this principle.[49] This approach is also endorsed by the Council of Europe in its *Recommendation No. R(94) 12 of the Committee of Ministers to Member States on the Independence, Efficacy and Role of Judges*[50] (hereinafter the Council of Europe Recommendation). It recommended that the independence of judges should also be explicitly guaranteed in national constitutional principles, in addition to the guarantee under the Convention for the Protection of Human Rights and Fundamental Freedoms (the ECHR).[51]

Apart from this broad principle, some detailed requirements related to jurisdiction and finality of judicial decisions have been laid down in the UN Principles. As the judiciary should have jurisdiction over all judicial issues, it is the judiciary which determines whether a case would be under its competence as defined by law.[52] Additionally, the finality of judicial decisions should be respected; they should not be overturned by the other branches.[53] The *Draft Universal Declaration on the Independence of Judiciary* (hereinafter 'the Draft Declaration')[54] has also further elaborated on institutional independence. It reiterates that the judiciary should have jurisdiction of all issues of a judicial nature. It explicitly provides that such issues such as its jurisdiction and competence should be within the jurisdiction of the judiciary itself.[55] Therefore, a displacement of the jurisdiction, which was previously the ordinary courts, by *ad hoc* tribunals is not permissible.[56]

Specific standards in relation to the independence of judiciary are available to the African Union. *The Principles and Guidelines on the Right to Fair Trial and Legal Assistance in Africa*[57] (hereinafter 'the African Union Principles and Guidelines') also deals with the jurisdiction issue. Article 4(c) states 'the judiciary shall have jurisdiction over all issues of a judicial nature.' Besides, it emphatically stipulates

---

[49] The UN Principles, Principle 1.

[50] Recommendation No. R(94) 12 of the Committee of Ministers to Member States on the Independence, Efficacy and Role of Judges, adopted by the Committee of Ministers on 13 October 1994 at 518th of the Minister's Deputies.

[51] The Council of Europe Recommendation, Paragraph 2(a).

[52] The UN Principles, Principle 3.

[53] The UN Principles, Principle 4.

[54] Draft Universal Declaration on the Independence of Judiciary, also known as Singhvi Declaration.

[55] The Draft Declaration, Paragraph 5(a). Similar provision is laid down in Beijing Statement of Principles on the Independence of Judiciary in the LAWSAIA Region, where it, in Paragraph 3(b), provides that 'the judiciary has the jurisdiction, directly or by way of review, over all issues of a justiciable nature'.

[56] Ibid.

[57] The Principles and Guidelines on the Right to Fair Trial and Legal Assistance in Africa, adopted as part of the African Commission's activity report at 2nd Summit and meeting of heads of state of African Union held at Maputo from 4-12 July 2003.

that the judiciary shall have 'exclusive' authority to decide whether a submitted case falls under its competence as defined by the law.

Similar provision has been laid down in the *Beijing Statement of Principles on the Independence of Judiciary in the LAWSAIA Region* (hereinafter the Beijing Statement),[58] where it provides at Paragraph 3(b) that 'the judiciary has the jurisdiction, directly or by way of review, over all issues of a justiciable nature.' In comparison, the Beijing Statement is weaker on the protection of jurisdiction as it does not clarify who is empowered to decide on the scope of judicial issues. As the terms 'of a judicial nature' and 'of a justiciable nature' need to be further clarified and defined, it is thus crucial for the judiciary to decide which subject matter should fall under its jurisdiction. Only by so doing can the judiciary prevent legislative intervention from shifting its jurisdiction by re-defining the scope of judicial nature. The institutional independence of the judiciary can thus be strengthened and safeguarded.

The finality of judicial decisions should also be ensured to preserve the judiciary's institutional independence. Judicial decisions should not be subject to revision by the other non-judicial authorities. In other words, legislatures and executives are not allowed to *retrospectively* reverse the result of judicial decisions.[59] That is, the juridical validity of the judicial decisions and their status as *res judiciata* should not be subject to actions of the other branches, no matter whether such actions would alter or confirm the judicial decisions concerned.[60] Legislative intervention with the aim to bring about specific result should also be prohibited. It should be noted nevertheless that this principle is without prejudice to amnesty, pardon, mitigation, or commutation by competent authorities.

The ECtHR has dealt with both the jurisdiction and the finality issues. In *Papageorgiou v. Greece*,[61] the Court was asked to declare that Greece had infringed Article 6(1) of the ECHR because Greece removed the court's jurisdiction over Papageorgiou's case. The Court firstly recognised legislative powers to regulate individual rights through the passage of new provisions. However, the Court then

[58] Beijing Statement of Principles on the Independence of Judiciary in the LAWSAIA Region, adopted by the Chief Justices of the LAWASIA region and other judges from Asia and the Pacific in Beijing 1995, and adopted by the LAWASIA Council in 2001.

[59] UN Principles, Principle 4; Paragraph 6 of Draft Universal Declaration; Article 2(a)(iv) of Principle I of Council of Europe Recommendation; Article 4(f) of the African Union Principles and Guidelines.

[60] International Commission of Jurists (ed), *International Principles on the Independence and Accountability of Judges, Lawyers and Prosecutors: A Practitioners' Guide* (International Commission of Jurists, Geneva 2004).

[61] *Papageorgiou v. Greece* (App no 24628/94) (1997) ECtHR Series 1997-VI no 54.

turned to *Stran Greek Refineries and Stratis Andreadis v. Greece*[62] and argued that 'the principle of the rule of law and the notion of fair trial enshrined in Article 6 [of the Convention] precluded the interference by the Greek legislature with the administration of justice designed to influence the judicial determination of the dispute.'[63] The Court *Stran Greek Refineries and Stratis Andreadis v. Greece* held that the applicant's right of fair trial was violated due to the legislative intervention 'in a manner which was decisive to ensure that the imminent outcome of proceedings in which it [the State] was a party was favourable to it.'[64] The Court then examined the case at dispute and ruled that Greece infringed the applicant's right of fair trial by legislating new provisions with the view to clarifying the meaning of law, removing the jurisdiction of the litigated cases from the courts and dictating relevant claims to be struck out.[65] Although the Court did not refer to the term of 'an independent and impartial tribunal', this holding is nevertheless relevant in light of the intervention of legislature: its effect, method and timing. The legislative intervention through an enactment of laws to affect an on-going litigated dispute undermined the independence of judiciary and violated the applicant's right to fair trial.

The case-laws of *Stran Greek Refineries and Stratis Andreadis v. Greece* are worth noting in detail, as they are highly relevant in determining and ascertaining the independence of Chinese judiciary. In 1972, Andredis concluded a construction contract with the Greek government, which was then a military regime. Stran Greek Refineries, was established as a subsidiary to Andredis in order to carry out the contract. After the democracy was restored, Greek government considered this contract prejudicial to national economy and, by relying on Article 2(5) of Law no. 141/1975, the Greek government terminated the contract. Disputes between Stran Greek Refineries and Greek government arose both before the arbitral tribunal and the civil court and both found largely against Greece.[66] The civil proceedings was appealed by the state to the Court of Cassation on 15 December 1986. Then the Greek Parliament enacted Law no. 1701/1987, which in Article 12 reads as follows:

> 1. The true and lawful meaning of the provisions of Article 2 para. 1 of Law no. 141/1975 concerning the termination of contracts entered into between 21 April 1967 and 24 July 1974 is that, upon the termination of these contracts, all their terms, conditions and clauses, including the arbitration clause, are ipso jure repealed and the arbitration tribunal no longer has jurisdiction.

[62] *Stran Greek Refineries and Stratis Andreadis v. Greece* (App no 13427/87) (1994) ECtHR Series A no 335.

[63] *Papageorgiou v. Greece*, para. 37.

[64] Ibid.

[65] Ibid paras. 38–40.

[66] Ibid paras. 6–18.

> 2. Arbitration awards covered by paragraph 1 shall no longer be valid or enforceable.
> 3. Any principal or ancillary claims against the Greek State, expressed either in foreign or local currency, which arise out of the contracts entered into between 21 April 1967 and 24 July 1974, ratified by statute and terminated by virtue of Law no. 141/1975, are now proclaimed time-barred.
> 4. Any court proceedings at whatever level pending at the time of the enactment of this statute, in respect of claims within the meaning of the preceding paragraph, are declared void.

As Law no. 141/1975 was based on the Greek Constitution allowing the new government to enact legislation within three months upon the entry into force of the constitution for the purpose of maintaining the legal stability, the First Division of Court of Cassation thus held that the subsequent amendments and the authoritative interpretations of Law 141/1975, in the form of ordinary legislation, were prohibited by the constitution.[67] However, the plenary session of the Court of Cassation maintained that 'the prohibition on supplementing or modifying the content of such laws does not mean that they may never be interpreted',[68] and that 'the purpose of such interpretation is not to amend the substance of the law interpreted, but to clarify its original meaning and to resolve disputes that have arisen in connection with its application or which may do so in the future.'[69] Basing on this reasoning, the Court of Cassation held that Article 12 of Law no. 1701/1987 was constitutional, and ruled against the Stran Greek Refinerie.

Before the ECtHR, the applicant contended that the legislative intervention had effectively removed the jurisdiction of this litigated case. The legislature had ruled on a case to which it was a party.[70] On the contrary, the Greek Government argued that the Parliament, the source of all power, was fully justified to authoritatively interpret the enacted laws. This reading was based on Article 77 of the Greek Constitution. Legislative interpretation in the form of legislation should not be regarded as an interference of the judiciary, as the latter could determine on its own whether such interpretation has violated the principle of the separation of powers. Judiciary could thus safeguard itself against improper intervention.[71] After examining the timing and manner in which of Article 12 of Law no. 1701/1987, was adopted the Court held that the legislature intervened in a manner so 'decisive to ensure that the imminent outcome of proceedings in which it was a party was favourable to it'[72] and thus infringed upon the applicant's right of fair trial.

[67] Ibid para. 21.
[68] Ibid para. 22.
[69] Ibid.
[70] Ibid para. 42.
[71] Ibid para. 43
[72] Ibid para. 50.

With regard to the finality of judicial decision, the jurisprudence of ECtHR has also touched upon this. In *Findlay v. the United Kingdom*, where the applicant complained that the court martial is not 'an independent and impartial tribunal', the Court examined the composition of the court martial and the influence of its convening officer. The Court observed that the convening officer played a significant role in deciding the charges against the applicant, the type of court martial and its composition, and the appointment of prosecuting and defending officers.[73] Additionally, members of the court martial were subordinate in rank to the convening officer.[74] Above all, the convening officer had the power, in certain circumstances, to dissolve the court martial both before and during the proceeding. The convening officer even acted as a 'confirming officer'; without his/her ratification, the decision of the court martial could not take effect.[75] The Court then concluded that the court martial is 'contrary to the well-established principle that the power to give a binding decision which may not be altered by a non-judicial authority.'[76] The Court thus held that the applicant's doubts on the independence of the court martial were objectively justified.

2. *Individual Independence*

As previously noted, individual independence refers to the autonomy of an individual judge in adjudicating a given case. A judge should be free from unwarranted interference both from other governmental branches and from the judiciary itself. There should be no 'any restrictions, improper influences, inducements, pressures, threats or interferences, direct or indirect, from any quarter or for any reason'.[77] In decision-making, a judge should be able to pronounce his/her decision freely. No matter of what grade or rank a judge is in the hierarchical organisation of the judiciary, the judge should enjoy full autonomy in making his/her decision independently from his/her colleagues and superiors.[78] The *Council of Europe Recommendation* also stipulated that sanctions against those who seeking to interfere the judicial decision-making should be imposed. The judiciary should not be obliged to report on the merits of the cases to anyone outside the judiciary.[79]

---

73 Ibid para. 74.
74 Ibid para. 75.
75 Ibid paras. 75, 77.
76 Ibid para. 77.
77 The UN Principles, Principle 2.
78 The Draft Universal Declaration, Art. 3.
79 The Council of Europe Recommendation, Paragraph 2(d).

Individual independence is also closely related to the administration of justice.[80] As pointed out, the institutional independence and the individual independence may not be always complementary to each other.[81] The judiciary as a whole may constitute as a hindrance to the autonomy of individual independent judges through the administration of justice. The administration of justice covers various elements, ranging from selection, training, appointment and removal of judges to remuneration and social welfare. Detailed rules have been laid down in *European Charter on the Statute for Judges and Explanatory Memorandum.*[82] As prescribed in the general principles, decisions in relation to the 'selection, recruitment, appointment, career progress or termination of office of a judge' should be made by an authority that is independent of the power of the legislature and the executive. This authority should be composed partly of judges, allowing them to elect their fellow judges.[83] An internal self-governance, by judges, inside the judiciary is indispensable for the administration of justice and essential to guarantee the individual independence. These elements of the administration of justice also affect the qualification of establishing 'an independent tribunal'.

In *Bryan v. the United Kingdom*,[84] the ECtHR was called upon to rule on whether a housing and planning inspector constitutes as 'an independent and impartial tribunal.' The Court held that "in order to establish whether a body could be considered 'independent', regard must be had, *inter alia*, to the manner of appointment of its members and to their term of office, to the existence of guarantee against outside pressures and to the question whether the body presents an appearance of independence."[85] Thus, a 'good administration' of justice does not only constitute a safeguard to individual independence, according to this holding, but it is also a factor to determine whether an entity could be qualified as an independent tribunal. This view is reaffirmed in *Findlay v. the United Kingdom*. The Court further elaborated on this view in *Incal v. Turkey*,[86] opining that, in determining whether a tribunal or a court is independent, the decisive point is whether the applicant's doubts about the independence of the tribunal can be held to be

[80] Both institutional independence and individual independence may be subject to interference through the administration of justice. In respect of institutional independence, it may concern with the appointment of judges in higher courts, budgetary issues, and the interaction of the judiciary and Ministry of Justice, which is normally allocated in the executive branch.

[81] A Winkler and J Zagel, 'The Independence of Judges' (1995) 46 Mercer Law Review 795, 798.

[82] European Charter on the Statute for Judges and Explanatory Memorandum, Strasbourg 8–10 July 1998 (DAJ/DOC(98)).

[83] European Charter on the Statute for Judges and Explanatory Memorandum, Art. 1.3.

[84] *Bryan v. the United Kingdom* (App no 44/1994) (1995) ECtHR Series A no 335.

[85] Ibid para. 37.

[86] *Incal v. Turkey* (App no 22678/93) (1998) ECtHR, ECHR 1998-IV 1547.

objectively justified.[87] An appearance of independence is thus important to clear the applicant's doubts.

Two major issues in relation to the administration of justice deserve to be further examined: promotion and discipline of judges for their performance or misconducts. Wherever there exists a system of promotion of judges, this promotion mechanism should be based on objective factors and standards, particularly on ability, integrity and experience in order to prevent this promotion mechanism from undermining individual independence.[88] To ensure its objectivity, as previously noted, substantial participation of judges in the decision-making process should be made available if these decisions are not directly decided by judges or by their representatives. This requirement is equally applicable to disciplining. There must be security with regard to the term of office of judges; the suspension of a judge from his/her duty or removal from his/her office should be only possible in accordance with the law. In case of suspension or removal, access to an independent and impartial judicial review should be provided against this decision.[89]

B. *Impartiality*

The impartiality of a court may be explored from two dimensions: the case and the parties. An impartial court suggests an absence of interest or stake in a particular case as well as an absence of bias, animosity or sympathy towards either party. In parallel to 'independence', global and regional instruments have also laid down some standards in relation to the impartiality of judiciary. Principle 2 of *the UN Principles* does not only prescribe the independence of judiciary, but also dictate the courts have to decide cases before them impartially based on facts and in accordance with the law. In addition, unfettered freedom should be available to the courts. Similar to *the UN Principles*, Paragraph 2(d) of the *Council of Europe Recommendation* sets out that cases should be impartially decided in accordance with the conscience of judges, their interpretation of facts, and the prevailing rules of the law. The *African Union Principles and Guidelines* spell out the impartiality of judiciary in more detail. The judiciary is obliged to base its decisions on objective evidence, facts and arguments.[90] The *African Union Principles and Guidelines* also prescribe three aspects for the determination of the impartiality of judiciary: equal position to act in the proceeding; the judge' expression of an opinion; and the existence of his/her own priority.[91] Concrete examples are also

87 Ibid para. 71.

88 UN Principles, Principle 13; The Principles and Guidelines on the Right to Fair Trial and Legal Assistance in Africa, Art. 4(o).

89 UN Principles, Principles 19–20; The Council of Europe Recommendation, Paragraph 3.

90 African Union Principles and Guidelines, Art. 5(a).

91 African Union Principles and Guidelines, Art. 5(c).

provided to demonstrate the undermining of the impartiality of the judiciary.[92] Above all, the *Bangalore Principles of Judicial Conduct*[93] stipulate, in detail, various norms of conduct in order to ensure the impartiality of the judiciary. Judges are obliged to disqualify themselves whenever there are doubts in relation to their ability in deciding the cases impartially.[94]

The ECtHR has also dealt with the impartiality of judiciary in a number of cases. The Court held, in *Castillo v. Spain*[95] that two tests should be applied in determining the impartiality of tribunals: a subjective test and an objective test. The subjective test relies upon 'the personal conviction of a particular judge in a given case';[96] the objective test is to ascertain 'whether the judge offered sufficient guarantees to exclude any legitimate doubt in this respect.'[97] The personal impartiality of a particular judge is presumed unless proof of the contrary is demonstrated.[98] With regard to the objective test, the Court held that confidence in the impartiality of the courts must 'inspire in the public',[99] which means that any factor leading the public to question the impartiality of the courts should be avoided. 'Accordingly, any judge in respect of whom there is a legitimate reason to fear a lack of impartiality must withdraw.'[100] In determining whether in a given case there is a legitimate reason to question the impartiality of a particular judge the decisive criterion is 'whether this fear can be held to be objectively justified.'[101]

These two tests have been repeatedly referred to in the jurisprudence of the ECtHR. The Court in *Incal v. Turkey*, a case-law referred to by *Castillo v. Spain* held that "as to the condition of 'impartiality' within the meaning of that provision, there are two tests to be applied: the first consists in trying to determine the personal conviction of a particular judge in a given case and the second in ascertaining whether the judge offered guarantees sufficient to exclude any legitimate doubt in this respect."[102] This view is also re-affirmed in *Findlay v. the United*

[92] African Union Principles and Guidelines, Art. 5(d).

[93] Draft Bangalore Principles of Judicial Conduct, adopted by the Judicial Group on Strengthening Judicial Integrity, as revised at the Round Table Meeting of Chief Justice held at the Peace Palace, The Hague, 25–26 November 2002.

[94] Draft Bangalore Principles of Judicial Conduct, Value 2.

[95] *Castillo Algar v. Spain* (App no 79/1997) (1998) ECtHR, ECHR 1998-VIII 3124.

[96] Ibid para. 43.

[97] Ibid para. 43.

[98] Ibid para. 44.

[99] Ibid para. 46.

[100] Ibid.

[101] Ibid.

[102] *Incal v. Turkey*, para. 65. For earlier cases, *see, e.g., Pullar v. the United Kingdom*, where the Court, in paragraph 30, held that, '[I]t is well established in the case-law of the Court that there are two aspects to the requirement of impartiality in Article 6 para. 1(Art. 6(1)).First, the tribunal must be subjectively impartial, that is, no member of the tribunal should hold any personal prejudice orbias. Personal impartiality is to be presumed unless there is evidence to the contrary. Secondly, the tribunal must also be impartial from an objective viewpoint, that is, it must offer

Kingdom.[103] As subjective impartiality is normally presumed, unless the contrary is proved, the operative part of the Court's jurisprudence is thus to answer whether the litigant's fear is objectively justified. Nevertheless, the Court seems not to offer a clear picture as to what factors should be taken into account in determining the existence of the 'objectively justified fear of impartiality'.

IV. Judicial Review in China: Law and Practice

A. *Progress So Far Made*

1. *Five-Year Court Reform Programme*

In 1999, the SPC issued its First Five-Year Reform Programme leading a series of judicial reforms. Since then, the SPC has adopted a second and third five-year reform programme covering the years 2004 to 2008 and 2009 to 2013 respectively. The Second Five-Year Reform Programme is comprised of seven dimensions: (1) litigation procedure systems; (2) the system of trial guidance and the mechanisms for the uniform use of law; (3) work systems and methods to enforce judgments; (4) reforming and perfecting trial organs; (5) the management of trials and the political affairs; (6) the system of judicial personnel management; (6) the internal and external supervision for People's Courts; and (7) continuing reform to the court system.

In the reform programme, the objective of establishing a judicial system under the socialist rule of law is reiterated. It also points to the role of the CCP, stating that People's Courts should be subjective to the party's leadership and guidance, and to the supervision of the NPC and the NPCSC. The courts should preserve, in its judicial system, the characteristic of socialist democracy. Such statements illustrate the political environment where China's judicial reform is situated and present the potential challenges and interferences ahead. However, the reform program also emphasises on the importance of 'justice and efficiency' in shaping the new judicial system while retaining its root in the Chinese societal context and borrowing other countries' experiences at the same time. The various objectives present complexities and conflicts of values within China's legal system and they constitute constraints of China's judicial reform and hinder its potential progress.[104]

---

sufficient guarantees to exclude any legitimate doubt in this respect.' In this case, the Court further refers to its previous case-law *Fey v. Austria* (judgment of 24 February 1993, Series A no. 255-A).

[103] *Findlay v. the United Kingdom*, esp. para. 73.

[104] For an updated review and comments on China's progress in judicial reform, *see* B L Liebman, 'China's Courts: Restricted Reform' (2007) 21 Columbia Journal Asian Law 1.

The reform programme also emphasises on the importance of the judicial interpretation, the case guidance system and the role of adjudicative committees. With the objective to unify legal applicable standards, to guide the work of lower courts, and to enrich and develop legal theory, the SPC will issue regulations on case guidance system. These regulations will address standards and procedures for selecting guiding cases and methods for issuing the guidance.[105] The procedures for the SPC to issue judicial interpretations should be reformed to ensure greater coherence. The SPC will regularly clean up, amend, abolish, compile judicial interpretations, and regularise the notification systems of judicial interpretations to the NPCSC.[106] Specialised criminal and civil/administrative adjudicative committees will be established under the SPC while the High People's Courts and the Intermediate People's Courts can establish specialised criminal committees and civil/administrative committees according to their needs.[107]

The judicial interpretation and the case guidance system are some peculiar practices in China's judicial systems. Judicial interpretations are normally handed down by the SPC with a view to clarify the meaning of certain legal text and guide lower courts in hearing a specific case. These judicial interpretations are of general application and gradually acquire legal-binding effects in Chinese legal system. Case guidance system is a mechanism for Chinese lower courts to refer cases with factual and legal complexities to higher courts, notably the SPC to deliver their opinions. Lower court may then decide the cases in accordance with these opinions. The designation of judicial interpretation and case guidance system aims to enhancing the uniformity of the interpretation and application of laws and regulations. Given the limited training and knowledge of the judges in lower courts, such practices from a realistic perspective have their merits. They contribute to the improvement of the adjudicative quality of the lower courts. However, such practices constitute as a stronger form of judicial law-making since the interpretation and guidance of the SPC is of general application and according to the SPC, such interpretation of law enjoys the same legal status as legislation. The legality and legal status of the judicial interpretation is also explicitly recognised and defined by *The Law on Legislation*.

Given the great threat derived from local protectionism, the reform programme takes a top-down approach. The SPC aims at ensuring a uniform interpretation and application of laws within China's judicial system through strengthening judicial interpretation and case guidance system and thus preventing an incoherent interpretation and application of laws and regulations. However, the pursuit and realisation of judicial independence should find their roots from the practices

[105] The Third Five-Year Court Reform Programme, Art. 13.
[106] The Third Five-Year Court Reform Programme, Art. 14.
[107] The Third Five-Year Court Reform Programme, Art. 23.

of local courts. Only when local courts have the courage and capacity to challenge the 'authoritative interpretations' with rational reasoned beliefs, can judicial independence be realised. Precluding the lower courts from interpreting and applying laws by themselves would not lead to the establishment of an independent and impartial judicial review, but on the contrary, would estrange from it. The same rationale applies to the adjudicating committee. Although it is seen as a device to enhance adjudicating quality, it nevertheless also affect the judicial independence, notably individual independence.

Following the Second Five-Year Court Reform Programme, in 2009 the SPC adopted its Third Five-Year Court Reform Programme[108] with a view to ameliorate the organisation of people's courts; to shape a sound criminal policy; to strengthen the training of judges; to raise the budgets of Chinese courts; and to ensure the citizens are benefitting from the judicial reform. With these objectives, the SPC would develop sentencing guidance and rules on evidence.[109] It would also clarify the relationship between higher courts and lower courts and strengthen the management and supervision of the people's courts.[110] Emphasis would also be placed upon the recruiting and training of judges to enhance the adjudication quality of the judicial system.[111]

2. *Judicial Interpretations in Relation to Trade-Related Issues*

Following China's accession, the SPC issued a number of interpretations with the aim to provide a prompt review of relevant administrative actions. Four judicial interpretations are worth of further elaboration here, namely:

(1) Regulation on Several Problems in the Trial of Trade-Related Administrative Litigation Cases;
(2) Regulation on the Application of Law in the Trial of Anti-Dumping Administrative Litigation Cases;
(3) Regulation on the Application of Law in the Trial of Anti-Subsidy Administrative Litigation.
(4) Interpretation by the Supreme People's Court and the Supreme People's Procuratorate on Several Issues of Concrete Application of Laws in Handling Criminal Cases of Infringing Intellectual Property.

[108] Notice Fa-Fa [2009] No. 14 (17 March 2009) <http://www.court.gov.cn/spyw/sfgg/201002/t20100223_1776.htm> Accessed 1 September 2011, in Chinese.
[109] The Third Five-Year Court Reform Programme, Arts. 2, 3.
[110] The Third Five-Year Court Reform Programme, Arts. 7–9.
[111] The Third Five-Year Court Reform Programme, Art. 14.

Regulation on Several Problems in the Trial of Trade-Related Administrative Litigation Cases defines the scope of trade-related administrative litigation cases and clarifies the standing for bringing a complaint, standard of review and applicable laws. The regulations, in Article 9 also explicitly adheres to consistent interpretation doctrine, stipulating that the one consistent with China's treaty obligations should apply when two reasonable interpretations of a legal text are available. The regulations, in Article 6, also instruct the courts to limit their review to the issue of legality and prohibit the courts from the inquiry on appropriateness of an administrative act. An administrative act may be struck down on the ground of infringement of procedural requirements, misuses or lacks of competence and failure to approach the evidence fairly.

Regulations on the Application of Law in the Trial of Anti-Dumping Administrative Litigation Cases defines the scope of the anti-dumping acts subject to administrative review. The regulations also lay down the rules on standing, defendant authority, jurisdiction, burden of proof, examination of evidence, and standard of review. The regulations, in Article 7(2) further provides that factual materials that are not included in the records during the anti-dumping investigations should not be presented as evidences to justify the anti-dumping decisions. Similar stipulations are included in the *Regulations on the Application of Law in the Trial of Anti-Subsidy Administrative Litigation.*

In response to an agreement between China's Deputy Premier Wu Yi and the US government at the 15th annual meeting of the Joint Commission on Commerce and Trade, the SPC and the Supreme People's Procuratorate (the SPP) issued a new judicial interpretation concerning the infringement of intellectual property rights. One of the most important elements contained in this new interpretation is that it lowers the numerical thresholds for an act infringing intellectual property rights to be criminally punishable. Prior to the request for consultation by the US, on 5 April 2007 the SPC issued another interpretation governing criminal prosecution of intellectual property rights infringement. It widened the scope of 'reproduction and distribution' governed by Article 217 of criminal law to include advertising for the sale of copyright-infringing products. It also lowered the thresholds for illegal copies and for determining 'serious' or 'especially serious' as referred to in Article 217 of criminal law.

As previously noted, the reason why these judicial interpretations are so important is that provisions in the relevant national legislations are often too vague, and the lower courts are not fully equipped with the knowledge to apply laws concerning the international trade. Judicial interpretations issued by the SPC, thus serve as guidance for the lower courts so that they can 'effectively and correctively' to apply the relevant legislations. It is expected, in so doing, that the coherence of the interpretation of the laws and the quality of adjudication can be enhanced. However, the following subsection explains these various interpretations serve only as 'effective and correct' applications of the laws and regulations in relation to external trade-related disputes. Efforts and progresses as to ensure the independence and impartiality of judiciary have not been satisfactorily made. As will be illustrated, the practice of judicial interpretation and the case guidance system are some of the factors that undermine the independence and impartiality of the Chinese judicial system and make China's judicial review difficult to pass the scrutiny of the WTO requirements.

B. *Task Half-Accomplished: the Independence and Impartiality of the Chinese Courts*

1. *The Administration of Justice*

Several legal instruments have been laid down in order to better the administration of justice in China. Three legal (policy) instruments are illustrative, particularly in their timing for enactment, legal status, and subject matter: *Law on Judges*; *Code of Conduct for Judges (for Trial Implementation)*; and *Opinions on Strengthening the Adjudicative Work with the aim to Providing Judicial Protection for the Construction of Innovative State*. *Law on Judges*, effectuated on 1 July 1995, lays down the framework for, *inter alia*, the appointment, removal, promotion and disciplining of judges. In general, it was an advanced legislation in light of the time of its enactment. While it is prescribed that the president of People's Courts should be appointed by the People's Congress at corresponding level,[112] the CCP has not been referred to in this act. Additionally, judges are obliged to decide a case impartially based on facts and in accordance with the law.[113] The minimum standard of legal education is also explicitly laid down in this act, with the aim to improve the quality of the judges and consequently that of the adjudication.[114] Nevertheless, as the very first article provides, the objective and purpose of this act is to ensure that 'People's Courts' adjudicate cases independently and that judges carry out their duties in accordance with the law. It appears that independence should be collectively enjoyed by the judiciary as a whole, namely, the People's Courts. In China, the power of independent adjudication is vested in courts, not in individual judges, and this suggests that judicial independence in China is usually understood in a collective sense. This explains why it is so difficult, if not

[112] Law on Judges of People's Republic of China (hereinafter Law on Judges), Art. 11.
[113] Law on Judges, Art. 7(2).
[114] Law on Judges, Art. 9(1)(vi).

impossible, to bring about individual independence under the Chinese judicial system.[115]

Ten years after the enactment of Law on Judges, on 4 November 2005. Code of Conducts for Judges (for Trial Implementation) was issued by SPC. As this Code of Conduct was specifically laid down for judges and it had been ten years since the enactment of Law on Judges, it thus serves as a good basis to examine the progress made and the change of mindset in relation to judicial independence. Surprisingly, Marx-Leninism, Mao and Deng are referred to in the very first article of this code of conduct. Western lawyers may also be bewildered to find that this code covers so detailed regulation, ranging from dress code[116] and manner[117] to specific issues on adjudicating a case, such as jurisdiction,[118] trial hearing,[119] and mediation.[120] This code of conduct can be seen as a mini-procedural law or a manual for the judges. This may suggest that the complexity of cases before the lower courts has already exceeded the capacity of the lower courts and detailed guidelines are necessary. It also reflects that the understanding of judicial function by the SPC. An 'effective and correct' application of laws and regulations is enforced by a centralised and top-down approach. Nevertheless, this code of conduct also deals with the independence and impartiality of judiciary. In Article 3, it is stipulated that judges shall adjudicate independently in accordance with the law and shall not be subject to interferences from administrative agencies, social groups and individuals. Judges should insist on their believed opinions and resist improper influences based on power, money and social relationships. They shall remain impartial to protect legitimate interests. The requirements of independence and impartiality do not deviate from the international standards. However, they do not offer much assistance in ensuring the independence and impartiality of Chinese courts, as the issue of the CCP has not resolved.

Opinions on Strengthening the Adjudicative Work with the aim to Providing Judicial Protection for the Construction of Innovative State,[121] issued on 11 January 2007, is even more illustrative. As its title suggests, courts are seen as an actor to carrying out policy goals. In the preamble, the central committee of the CCP is explicitly referred to. Various policy goals have been identified in these opinions. They also points out that the main task is to focus on intellectual property rights, due to the pressure of China's trading partners, notably the US and the EU.

---

[115] K Zou, *China's Legal Reform* (Martinus Nijhoff Publishers, Leiden, Boston 2006) 150.

[116] Code of Conduct for Judges (for Trial Implementation, hereinafter Code of Conduct of Judges), Art. 6.

[117] Code of Conduct for Judges, Art. 7.

[118] Code of Conduct for Judges, Chapter II.

[119] Code of Conduct for Judges, Chapter III.

[120] Code of Conduct for Judges, Chapter IV.

[121] Notice Fa-Fa No 1 (11 January 2007) <http://www.chinacourt.org/flwk/show1.php?file_id=115565> accessed 1 September 2011.

Following China's WTO entry, the increase in international trade related disputes has significantly reshaped the composition of case genre in the Chinese courts. But with regard to the independence and impartiality, as these opinions seem to address solely upon the everyday practices of the Chinese courts, it is questionable how much progress has been actually made so far.

2. *Legislative Interpretation and Judicial Interpretation*

The Constitution assigns the competence to interpret the national law and the Constitution itself to the NPC or the NPCSC whereas the *Organic Law of People's Courts* authorises the SPC to give guidance on judicial interpretation for questions concerning specific application of laws and decrees in the judicial proceedings for practical reasons. As prescribed, the courts, specifically the SPC, can only interpret laws and decrees during judicial proceedings. On June 10, 1981, in the 19th Meeting of the Standing Committee of the Fifth National People's Congress, a resolution to improve the interpretation of laws and decrees had been adopted. Even though the 1982 constitution have not been drafted yet at that point, the limitation in competence of judicial interpretation has remained the same, as the competence to interpret the constitution and national laws was not amended in the 1982 constitution.

Given the necessity to provide more legislation and better interpretation on the laws in order to improve the socialist legal system, it was decided in the resolution that:

> (1) In cases where the limits of articles of laws and decrees need to be further defined or additional stipulations need to be made, the Standing Committee of the National People's Congress shall provide interpretations or make stipulations by means of decrees.
> (2) Interpretation of questions involving the specific application of laws and decrees in court trials shall be provided by the Supreme People's Court. Interpretation of questions involving the specific application of laws and decrees in the procuratorial work of the procuratorates shall be provided by the Supreme People's Procuratorate. If the interpretations provided by the Supreme People's Court and the Supreme People's Procuratorate are at variance with each other in principle, they shall be submitted to the Standing committee of the National People's Congress for interpretation or decision.[122]

[122] Resolution of the Standing Committee of the National People's Congress on Providing an Improved Interpretation of the Law, An unofficial English version can be downloaded at <http://www.novexcn.com/interp_of_law.html> accessed 1 September 2011. The resolution covers four paragraphs. The third paragraph deals with those interpretations which fall beyond the scope of judicial and procuratorial affairs while the fourth paragraph deals with the interpretation of local regulations.

One cannot decipher any clear line between 'further definition', 'additional stipulation' and 'the specific application of laws and decrees.' As prescribed in the second paragraph of this resolution, the SPC can only give the judicial interpretations when the specific application of laws and decrees during court trials is needed. In other words, only when these two conditions, namely 'the specific application of laws and decrees' and 'during court trials', are satisfied can the SPC hand down judicial interpretations. However, this does not seem to be the case. Some literature even argues that the SPC has continuously gone beyond its competence since either the NPC or the NPCSC has hardly made any interpretations except the Hong Kong Basic Law cases.[123]

Doubts may also arise with regard to how and when the the NPC and the NPCSC will hand down its legislative interpretation and its potential threats of such to particular cases during trial proceedings. The ECtHR clearly laid down in *Stran Greek Refineries and Stratis Andreadis v. Greece* ruled out the permissibility of 'decisive to ensure that the imminent outcome of proceedings in which it was a party was favourable to it.'[124] Such legislative intervention would have infringed the applicant's right of fair trial by an independent and impartial tribunal. This holding is of great relevance in the current context. First, the most telling part of this holding is that legislature is prohibited from interfering with the judicial proceeding by means of legislative intervention to ensure a particular outcome. This holding should not be limited to cases to which the State is a party. Nevertheless, if it is the case, an infringement on the right to fair trial at the independent and impartial tribunals is manifest. The Greek government's argument may also be employed by the NPC and the NPCSC. The NPC, through which the people exercise state power, is the source of all powers and its authoritative competence to interpret the constitution and laws are explicitly recognised by the Constitution. However, as made clearly by the ECtHR, this argument cannot sustain. It should also be noted that the WTO obligation to provide an independent and impartial judicial review is an international obligation, which means China cannot justify its derogation on the ground of its constitutional system. The international obligation binds not only its executive powers, but also its legislature and judiciary.

[123] Liu (n 43) 59–62. Further initiatives to clarify the allocation of jurisdiction and to strengthen legislative interpretation can be found in *Law on Legislation*, and *Working Procedures Governing Notification and Review of Administrative Regulations, Regional Laws, Autonomous Decrees and Special Decrees, Regulations of Special Economic Zones* and *Working Procedures Governing Notification and Review of Judicial Interpretations*.

[124] *Stran Greek Refineries and Stratis Andreadis v. Greece*, para. 50.

3. *Adjudicative Committee*

One of the important features of the Chinese judicial system is the existence of adjudicative committee[125] and its legal basis is founded upon the *Organic Law of People's Courts*. The main task of the adjudicative committee is to 'sum up judicial experience and to discuss important or difficult cases and other issues related to the judicial work'.[126] The president of the court or a presiding judge may refer a particular case (usually the important or difficult cases) to adjudicative committee when necessary. The adjudicative committee would discuss and decide the case based on a summary presentation by the presiding judge of that case as well as any documents presented. Subsequently, a collegial panel should carry out the decision of the adjudicative committee.[127]

Such practices deviate from international standards on judicial independence, in particular on individual independence. As noted above, an individual judge when adjudicating a case should make the decision based on facts and in accordance of the law. It must be based on the judge's own examination of facts and interpretation of laws. The adjudication committee introduces improper interferences and undue influences from the president or vice-president of the courts and other judges not hearing this case. These interferences and influences are improper and undue in the sense that there is no space for individual decision-making process. It does not matter whether decisions made by adjudicative committee are more 'correct' or not, as the essence of the judicial function is to decide a case based on one's own assessment of the facts as well as one's own interpretation of the law. As the ECtHR has repeatedly pointed out, the independence of tribunals should be sufficient to exclude any legitimate doubts. Even appearance is of relevance. It is difficult, if not impossible, to exclude legitimate doubts of litigants when cases are not directly and exclusively decided by judges sitting before them but rather behind the courtroom instead, where an opportunity even to be heard

---

[125] Views among Chinese scholarship on the abolishment of adjudicative committees are also diverse, sometimes to the opposite. A stipulating debate between Suli Zhu and Weifang He reflects best this divergence. *See* W He, 'Two Problems of the Administration of Justice in China (Zhongguo sifa guanli zhidu de liang ge wentí)' (1997) 6 China Social Science (Zhongguo shehui kexue) 117 (in Chinese); W He, 'Some Comments on the Adjudicative Committees (Guanyu shenpan weiyuanhui de ji dian pinglun)' (1999) 1 Beijing University Law Review (Beida falu pinglun) 265 (in Chinese); S Zhu, 'Examination and Reflection on the Adjudicative Committee in Chinese Local Courts (Jiceng shenpan weiyuanhui zhidu de kaocha ji sikao)' (1999) 1 Beijing University Law Review (Beida falu pinglun) 320 (in Chinese).

[126] Organic Law of People's Court of the People's Republic of China, Art. 11.

[127] R C Brown, *Understanding Chinese Courts and Legal Process: Law with Chinese Characteristics* (Kluwer Law International, The Hague; Boston 1997) 76–77.

is not provided. In this case, the litigants' doubts on the independence may be objectively justified.

It should also be pointed out that the objective and purpose to include the 'independent and impartial judicial review' in China's Accession Protocol is to better protect the rights and interests of individual economic actors through the prompt review of relevant administrative actions by independent and impartial tribunals. It is expected that this obligation may contribute to judicial independence in China. However, it seems that the Chinese judiciary is not going on the right, if not opposite, direction. This can be clearly illustrated by the two judicial interpretation issued by the SPC with regard to the protection of intellectual property rights. The second judicial interpretation is aimed at lowering again the thresholds for the determination of 'serious' or 'especially serious' infringement of intellectual property rights so as to mitigate the pressure from the US. Judiciary is seen as an instrument to meet policy goals and the SPC dominates the competence of judicial interpretation. Lower courts should thus abide by the judicial interpretation issued by the SPC. However, as this chapter emphatically argues, a centralised judicial interpretation dominated by the SPC will not bring about real independent and impartial judges in China. Inferior judges should be encouraged and obliged to apply the law in accordance with their own reading and interpretation. They should refrain from relying on the SPC for the finding of facts and interpretation of laws.

4. *Case Guidance System*

One major competence of the SPC conferred by the Constitution is to supervise the lower courts.[128] The adjudicative committee of the SPC uses this competence of 'summing up judicial experience and of discussing important or difficult cases and other issues relating to the judicial work of judicial interpretation of national laws', by issuing a variety of 'decisions', including opinions, instructions, and official replies to lower courts. Those decisions can appear in the forms of official opinions, letters, notices, explanations and so on.

The case guidance system shares the same weakness as the adjudicative committee. After seeking official relies from the SPC, the lower courts are obliged to decide the present case according to these official replies. In other words, those who decide on the cases are not those judges sitting in front of the litigants, but those in Beijing. This system prevents the litigants from presenting evidence and arguments to those judges who really decide their cases. Litigants have no idea on how these decisions are made, and are not sure whether those judges place the same emphasis as they do. The independence of those judges sitting before

---

[128] Constitution (China), Art. 127(2).

litigants is doubtable, as they are subordinate to their superiors. They should decide the case according to the SPC's assessments of facts and interpretation of laws instead of their own. Individual independence of every single judge is of no less, if not more, importance than institutional independence. The image of judiciary cannot be mapped as a whole if there are no tiny pieces of every single judge. One should not always perceive the judiciary collectively as a single entity. Independents judges are the foundation for establishing an independent judiciary. This view can also be supported by those international instruments mentioned above, which place emphasis on not only institutional independence but also individual independence.

In 2010, the SPC issued *Opinion Concerning the Standardisation of Trial Work between Higher Level and Lower Level Courts* (the Opinion)[129] aiming to lessen the tendency of the lower courts to seek instructions from the higher court and to avoid shouldering their owning responsibility. This Opinion is intended to prohibit the practice of seeking guidance on factual or evidentiary aspects when hearing a case through establishing a mechanism barring the lower courts from transferring cases to higher courts for ruling except for the following: major, difficult, and complex cases; new categories of cases; cases with general legal implications and applicability; and cases inappropriate for trial in the lower courts.[130] Article 9 of the Opinion authorises provincial higher courts to issue interpretation on general application to guide the lower courts; this competence has been widely exercised by the SPC. By emphasising on the legal aspects of interpretation or guidance, the Opinion aims to correct the tendency of lower courts to seeking instructions from higher courts and to prevent higher courts from interfering with the adjudicating processes of the lower courts.

V. Short Conclusion

This chapter has examined the scope and nature of China's WTO obligation to provide an independent and impartial judicial review. It first presents the trend within the WTO to strengthen domestic judicial review and then analyses why this obligation is embodied in China's Accession Protocol. The requirements laid down by Section 2(D) of China's Accession Protocol are more stringent than the 'prompt review' of administrative actions. The scope of China's obligation to provide an 'independent and impartial judicial review' is also wider than the existing provisions in the WTO agreements. This chapter then examines the existing WTO

[129] Notice Fa-Fa No. 61 (28 December 2010) <http://www.court.gov.cn/qwfb/sfwj/yj/201104/t20110427_19930.htm> accessed 1 September 2011, in Chinese.

[130] The Opinion, Art. 3.

jurisprudence in order to clarify the criteria of 'independence' and 'impartiality', and finds that no sufficient and clear guidance has been provided. In light of Article 3.2 of the DSU, this chapter then argues that it is feasible to refer to and examine international standards as well as jurisprudence in the ECtHR. This chapter thus discusses various global and regional standards on independence and impartiality and explores the jurisprudence laid down by the ECtHR. Based on these standards and jurisprudence laid down by the WTO and other international legal instruments and international tribunals, this chapter then presents the efforts and progresses that China has made so far to establish an 'independent and impartial judicial review' and then examines the compatibility of this judicial review with other standards outlined in previous sections. This chapter finds that the administration of justice, the practices of legislative interpretation, and the adjudicative case guidance system cannot pass the scrutiny of the WTO panel/ Appellate Body if a case is brought under the WTO Dispute Settlement Mechanism.

CHAPTER SIX

TWENTY YEARS AFTER LIBERALISATION: IS IT TIME FOR TAIWAN'S COURTS TO FACE WITH CROSS-STRAIT TRADE?

I. Introduction

This chapter aims to explore the role of Taiwan's courts in foreign trade relations, specifically in foreign trade relations with China. It will examine the jurisprudence laid down by the Taiwanese courts, notably by the Constitutional Court. The case-laws are to be examined from two perspectives: the perspective of the WTO law and the perspective of Taiwan's constitutional/national law. It will then point to the conflicts between these two perspectives and propose an answer to resolve these conflicts.

The relevance of the WTO law is comprehensible as Taiwan still adopts and maintains a large number of discriminatory restrictions on trade against China. Since these trade restrictive measures may affect rights and interests of individuals an enterprises, domestic constitutional and legal framework may also come into play. Since more and more natural and legal persons are engaging in economic activities with China, such as trade and investments, their rights and interests both under the WTO Agreement and under domestic constitutional/legal framework may be limited by arbitrary and capricious restrictions. Judicial review on foreign trade relations is thus of great significance, particularly in light of the long-established self-restraint approach of the Taiwanese courts in this sphere.

In addition, WTO law and national constitutional law are interrelated. The story of Chinese immigrants, who mostly come to Taiwan through marriages, is telling. Under Taiwan's existing regulatory regime on China trade, these Chinese immigrants suffer from discriminatory treatments in terms of WTO law. For example, their qualification and equivalency for their education, profession and certification may be treated less favourable than that of nationals of other Members. Even after they acquire Taiwanese nationality, they continue to face discrimination and unequal treatments. Equal protection of rights under the national constitution thus adds additional complexities to this issue.

Bearing these in mind, this chapter will firstly examine the legal status of the WTO Agreement under the constitutional framework of Taiwan, and its judicial practice in the field of foreign trade relations, in particular its trade relations with China. Based on this analysis, this chapter aims to find out whether a discernable approach or pattern can be registered. After these, this chapter will then propose to redefine, through two related cases on China's education services and the recognition of Chinese diploma, the role of Taiwanese courts in foreign trade relations with China.

II. The legal Status of WTO Agreement in Taiwan's Constitutional Framework

This section deals with the legal status of the WTO Agreement under Taiwan's domestic constitutional framework. It will start with the legal status of treaties and international agreements and then examine the WTO Agreement as a specific case. After examining national constitutional/legal provisions governing this issue, this section will investigates the relevant jurisprudence on the legal status of treaties and international agreements in Taiwan. It will mainly focus on three aspects: the scope of treaties and international agreements and corresponding ratification/incorporation procedures; direct effects of treaties and international agreements; and legal hierarchy between international law and national legislation. In relation to the WTO Agreement, the chapter will start with its legislative history and then examine relevant jurisprudence in the courts.

A. *Legal Status of Treaties/International Agreements on Taiwan*

1. *Scope of Treaties and International Agreements and Corresponding Deliberation/Ratification Procedures*

In 1992 Koo Chen-fu, the President of Straits Exchange Foundation (the SEF) in Taiwan, and Wang Daohang, the President of the Association for Relations across the Taiwan Straits (the ARATS) in China, signed four agreements in Singapore.[1] Controversies arose as to whether these four agreements needed to be deliberated by the Legislative Yuan (the Congress of Taiwan). It was, and still is, not clear due to two reasons. Firstly, the Taiwanese Constitution does not clearly set out that the scope of treaties and international agreements that needed to be deliberated by the Legislative Yuan and subsequently be ratified by the president. Secondly and maybe more importantly, whether the relationship between China and Taiwan could be deemed as 'international', and should thus be governed by international law, is subject to dispute.

This issue was subsequently referred to the Constitutional Court due to the request of one-third of the deputies of Legislative Yuan. On 24 December 1993, the Constitutional Court clarified the scope of 'treaties and international agreements'

[1] For the background and results of this negotiation and other relevant meetings between Koo and Wang, *see* Straits Exchange Foundation (ed), *Talks and Meeting between Koo and Wang* (*Gu wang huitan yu gu wang huiwu*) (Straits Exchange Foundation, Taipei 2001).

in its *Judicial Yuan Interpretation* No. 329: a 'treaty' means an international legally-binding agreement concluded between Taiwan[2] and other nations or international organisations that relates to 'important issues' to the state or to the rights and obligations of its people regardless of the entitlement of the agreement being 'treaty', 'convention' or 'agreement'. Clearly, such agreements with 'ratification clauses' should be deliberated by the Legislative Yuan. In addition, other international agreements which fall into the scope of this interpretation, namely those relating to 'important issues' to the state or to the rights and obligations of its people, should also be deliberated by the Legislative Yuan. This interpretation nevertheless excludes those treaties or international agreements that are authorised by laws or pre-determined by the Legislative Yuan and those whose contents that are identical to national laws. Treaties and international agreements deliberated and ratified by the Legislative Yuan shall enjoy the same legal status as national legislations. Nevertheless, in respect of the controversy agreements signed by Koo and Wang, the Constitutional Court briefly noted that 'the agreements concluded between Taiwan and [mainland] China are not international agreements to which this interpretation relates.'[3] Based on this reasoning, the Constitutional Court thus concluded that 'whether or not these four agreements should be sent to the Legislation Yuan for deliberation is not included in this interpretation.'[4]

According to the Constitutional Court, whether an international agreement should be referred to the Legislative Yuan for deliberation, as dictated by Article 58(2) and 63[5] of the Constitution, depends on the content of the international

[2] Here, the terms employed by the Constitutional Court is 'Republic of China', the official name of Taiwan. Nevertheless, China is normally referred to 'People's Republic of China'. It could be confusing if both 'People's Republic of China' and 'Republic of China' are simultaneously used in this work. Therefore, with the same reason provided in Chapter I, this Chapter uses the term Taiwan when 'Republic of China' is referred to, unless the context requires otherwise.

[3] Judicial Yuan Interpretation of the Constitutional Court, No 329, available at <http://jirs.judicial.gov.tw/ENG/FINT/FINTQRY03.asp?total=1&seq=1&cno=329> accessed 1 September 2011. A multilingual website bearing legal bases and jurisprudence of the Constitutional Court can be reached at the above link. This may not be reproduced in this Chapter except as necessary. It should be noted that this case was decided on 24 December 1993, when the democratisation and of Taiwan just started. On 7 July 1999, in an interview by Deutsche Welle radio station, the former President Lee Tung-hui remarked that the cross-strait relationship is 'at least a special state-to-state relationship. Whether the agreements signed by China and Taiwan are 'international' agreements may be subject to dispute today. Further on this point, *see* T-L Hsu, et al. (eds), *The Special State-to-State Discourse and Taiwan's National Identity* (*Liang guo lun yu Taiwan guojia dingwei*) (Xunlin Press Taipei 2000).

[4] Ibid.

[5] Article 58(2) of Taiwan's constitution reads, 'statutory or budgetary bills or bills concerning martial law, amnesty, declaration of war, conclusion of peace, *treaties*, and other important affairs, all of which are to be submitted to the Legislative Yuan, as well as matters that are of common concern to the various Ministries and Commissions, shall be presented by the President and various Ministers and Chairmen of Commissions of the Executive Yuan to the Executive Yuan Council for decision.' Article 63 reads, "the Legislative Yuan shall have the power to decide by resolution upon statutory or

agreement concerned. In the case of a legally binding international agreement containing 'important issues' relating to the state or to the rights and obligations of the people, the deliberation procedure should be followed. As far as the deliberation procedure is concerned, it makes no difference whether the pertinent international agreement carries the title of 'treaty', 'convention' or 'international agreement'. However, the interpretation of the Constitutional Court does not offer any guidance on the nature of the agreements that were concluded between Taiwan and China. The controversy before the Constitutional Court remains unresolved.

2. *Direct Effects of Treaties and International Agreements*

Taiwan's Constitution does not provide guidance on the direct effect of international agreements. A Supreme Court case and a Supreme Administrative Court case are relevant in this regard. When dealing with the legal status of the *Treaty of Friendship, Commerce and Navigation between United States of America and Republic of China* in Taiwan, the Supreme Court opined that the treaty concerned was signed on 4 November 1946 and subsequently ratified by the Legislative Yuan. In light of the wording of 'respect of treaties' in Article 141 of the Constitution and the deliberation procedure as set out in Article 63, this treaty should enjoy the same legal status as national legislation and be applied in the domestic courts.[6] According to the Supreme Court, whether an international agreement signed by Taiwan enjoys the same legal status as national legislation and whether it can be applied in domestic courts rely mainly upon the deliberation procedures. If an international agreement is deliberated by the Legislative Yuan and ratified by the president, it should enjoy a legal status that if of equal to national legislation. The Supreme Court relies its reasoning mainly upon the constitutional provision that directs the State to respect treaties.

In a letter to the Ministry of the Administration of Justice, the Judicial Yuan stated that the *Treaty of Friendship, Commerce, and Navigation between United States of America and Republic of China* is self-executing in nature and thus can be directly applied by the courts.[7] Whether the ruling of the Supreme Court is influenced by the letter is unclear since this letter is not explicitly referred to in this case. Further, whether the Supreme Court intends to distinguish the self-executing treaties from the non-self-executing ones is also subject to dispute.

budgetary bills or bills concerning material law, amnesty, declaration of war, conclusion of peace or *treaties*, and other important affairs of the State." (emphasis added).

[6] Tai-Shang-Zhi No. 1412 (1985) <http://jirs.judicial.gov.tw/Index.htm> accessed 1 September 201. Cases and of Taiwanese courts can normally be found in the database referred above by providing years and case numbers. This Chapter may not specify except as necessary.

[7] Xun-ling-Zhi No. 449 (27 July 1931).

From the aforementioned holdings, one may be tempted to draw the conclusion that once an international agreement has been deliberated by the Legislative Yuan, it should enjoy the same status as national legislation and can be applied by Taiwanese courts. This position is nevertheless far from settled.

In a recent case concerning the effective protection of inventions, trademarks and trade names, as provided in Article IX, the Supreme Administrative Court held that international law and national law are two parallel legal systems and both may constitute a part of the legal source of the administrative law. However, international law may be relied upon by domestic courts only subject to certain limits and conditions. The relevant treaty or international agreement should be 'clear and specific' in its content so that it may thus be relied upon by the domestic courts. Otherwise, the treaty or international agreement in question should be transformed into national legislation so that domestic courts can apply. Since the content of 'effective protection' as set out in Article IX has not been clearly and specifically defined, domestic courts are unable to directly to apply this provision.

The Supreme Administrative Court further added that, while general international law normally ranks above national law on the legal hierarchy, it is only when the pertinent international agreement contains 'clear and specific in its content' that an international agreement can be applied in domestic courts. As a result of the application of the international agreement, the conflicting domestic law should be made inapplicable.[8] However, the Supreme Administrative Court has given little guidance on the requirement of 'clear and specific' in its content. In addition, whether the Supreme Administrative Court intended to refer to the concept of 'self-executing' or 'direct applicability' is also unclear.

3. *Legal Hierarchy between International Law and National Law*

Divergent views exist in relation the legal hierarchy between treaties or international agreements and national legislation. In the *Judicial Yuan Interpretation* No. 329, the Constitutional Court held that treaties or international agreements deliberated by the Legislative Yuan shall enjoy the same legal status as national legislation. In the case of a conflict between those deliberated treaties and international agreements and the national legislation, the Supreme Court held the rule of *lex specialis* applies. As treaties and international agreements are *lex specialis*, the courts are obliged to apply relevant treaties and international agreements.[9] The Supreme Administrative Court qualified the primacy of treaties and international agreements to only those whose content that are clear and specific. Only

[8] Supreme Administrative Court, Pan-Zhi No. 181 (2004).

[9] Supreme Court Judgment, Tai-Fei-Zhi No. 69 (1984).

when the condition of clarity and specificity is satisfied with can these treaties and international agreements be directly applied in domestic courts, and thus enjoy higher legal hierarchy than national legislation.

There are some subtle differences among the jurisprudence of the Constitutional Court, the Supreme Court and the Supreme Administrative Court. The Constitutional Court clarifies the procedural requirement for treaties and international agreements to be directly applicable in domestic courts as prescribed in the Constitution, namely to be deliberated by the Legislative Yuan. Both the Supreme Court and the Supreme Administrative Court share this view on the needed procedural requirement. Nevertheless, in respect of the legal hierarchy, the Constitutional Court viewed that these deliberated treaties and international agreements should have the same legal status as national legislation. In contrast, the Supreme Court held that as the relevant treaties and international agreements are *lex specialis* in nature, they should exclude the application of conflicting national legislation. Further, the Supreme Administrative Court qualified the primacy of treaties and international agreements to only those provisions that contain clear and specific rights and obligations. Without such clear and specific content, the pertinent treaties or international agreements cannot be relied upon by domestic courts and cannot enjoy a higher position on the legal hierarchy.

Notwithstanding their minor differences, these three courts have never dealt with conflicts between the national Constitution and the deliberated treaties and international agreements. Thus naturally, none of these courts touched upon the issue whether a violation of the deliberated agreements would also constitute an infringement to the Constitution, especially in light of the fact that Taiwanese Constitution directs the state to 'respect the treaties' to which Taiwan is a party.

B. *Legal Status of WTO Agreement in Taiwan*

1. *Legislative History*

With regard to the legal status of the WTO Agreement in Taiwan, Taiwan's Accession to the WTO was approved on 11 November 2001 at the Doha Ministerial Meeting. In respect of the deliberation and ratification processes, the Accession Protocol was deliberated by the Legislative Yuan of Taiwan on 16 November 2001 and ratified by the president on 20 November 2001. In light of this deliberation process, one may be safe to say that the WTO Agreement enjoy the same legal status as national legislation according the jurisprudence of the Constitutional Court, since the procedural requirement has been met. However, the same difficulty persists. It is not entirely clear whether one should adopt the approach proposed by the Supreme Court: the WTO Agreement should prevent the application of national legislation that is in conflict with the Agreement. Or, should one adopt the approach proposed by the Supreme Administrative Court: only those provisions in the WTO Agreement with clarity and specificity may have primacy over the national legislation? This issue becomes even more complicated when (trade) relation with China is at stake, as the Constitution demanded for a different type authorisation, a special legislation, from the Legislative Yuan to regulate the relationship between Taiwan and China.[10]

2. *Relevant Jurisprudence*

Since Taiwan's accession to the WTO, private litigants have occasionally relied upon WTO laws to challenge domestic measures. Nevertheless, the courts seldom deal with debates on the legal status of the WTO Agreement in Taiwan; neither do they touch upon the substantial rules provided therein. In an earlier case, the Taipei Higher Administrative Court when dealing with a case related to the Information Technology Agreement (the ITA) held that, as the product concerned does not fall into the scope of products provided in Attachment A to the Annex of the ITA, Taiwan is not obliged to offer zero-tariff treatment to such product. Following this reasoning, the court concluded that potential trade disputes with other Members as well as possible trade retaliations did not exist.[11] In this case, the court did not clarify on the legal status of the ITA within Taiwan's domestic legal system. Instead, it jumped to an examination on whether the disputed administrative measures are covered by Taiwan's commitments under the ITA. It appears that the court viewed that the ITA can be relied upon by private parties to challenge administrative measures and may possess a higher status in the legal hierarchy. Otherwise, there would be no need for the court to examine the scope of Taiwan's ITA commitments (and the conformity of the administrative measures in question).

In a case relating to anti-dumping measures, the plaintiff relied upon the Anti-Dumping Agreement (the ADA) to challenge the legality of anti-dumping measures imposed by administrative agencies. The plaintiff referred to Article 3.4 and 3.7 of the ADA to challenge the agencies' determinations on the possibility of increased imports and the impact of dumped imports on the domestic industry. While the plaintiff referred to the ADA in his arguments, the court nonetheless disregarded the plaintiff's argument and ruled the case before it based merely upon domestic anti-dumping laws and regulations.[12]

In a recent case, a trader who imports products mainly from China bid for a government procurement contract from the Police Agency of the Ministry of Interior (the MOI) on 'rapiscan eagle fixed site', a device for cargo and vehicle inspection to be installed at the customs. The MOI excluded the bid of this trader

[10] *See* further, *infra* text to (n 16) *et seq*.
[11] Taipei Higher Administrative Court, Jian-Zhi No. 562 (2003).
[12] Taipei Higher Administrative Court, Su-Zhi No. 562 (2002).

on the ground that the bid, if successful, would be supplied with Chinese products. After arbitration, this case was referred to the administrative court where it found once again against the trader. The court held that since neither Taiwan nor China was a party to the Government Procurement Agreement (the GPA), Taiwan's government procurement was thus not bound by the GPA. In light of the political enmity between China and Taiwan and with national security at stake, the Police Agency's decision to exclude Chinese products in this bid was justified.[13] The court did not clarify on the legal status of the GPA in Taiwan's national legal system since Taiwan is not a party to the GPA. Nevertheless, the court seemed to imply that the GPA could be relied upon by the plaintiff if Taiwan had been a party.[14]

In light of these cases noted above, it is safe to say that the courts in Taiwan tend to examine the legality and reasonableness of administrative measures in light of their conformity with WTO law. With regard to the GPA, since Taiwan at that time was not a party to this agreement, Taiwan's courts were thus no position to rely upon it. Taiwanese courts tend to allude directly to laws and rules provided within the WTO agreements without clarifying the legal status of these agreements in the first place. In general, one may be tempted to say that Taiwan's courts make no distinction between the WTO Agreement and other treaties and international agreements. Therefore, the legal status of the WTO Agreement within Taiwan is also ambiguous: it is not clear whether the primacy of the WTO Agreement would be conditional upon the clarity and specificity of its content. The relationship between the Constitution and the WTO Agreement is also unclear. In respect to trade with China, the aforementioned government procurement case illustrates its complexity. The argument for political enmity and national security has its weighting on this matter. This argument may be reinforced by the Taiwanese Constitution which authorises the legislature to regulate Taiwan-China relations differently. Moreover, given different discriminatory laws and regulations, Taiwanese courts may tend to refer merely to domestic law and disregard WTO rules. The following section will deal with the existing constitutional/legal framework governing foreign (trade) relations with China.

III. Constitutional/Legal Framework Governing (Trade) Relations with China

This section will examine the existing constitutional/legal framework governing foreign (trade) relations with China. It will also analyse the existing relevant

[13] Supreme Administrative Court, Pan-Zhi No. 1881 (2005).

[14] It should be noted that Taiwan's *Government Procurement Act*, in Article 17.1, provides that '[T]he participation of foreign suppliers in the procurement by each entity shall be governed by the requirements set forth in the treaties or agreements to which this nation is a party'. Based upon this arrangement, requirements set forth in the treaties or agreements to which Taiwan is a party becomes applicable law and can be directly relied upon in domestic courts.

jurisprudence. The constitutional/legal framework focuses mainly on Article 11 of the Amendment to the Constitution and the *Statute Governing Relations between People of the Taiwan Area and Mainland Area* (last amended on 1 September 2010).[15] It will also investigate into the relevant administrative regulations by focusing on trade in goods and trade in services. In respect of jurisprudence, it will examine several decisions made by the Constitutional Court on issues such as the delimitation of national territory; the definition of international agreement and its application to agreements concluded between Taiwan and China; restriction on the entry of Chinese nationals into Taiwan; and restriction for naturalised Chinese nationals to hold public offices.

A. *Constitutional/Legal Framework*

1. *Constitutional Arrangements*

In 1987, Taiwan abolished its long-lasting marital law and moved towords democratisation. In the same year, the ban on Taiwanese travelling to China was lifted so that people who followed the Nationalist Party (the Kuomintang or the KMT) to Taiwan in 1949 could go back to China for family reunion. Since then, Taiwan has gradually relaxed its relationship with China and its perception towards China. Thus its Constitution has been constantly reshaped. After a series of constitutional reform, several articles have been added to the original constitutional text as an Amendment. Article 11 of the Amendment to the Constitution provides that 'rights and obligations between the people of the Chinese mainland area and those of the free area, and the disposition of other related affairs may be specified by law.'[16] In this provision, 'Chinese mainland' refers to People's Republic of China while the 'free area' refers to Taiwan. This constitutional provision itself does not regulate the relations between Taiwan and China, but delegates the regulatory authority to legislature. This delegation may suggest that the Constitution intends to authorise the legislature to regulate China affairs in such a way that may deviate from the existing national legislation. It may also be argued that different treatments or even discriminatory treatments against Chinese nationals are intended by the Constitution.

2. *National Legislation and Relevant Regulations*

With the delegation of the Constitution, the Legislative Yuan enacted the *Statute Governing Relations between People of the Taiwan Area and Mainland Area* (hereinafter the *Statute*), which lays down a comprehensive regulatory framework

[15] An English version is available at the Law and Regulations Database of Republic of China (Taiwan) <http://law.moj.gov.tw/eng/index.aspx> accessed 1 September 2011.

[16] This amendment was firstly added into the Constitution as Article 10 on 1 May 19999, now renumbered as Article 11.

governing Taiwan's relations with China. The term 'Taiwan area' refers to Taiwan and the term 'mainland area' refers to People's Republic of China.[17] Since its promulgation in 1992, this *Statute* has been frequently amended because of the changing political climate between Taiwan and China.

The *Statute* addresses trade in goods and trade in services between Taiwan and China in great detail. Contrasting these two aspects, the *Statute* mentions little on trade related intellectual property rights. This arrangement may be understandable since services trade relates closely to the free movement of natural persons from China into Taiwan and the commercial presence of Chinese legal persons in Taiwan, which necessitates a high degree of regulation in this regard.[18] Regulation on trade in goods may also impact on trade-related intellectual property rights owned by Chinese national/legal persons. Even though the intellectual property rights owned by Chinese nationals and enterprises are recognised and protected in Taiwan, the restriction on Chinese imports can effectively exclude these Chinese products from entering into the market. Therefore, the regulation on trade in goods simultaneously regulates trade-related intellectual property rights and lessens the need of a high degree of regulation in the area of intellectual property rights.

However, apart from trade issues, the *Statute* also imposes strict control on inbound and outbound investments which the *Statute* virtually classified as a part of trade in financial services.[19] Although investment issues are part of the Single Undertaking of the WTO Agreement, the Agreement on Trade-Related Investments Measures (the TRIMs Agreement) limits its application of only to 'investment measures related to trade in goods'.[20] In addition, Article 2.1 of the TRIMs Agreement refers to Article III and Article XI of the GATT 1994. By acting inconsistent with these two articles of the GATT 1994, a Member thus breaches its obligation under the TRIMs Agreement. Since any WTO-inconsistent trade-related investment measure adopted or maintained by Taiwan should eventually be examined in accordance with these GATT 1994 articles, this chapter will thus not examine Taiwan's investment regulatory regime in isolation. Above all, given the wide diversity among different types of services trade, it is impossible and infeasible to examine all the listed categories under services trade. In light of the fact that financial services are among the most regulated areas in Taiwan, they prove to be an illustrative example of Taiwan's regulatory regime on trade in services with China. Therefore, the following will firstly analyse Taiwan's regulatory regime on

---

[17] The *Statute*, Art. 2.

[18] Except mode 1 (cross-border supply), mode 2 (consumption abroad), mode 3 (commercial presence) and mode 4 (presence of natural persons) may all relate to the entrance into Taiwan of Chinese legal/natural persons.

[19] *See, e.g.*, the *Statute*, Art. 35(1), 36(2), 73.

[20] The Agreement on Trade-Related Investments Measures (the TRIMs Agreement), Art. 1.

trade in goods between Taiwan and China and then examine trade in financial services.

a. *Trade in Goods*

Article 35 of the *Statute* lays down a general regulatory framework for trade and other related economic activities with China: investment and technical cooperation in China, general and vague idea of commercial behaviour, and trade between Taiwan and China. Under the second paragraph of Article 35, individuals, juristic persons, organisations or other institutions in Taiwan may engage in commercial behaviour with Chinese individuals, juristic persons, organisations or other institutions. The Ministry of Economic Affairs (the MOEA), in consultation with other competent authorities may prohibit or require to obtain permission for these commercial behaviour. With the delegation of the *Statute*, the MOEA issues a *Regulation Governing the Permission of Commercial Behaviour in China* (last amended on 1 March 2004, hereinafter the *Commercial Behaviour Regulation*).[21] This *Commercial Behaviour Regulation* lays down a low threshold for the permission of the MOEA by submission a project plan stating the category, the content, the time period and the place of which the commercial behaviour was engaged.[22] If the commercial behaviour extends to trade activities, it falls under the scope of Article 35(3) of the *Statute*. Any natural and legal person, organisation or other institution in Taiwan may be permitted by competent authorities to engage in trade activities with China. The second sentence then delegates the competent authorities, upon the approval of the Executive Yuan (the Cabinet of Taiwan), to regulate the permission in question; for example the liberalised items; conditions and procedures for liberalisation and its suspension; and relevant provisions for import/export administration.[23]

In accordance with Article 35(3) of the *Statute*, the MOEA in 1993 adopted the *Regulation on the Permission of Trade between Taiwan and China* (last amended on 12 December 2008, hereinafter the *China Trade Regulation*).[24] Similar to the *Statute*, the *China Trade Regulation* has also been frequently revised. Trading activities between Taiwan and China are defined as 'imports and exports of goods between Taiwan and China, and other relevant subjects'.[25] Further, while trade between Taiwan and China is conditional upon obtaining permission from the competent authorities, the application for such permission may nevertheless be waived.[26]

[21] MOEA Order, Shang-Zhi No. 201625 (1994) <http://www.moeaic.gov.tw/> accessed 1 September 2011.

[22] The *Commercial Behaviour Regulation*, Art. 5(2).

[23] The *Statute*, Art. 35(3).

[24] MOEA Order, Mao-Zhi No. 083651 (1993), available at the Law and Regulations Database of Republic of China (Taiwan) <http://law.moj.gov.tw/eng/index.aspx> accessed 1 September 2011.

[25] The *China Trade Regulation*, Art. 4(1).

[26] The *China Trade Regulation*, Art. 4(3).

The *China Trade Regulation*, in Article 7, lists 13 categories of Chinese goods eligible for importation Taiwan. Among these 13 items, the competent authorities can decide which items to liberalise and announce its decisions through public notices.[27] Article 9 reinstates the permission requirement for trade between Taiwan and China, but the competent authorities may waive the application for such permission through a public notice.[28] Prior to the inking of the direct transportation agreements concluded between Taiwan and China,[29] Article 5 of the *China Trade Regulation* dictated the shipment of goods was to be carried out through a third port or an exterritorial transportation zone.[30] As a result of the liberalisation of direct transportation across the Taiwan Strait, this article was removed.

b. *Trade in Financial Services*

Upon Taiwan's accession the WTO, its market access for financial services has been largely liberalised. For example, while Taiwan remains unbound on financial services in mode 1 (cross-border supply) and mode 4 (presence of natural persons), there is no limitation albeit with certain exception on market access for mode 2 (consumption abroad) and mode 3 (commercial presence). The commercial presence of banking and other financial services (excluding insurance, securities and futures) may be established in the form of commercial banks, branches of foreign banks, offshore banking branches of banks, foreign exchange brokerage firms, credit card institutions and bills finance companies.[31] Taiwan also permits the opening of foreign currency deposit accounts abroad and the transferring of funds to these accounts.[32] In spite of these commitments, banking and other financial services provided by Chinese service suppliers are still subject to strict restrictions in Taiwan.

In 2003, Article 73 of the *Statute* was amended in order to liberalise investment from China.[33] This revision also aims to provide a legal basis for the commercial presence of Chinese banking enterprises in Taiwan. Upon obtaining permission from the competent authorities, any natural and legal person, organisation, or other institution from China or their subsidiaries in third area may engage in investment activities in Taiwan.[34] Following conventional practices, the *Statute*

[27] The *China Trade Regulation*, Art. 7(1), first indent.

[28] The *China Trade Regulation*, Arts. 9(1), first indent, 9(3).

[29] *See infra* Chapter VII, text to (n 103) *et seq.*

[30] The *China Trade Regulation*, Art. 5 (deleted).

[31] WTO, *Protocol on the Accession of the Separate Customs Territory of Taiwan, Penghu, Kinmen and Matsu* (Cambridge University Press, Cambridge 2003) 862.

[32] Ibid.

[33] It should also be noted that Taiwan makes a horizontal commitment in relation to investment in mode 3 (commercial presence). Unless specified in the specific sectors, foreign business and individuals may directly invest in Taiwan. No limitation exists either with respect to portfolio investment in companies whose shares are listed in Taiwan's securities markets. Ibid 835.

[34] The *Statute*, Art. 73(1).

then directs the competent authorities, upon obtaining approval from the Executive Yuan, to draft rules governing the 'qualifications of investors, permission requirements, procedures, investment means, business items and amount limits, investment percentage, foreign exchange settlement, review and determination, re-investment, filing items and procedures, application format and any other requirements.'[35] Judging from the language used in the legal text of the *Statute*, it appears that that Chinese investment in Taiwan has long been liberalised. However, the long-awaited implementing rules, *Regulation on the Permission of Chinese Investment in Taiwan*,[36] were finally adopted by the MOEA on 3 July 2009, six years after the revision of the *Statute*. As of 1 September 2011, four Chinese banks have been allowed to establish a representative office in Taiwan: Bank of China, Bank of Communications, China Merchants Bank, and China Construction Bank.

On the topic of Chinese banks' commercial presence, another element should also be noted: the acquisition, creation and transfer of a legal right over a real property. On this matter, the *Statute* regulates quite differently. Article 69 provides the legal basis and the conditions upon which to gain the permission from the competent authorities for Chinese individuals, juristic persons, organisations, institutions, or their subsidiaries in third area to acquire, create or transfer any right over any real property in Taiwan.[37] The *Statute* then instructs the competent authorities to draft rules governing 'the qualifications of applicants, permission requirements, permitted uses, application procedures, filing items, required documents, review means, the disposition for uses not in accordance with the permitted uses and any other requirements.'[38] With this delegation, the Ministry of Interior (the MOI) was able to issue the *Regulation Governing Permission for Chinese People to Acquire, Create or Transfer Rights over Real Property in Taiwan* (hereinafter the *Real Property Regulation*).[39] However, it still contains various restrictions for Chinese personnel to acquire, create or transfer real property rights in Taiwan.

With regard to Taiwanese service providers in China, the *Statute* also lays down strict conditions for financial services activities in which they can engage. According to Article 36(1) of the *Statute*, any financial, insurance, securities or futures institution in Taiwan, and any of its overseas branches, with the permission of the Ministry of Finance (the MOF), may conduct direct commercial

---

[35] The *Statute*, Art. 73(2).

[36] MOEA Order, Jing-Shen-Zhi No. 09802085680 (2009), available at the Law and Regulations Database of Republic of China (Taiwan) <http://law.moj.gov.tw/eng/index.aspx> accessed 1 September 2011, Chinese version only.

[37] The *Statute*, Art. 69(1).

[38] The *Statute*, Art. 69(2).

[39] MOI Order, Tai-Nei-Di-Zhi No. 0910071523 (2002).

behaviour with any natural and legal person, organisation, or other institution in China. The second paragraph further provides that any of these Taiwanese natural and legal person, organisation or institution wishing to establish a branch in China should apply for the permission from the MOF.[40] The *Statute* then authorises the MOF, after receiving approval from the Executive Yuan, to draft a regulation governing 'the permission requirements, business scope, procedures, administration, restrictions and any other requirements'[41] as referred to in Article 36(1) and 36(2).

The MOF subsequently in 1993 adopted the *Regulation Governing the Permission for the Business Dealing of Banking Service between Taiwan and China* (last amended 16 March 2010, hereinafter the *Banking Service Regulation*).[42] With approval for the competent authority, Taiwanese banks' overseas branches and offshore banking units may engage in the following financial activities with individuals, juristic persons, organisations, other institutions in China and with their branches in a third area:

1. Accepting deposits;
2. Outward and inward remittance business;
3. Export-related foreign exchange business, including export bill negotiation, export bill collections, advice of letters of credit and bonding business;
4. Import-related foreign exchange business, including issuance of letters of credit, acceptance of drafts, import foreign exchange settlements, and import bill collections;
5. Acting as a collecting and paying agent;
6. Credit extension business;
7. Factoring business;
8. Interbank transactions related to business specified in the preceding seven subparagraphs; and
9. Other businesses as approved by the Competent Authority.[43]

In respect of these permitted financial activities, some points should be noted. Firstly, they should be conducted through Taiwanese banks' overseas branches or overseas banking units. Secondly, since one of the major purposes to allow Taiwanese banks to engage in financial activities in China is to satisfy the collecting and paying needs resulting from trading activities of Taiwan-invested enterprises, a clear link between these financial services and trade activities is visible. By 1 September 2011, eleven Taiwanese banks have established branches or representative offices in China. Thirdly, the *Banking Regulation* also deals with

[40] The *Statute*, Art. 36(2), first sentence. The second sentence then further provides that in case where this individual, juristic person, organisation or institution establishes a branch in China, its investment in China is subject to the regulation of Article 35 of the same Statute.
[41] The *Statute*, Art. 36(3).
[42] BOF Order, Tai-Tsai-Rong-Zhi No. 820178343 (1993).
[43] The *Banking Service Regulation*, Art. 11.

foreign exchange activities. Article 13 of this regulation provides that only the designated foreign exchange banks listed therein and the Chunghwa Post Company may conduct foreign currency activities with individuals, juristic persons, organisations, and other institutions in China and with their branches established in a third area.

Article 38 of the *Statute* was amended in order to provide the legal basis for those designated banks and the Chunghwa Post Office to conduct foreign exchange activities and to permit the circulation of Chinese Yuan in Taiwan. Before the conclusion of a clearing agreement between Taiwan and China or the establishment of a bilateral settlement mechanism on currency exchange, the *Act on the Control of Foreign Exchange* shall apply *mutatis mutandis* to the regulation of Chinese currency in Taiwan.[44] Article 38(2) of the *Statute* then directs the Financial Supervision Committee (the FSC) and the Central Bank to issue regulations governing Chinese currency flowing into and out of Taiwan prior to the signature of a clearing agreement or bilateral settlement mechanism. Article 38(4) of the *Statute* then delegates the management of regulating Chinese Yuan in Taiwan to Central Bank and the FSC. Being preoccupied over the failure to guarantee a sufficient supply of Chinese Yuan, the Central Bank originally maintained that liberalisation should be divided into two steps: firstly the free conversion of Chinese Yuan into New Taiwan Dollars and secondly the offer for sale of Chinese Yuan in Taiwanese banks. This position has not been supported by the Executive Yuan. In order to guarantee a sufficient supply of Chinese Yuan in the Taiwanese banks, the Central Bank has relied mainly upon currency deposited by Taiwanese individuals and enterprises returning from China and currency exchanged by Chinese tourists in Taiwan. When an insufficiency of the supply occurs, the Central Bank may purchase Chinese Yuan for the foreign exchange market of a third country as there is a lack of formal arrangements between Taiwanese Central Bank and the People's Bank of China.[45]

B. *Relevant Jurisprudence on (Trade) Relations with China*

1. *Delimitation of the Boundary of National Territories*

In 1992, Taiwan applied for its GATT membership as a separate customs territory of which the 'full autonomy in the conduct of its external commercial relations

---

[44] The *Statute*, Art. 38(3).

[45] According to the statics of the Central Bank of Taiwan, up to 15 July 2008, 15 banks (1570 branches) are approved to engage in Chinese exchange activities. During the period from 30 June to 15 July, the buy-in for the Chinese currency amounted to 102.76 million Yuans, while the sell-out amounted to 238.06 million Yuans. Liberalisation of Chinese Currency Exchange in Taiwan and its Implementation, Press release, No. 46 (2008) <http://www.mac.gov.tw/ct.asp?xItem=44825&ctNode=5649&mp=1&xq_xCat=2008> accessed 1 September 2011, in Chinese.

and of the other matters provided for' is limited to Taiwan, Penghu, Kinmen and Matsu. One year after, Taiwan's Constitutional Court was called upon to delimit the boundaries of Taiwan's national territory of the Republic of China. During 1993 budgetary review, especially the budget for the Mainland Affairs Council (the MAC) in charge with China affairs, the deputy of the opposition party at the Legislative Yuan referred to the Constitutional Court for the interpretation for the term 'according to its existing national boundaries' as provided in Article 4 of the Constitution. That is, it would be problematic, and unthinkable for Taiwan to maintain internal a stand that, under its official title of Republic of China, its national territory still extends to mainland China while at the same time externally recognises its limit in the full autonomy of external commercial relations.

Nevertheless, the Constitutional Court chose not to address this issue. Relying upon the 'political question' doctrine, the Constitutional Court denied the application for an interpretation on national territory. According to the Constitutional Court, the reason why the drafters of the Constitution chose not to enumerate the components of its territory was based upon historical and political considerations.[46] In light of this legislative policy not to identify all the components of its territory, the delimitation of national territory is not subject to judicial review according to the constitutional principle of separation of powers. Based on this reasoning, the Court held as followed:

> Instead of enumerating the components, Article 4 of the Constitution provides that the national territory of the Republic of China is determined 'according to its existing national boundaries.' Based on political and historical reasons, a special procedure is also required for any change of territory. The delimitation of national territory according to its history is a significant political question and thus it is beyond the reach of judicial review.[47]

What is at stake in this present case is the relationship between China and Taiwan. It goes beyond trade relations with China and covers, *inter alia* national security and foreign relations. The Constitutional Court strictly restrained itself from stepping into this field. Consequently, it referred to the 'political question' doctrine and rejected the application for an interpretation. As the first of a series of cases on relations with China, the Constitutional Court took a very cautious approach. It had to wait until it got more experienced in that regard so that it could step in with greater confidence.

[46] *Judicial Yuan Interpretation* No. 328. <http://www.judicial.gov.tw/constitutionalcourt/> accessed 1 September 2011. All of the judicial interpretations of the Constitutional Court, with multilingual translations are available on the aforementioned website. This chapter will not reproduce the hyperlink unless necessary.

[47] Ibid.

2. *Agreements between Taiwan and China as 'Treaty' in Terms of Taiwan's Constitution*

Immediately after the aforementioned national territory case, the Constitutional Court was called upon to define the term 'treaty' as contained in Article 38, Article 58(2) and Article 63 of the Constitution. More specifically, the Constitutional Court was to decide whether the agreements signed by Taiwan and China are 'international' agreements. While the Constitutional Court addressed the scope of 'treaties' subject to the deliberation procedures,[48] the Court did not answer whether the agreements signed between Taiwan and China were subject to the same congressional oversight. The Court only hinted that those agreements are not 'international' in the sense of 'State to State' or 'inter-State'. It thus indirectly clarified its perception on the relationship between Taiwan and China. At this stage, the Constitutional Court did not see this relationship as one between two states.

While the substance of this interpretation appears to be awkward, the Constitutional Court in this case seems to take a more activist approach on Taiwan's relations with China. Nevertheless, it is paradoxical that within one month, the Constitutional Court had a different perception on this issue. While the Constitutional Court denied to rule upon the question whether the national territory extends to mainland China in its *Judicial Yuan Interpretation* No. 328, it felt was competent to interpret the relationship between Taiwan and China (not 'international'). It clearly contradicts its position in the previous case where the 'political question' doctrine was preferred. Nevertheless, it should also be noted that, while the majority of the Constitutional Court decided to interpret the scope of the 'treaties', some Justices disagreed on this decision. They have dissented individually, but their arguments are similar, based mainly upon the 'political question' doctrine.[49]

3. *Restriction for the Entry of Chinese Nationals into Taiwan*

The issue of Taiwan's relations with China came before the Constitutional Court once again in 1999 which called into question the scope of the constitutional guarantee of individual rights. In a case related to the re-entry into Taiwan of a Chinese national, who is the spouse of a Taiwanese citizen, the Constitutional Court was called upon to review the legality of several delegated regulations: the *Regulation Governing the Entry Permission to Taiwan for the People from China* and the *Regulation Governing Permanent or Temporary Residence Permission for the People from China*. Article 10(3) of the *Statute* directs the MOI to adopt, after submitting

[48] Ibid.

[49] *See* dissenting opinion of Justice Te-Sheng Zhang; Yu-Ling Yang; Zhi-Peng Li; Zhong-Sheng Li.

the drafting rules to the Executive Yuan for approval, a rule governing the entry into Taiwan of Chinese citizens. Article 17(7) of the *Statute* (amended and renumbered as 17(9)) instruct the MOI in conjunction with the authorities concerned, upon receiving the approval for the Executive Yuan, to drat the rules governing 'the requirements, procedures, means, restriction, revocation, or annulment of permission and any other requirements for residency, long-term residency or permanent residency' as referred to in Article 18 and Article 19(1) to 19(5).

In this case, the legal status of Chinese nationals in Taiwan is at stake. The Constitutional Court had to examine the legality of these two delegated regulations adopted by the MOI. To resolve the dispute before it, the Constitutional Court had also to clarify the relationship between the *Statute* and Article 11 of the Amendment to the Constitution. However, the Constitutional Court took a narrow and shallow approach. Relying mainly upon its jurisprudence on the principle of 'legal reservation' (Vorbehalt des Gesetzes) and upon the clarity and definitiveness of the delegation, the Constitutional Court upheld the legality of the regulations at issue.[50]

According to the Court, the delegation of the legislative duties to the executive branch as contained within the *Statute* is explicit and concrete since the construction of a legislative intent could be sought from the entirety of the relevant context. These two regulations adopted by the MOI are meant to protect the security and welfare of Taiwan's people. They are in accordance with the legislative purpose of the *Statute* and within the scope of its delegation. The Court then touched upon the principle of proportionality as enshrined in Article 23 of the Constitution. The Court reinstated the legal text under this article that rights and freedoms conferred by the Constitution may be restricted by law in order to prevent the infringement upon others' freedoms, to avert an imminent crisis, or to maintain social order and to enhance public welfare. Then it briefly stated that the measures set out in these two regulations are essential to protect security and welfare of people in Taiwan. Their legality in terms of proportionality should thus be sustained.[51]

The Court did not clarify the role of Article 11 of the Amendment to the Constitution in relation to rights provided therein. Nor did the Court answer to what extent the constitutional rights may be extended to those Chinese nationals who reside in Taiwan. Further, the Court failed to address on the constitutionality of the *Statute*. Nothing has been said as to whether the *Statute* may infringe the constitutional rights of these Chinese nationals. The Court took a rather

[50] The jurisprudence of Taiwan's Constitutional Court has been greatly influenced by German legal schools. The Court repeatedly emphasises on 'Vorbehalt des Gesetzes', and then examines the clarity and definitiveness of delegation to the administrative power in terms of the purpose, scope, and content. *See, e.g., Judicial Yuan Interpretation* No. 443.

[51] *Judicial Yuan Interpretation* No. 497.

deferential approach in reviewing the case before it. Without clearly defining the scope of security and welfare enjoyed by Taiwanese people, the Constitutional Court upheld the legality of the disputed regulations and granted great discretionary power to both the legislature and the administration.

4. *Restriction for Naturalised Chinese Nationals to Hold Public Offices*

In 2006, another case relating to rights and freedoms of those Chinese nationals who are married with Taiwanese nationals was brought before the Constitutional Court. Nevertheless, this time the issue was the equal protection of Taiwanese citizens, instead of the relation between Chinese people and Taiwanese people. A Chinese national after her marriage with a Taiwanese citizen and being a resident in Taiwan finally acquired her Taiwanese nationality. With this Taiwanese status, she participated in an examination for public offices and passed the examination. Nevertheless, she was disqualified and excluded from civil service due to her original Chinese nationality status. After administrative review and administrative litigation, this case was brought before the Constitutional Court where the remedies were eventually denied.

According to Article 21(1) of the *Statute,* as amended and promulgated on 20 December 2000, unless he or she has had a household registration in Taiwan at least ten years, a Chinese national may not register as a candidate for any public office, serve in any military, governmental or educational organisation or state enterprise nor organise political party. One of the requirements for this household registration is to have a Taiwanese nationality status. Therefore, Chinese nationals can only participate in the aforementioned activities after ten years from acquiring their Taiwanese citizenship. The issue before the Constitutional Court was thus on the constitutionality of this provision in terms of the equal rights protection and the principle of proportionality. Compared to the case of the entry of Chinese citizen, an even clearer and stronger tone of deference to legislature can be evinced.

The Court started its reasoning by clarifying the equal rights protection as enshrined in Article 7 of the Constitution. According to the Court, while under Article 18 of the Constitution all citizens of Taiwan, irrespective of sex, religion, race, class, or party affiliation, shall be equal before the law and thus shall enjoy equal rights in taking public examinations and in holding public offices, it does not nevertheless exclude the possibility of differential treatments based on reasonable differentiation. Equality as set out in the Constitution refers to substantial equality, where different treatments may be justified based upon the nature of subject matters.[52]

---

[52] *Judicial Yuan Interpretation* No. 618.

In upholding the constitutionality of Article 21(1) of the *Statute*, the Court referred to Article 11 of the Amendment to the Constitution which authorises the legislature of regulate the relations between Taiwan and China. While the Constitutional Court did not clarify the relevance of this delegation, it did shield the *Statute* from being the basis for the challenging of its constitutionality. One may argue that in light of this delegation, the *Statute* is presumably constitutional. This explains why the Constitutional Court took a highly deferential approach in this case. According to the Constitutional Court, when cross-Taiwan-Strait relations are at stake, numerous social-political-economical factors need to be evaluated and balanced. Unless there is a clear and manifest oversight, the Constitutional Court should show due respect to decisions made by the legislative branch which represents diverse opinions of people and should be better informed.[53]

Based on this deferential approach, the Court reviews the constitutionality of the *Statute* in light of the proportionality principle, as enshrined in Article 23 of the Constitution. The Court firstly pointed to the duty of loyalty to the State of a public functionary. It further elaborated that a public functionary, entrusted with public authorities, should bear in mind the overall interests of the State when carrying out his/her official duties. In doing so, he/she may take every action and adopt every policy possible that he/she considers in the best interests of the state. The Court then emphasised the status quo of cross-Taiwan-Strait relations: Taiwan and China are two separate and antagonistic entities with significant differences in essence between each other particularly in respect of their political, economic and social systems. Such systems are the context in where the security of Taiwan, the welfare of its people and the constitutional structure of a free democracy therein are to be ensured and preserved. Based on this reasoning, the Constitutional Court then concluded that Article 21(1) of the *Statute* does not run counter to the legislative intent under Article 11 of the Amendment to the Constitution. Different treatments for those Chinese nationals who acquire Taiwanese nationality – barring them for public offices – can be justified by equality rights protection and the proportionality test, as there has been no clear and manifest oversight in the legislative decision.[54]

The special delegation set out under Article 11 of the Amendment to the Constitution and the status quo of two separate and antagonistic entities with significant differences are the two cornerstones of the Constitutional Court's reasoning. Since the Constitution has authorised the legislature the power to regulate the relations between Taiwan and China with a special law, it envisages different or discriminatory treatments. In light of the intention of the Amendment drafters, different treatments towards Chinese nationals in the *Statute* should be respected by

[53] Ibid.
[54] Ibid.

the Constitutional Court. In accordance with this deferential approach, the Court further upheld the constitutionality of the *Statute* in terms the proportionality principle. The Court seemed to have little difficulty to reach this decision since the security of Taiwan, the welfare of its people and the constitutional structure of a free democracy were at stake. The reasoning of the Constitutional Court may nevertheless problematic. Firstly, the Constitutional Court failed to articulate clearly the concept of national security and what it entails. Secondly, it seemed that the Constitutional Court tended to take a deferential approach when it was called to examine the relations between Taiwan and China. The Constitutional Court, in relying on a vague concept of national security and endorsing broad scope of manoeuvre to the political branches, failed to discharge its constitutional obligation to ensure that the Constitution is fully respected.

C. *Short Conclusion: Approaches or Patterns*

With regard to trade relations with China, parallel development in the legal regulation and judicial jurisprudence can be seen. Regardless of a number of WTO-inconsistent regulations relating to cross-Taiwan-strait trade relations, Taiwan's regulatory regime governing this subject matter has been gradually liberalised. A first step in this liberalisation took place in the area of trade in goods. With the increase trade volume between Taiwan and China, there was need for liberalisation in services trade. The liberalisation of services trade came for two directions. Not only has Taiwan's market access been gradually opened to Chinese services providers, but Taiwan's service providers into China have also been 'liberalised'. Due to the great volume of Taiwanese investments in China, liberalisation in the financial services, notably the banking services, to sustain these investments has long been overdue. In response to this need, commercial presence of Taiwanese banks in China is thus inevitable.

With the surging trade volume accompanied by other trade-related issues such as the entry of Chinese nationals into Taiwan and their residence therein, Taiwanese courts are forced to face with the issues of the relations between Taiwan and China. The cases before the courts may relate to trade and economic activities; they may well concern non-trade related issues, such as civil and political rights. The Constitutional Court has long adopted a deferential approach on the relations between Taiwan and China. Among the examined cases, the Constitutional Court firstly rejected a case on national territory based on the 'political question' doctrine. Then the Court interpreted the meaning of 'treaty' within the Constitution but failed to provide no answer for the main question: whether the agreements signed between Taiwan and China are to be deemed as 'international'. With regard to Chinese-Taiwanese and their right to hold public offices as naturalised Chinese, the Court directed such decision to the discretion power of the legislature.

While a flood of cases related to China relations is inevitable and irresistible, the Court seems to react awkwardly in this regard. So far, under the shadow of national security it has not developed a good approach to deal with cases on cross-Taiwan-strait relations. In light of this, the following section will propose an approach to resolve the conflicts between WTO rules and Taiwanese laws and regulations maintained in the name of national security. It focuses on how the relevant WTO rules may complement Taiwanese Constitution in eliminating WTO-incompatible discriminatory measures against China.

IV. Case Study in Relation to Chinese Education Services and Recognition Diplomas of Chinese Diplomas

This section will examine two related criminal cases handed down by the Taipei District Court and the Taiwan Higher Administrative Court. The first case concerns the application of Article 23 and 82 of the *Statute* which criminalise the acting as an intermediary for Chinese education institution without prior approval from the competent authorities. The second case relates to a moratorium in recognising Chinese diplomas. Both cases involve the complex issues elaborated above and are good illustrative examples to explore how Taiwanese courts should deal with the relations between Taiwan and China.

A. *Criminalisation of Recruiting for Chinese Education Institutions*

Article 23 of the *Statute* prohibits any Taiwanese natural and legal person or other institution from recruiting or acting as an intermediary for Chinese education institutions without prior approval from the competent authorities; Article 82 of the *Statute* then imposes criminal penalty of maximum one year imprisonment, detention, or in lieu thereof or in addition thereto, a fine of no more than one million New Taiwan Dollars. As of 1 September 2011, the Ministry of Education (the MOE) has not adopted any rule to permit Taiwanese natural or legal persons or institutions to recruit or act as an intermediary for Chinese education institutions.

In accordance with Article 82, the courts have handed down a number of decisions that find the defendants guilty. Taiwan Taipei District Court 96-Yi-Zhi No. 1288 (2007) is one of those examples. In 2007, the defendants were charged with a criminal infringement for their violation of Article 23 of the *Statute* by introducing a number of Chinese universities to Taiwanese students through advertisements in newspapers and on the internet. Subsequently, the defendants entered into contracts with eleven Taiwanese students that guaranteed their admissions into Chinese universities. In accordance with these contracts, the defendants took these Taiwanese students to Beijing to receive pre-examination supervision and to Hong Kong to participate in the entrance examination for the China Legal-Political University. Nine of eleven Taiwanese students were eventually admitted by China Legal-Political University.

Article 82 of the *Statute* criminalises the acts specified in Article 23 and reads as follows:

> [A]ny individual, juristic person, organisation, or other institution of the Taiwan Area, the Mainland Area or any other area may be permitted to recruit students or act as an intermediary in the Taiwan Area for any educational institution of the Mainland Area. Rules governing the granting of the referred permission shall be drafted by the Ministry of Education and submitted to the Executive Yuan for approval.

Article 82 provides the legal basis for the state to issue fines and impose criminal penalty. Relying upon Article 82 of the *Statute*, the prosecutor thus claimed that the acts of defendants were in violation of Article 23 of the *Statute*, and thus constituted as a criminal offense as prescribed in Article 82. The district court subsequently found the defendants guilty. According to the district court, whereas the second sentence of Article 23 of the *Statute* directs the competent authority to draft rules governing the procedure to obtain permission for acting as an intermediary for Chinese education institutions, the relevant rules have not yet been released. The acts of the defendants thus infringed Article 23 of the *Statute* and should be subject to criminal penalty as laid down by Article 82 of the *Statute*.[55] This decision was subsequently repealed by the higher court that based its reasoning mainly upon the regulation of 'acting as an intermediary' in Taiwan's Civil Code. According to the higher court, to act as an intermediary should be interpreted in accordance with the spirit of the Civil Code. In the present case, the defendants did not act as an intermediary for Chinese education institutions as the defendants did not receive payments from the institutions in return. In essence, the admission of those Taiwanese students into Chinese universities depended on the result of the entrance examination instead of the acts of the defendants. In view of these facts, the higher court found the defendants not guilty.[56]

The case handled by Taiwan Taipei District Court in 96-Yi-Zhi No. 1288 (2007) is one of the numerous cases related to the recognition of the Chinese diploma. The fundamental issue in this case is whether the state can criminalise an act would be legal should the state implement/fulfil its international obligations, and whether a defendants can rely upon both an international agreement and a national constitution for his/her plead not guilty. When approaching this case from a constitutional dimension, one not only needs to clarify the legal status of the WTO Agreement with in Taiwan's domestic legal system, but also has to pay due regard for Taiwan's established jurisprudence.

---

55 Taiwan Taipei District Court, Yi-Zhi No. 1288 (2007).

56 Taiwan Higher Court, Shang-Yi-Zhi No. 2199 (2007).

B. *Recognition of Chinese Diplomas*

Another issue involving the Chinese education services sector relates to the recognition of Chinese diplomas. While Article 22 of the *Statute* provides the legal basis for recognising Chinese diplomas and the MOE has also adopted the *Regulation on the Examination and Recognition of Chinese Diplomas* (hereinafter the *Chinese Diplomas Regulation*) to deal with this subject matter, the MOE has maintained a moratorium in the recognising of Chinese diplomas, which was eventually lifted in August 2010. This case took place prior to lift of the moratorium.[57] The plaintiff, after her marriage with a Taiwanese citizen, entered and resided in Taiwan. Subsequently, she acquired her Taiwanese citizenship on 2 September 2004. One day later, she applied to the MOE for the recognition of her the diploma which she acquired in China in 1994. This application was rejected by the MOE on 10 September 2004 on the ground that the review and recognition of Chinese diplomas of higher education were not permitted and that the notification of the diplomas acquired was also unavailable.[58] After an administrative review, this case was brought into the administrative court and the court ruled in favour of the plaintiff on 4 May 2005.

In this case, the plaintiff argued that unjustified different and discriminatory treatments during the recognition of diplomas towards foreign spouses of Chinese nationality from other nationalities infringed her equal rights protection as enshrined in the Constitution. Those Chinese nationals, who are married to Taiwanese citizens, should be able to refer to the *Chinese Diplomas Regulation* for the examination and recognition of their Chinese diplomas after acquiring the nationality of Taiwan.[59] According to the existing MOE policy, Chinese higher education diplomas are not recognised in Taiwan. In contrast, spouses of other nationalities can refer to the *Regulation Governing the Examination of Foreign Diplomas* (hereinafter the *Foreign Diplomas Regulation*) once they acquire their residence in Taiwan. These different and unfavourable treatments were not based on the nature of things (Natura Rerum) and could not be justified.[60] Additionally, the MOE's refusal to recognise the effect of the plaintiff's higher education received in China would prevent her from taking public examination, holding public offices, and from being qualified to provide professional services in Taiwan.[61] These unjustified and discriminatory treatments also infringed her right to life, work, to own property and her right to take public examinations and to hold public offices as

---

[57] Taipei Higher Administrative Court, Su-Zhi No. 582 (2005). The court here refers to the concept of 'subjektiv-öffentliches Recht'.

[58] Ibid.

[59] Ibid.

[60] Ibid.

[61] Ibid.

provided under Article 15 and 18 of the Constitution.[62] On the other hand, the MOE asserted that the examination and recognition of Chinese diplomas relates to the sustainable development and allocation of human resource in higher education. Thus this issue should be considered in the context of other China policies and the political sensitivity between Taiwan and China.[63] As this issue also would have an impact on employment, reorganisation of human resource and social security, it could not be decided solely by the MOE. Moreover, in light of public interests, the decision not to recognise Chinese diplomas on the constitutional level should be deemed proportionate as set out under Article 23 of the Constitution.[64]

In contrast to the human rights arguments advanced by the plaintiff and the policy arguments maintained by the MOE, the court rules this case mainly on the ground of administrative law principles. According to the Court, Article 22 of the *Statute* directs the competent authorities to draft rules governing the recognition of the diplomas for those Chinese nationals who have a permanent residency in Taiwan.[65] The MOE, upon the approval of Executive Yuan subsequently adopted the *Chinese Diplomas Regulation* on 24 October 1997.[66] Article 22 of the *Statute* and the *Chinese Diplomas Regulation* are mandatory in nature and the MOE does not enjoy discretionary power. The MOE was obliged to decide whether or to recognise the diplomas based solely upon the positive and passive conditions as set out in Article 7 and 9 of the regulation. The plaintiff had a subjective right under Article 22 of the *Statute* and the *Chinese Diplomas Regulation*. Based on this reasoning, the Court repealed the decision of administrative review and ordered the MOI to accept the plaintiff's application to examine and recognise her Chinese diploma.

During the appellate proceedings, the Supreme Administrative Court repealed the decision of the Taipei Higher Administrative Court and remanded the case to be redirected back to Taipei Higher Administrative Court.[67] According to the Supreme Administrative Court, the *Chinese Diploma Regulation* should be applicable to Chinese nationals residing in Taiwan. Since the applicant had already obtained her Taiwanese citizenship, it would thus questionable whether the *Chinese Diploma Regulation* could be applicable in this case.[68] In other words,

[62] Article 15 of the Constitution reads that 'the right to life, the right to work and the right of property shall be guaranteed to the people'.

[63] Taipei Higher Administrative Court, Su-Zhi No. 582 (2005).

[64] Ibid.

[65] Article 22 provides that 'for any of the people of the Taiwan Area or any of the people of the Mainland Area permitted to have a permanent residency in the Taiwan Area, rules governing its examination and the recognition of its education in the Mainland Area shall be drafted by the Ministry of Education and submitted to the Executive Yuan for approval'.

[66] Regardless of Article 22 of the *Statute*, and the *Chinese Diplomas Regulation*, the MOE openly and officially denies the possibility for this examination and recognition.

[67] Supreme Administrative Court, Pan-Zhi No. 602 (2008).

[68] Ibid.

the recognition of a Taiwanese national's diploma obtained in China is governed by other laws or regulations, rather than the *Chinese Diploma Regulation*. This holding linked back to the identity and legal status of a naturalised Chinese in Taiwan. While it is the Chinese diploma subject to discriminatory treatment, the discrimination is directed against a Taiwanese citizen.

This case resembles with the afore-mentioned restriction for naturalised Chinese to hold public offices. In fact, the plaintiff in this case argued that the MOE's refusal to recognise her diploma had infringed her constitutional rights to take public examinations and hold public offices. The decisions by this administrative court and the Constitutional Court are completely different in terms of the results and their approaches. In this case, both the *Statute* and the *Chinese Diplomas Regulation* can be the legal basis for the plaintiff's application. The MOE refuses the plaintiff's application upon policy grounds. Consequently, the court only has to ensure that the *Statute* and the *Chinese Diplomas Regulation* are being abided to. Since the *Statute* and the *Chinese Diplomas Regulation* oblige the MOE to decide whether or not to recognise the diploma concerned according to the criteria set out therein, the court thus had little difficulty in revoking the decision of the MOE and in ordering it to accept the plaintiff's application. As this case relates only to the recognition of Chinese diplomas, national security may not be a concern. In contrast, holding public offices could be, according to the legislature and endorsed by the Constitutional Court, related to national security. The public office case relates to the prohibitions within the *Statute*, where the legislature clearly expressed its evaluation and balance in the form of a congressional legislation. In particular, this congressional legislation is specially authorised by the Constitution. The Constitutional Court is thus in a more difficult position than the administrative court as the Constitutional Court has to balance between the individual right to hold public offices as enshrined in the Constitution and the congressional will which intentionally bars Chinese nationals, even after obtaining Taiwan nationality, from civil services.

In the Chinese diploma case, the plaintiff relied on human rights arguments whereas the MOE resorted to the policy arguments of political sensitivity. In contrast, the court ruled mainly upon principles of administrative law. Insofar as the diploma case is concerned, the Higher Administrative Court's decision has its merit. A narrow and shallow approach may be sufficient to resolve this present case. Nevertheless, in light of the policy arguments based on political concerns that the MOE greatly and emphatically relied upon during the proceedings, a different approach is needed in order to balance the MOE's political sensitivity arguments with the plaintiff's human rights arguments. The holding of the Supreme Administrative Court adds complexities to this issue. It points to the identity and legal status of a naturalised Chinese in Taiwan. Differential treatment based simply upon her prior Chinese nationality according to this approach is difficult to justify.

C. *Complementarities between WTO Rules and National Constitution*

It is essential to stress the constitutional significance of the WTO Agreement in Taiwan. Taiwan's accession to the WTO is not only of economic importance, but also of constitutional importance. The competence and capacity to carry out its WTO obligations and to normalise trade relations with China help to shape the internal and external constitutional identities of Taiwan. This thus clarifies the weight of the MOE's policy arguments based on national security, political sensitivity and public interests in the Chinese diploma case. The adherence to those policy arguments would prevent potential constitutionalisation of the relations between Taiwan and China and thus prevents a normalised constitutionalism. Taiwan's national constitution is interconnected with the national legal system and the WTO treaty constitution. Arguments based on WTO non-discrimination principles and national equal rights protection can complement each other in order to limit the abuse of public power. To propose a better approach to resolve issues in these two cases, one has to examine Taiwan's education services commitments and the legal status of WTO Agreement in Taiwan's domestic legal system.

While equal rights protection under the national constitution prevent unjustified discriminatory treatments towards Chinese spouses from other foreign spouses, the Most-Favoured-Nation Treatment under WTO law also prevents Taiwan from singling out Chinese education services and refusing to recognise its diplomas. In the context of this case, these two issues are extremely relevant in the recognition of Chinese diplomas.

In respect of Taiwan education services commitments (CPC, 9222, 9223, 9224, 923, 924 and 929), there is no limitation on the market access in cross-border supply and consumption.[69] Nevertheless, Article 23 of the *Statute* provides that the recruiting students or acting as an intermediary for any Chinese education institution may be permitted if the condition of obtaining approval from the competent authorities is met. The *Statute* then directs the MOE to draft a rule governing the permission procedures, which has so far yet to be issued. Criminal penalty can be imposed when failure to acquire the appropriate permissions.[70] As the market access of education services in higher education (CPC, 923) is being liberalised, restrictions on Taiwanese citizens barring studying in China or other incidental recruiting or intermediary activities cannot be justified.

The legality of Article 23 and 82 of the *Statute* which prohibit the recruitment for Chinese education institutions and criminalise the act cannot be sustained, even under the Taiwanese domestic legal system, since they are in conflict with the international agreement, namely, the WTO Agreement that enjoys higher

[69] WTO (n 31) 857.

[70] The *Statute*, Art. 83.

status on the legal hierarchy. One may be tempted to refer to Article 11 of the Amendment of the Constitution as a justification for the discriminatory treatment. Here, it is worthy of a closer look at the legal text again. It reads as followed:

> Rights and obligations between the people of the Chinese mainland area and those of the free area, and the disposition of other related affairs may be specified by law.

According to this provision, the Constitution merely delegates the power to the legislature to regulate the rights and obligations between Chinese people and Taiwanese people and other related affair. The drafters do not offer any hint on the shape and content of this regulatory regime. One may thus be tempted to conclude that the amendment provides a leeway for the legislature to outline this regulatory regime in a way that may not be subject to the rule of law and the principle of fundamental rights as enshrined in the Constitution. This position is nevertheless groundless. The constitutional amendment does not envisage a regulatory regime outside of the constitutional order. Neither does it endorse a *carte blanche* for the legislature. To be more precisely, the legal text says nothing about the deviation permitted for this regulatory regime from the existing constitutional framework. Consequently, the regulatory regime on cross-Taiwan-strait relations should be consistent with the constitutional guarantee on the rule of law and fundamental rights.

As dictated by the Constitution, Taiwan should respect of all treaties to which it is a party.[71] In other words, Taiwan should honour its international obligations as set out in the WTO Agreement. Taiwan's constitutional obligations under the WTO Agreement are not incompatible with Article 11 of the Constitutional Amendment since Article 11 does not intentionally derogate from Taiwan's international obligations. It does not oblige the legislature to regulate the cross-Taiwan-strait relations in a WTO-inconsistent way. On the contrary, legislature is under its constitutional obligation to respect treaties and to enact a WTO-consistent regulatory regime.

On the other hand, the constitutional guarantee on human rights also comes to the same conclusion. As enshrined in Article 15 and elaborated by various Constitutional Court interpretations, such as Judicial Yuan Interpretation No. 404, 411, 510 and 514, right to work as a fundamental right under constitutional protection may be subject to reasonable limitation. In determining whether a limitation is reasonable or not, the Constitutional Court has consistently referred to the concept of 'public interests'. In the criminal litigation cases, the main issue is whether a regulatory measure which runs contrary to the state's international obligation

---

[71] Taiwan's Constitution, Art. 141.

can be considered reasonable. In other words, does the Constitutional Court have to take into account of Taiwan's international obligation when deciding whether a regulatory measure is reasonable or not. This seems to be dependent on one's perception of constitutionalism as to how much policy space and scope of manoeuvre[72] should be left to political branches. The danger of policy space and scope of manoeuvre is that the political branches, in particular the executive branch, would be tempted to demand for larger policy space and to claim looser legislative oversight and judicial control but at the same time, to advance the same arguments based on the confidentiality and complex of foreign trade affairs domestically to achieve the greatest amount of freedom. The result of such tends to be a set of conflicting regulatory measures based solely on the discretion of the executive branch. This would also bring about the conflict, between international legal order and national order, and would undermine the legal certainty of the system and infringe on the reasonable expectation of individuals' rights and freedoms. Finally, this yields to an abuse of governmental powers.

The aforementioned position can also find its support from the positive law perspective. As clarified above, international agreements, including the WTO Agreement, enjoy a higher status on the legal hierarchy than national laws even if according to Taiwan's constitutional framework and the existing jurisprudence. Taking the stricter approach as adopted by the Supreme Administrative Court, Taiwan's WTO commitment relating to higher education services should be directly applicable in Taiwanese courts given its specific and unconditional nature. Therefore, Article 23 of the *Statute,* which imposes restrictions on Taiwanese citizens for the recruiting and acting as an intermediary for Chinese higher education institutions, infringes Taiwan's WTO obligation and should thus be disapplied. Its legality under Taiwan's domestic legal system cannot be upheld. Given the illegality of the Article 23 of the *Statute*, Article 82 of the same *Statute* which criminalises the act as referred to in Article 23, namely the recruiting or acting as an intermediate for Chinese higher education institutions without prior authorisation from the MOE, cannot be sustained. In other words, since the restrictions imposed by Article 23 is incompatible with Taiwan's commitment under the educational services schedule, its legality cannot be upheld both in accordance with the WTO law and with Taiwan's domestic legal framework. Article 82 of the *Statute,* by criminalising an act justifiable under Taiwan's international law obligations, is unconstitutional. The case law laid down by Taiwan Taipei District Court in 96-Yi-Zhi No. 1288 (2007) is therefore flawed.

---

[72] On this point, *see* the debates between Griller and Eeckhout, S Griller, 'Judicial Enforceability of WTO Agreement in European Union: Annotation to Case C-149/96 Portugal v. Council' (2000) 3 Journal of International Economic Law 441; P Eeckhout, 'The Judicial Enforcement of WTO Law in European Union: Some Further Reflections' (2002) 5 Journal of International Economic Law 91.

Regarding the Chinese diploma case, the pertinent issue relates to the mutual recognition as regulated by Article VII of the GATS. Paragraph 1 provides the possibility for a Member to recognise the 'education or experience obtained, requirements met, or licenses or certifications granted in a particular country' in considering whether the criteria or standards for the authorisation, licensing or certification of services suppliers are met. This recognition may be achieved either through harmonisation or based upon Mutual Recognition Arrangements (the MRAs).[73] In the absence of MRAs, a Member may also accord recognition autonomously on the condition that it provides an opportunity for any other Member to demonstrate to its 'education, experience, licenses, or certifications obtained or requirements met' to be recognised as well.[74] Further, this recognition should not be in a discriminatory manner.[75] In this present case, singling out education received in China and denying the recognition of is apparently incompatible with Article VII of GATS, in particular paragraph 3.

Lastly, it should also be pointed out that Taiwan's regulatory measures in relation to Chinese diplomas are also inconsistent with Article VI:1 which dictates a Member to administer all measures of general application affecting trade in services 'in a reasonable, objective and impartial manner.' While the WTO has not developed a detailed set of rules in relation to the recognition of education, fundamental non-discriminatory principles should be respected. The measure adopted by the MOE in this present case clear deviated from this requirement.

Lastly, with a shift in regulatory power to trans-national or even global level, domestic regulatory agencies are subject to the control of various global laws, rules and standards. A domestic regulatory measure affects not only national enterprises and individuals but also foreign enterprises and individuals. Taiwan's courts cannot isolate themselves from this trend. The jurisprudence of Taiwan's courts has not dealt with the conflicts between the national constitution and its international obligations. The importance of Article 11 of the Amendment to the Constitution should be carefully weighed. As argued above, since the WTO Treaty constitution and national constitution complement with each other, courts are under their constitutional obligation to ensure the compliance to these global norms. Taiwanese courts should refrain itself from readily referring to Article 11 of the Amendment of the Constitution and from relying on national security arguments.

---

[73] GATS, Art. VII:1.
[74] GATS, Art. VII:2.
[75] GATS, Art. VII:3.

V. Short Conclusion

The objective of this chapter is to propose a better approach for Taiwan's courts to deal with cases relating to cross-Taiwan-strait trade relations. It firstly examines the legal status of treaties and international agreements within Taiwan's national legal system. Based on this, it then explores the role of the WTO Agreement in Taiwan, focusing on the legal hierarchy, direct effects and relevant jurisprudence. While there are some arguments based on WTO law in the analysed cases, the courts do not clarify those issues. This chapter then investigates the regulatory regime on cross-Taiwan-strait trade relations, focusing on Article 11 of the Amendment to the Constitution, the *Statute Governing the Relationship between People in Taiwan Area and Mainland Area,* and other relevant administrative regulations. This chapter then examines a series of Constitutional Court cases relating to relations between Taiwan and China. It begins with the delimitation of national territory and the definition of 'treaty' as set out in Taiwan's Constitution and the nature of agreements signed between Taiwan and China. Then it deals with restriction on Chinese nationals who are married with Taiwanese citizens as they re-enter into Taiwan and on their right to hold public offices. Lastly, this chapter uses two related cases handed down by Taipei District Court and Taipei Higher Administrative Court to illustrate the strengths lent by WTO rules for Taiwanese courts to overcome the obstacle of Article 11 of the Amendment to the Constitution and the policy arguments heavily relied upon by the administrative agencies. It argues that Taiwanese courts should refrain from referring to Article 11 of the Amendment and national security arguments for the justification of WTO-incompatible discriminatory measures. On the contrary, they are under their constitutional obligation to ensure both the WTO Treaty constitution and national constitutional are respected. In so doing, judicial governance in trade relations with China can thus not only contribute to Taiwan's faith in the implementation of international obligations under the WTO Treaty constitution, but also guarantee the rights and freedoms, such as right to work, freedom of profession and equal rights protection as enshrined in Taiwan's constitution.

CHAPTER SEVEN

TRADE DISPUTE RESOLUTION BETWEEN CHINA AND TAIWAN: AN INDIRECT APPROACH THROUGH THIRD PARTY PARTICIPATION

I. Introduction

This chapter examines the resolution of trade disputes between Taiwan and China on three platforms: the WTO Dispute Settlement Mechanism; dispute resolution mechanisms as contained within bilateral agreements, notably the Economic Cooperation Framework Agreement (the ECFA); and domestic trade regulatory regimes. So far, Taiwan and China have no directly complained against each other under the WTO Dispute Settlement Mechanism. Nevertheless, this does not suggest there is an absence of interaction between Taiwan and China at this multilateral forum. Both China and Taiwan actively intervene as third parties in the WTO Dispute Settlement Mechanism. Their positions in these complaints they intervene may converge or diverge. They may take the same position; they may well argue with each other. Taiwan has intervened as a third party participant in those complaints brought against/by China; China has also participated as a third party in the complaint brought by Taiwan. One may thus explore the interaction between Taiwan and China in the WTO Dispute Settlement Mechanism through this indirect approach.

In addition to the multilateral framework, since the Ma administration in 2008, Taiwan and China has concluded a number of bilateral agreements. The dispute settlement mechanism provided therein is also worth exploring even though that regulatory framework is rather primitive. In addition to multilateral and bilateral forum, both Taiwan and China have adopted several trade defence measures against each other. The legality of these trade defence measures may be challenged in domestic courts.

This chapter is organised as followed: following this introductory section, Section II will examine the interaction between China and Taiwan in the WTO Dispute Settlement Mechanism. As there is no direct complaint against each other, the analysis will focus on their interactions through the lens of third party intervention. This section begins with a survey of the existing WTO law and practices in relation to third party participation in the WTO Dispute Settlement Mechanism. Then it examines Taiwan's third party participation in complaints brought against/by China and China's third party participation in complaint brought by Taiwan. This section will end with an overall evaluation of their interactions within the WTO Dispute Settlement Mechanism.

Section III will examine those dispute settlement mechanisms as contained within bilateral agreements signed between Taiwan and China; these agreements range from agreements such as the ones permitting direct-transportation across-Taiwan-Strait to the ECFA. Section IV will deal with trade disputes at the domestic level focusing on several trade defence measures. In response to a series of safeguard measures on steel products in 2002, China imposed safeguard and anti-dumping measures against Taiwanese steel products. By contrast, Taiwan initiated anti-dumping and special safeguard investigation against Chinese towelling products. These measures will be examined in detail with a view to illustrate trade disputes in domestic level. Section V then ends with a short conclusion of this chapter.

II. Interaction between China and Taiwan within the WTO Dispute Settle Mechanism

This section will start with an analysis of the WTO law and practices on third party participation under its WTO Dispute Settlement Mechanism. After clarifying the objective of third party participation in the WTO Dispute Settlement Mechanism, the section will go on examining third party rights during the WTO panel/ Appellate Body proceedings. It will also touch upon the issue of 'enhanced third party rights'. With an introduction of general law and practice on third party participation, this section will then examine Taiwan's third party participation in complaints brought about by/against China and China's third party participation in the complaint brought about by Taiwan.

As of 1 September 2011, twelve WTO complaints have been brought against China. Three cases were settled by mutually satisfactory agreements during the consultation processes and there were thus no need for request for the establishment of a panel. These three cases are *China – Value-Added Tax on Integrated Circuits*[1](the first complaint), *China – Measures Affecting Financial Information Services and Foreign Financial Information Suppliers*[2] and *China – Measures concerning Wind Power Equipment*[3] (the latest complaint). Among these three settled complaints, Taiwan intervened in the first complaint through a joint-consultation

[1] WTO, *China—Value-Added Tax on Integrated Circuit s*(*China – Integrated Circuits*), request for consultation by the US (23 March 2004) WT/DS309/1.

[2] WTO, *China—Measures Affecting Financial Information Services and Foreign Financial Information Suppliers (China – Financial Information Service), request for consultations by the EC, the US and Canada* (5 March 2008) WT/DS372/1; (5 March 2008) WT/DS373/1; (23 June 2008) WT/DS378/1.

[3] WTO, *China—Measures concerning Wind Power Equipment* (*China – Wind Power Equipment*), *request for consultation by the EU* (6 January 2011) WT/DS419/1.

request, which was eventually not accepted by China. Given that whether to accept the joint-consultation request or not depends solely on the attitude of the responding Member and no remedy is offered; in the subsequent complaints, Taiwan thus shifted its approach by participating in the WTO panel/Appellate Body proceeding through the third party participation apparatus, since Taiwan can simply reserves its rights or notify the Secretariat of its intent to participate as a third party without being subject to the consent of China.

Two cases are still in the consultation phase and the request for the establishment of a panel has not yet made. These two cases are *China – Grants, Loans, and Other Incentives*[4] and *China – Provisional Anti-Dumping Duties on Certain Iron and Steel Fasteners from the European Union.*[5]

The remaining seven cases have gone through the panel/Appellate Body proceedings and are now at different stages of the procedures. Among these seven cases, one case was eventually settled at the panel proceedings. Up to date, six complaints have gone through the panel proceedings. Among these seven cases coming into the panel/Appellate Body proceedings, the Dispute Settlement Body (the DSB) has just established a panel for *China – Countervailing and Anti-Dumping Duties on Grain Oriented Flat-rolled Electrical Steel from the United States* (*China - GOES*)[6] and another one for *China – Measures Affecting Electronic Payment Services* (*China – Electronic Payment Services*).[7] Since the two panels have recently been established, whether Taiwan would follow its practice to participate as a third party remains to be seen.

Taiwan has reserved its third party rights and anticipated in the panel proceedings of the other cases with different degrees of intensity: *China—Measures Affecting Imports of Automobile Parts* (*China – Auto Parts*)[8]; *China – Certain Measures Granting Refunds, Reductions or Exemptions from Taxes and Other Payments* (*China – Taxes*);[9] *China – Measures Affecting the Protection and Enforcement of*

[4] WTO, *China – Grants, Loans and Other Incentives, request for consultation by the US, Mexico and Guatemala* (7 January 2009) WT/DS387/1; (8 January 2009) WT/DS388/1; (22 January 2009) WT/DS390/1.

[5] WTO, *China – Provisional Anti-Dumping Duties on Certain Iron and Steel Fasteners from the European Union* (12 May 2010) WT/DS407/1.

[6] WTO, *China – Countervailing and Anti-Dumping Duties on Grain Oriented Flat-rolled Electrical Steel from the United States* (*China – GOES*), *request for consultation by the US* (20 September 2010) WT/DS414/1.

[7] WTO, *China – Certain Measures Affecting Electronic Payment Services* (*China – Electronic Payment Services*), *request for consultation by the US* (20 September 2010) WT/DS413/1.

[8] Panel Reports, *China – Measures Affecting Imports of Automobile Parts* (*China – Auto Parts*), WT/DS339/R, WT/DS340/R, WT/DS342/R and Add.1 and Add.2, adopted 12 January 2009, as upheld (WT/DS339/R) and as modified (WT/DS340/R, WT/DS342/R) by Appellate Body Reports WT/DS339/AB/R, WT/DS340/AB/R, WT/DS342/AB/R.

[9] WTO, *China—Certain Measures Granting Refunds, Reductions or Exemptions from Taxes and Other Payments* (*China – Taxes*), *request for consultation by the US and Mexico* (7 February 2007)

Intellectual Property Rights (*China – Intellectual Property Rights*);[10] *China – Measures Affecting Trading Rights and Distribution Services for Certain Publications and Audiovisual Entertainment Products* (*China – Trading Rights and Distribution Services*);[11] and *China – Measures Related to the Exportation of Various Raw Materials* (*China – Raw Materials Export*).[12]

Regarding Taiwan, it has filed three complaints against the United States (the US), India and the European Union (the EU) but only one of which has gone through to the panel proceedings: the *EC – IT Products* case. In that complaint, China also participated as a third party and stood in line with Taiwan.

In view of the development in the WTO Dispute Settlement Mechanism, this section, after a general introduction of WTO law and practice on third party participation, this section will firstly examine Taiwan's third party participation in complaints brought about against/by China, and then China's third party participation in the *EC – IT Products* brought about by Taiwan.

A. *WTO Law and Practices on Third Party Intervention*

1. *The Objectives of Third Party Intervention*

The WTO being a multilateral trading system by nature provides opportunities for Members other than parties to the dispute to participate in the dispute settlement proceedings. Members' third party participation in the proceedings helps to 'multilateralise' the dispute. Third party participation is aimed to ensure that rights and interests of the other Members not parties to the dispute under the covered agreements are not prejudiced. This is particularly true when parties to the dispute have reached mutually satisfactory agreements. Third party participation may also contribute to due process in the WTO panel/Appellate proceedings, as it offers an opportunity for a Member other than parties to the dispute to submit a third party submission, to receive the first submission of parties and to make an oral statement in the first substantial meeting. Members' third party participation

---

WT/DS358/1; (28 February 2007) WT/DS359/1. A mutual agreement was reached between China and the complaining Members during the panel proceedings. WTO, *China - Certain Measures Granting Refunds, Reductions or Exemptions from Taxes and Other Payments - Request for the Establishment of a Panel by the United States* (13 July 2007) WT/DS358/13; WTO, *China - Certain Measures Granting Refunds, Reductions or Exemptions from Taxes and Other Payments - Notification of Mutually Agreed Solution* (13 February 2008) WT/DS359/14.

[10] Panel Report, *China – Measures Affecting the Protection and Enforcement of Intellectual Property Rights* (*China – Intellectual Property Rights*), WT/DS362/R, adopted 20 March 2009.

[11] Panel Report, *China – Measures Affecting Trading Rights and Distribution Services for Certain Publications and Audiovisual Entertainment Products*, WT/DS363/R and Corr.1, adopted 19 January 2010, as modified by Appellate Body Report WT/DS363/AB/R.

[12] WTO, *China – Measures Related to the Exportation of Various Raw Materials* (*China – Raw Materials Export*) WT/DS394/R, WT/DS395R, WT/DS398R (on appeal).

also helps the WTO panel/Appellate Body to reach better-informed decisions, after considering perspectives different from those of the complaining and responding Members.[13] Third party participation may also help to prevent potential violation, to enhance the security and predictability of this world trading system, and to contribute to its transparency.[14]

Members may also take advantage of the third party participation scheme as a means of surveillance and exert pressure to the parties to the dispute not to settle the case in a manner that is incompatible with WTO rules, and can thus ensure that their rights and interests under the WTO Agreement. As Busch and Reinhardt observe, with the participation of third parties, the parties to a dispute tend to litigate the cases until the final ruling of the WTO panel/Appellate Body is made available.[15] Third party participation is an also important designation to widen the participation of its Members, given most developing country Members and least developed country Members usually experience a lack of capacity and resource. Due to limited capacity and resources, third party participation may be a good alternative for developing countries to shield their interests in the WTO Dispute Settlement Mechanism. In addition, it be used to training the officials of developing countries or newly-acceded Members and may be viewed as a capacity building mechanism for these developing countries.[16]

In light of these, third party participation is of 'systemic' value to the WTO Dispute Settlement Mechanism, benefitting both the WTO system and its Members. With the participation of third parties, the WTO dispute settlement mechanism can strengthen its transparency and due process, widen its scope of participation of the Members and reach better informed decisions.

2. *WTO Law and Practices in Relation to Rights and Obligations of Third Party Participation*

Two legal instruments govern the framework of third party intervention in the WTO panel/Appellate Body proceedings: the Understanding on Rules and Procedures Governing the Settlement of Disputes (the DSU) and the Appellate Body's

---

[13] N Covelli, 'Member Intervention in World Trade Organization Dispute Settlement Proceedings After EC-Sardines: The Rules, Jurisprudence, and Controversy' (2003) 37 Journal of World Trade 673, 673.

[14] N H Yenkong, 'Third Party Rights and the Concept of Legal Interest in World Trade Organization Dispute Settlement: Extending Participatory Rights to Enforcement Rights' (2004) 38 Journal of World Trade 757, 761.

[15] M L Busch and E Reinhardt, 'Three's a Crowd: Third Party and WTO Dispute Settlement' (2006) 58 World Politics 446, 448.

[16] *See, e.g.*, F Pierola, 'Third-party Participation in WTO Dispute Settlement Proceedings for Training Purposes' (2007) 2 Global Trade and Customs Journal 367, 367-368.

Working Procedures for Appellate Review (the Working Procedures).[17] Prior to the panel proceedings stage, third party participation during the consultation phase is possible through the request for joint-consultation should the Members have 'substantial trade interests' in this matter.[18] In order to join the consultations, a third party needs to notify its intent within ten days from the date the request for consultations is circulated. The acceptance of this joint-consultation request depends solely on whether 'the Member to which the request for consultations was addressed' agree that the third party has substantial trade interests. While a third party is refused to be joined in the consultation can initiate its own consultation, no remedy is provided under the DSU.[19]

At the panel stage, third parties are entitled to receive the parties to the disputes' first submissions, to make their written submissions, and to be heard at the first substantial panel meeting.[20] They may also comment on the disputing parties' first submissions and on the questions addressed to them at this first substantive session.[21] However, third parties are not able to participate in the subsequent sessions.

As for proceedings before an Appellate Body, the Working Procedures allow three categories of third party participants to participate in the proceedings. The major distinctions are whether those Members file a written submission or notify the Secretariat of their intent to appear at the oral hearing within 21 days of the date on the notice of appeal and whether they aim to influence the result of the appellate proceedings. The first category is a Member which wishes to 'actively' influence the result of the appellate review. It has to file a written submission with grounds and legal arguments to support its position within the time constraint. It may also make an oral statement and/or respond the questions addressed to them.

The second category is a Member which notifies the Secretariat of its intent to 'passively' appear at the oral hearing.[22] A 'passive' third party is free to decide whether it wishes to make an oral statement or not. The third category relates to Member which does not file a written submission or notify the Secretariat of its intent to participate as a third party, but nonetheless wishes to appear at the oral hearing. In accordance with the discretionary power of the Appellate Body, this third category of third parties may be offered an opportunity to make an oral statement or to respond questions. Importantly the exercise of this discretion

[17] WTO, *Appellate Body - Working Procedures for Appellate Review* (hereinafter the Working Procedure) (16 August 2010) WT/AB/WP/6.

[18] DSU, Art. 4.11.

[19] G Marceau, 'Consultations and the Panel Process in the WTO Dispute Settlement System' in R Yerxa and B Wilson (eds), *Key Issues in WTO Dispute Settlement: The First Ten Years* (Cambridge University Press, Cambridge 2005) 31-32.

[20] DSU, Art. 10.2-3.

[21] DSU, Appendix 3.6, 3.8.

[22] Working Procedures, Art. 24.2.

should take into due account of the 'due process' requirement.[23] Since a Member may always make a request to intervene as a third party, in light of this, the 21 days' time constraint appears to be unnecessary.[24] It may overcomplicate the appellate review process and cause unnecessary delay for proceedings before the Appellate Body.

While third parties are encouraged to make a written submission to facilitate the appellate proceedings, this is not obligatory.[25] In respect of written response during the appellate proceedings, whenever the Appellate Body addresses to participants of the case or requests for memoranda, the response or requested memoranda should be made available to third parties. The third parties should also be offered an opportunity to comment on the response and the requested memoranda.[26]

3. *Legal Effect of Panel/Appellate Body Decisions on Third Parties*

The procedural rights relating to third party may suffice for a Member which simply wishes to present their views before the panel and intends only to influence the panel decisions without being bound by them. Even though the panel is obliged to take due account of the 'interests of parties to the dispute and those of other Members under a covered agreement',[27] for a Member with pressing interests at stake, these procedural rights are nonetheless inadequate.[28] In addition, as Yenkong rightly points out, the more fundamental issue in ascertaining the sufficiency of third rights relate to whether third parties can obtain a particular remedy when the panel finds the disputed measures to be WTO-inconsistent, or whether third parties can influence the implementation of the rulings and recommendations handed by the WTO Dispute Settlement Body (the DSB).[29]

With regard to the remedy, a good starting point is still the distinction between the parties to the dispute and third parties. As the Panel in *US – 1916 Act* rightly pointed out, this distinction is an underlying principle in the DSU and the line should not be blurred. It is also clearly set out that the possibility of compensation and suspension of concessions provided under the DSU is reserved only for the complaints of which the benefits under the covered agreement are directly or indirectly nullified or impaired. As *res judicata* is only limited to the parties to

---

[23] Working Procedures, Art. 27.3(c).

[24] For criticism of this lenient rule, and admittance of this third category of third participants being left to the discretion of the Appellate Body, *see, e.g.*, Covelli (n 13) 680-686.

[25] Working Procedures, Art. 24.3.

[26] Working Procedures, Art. 28.

[27] DSU, Art. 10.1.

[28] Covelli (n 13) 675.

[29] Yenkong (n 14) 763.

the dispute, it is not binding on third parties. Therefore, 'remedy' in the form of compensation and suspension of concessions is not, and should not be made available to third parties. However, with the removal or elimination of WTO-incompatibilities, third parties share the benefit of WTO compliance. This reflects the spirit enshrined in the DSU that reads: 'neither compensation nor the suspension of concessions or other obligations is preferred to full implementation of a recommendation to bring a measure into conformity with the covered agreements.'[30]

This also points to the importance of a correct reading of the relationship between complying with the WTO panel/Appellate Body ruling and suspending concessions and mutually agreed compensation. As Griller argues, the obligation to comply with the WTO panel/Appellate Body reports is unconditional, and compensation is not an 'alternative to compliance, but a temporary measure available",[31] when recommendations and rulings are not duly enforced. Comparing relevant provisions of the DSU in a systemic manner – namely, condition of compensation, prompt compliance, preference to full implementations, and surveillance of the implementations of recommendations and rulings – Griller further argues that 'the binding force of the panel and Appellate Body reports is unconditional, and there is no authorisation to depart from such findings, even on a temporary basis'.[32]

This view is supported by the Arbitrators in *EC – Bananas III* (*US*) (*Article 22.6 – EC*). The Arbitrators, after referring Article 22.1 of the DSU, decided that 'the authorisation to suspend concessions or other obligations [was] a temporary measure pending full implementation by the Member concerned,' and that 'this *temporary* nature [indicated] that it [was] the purpose of countermeasures to *induce compliance*'.[33] This illustrates the preference of WTO compliance to compensation. It also clarifies the importance of ensuring compliance with the WTO panel/Appellate Body ruling, in particular from the perspectives of third parties. In order to ensure full compliance with the WTO panel/Appellate Body ruling, third party participation in both the Compliance Panel and the Arbitration Panel enjoys equal significance. Third party participation would help to ensure that the authorised countermeasures will not deviate from the WTO rules and that the mutually-satisfactory agreement, if any, stays WTO-consistent.

---

[30] DSU, Art. 22.1.

[31] S Griller, 'Judicial Enforceability of WTO Agreement in European Union: Annotation to Case C-149/96 *Portugal v. Council*' (2000) 3 Journal of International Economic Law 441, 451.

[32] Ibid.

[33] Decision by the Arbitrators on WTO, *European Communities – Regime for the Importation, Sale and Distribution of Bananas – Recourse to Arbitration by the European Communities under Article 22.6 of the DSU – (EC – Bananas III (US) (Article 22.6 – EC))* (9 April 1999) WT/DS27/ARB, para. 6.3 (emphasis original).

B. *Taiwan's Third Party Participation in Complaints Brought about by/against China*

The above subsection examines the objectives to include third party participation in WTO law and practice. It covers different phases of the WTO Dispute Settlement Mechanism, ranging from the joint-consultation to the panel/Appellate Body proceedings. It clarifies what third party participatory rights that Members like Taiwan may enjoy if they intervene as a third party. Following the noted generalisations, this subsection examines Taiwan's third party participation in complaints brought about by/against China. Taiwan has intervened as a third party in all complaints brought about against China. This subsection explores and ascertains whether Taiwan's position is in line with China. Varying in the depth of participation, Taiwan has participated as a passive observer, as an active third party participant and as a third party participant with enhanced third party rights.

Among those complaints brought about by/against China that have entered into the panel proceeding stage, Taiwan has acted as a passive observer in five cases: *US – Anti-Dumping and Countervailing Duties*, *US – Tyres*, *China – Auto Parts* and *China – Trading Rights and Distribution Services,* and *China – Raw Materials Export*. For the other cases, Taiwan has intervened as an active third party by making either written submissions or oral statements or both. In *US – Poultry*, Taiwan even sought for enhanced third party rights, albeit without success, by alluding to the European Union's request for enhanced third party rights.

1. *Taiwan's Third Party Participation in The Complaint Brought by China*

a. *US – Steel Safeguards*

On 20 March 2002, the US imposed definite safeguard measures on certain steel products from various origins including China and Taiwan and this initiative led to other WTO Members setting similar safeguard measures against similar steel products. On 19 November 2002, China adopted safeguard measures against Taiwanese steel products. China, among others Members, referred these safeguard measures to the WTO Dispute Settlement Mechanism and a single panel was established to examine the WTO consistency of the steel safeguard measures adopted by the US. At the same time, Taiwan, relying on Article 4 of the DSU, requested for consultations with the US and intervened as a third party in the complaint against the US brought by China.

In this dispute, China structured its complaint mainly on the following claims: unforeseen developments, the definition of 'domestic industry', increased imports, serious injury or threat of serious injury, causation and parallelism. As a third party participant, Taiwan argued against the WTO-inconsistency of the US safeguard measures and touched upon similar issues: unforeseen developments, the definition of 'domestic industry', serious injury, and causation. The Panel exercised judicial economy and examined only on the requirements of unforeseen development, increased imports, causation and parallelism. Since China, Taiwan and the Panel all chose to review the notion of unforeseen developments and causation, these concepts will be explored in depth in the following subsections with a view to ascertaining whether and how China and Taiwan might have 'cooperated' in this complaint against the US.

i. *'Unforeseen Developments'*. Regarding 'unforeseen developments', China argued that because the Second Supplementary Report (the SSR) by the International Trade Commission of the US (the USITC) was released after the decision to impose safeguard measures was made, it could not constitute as a basis for the justification of the existence of 'unforeseen developments'. Even if the Supplementary Report might be taken into consideration for the justification, China claimed that it failed to provide a reasoned and adequate explanation of the taking place of 'unforeseen developments'.[34] According to China, while the legal standard for determining what constitutes an unforeseen development is relatively subjective, the unexpectedness of a development is something that can be demonstrated.[35] Consequently, the USITC has to demonstrate in its report this unexpectedness in an adequate and reasoned manner.

China rejected the US' claim that the Asian and Russian financial crises, the continued strength of the US market and the appreciation of US currency could be constituted as 'unforeseen developments'. China argued that Asian and Russian financial crises were macroeconomic events that only affected domestic industries and a direct relationship between these events and an increase in steel importation did not exist.[36] Moreover, fundamental economic principle sets out that the currency of a country with a robust economy and low inflation will appreciate against other currencies. In view of the strong economy and low inflation of the US during the 1990s, it is thus groundless to claim the strong US currency could be unexpected.[37]

China argued that the phrase 'as a result of' as set out in Article XIX:1(a) of GATT 1994 indicated that there should be a 'causal link' between the 'unforeseen developments' and the 'increased imports' which allegedly caused or threatened to cause serious injury to the domestic industry.[38] Particularly, those conditions for

---

[34] Panel Reports, United States – Definitive Safeguard Measures on Imports of Certain Steel Products (US - Steel Safeguards), WT/DS248/R, WT/DS249/R, WT/DS251/R, WT/DS252/R, WT/DS253/R, WT/DS254/R, WT/DS258/R, WT/DS259/R, and Corr.1, adopted 10 December 2003, modified by Appellate Body Report, WT/DS248/AB/R, WT/DS249/AB/R, WT/DS251/AB/R, WT/DS252/AB/R, WT/DS253/AB/R, WT/DS254/AB/R, WT/DS258/AB/R, WT/DS259/AB/R, DSR 2003:VIII, 3273 paras. 7.96, 153, 155.

[35] Panel Reports, *US – Steel Safeguards*, para. 7.101.

[36] Panel Reports, *US – Steel Safeguards*, paras. 7.116, 183.

[37] Panel Reports, *US – Steel Safeguards*, para. 7.112.

[38] Panel Reports, *US – Steel Safeguards*, para. 7.118.

the impositions of safeguard measures should be situated in a 'logical continuum'. This logical continuum begins with a tariff concession and/or the acceptance of a WTO obligation that is followed by the 'unforeseen developments' giving rise to 'such increased imports'. The result of 'such increased imports' brought about by such 'unforeseen developments' should also satisfy with those conditions set out for in Article XIX of the GATT 1994 and Article 2.1 of the Agreement on Safeguards (the ASG). The increased imports then in turn caused the 'serious injury' as defined in Article 4.1(a) of the ASG.[39] A separate 'logical continuum' should exist for each of the products that were subject to safeguard measures.[40]

In respect of 'unforeseen developments', Taiwan argued that the requirements set out in Article XIX:1(a) of the GATT 1994 should be read together with the three conditions laid down by Article 2.1 of the ASG: 'increased imports', 'serious injury or threat of serious injury' and 'causation'. The logical connection as dictated by Article XIX:1(a) of the GATT 1994 could be established only when all of the requirements and conditions were duly met. Emphasis had been placed on establishing that the increased imports had caused serious injury or threatened to cause serious injury to the domestic industry and such should be a result of the unforeseen developments. The logical connection would also apply to the acceptance of the WTO obligations, which include tariff concessions incurred by the US under the GATT 1994. Taiwan claimed that the logical connection dictated by Article XIX:1(a) of the GATT 1994 should not be reduced to a 'sequential relationship' as asserted by the US. Taiwan further argued that macroeconomic factor should not be regarded as a potential unforeseen development. In particular, Taiwan asserted that, the Russian financial crisis cannot be qualified as an unforeseen development, since at the time point for the determination of a development unforeseen or not, namely, the conclusion of the Uruguay Round in 1994, Russian exports into the US were much higher.[41]

The Panel recognised the Asian and Russian crises as unforeseen developments[42] and admitted SSR as a basis to justify the imposition of the safeguard measures, as the SSR was issued before the actual imposition, though after the decision for the imposition, of the safeguard measures.[43] The Panel nevertheless found that, even when reading all the reports issued by the USITC together, there was no adequate and reasoned explanation for establishing 'unforeseen developments.' The Panel held that although the legal standard for determining unforeseen development is subjective, this subjectivity does not discharge the

39 Panel Reports, *US – Steel Safeguards*, para. 7.121.
40 Panel Reports, *US – Steel Safeguards*, para. 7.122.
41 Panel Reports, *US – Steel Safeguards*, para. 8.12.
42 Panel Reports, *US – Steel Safeguards*, paras. 10.68-101.
43 Panel Reports, *US – Steel Safeguards*, paras. 10.47-58.

obligation for an importing Member to demonstrate the unexpectedness of a development in a reasoned and adequate explanation. Besides, the unexpectedness of each product subject to safeguard measures should be demonstrated independently, and should be duly reflected in the competent authority's published reports.[44] The Panel first referred to the holding by the Appellate Body stating that the phrase 'as a result of' in Article XIX:1(a) of GATT 1994 as a logical connection that exists between the first two clauses of that Article.[45] The Panel then opined that

> 'a logical connection must be demonstrated to have existed between the elements of the first clause of Article XIX:1(a) – 'as a result of unforeseen developments and of the effect of the obligations incurred by a Member under this Agreement, including tariff concessions' – and the conditions set forth in the second clause of that Article – 'increased imports causing serious injury' – for the imposition of a safeguard measure'.

According to this holding, a logical connection must be demonstrated 'as a result of unforeseen developments and of the effect of the obligations incurred by a Member' under the WTO Agreement and the 'increased imports causing serious injury'. Based on this criterion, the Panel then continued to examine those reports issued by the USITC. It found that the initial report of the USITC did not address the issue of 'unforeseen developments' *per se* and that, while the SSR refers to the Asian and Russian Crises as unforeseen developments, the logical connection between these crises and specified increased steel imported products has not been established.[46] In view of these findings, the Panel therefore found against the US on its claim of 'unforeseen developments'.

In relation to 'unforeseen developments', one may say that Taiwan argued concurrently with China against the US. Firstly, both Taiwan and China argued that Article 2.1 of the ASG set out the requirement of 'unforeseen developments' should not be read in isolation from other conditions. They both emphasised a form of 'causal link' between the unforeseen developments and the increased imports should be demonstrated in the USITC reports: Taiwan employed the term 'logical connection' while China used 'logical continuum'. The requirement of 'unforeseen developments' could not be met by a mere reference to a macroeconomic event, such as Asian and Russian financial crises. A specific link between the unforeseen development and a particular sector of domestic industries should be delineated. Based on this, they rejected the Russian crisis as an unforeseen development upon which the USITC could rely, since a direct relationship between the Russian crisis

[44] Panel Reports, *US – Steel Safeguards*, paras. 10.41-45.
[45] Panel Reports, *US – Steel Safeguards*, para. 10.104.
[46] Panel Reports, *US – Steel Safeguards*, paras. 10.117-126.

and an increase in steel imports had not been demonstrated in the USITC report. While the Panel accepted the Asian and Russian crises as unforeseen developments, it nevertheless agreed mostly with China and Taiwan on the relationship between the requirement of 'unforeseen developments' and the three conditions set out in Article 2.1 of the ASG.

ii. *'Causation'.* Regarding the causation issue, China referred to the Appellate Body jurisprudence in *United States – Definitive Safeguard Measures on Imports of Wheat Gluten from the European Communities* (*US – Wheat Gluten*)[47] where the causal link between increased imports and serious injury was defined as 'a genuine and substantial relationship of cause and effect'. Based on this interpretation, China argued that the competent authority should, upon the first opportunity, establish the coincidence between increased imports and serious injury, and then conduct the non-attribution 'explicitly and expressly through a reasoned, clear, unambiguous and straightforward explanation'.[48] When such a relationship could not be established, the competent authority should justify the existence of a causal link with a compelling analysis. Explanation on the existence of causal link should always be provided.[49] When addressing the requirement of non-attribution, China argued that the competent authority should separate and distinguish the injurious effects caused by the increased imports from those caused by other factors. Only when those injurious effects caused by other factors were determined could a causal link between the increased imports and serious injury be truly established, since by non-attribution, the injury caused by increased imports to a domestic injury had to be clarified.[50] Relying upon the jurisprudence of the Appellate Body, China further argued that whether the relationship of cause and effect between increased imports and serious injury was genuine and substantial should be determined by the injurious effects caused by the increased imports in relation to the 'interplay', namely the collective weight of all other factors instead of each single other factor.[51]

In respect of causation, Taiwan referred to Article 4.2(b) of the ASG, which highlighted of two requirements: the existence of a causal link and non-attribution. According to Taiwan, the US needed to establish a causal link between increased imports and serious injury, and from which to exclude the

[47] Appellate Body Report, *United States – Definitive Safeguard Measures on Imports of Wheat Gluten from the European Communities*, WT/DS166/AB/R, adopted 19 January 2001, DSR 2001:II, 717.

[48] Panel Reports, *US – Steel Safeguards*, para. 7.832

[49] Panel Reports, *US – Steel Safeguards*, para. 7.925.

[50] Panel Reports, *US – Steel Safeguards*, paras. 7.975,1039.

[51] Panel Reports, *US – Steel Safeguards*, paras. 7.1051-1056, *see* also paras. 7.1050-7.1058, esp. para. 7.1053.

injury caused by other factors. Thus the 'substantial cause' test adopted by the US in the alleged measures was WTO-incompatible since the US could not establish a causal link as dictated by Article 4.2(b) of the ASG. According to Taiwan, while the relationship between the cause and effect of increased imports as compared to one single other factor may be substantial, it is not when the increased imports are compared to other factors as a whole. Taiwan also emphasised that the US had failed to separate and distinguish other factors causing injury to its domestic industry and thus had violated its obligation under the ASG.[52]

In response to the arguments put forward by China and Taiwan, the Panel referred to *US – Wheat Gluten* as the starting point of its jurisprudence, and the Appellate Body of that case concluded that the 'causal link' effectively requires a 'genuine and substantial relationship between cause and effect'. The Panel nevertheless declared that this holding by the Appellate Body offered little help. The Panel then stated that three elements have to be clarified when determining the existence of a causal link: (a) the standard or threshold to determine the existence of a genuine and substantial relationship between cause and effect; (b) the way in which a causal link can be established; and (c) how non-attribution is to be performed and its relation with the overall demonstration of the causal link.[53]

Relying on *US – Wheat Gluten,* the Panel concluded that the establishment of the 'causal link' as set out in Article 4.2(b) of the ASG does not necessarily prevent other factors from contributing to the injury of a domestic industry. To support its findings, the Panel also referred to *United States – Safeguard Measures on Imports of Fresh, Chilled or Frozen Lamb Meat from New Zealand and Australia* (*US – Lamp*) where the Appellate Body reiterated that the ASG does not require the increased imports alone to be capable of causing, or threatening to cause, serious injury.[54] While the Panel rejected China and Taiwan's arguments that the factors other than increased imports should not be taken into account when establishing a casual link, it nevertheless agreed with their views that the competent authorities should identify, distinguish and assess the other injurious factors. The Panel also accepted their view that increased imports, as opposed to the collective weight of injurious effects caused by the factors other than increased imports should establish a genuine and substantial relationship to the serious injury.[55]

According to the Panel, although the 'substantial cause test' does not violate the obligation under Article 4.2(b) of the ASG in itself, the competent authorities would have to explicitly establish that 'the effect of the other factors on the

[52] Panel Reports, *US – Steel Safeguards*, para. 8.14.
[53] Panel Reports, *US – Steel Safeguards*, para. 10.287
[54] Panel Reports, *US – Steel Safeguards*, paras. 10.288-290.
[55] Panel Reports, *US – Steel Safeguards*, para. 10.332.

situation of the domestic industry had not been attributed to the increased imports'.[56] This should be supported by a 'reasoned and adequate explanation'. The Panel further noted that since the purpose of the non-attribution is to identify, distinguish and assess the other injurious factors, the exercise of non-attribution calls for an overall assessment of those other factors. As the Panel put it, 'Article 4.2(b) is not concerned with the relative importance of individual factors as between themselves or as compared with increased imports'.[57] Rather, Article 2 and 4 of the ASG are concerned with the injurious effects of the increased imports as distinct from the injurious effect of *all* other factors.[58] The Panel then applied this approach to those products subject to the safeguard measures and found that most of the measures were inconsistent with Article 4.2(b), as the US failed to identify, separate, distinguish and assess the nature and extent of the injurious effects of the other factors so that these injurious effects could not have attributed to the increased imports. In addition, the US failed to provide a reasoned and adequate explanation on the existence of a 'causal link' between increased imports and serious injury and the effect of such on its relevant domestic producers.[59]

Regarding the issue of causation, Taiwan took a similar position as China did on the major points, even referring to almost the same authorities. In finding a causal link between increased imports and serious injury to a domestic industry, they identified two requirements as set out in Article 4.2(b) of the ASG: the establishment of a causal link and non-attribution. They emphasised on the importance of non-attribution and maintained that the injurious factors, other than increased imports, should be identified, distinguished and assessed. According to them, when performing a non-attribution analysis, what is at stake is the collective weight of all other factors, instead of an individual factor. Whether a genuine and substantial relationship between cause and effect can be established depends on the injurious effects caused by increased imports in relation to those caused by all other factors as a whole. This collective weight argument took prime importance in the Panel's finding on causation.

b. *EC – Fasteners*

The *EC – Fasteners* dispute involved anti-dumping measures imposed by the EU against Chinese fasteners. The main issue before the Panel relates to the scope of

[56] Panel Reports, *US – Steel Safeguards*, para. 10.334.

[57] Panel Reports, *US – Steel Safeguards*, para. 10.332.

[58] Ibid (emphasis added).

[59] Regarding China's claim based on causation, The Panel finds against the United States on CCFRS, tin mill, hot-rolled bar, cold-finished bar, rebar, welded pipe, FFTJ, and stainless steel bar. Only stainless steel rod, stainless steel wire are found to be provided with a adequate and reasoned explanation and thus be consistent with Article 4.2(b) of the ASG. *See* Panel report, *US – Steel Safeguards*, para. 12.2.

'the product concerned' and of the 'like product.' In this complaint, Taiwan claimed that it had systemic interests in ensuring a fair and objective interpretation and application of the ADA and clarified that it would not take a position on the merit of the dispute.[60] Taiwan further stated that without prejudging the validity of the dispute's factual arguments, it disagreed with the view of the EU that Article 2.1 and 2.6 of the ADA are irrelevant to the selection of 'the product concerned'.[61] It attached utmost importance to the intertwined relationship between these two articles in determining the scope of 'the product concerned' and the 'like product' definition,[62] and thus urged the Panel to clarify on the question of how much latitude an investigating authority may have in determining the scope of these two terms so as to preserve the balance under the ADA.[63]

With respect to the legal arguments pertaining to the scope of 'the product concerned' and the 'like product'. Taiwan seemed to stand by China and disagree with the EU. Nonetheless, judging from the ruling of the Panel, Taiwan seemed to have missed the point. The Panel held that the legal text of Article 2.1 of the ADA merely provides that 'a product is to be considered as being dumped' without establishing any obligation relating to the scope of 'a product'.[64] Article 2.6 aims to define the scope of 'like product' but does not provide a definition for 'product' or 'product under consideration' as 'product' needs to be determined before becoming a comparator for 'like product'.[65] The Panel further referred to *United States—Final Dumping Determination on Softwood Lumber from Canada* (*US – Softwood Lumber V*) where the Panel held that when a clear rule on the 'product under consideration' may be appropriate from a policy perspective, it is a matter for the Members to address during the negotiation. The Panel is not in a position to create an obligation which does not exist in the ADA.[66] In view of the ruling of the Panel, Taiwan's intervention in this dispute seemed to be irrelevant.

Apart from the legal arguments presented by Taiwan through its third party participation, another point worth noting in this complaint would be the nomenclature issue faced by Taiwan. In its oral statement, Taiwan used the abbreviation of 'TPKM' as its name. This terminology was objected by China; China subsequently requested the Panel to refer to Taiwan as 'Chinese Taipei'. After seeking comments from the parties to the dispute (the EC did not comment on this point), the Panel granted the request 'in the absence of any objection, and in light of the

---

[60] *European Communities — Definitive Anti-Dumping Measures on Certain Iron or Steel Fasteners from China* (*EC – Fasteners*), WT/DS397/R, adopted 28 July 2011, as modified by Appellate Body Report WT/DS397/AB/R, D-16.

[61] Panel Report, *EC – Fasteners*, para. 7.256.

[62] Ibid.

[63] Panel Report, *EC – Fasteners*, D-18.

[64] Panel Report, *EC – Fasteners*, para. 7.263.

[65] Panel Report, *EC – Fasteners*, para. 7.267.

[66] Panel Report, *EC – Fasteners*, para. 7.275.

sensitivities of Members'.[67] This again illustrated the complexities and political sensitivities of the interactions between Taiwan and China in the multilateral WTO forum.

c. *US – Poultry*

In *EC – Poultry*, a dispute over the SPS measures, Taiwan and the EU requested for enhanced third party rights which included the right to receive second submission from the parties to the dispute and other documents associated with the second substantive meeting; the right to observe the second substantive meeting of the Panel; and the right to make a brief statement during that meeting.[68] Taiwan argued that during the first substantive meeting, there was no in-depth discussion on the compatibility of the contested measures within the SPS Agreement and thus urged the Panel to exercise its discretionary authority and grant enhanced third party rights in accordance with due process of the law. With enhanced third party rights, third parties would be able to assist the Panel to reach a correct interpretation of the covered agreements but at the same time would not blur the distinction drawn in the DSU between parties and third parties.[69]

In response to this enhanced third party rights request, the Panel, after consulting with the parties and other third parties, held that 'views and interests of the third parties have been full taken into account during the Panel proceedings'. In the present case, the Panel saw there was no need to deviate from the rights as set out in Article 10.2 of the DSU and thus decided not to grant enhanced third party rights.[70] Taiwan's third party participation did not involve any substantive issue, from both the factual and legal perspectives. Taiwan focused on the procedural issue by joining the EU in requesting enhanced third party rights. This initiative is of great importance to Taiwan in relation to its interaction with China since there has yet been any direct complaint against each other between Taiwan and China due to political concerns. Enhanced third party rights thus may contribute to Taiwan's participation in complaints brought by/against China.

2. *Taiwan's Third Party Participation in Complaints Brought about against China*

a. *China – Integrated Circuits*

After the US requested for consultations with China on value-added tax on integrated circuits,[71] Taiwan issued a joint-consultation request. In the

---

67 Panel Report, *EC – Fasteners*, para. 6.7.

68 Panel Report, *United States – Certain Measures Affecting Imports of Poultry from China* (*US - Poultry*), WT/DS392/R, adopted 25 October 2010, para. 5.37.

69 Panel Report, *US – Poultry*, para. 5.38.

70 Panel Report, *US – Poultry*, para. 7.58.

71 WTO, *China - Value-Added Tax on Integrated Circuits - Request for Consultations by the United States* (23 March 2004) WT/DS309/1.

communication, Taiwan stated that, being one of China's major integrated circuit suppliers with the total value about US$ 1.8 billion of exports in 2003, it had a 'substantial interest' as well as 'systemic interest' in this matter. Based on these interests, Taiwan thus duly requested to be joined in the consultations.[72] In the meantime, the EU,[73] Japan[74] and Mexico[75] had also requested to be made part of this consultation. In a communication dated 28 April 2004, China notified the DSB that it had accepted the requests of the EU, Japan and Mexico to join the consultations without mentioning of its refusal for Taiwan.[76] Nevertheless, since the accepted requests did not include Taiwan's, it was thus rejected.

As provided in Article 4.11 of the DSU, a Member other than the consulting parties can, within 10 days after the circulations of the requests for consultations, request to be made part of the consultations if it considers that it has 'substantial trade interests' in these consultations. This request for joint-consultations can be rejected if the Member to which the request for consultations was addressed considers that the claimed 'substantial trade interest'[77] does not exist. The only requirement for joint-consultation is that the requesting Member should have 'substantial trade interests'. Taiwan, citing the total values of exports and proving itself as one of the major suppliers in these products, that it had 'substantial trade interests' in this matter.

---

[72] WTO, *China – Value-Added Tax on Integrated Circuits – Request to Join Consultations – Communication from the Separate Customs Territory of Taiwan, Penghu, Kinmen and Matsu* (5 April 2004) WT/DS309/5.

[73] WTO, *China – Value-Added Tax on Integrated Circuits – Request to Join Consultations – Communication from the European Communities* (30 March 2004) WT/DS309/2.

[74] WTO, *China – Value-Added Tax on Integrated Circuits – Request to Join Consultations – Communication from Japan* (1 April 2004) WT/DS309/3.

[75] WTO, *China - Value Added Tax on Integrated Circuits – Request to Join Consultations – Communication from Mexico* (5 April 2004) WT/DS309/4.

[76] WTO, *China - Value-Added Tax on Integrated Circuits - Acceptance by China of the Requests to Join Consultations* (28 April 2004) WT/DS309/6.

[77] The DSU lays down different requirements for joint-consultation and third-party intervention in the panel proceeding. A Member wishing to request to be joined in the consultation should have 'substantial trade interest' while third-party intervention in the panel proceeding needs only 'substantial interest', which 'systemic interest' may well satisfy this requirement. However, it is also argued by some Members that 'substantial trade interest' should not be read in purely commercial terms. For example, Canada argued in *US – Section 306 of the Trade Act of 1976 and Amendments Thereto* (*US – Section 306 Trade Act*) that substantial trade interest should not be interpreted as 'limited to an immediate commercial interest'. Rather, it should be 'wide enough to encompass both commercial and systemic interest'. *See* WTO, *United States - Section 306 of the Trade Act of 1974 and Amendments Thereto - Request to Join Consultations - Communication from Canada* (27 June 2000) WT/DS200/8. Additionally, in rebutting the US's refusal to be joined in the consultation, Japan argued that substantial trade interest should also include interest 'of systemic nature.' *See* WTO, *United States - Section 306 of the Trade Act of 1974 and Amendments Thereto - Communication from Japan* (3 August 2000) WT/DS200/12.

As clarified by the Chairman of the DSB in its communication, dated on 17 July 2000, 'pursuant to the wording of Article 4.11, third-party Members may participate in such consultations only with the approval (acceptance) of the defending Member'.[78] Consequently, although China's denial for Taiwan's request to be joined in the consultation was not justifiable, no remedy is offered by the DSU on this point. This is based on the rationale that the requesting Member can, in any event, refer to the consultation provisions to request their own consultations.[79] Further, while the DSU sets a lower threshold for third party participation in the Panel proceedings, Taiwan did not benefit from this lower threshold.[80] Since this case was later settled with a mutually satisfactory agreement,[81] and consequently no panel has been established, Taiwan was not able to take advantage of the lower bar of the third party participation in the panel proceedings.

b. *China – Intellectual Property Rights*

Following *China – Auto Parts*, Taiwan participated as an active third party participant in *China – Intellectual Property Rights*. In this case, Taiwan argued against the WTO-compatibility of China's regulatory regime on intellectual property rights. In its written submission, Taiwan emphasised that the TRIPS Agreement lays down a minimum standard for intellectual property rights protection and then pointed out that the Panel's function is to review domestic legislations. In referring to *US – Section 301 Trade Act,* Taiwan argued that *China's Copyright Law* should not be interpreted 'as such'. Instead, the Panel needed to establish the meaning of Chinese domestic law based on facts presented to it. Nevertheless, this should be done solely for the purpose of determining whether China had violated its WTO obligations under the TRIPS Agreement.[82]

After briefly elaborating on the ruled of interpretation and burden of proof,[83] Taiwan then turned to relevant articles in this case, namely Article 61 and 46 of the TRIPS Agreement. According to Taiwan, a numerical threshold, as laid down by the *Judicial Interpretation* of the Supreme People's Court (the SPC) may not be

[78] This Chairman's communication addressed Japan's rebuttal for refusal of the US for its request for joint-consultation, *see* WTO, *United States - Section 306 of the Trade Act of 1974 and Amendments Thereto - Communication from the Chairman of the Dispute Settlement Body* (3 August 2000) WT/DS200/13.

[79] Taiwan could certainly request for consultation independently under Article 4.3 of the DSU. However, Taiwan seemed to take a cautious approach and chose not to prompt to it.

[80] In practice, there is virtually no barrier for the third party participation at the panel proceeding stage since Members may simply reserve their rights to intervene as a third party at the DSB meeting. Parties to the dispute are not in a position to object to it.

[81] WTO, *China - Value-Added Tax on Integrated Circuits - Joint Communication from China and the United States* (16 July 2004) WT/DS309/7.

[82] Panel Report, *China – Intellectual Property Rights*, Annex C-16, Executive Summary of the Third Party Submission by Chinese Taipei, para. 5.

[83] Ibid paras. 8-15.

capable of capturing all wilful infringements on a commercial scale, and was unable to meet the minimum standard as dictated by Article 61.[84] Regarding Article 46 of the TRIPS Agreement, Taiwan suggested a two-step approach to examine the WTO-compatibility of *China's Copyright Law*. Taiwan maintained that works before passing the content review cannot be distributed and cannot be protected by the *China's Copyright Law*. In case of the passage of content review with revised version, the original version of works could not enjoy protection from intellectual property rights. An intellectual property rights protection conditional upon content review is WTO-inconsistent. Taiwan further pointed to the contradictory statements within China's first submission. On the one hand, China claimed that only those works that failed to pass the content review are not protected under *China's Copyright Law*; on the other hand, China claimed that works are under intellectual property protection notwithstanding the fact that they are under the process of content review.[85] Taiwan argued that these two statements obviously contradicted with each other.

In terms the Panel's findings, Taiwan's arguments would only be valid in respect to the content review on the *China's Copyright Law*. Since Taiwan's argument relating to the content review did not differ substantially from arguments of the complainant and other third parties, it would be difficult to ascertain the relevance of Taiwan's argument. Furthermore, while arguing that the threshold prescribed by *China's Criminal Law* and judicial interpretations issued by the SPC cannot capture all categories of wilful trademark counterfeiting and copyright piracy 'on a commercial scale', this argument seemed to lack the support of the Panel.[86] Regardless of the limited merit in Taiwan's legal arguments, it is worth noting that in this complaint, Taiwan took the position against China and argued that *China Copyright Law* is WTO-inconsistent. In view of this, Taiwan appears more confident in arguing with China in this multilateral forum.

C. *China's Third Party Participation in Complaints Brought About by/against Taiwan*

As of 1 September 2011, Taiwan has filed three complaints but only one of which has entered into the panel proceedings; no complaint has been brought against

---

84 Ibid para. 18.

85 Ibid para. 33.

86 Panel Report, *China – Intellectual Property Rights*, para. 7.492. Taiwan listed multiple local to be taken into consideration in the determination of wilful trademark counterfeit and copyright piracy as such should be decided on a case-by case basis. The factors identified were nature of the infringed rights, value and price in the market, motive and purpose of act, method and scale of infringement, damage caused, profit gained, cultural background, advancement of modern technology and living standards.

Taiwan. In the complaint brought by Taiwan, namely, the *EC – IT Products*, China is participating as a third party. This initiative may well be explained by economic interests in view of the huge volume of Chinese information technology products exporting into the EU market; it is also a good case to explore the interaction between Taiwan and China in the WTO Dispute Settlement Mechanism.

The *EC – IT Products* concerns three categories of products: flat panel display devices, set-top boxes with a communication function; and multifunctional digital machines. China chose to focus on flat panel display devices. China claimed that it had 'systemic interests in the interpretation of the EC's Schedule of Concessions that implements EC's commitments under the ITA',[87] and then pointed to the general rule on interpretation as set out in the Vienna Convention on Law of Treaties.[88] According to China, the two sources of text needed to be interpreted in light of this present case, namely the tariff heading 8471.60.90 and its corresponding product descriptions, and the Headnote Table that includes all products of Attachment to the ITA.[89] In addition, the HS 1996 and the ITA also served as a context for the interpretation of the EC's schedule.[90]

Overall, China's written submission and oral statement were related to how to interpret the EC's schedule. Since the interpretation approach proposed by China is the established approach adopted by the WTO panel/Appellate Body, China's third party participation in this complaint in effect did not add much input to the panel proceedings. Nonetheless, it served as a symbolic significance in observing its interaction with Taiwan in the multilateral WTO forum. In other words, not only does Taiwan intervene as a third party participant in complaints brought by/against China, China also intervenes as a third party participant in complaint filed by Taiwan. Their interactions in the WTO Dispute Settlement Mechanism are not one-directional but mutual-interactive.

D. *Short Conclusion*

This section deals with the interaction between Taiwan and China in the WTO Dispute Settlement Mechanism through the lens of third party participation. This section begins with the objectives of third party participation in the dispute settlement proceedings and the existing WTO law and practice in this respect. It then examines Taiwan's third party participation in complaints brought about

[87] Panel Report, *European Communities and its member States – Tariff Treatment of Certain Information Technology Products (EC – IT Products)*, WT/DS375/R, WT/DS376/R, WT/DS377/R, adopted 21 September 2010, Annex E-2, Executive Summary of the Third Party Submission by China, para. 1.

[88] Ibid para. 2.

[89] Ibid para. 3.

[90] Ibid para. 4.

against/by China. In those cases where China was the complaining Member, Taiwan sometimes cooperated with China in arguing against the responding Members. Taiwan had also argued against China when China was the responding Member. In these complaints, three levels of participation can be seen: passive observer, active third party participants, and third party participants claiming enhanced third party rights. Conversely, when Taiwan acted as the complaining Member, China also participated as a third party. To some extent, China stood in line with Taiwan arguing against the responding Members. Through the lens of third party participation, this section saw the interaction, with different intensities, between Taiwan and China in the WTO Dispute Settlement Mechanism.

III. Dispute Settlement Mechanism in Bilateral Taiwan-China Agreements

Since 20 May 2008, a series of liberalisation measures have been adopted under the Ma administration. In addition to unilateral actions, Taiwan and China have also concluded a number of bilateral agreements. The conventional practice for the conclusion of these agreements is through specially-designated organisations: the Straits Exchange Foundation (the SEF) on behalf of Taiwan and the Association for Relations Across the Taiwan Straits (the ARATS) on behalf of China. After more than ten years of suspension, the SEF and the ARATS reopened negotiations at Beijing on 12 June 2008 which resulted in an agreement allowing the Chinese tourists to travel to Taiwan[91] and minutes on charter flights between Taiwan and China.[92] The Chinese Tourists Agreement effectuated the liberalisation of Chinese tourists to Taiwan up to a quota of 3000 persons per day.[93] Travelling should be conducted through group tourism.[94] On 1 January 2011, the quota has been increased to 4000 persons per day. Since 28 June 2011, the requirement of group tourism has also been lessened with the permission of 500 independent tourists per day. The Charter Flights Minutes provide the legal basis for charter flights for passengers between Taiwan and China during the weekends, defined as from

[91] Cross-Strait Agreement Signed between SEF and ARATS Concerning Mainland Tourists Travelling to Taiwan, Beijing, 23 June 2008 (hereinafter, the Chinese Tourists Agreement), an official English translation version is available at <http://www.sef.org.tw/> accessed 1 September 2011.

[92] SEF-ARATS Minutes of Talks on Cross-Strait Charter Flights, Beijing, 11-14 June 2008 (hereinafter, the Charter Flights Minutes); an official English translation version is available at <http://www.sef.org.tw/> accessed 1 September 2011.

[93] Special Arrangements Concerning Cross-Strait Tourism, Annex I to the Chinese Tourists Agreement, Art. 1.

[94] Chinese Tourists Agreement, Art. 2.1.

Friday afternoon to Monday morning.[95] The Charter Flights Minutes prelude the direct transportation agreements between Taiwan and China which eventually lifted the transhipment requirement via a third port.

Six rounds of negotiations headed by, Chiang Pin-Kung, the president of the SEF and Chen Yunlin, the President of the ARATS, have been conducted, resulting in 15 agreements covering a various subject matters. The first two rounds were meant to open up Taiwan for Chinese tourists and to liberalise direct air and sea transport between Taiwan and China. As the second round of negotiation was conducted in the midst of Chinese food safety scandal, a food safety agreement was thus included on the agenda. The third and fourth rounds of negotiations were dealt with sectoral issues such as financial and monetary cooperation;[96] mutual judicial assistance;[97] agricultural products;[98] standards, metrology and inspection and accreditation;[99] and fishing crew affairs.[100] At the fifth round, these agreements on sectoral applications then led to the conclusion of a compressive cooperation agreement, the ECFA. Sideline to the ECFA negotiation, Taiwan and China also concluded an agreement on cooperation in intellectual property rights protection.[101] The sixth round then saw a more sophisticated and legalistic approach in designing the cooperation on medical and health issues. This section will examine the direct-transportation agreements, sectoral bilateral agreements and then the ECFA. It will also investigate the dispute settlement mechanisms as contained within these agreements.

---

[95] Annex to the Charter Flights Minutes, Time, Destination, and Flights of Cross-Strait Charter Flights, Art. 1.

[96] Cross-Strait Financial Cooperation Agreement, Nanjing, 26 April 2009 (hereinafter, the Financial Cooperation Agreement), reprinted in *The Third Round of Chiang-Chen Talks: Economic and Trade Matters* (Mainland Affairs Council, the Executive Yuan, Taipei, 2009) 17.

[97] Ibid, 18.

[98] Cross-Strait Agreement on Cooperation of Agricultural Product Quarantine and Inspection (hereinafter, the Agricultural Products Agreement), Taichung, 22 December 2009, reprinted in *Three Agreements of the Fourth Chiang-Chen Talks* (Mainland Affairs Council, the Executive Yuan, Taipei, 2009) 1.

[99] Cross-Strait Agreement on Cooperation in Respect of Standards, Metrology, Inspection and Accreditation (hereinafter, the Standards, Metrology, Inspection and Accreditation Agreement), Taichung, 22 December 2009, reprinted in *Three Agreements of the Fourth Chiang-Chen Talks* (Mainland Affairs Council, the Executive Yuan, Taipei, 2009) 5.

[100] Cross-Strait Agreement on Cooperation in Respect of Fishing Crew Affairs (hereinafter, the Fishing Crew Affairs Agreement), Taichung, 22 December 2009, reprinted in *Three Agreements of the Fourth Chiang-Chen Talks* (Mainland Affairs Council, the Executive Yuan, Taipei, 2009) 9.

[101] Cross-Strait Agreement on Intellectual Property Rights Protection and Cooperation (hereinafter, the Intellectual Property Rights Agreement), an unofficial English version is available at <http://www.tipo.gov.tw/en/MultiMedia_FileDownload.ashx?guid=c0f78ebe-e402-4df5-9de1-76b4faf32696> accessed 1 September 2011.

A. *Direct Transportation Agreements*

Prior to the Ma administration, transportation between Taiwan and China had to pass through via a third port, normally, Hong Kong or Macau. A direct flight or shipment between Taiwan and China was not possible. One of the fundamental regulatory changes under the Ma administration was the conclusion of direct transportation agreements between Taiwan and China. The second round of the Chiang-Chen negotiations held in Taipei on 4 November 2008 led to the conclusion of four agreements pertaining to the cooperation of food safety,[102] direct air transport,[103] sea transport,[104] and postal service.[105] With the effectuation of the Sea Transport Agreement and Air Transport Agreement, the requirement of transhipment through a third-port was lifted and direct sea/air transportation between Taiwan and China was thus permitted. Direct passenger and cargo charter flights can now be conducted by airline companies that are capitalised and registered on either side of the Taiwan Strait, namely Taiwan and China.[106] In order to implement this direct air transport agreement, air traffic control agencies in Taiwan and in China should establish procedures for the direct handover of air traffic control.[107] A direct cross-strait air transport path has been opened through a northern line across the Taiwan Strait, from Taipei to Shanghai Flight Information Regions. Due to the huge demand of aviation market, a southern route and a second northern route were opened by virtue of the Cross-Strait Air Transport Supplementary Agreement concluded at the third round of negotiation held on 26 April 2009.

In respect to direct sea transport, vessels owned and registered on either side of Taiwan Strait, i.e. Taiwan and China, could engage in direct cross-strait transport of passengers and cargo.[108] With regard to the controversial flag-flying issue, it was agreed that, 'vessels registered on either side of the Taiwan Strait shall not fly their flag on the stern or mainmast of the vessel between entering and leaving the other side's port, but shall fly their company flag for vessel identification'.[109]

---

[102] Cross-Strait Food Safety Agreement, Taipei, 4 November 2008 (hereinafter, the Food Safety Agreement), an official English version is available at <http://www.sef.org.tw/> accessed 1 September 2011.

[103] Cross-Strait Air Transport Agreement, Taipei, 4 November 2008 (hereinafter, the Air Transport Agreement),an official English version is available at <http://www.sef.org.tw/> accessed 1 September 2011.

[104] Cross-Strait Sea Transport Agreement, Taipei, 4 November 2008 (hereinafter, 'the Sea Transport Agreement), an official English version is available at <http://www.sef.org.tw/> accessed 1 September 2011.

[105] Cross-Strait Postal Service Agreement, Taipei, 4 November 2008 (hereinafter, the Postal Service Agreement), an official English version is available at <http://www.sef.org.tw/> accessed 1 September 2011.

[106] The Air Transport Agreement, Art. 2.

[107] The Air Transport Agreement, Art. 1.1.

[108] The Sea Transport Agreement, Art. 1.

[109] The Sea Transport Agreement, Art. 3.

The sovereignty controversies had been avoided but unresolved. Another issue of great economic interests was the flag-of-convenience vessels owned by the shipping companies of Taiwan and China that may undertake direct cross-strait sea transport if they have already been engaging in offshore shipping centre transport ('testing point for direct shipping'), cross-strait third-territory container line transport, and sand and gravel transport before the signature of this agreement.[110] This has the effect of limiting the scope of application to Taiwanese capitalised flag-in-convenience vessels. In contrast, vessels capitalised in Taiwan or China but registered in Hong Kong may benefit from this direct air transport agreement.[111] In total, China has liberalised 63 ports, including 48 seaports and 15 river ports while Taiwan has liberalised 11 ports.[112]

Finally, as dictated by Article 95 of the *Statute*,[113] the Air Transport Agreement and the Sea Transport Agreement should refer to the Legislative Yuan (the Congress of Taiwan) for resolution, while the Food Safety Agreement and the Postal Agreement would only need to notify the Legislative Yuan. However, the Legislative Yuan did not make any resolution on the approval of the Sea Transport Agreement and Air Transport Agreement. These two agreements were effectuated by virtue of Article 95 of the *Statute* which provided that if the Legislative Yuan failed to adopt any resolution after one month after its consent was requested, the consent is deemed to be granted. As a result, the direct-transportation between Taiwan and China has effectuated without any congressional resolution.

B. *Sectoral Agreements between Taiwan and China*

Subsequent to the Food Safety Agreement, several bilateral agreements with sectoral coverage were concluded in the third and fourth rounds of Chiang-Chen talks. In general, these bilateral sectoral agreements were cooperation agreements in nature with loosely-designed regulatory frameworks and few legal-binding substantive obligations, reflected in the size of the agreements, being 15 articles in average. This subsection would examine those bilateral agreements with utmost trade and economic relevance, namely, the Financial Cooperation Agreement, the Agricultural Products Agreement and the Intellectual Property Rights Agreement.

---

[110] Annex to the Sea Transport Agreement, Art. 2.

[111] Annex to the Sea Transport Agreement, Art. 1.

[112] Annex to the Sea Transport Agreement, Art. 3.

[113] Article 95 of the *Statute* reads: [t]he competent authorities shall request the consent of the Legislative Yuan before permitting direct business transactions or direct sea or air transportation between the Taiwan Area and the Mainland Area, or permitting the people of the Mainland Area to enter into the Taiwan Area to work, and if the Legislative Yuan fails to adopt any resolution within one month after the request during its session, the consent is deemed granted.

1. *The Financial Cooperation Agreement*

With the growing in trade activities across the Taiwan Strait, the demand for financial services supporting these trade activities surges and thus calls for a stable financial market across the Strait. The Financial Cooperation Agreement is thus an instrument to meet this demand. This agreement governs two main fields: the financial supervision and the monetary management.

Regarding financial supervision, the Parties agreed that the financial supervisory institutions of the two sides should establish a cooperation mechanism for the supervision of banking, securities, future and insurance industries.[114] Under the framework of this cooperation mechanism, the supervisory institutions may also make specific arrangements in accordance with industry practices.[115] Some observations should be made here. The Financial Cooperation Agreement was concluded by the SEF and the ARATS, two specially-designated organisations for cross-Taiwan-Strait affairs. Nevertheless, this Financial Cooperation Agreement then directs the relevant financial supervisory institutions to establish a cooperative mechanism under which they can make specific arrangements. The governments delegated public authorities to these specially-designated organisations to negotiate the Financial Cooperation Agreement; this Financial Cooperation Agreement provided the legal basis for the public authorities, namely the financial supervisory institutions, to cooperate and to make specific arrangements. This practice may create legitimacy concern as the agreements were signed by the SEF and the ARATS, where they only need only to notify the Legislative Yuan, so the congressional oversight could be found insufficient. However, these agreements turned out to be the legal basis for the public authorities to act in certain areas. A weak parliamentary participation seemed to be unable to sustain the subsequent measures adopted by the public authorities.

With respect to monetary management, the Parties put forward their objective to establishing a currency settlement mechanism with a view to foster cooperation in monetary management. The first step toward this goal is to liberalise cash exchange, supply and flowback operations activities of the commercial banks and to strengthen anti-counterfeiting technological cooperation.[116] Allowing commercial banks to conduct the aforementioned activities are meant to meet the practical needs arising from Taiwan's numerous businessmen travelling to and from China and from Taiwan's opening up to Chinese tourists. But in the absence of a currency settlement agreement, how to deal with the currency held by each other remains unclear. In addition, there used to a shortage of Chinese Renminbi in

[114] The Financial Cooperation Agreement, Art. 1(1), first subparagraph.
[115] The Financial Cooperation Agreement, Art. 1(1), second subparagraph.
[116] The Financial Cooperation Agreement, Art. 1(2).

Taiwanese banks due to the limited supply channels, mainly through buying from Taiwanese businessmen, Chinese tourists and sometimes from foreign banks.

One of the few substantive commitments as contained within the Financial Cooperation Agreement relates to the establishment of entities of financial institutions in two sides. The financial supervisory institutions are instructed to pursue liberalisation of financial services through commercial presence in the spirit of reciprocity with the difference of market size taken into consideration with a view to maintaining the well functioning of market on financial services.[117]

The financial supervisory institutions of the Parties will also continue to negotiate on the criteria for establishing an entity or for acquiring equity stakes in entities and the scope of businesses permitted.[118] In deciding whether or not to allow the establishment of an entity or the acquisition of equity stakes in entities, the Parties agreed to consult and to seek opinions from each other. Overall, this obligation remains very vague. It points towards the direction of liberalisation in establishment or the acquisition of equity stakes of entities by financial institutions. Substantive rules pertaining to the scope of and conditions for liberalisation were left to further negotiations at a later stage. The only clear requirement imposed by the Financial Cooperation Agreement is the consultation obligation in handling the application for establishing an entity or acquiring equity stakes of entities.

In terms of institutional design, a loosely-cut liaison body is set out under the Financial Cooperation Agreement. The Parties would appoint a contact person within the financial supervisory institutions and the monetary management institutions to be responsible for liaising implementation matters covered by the agreement.[119] As to those matters going beyond the scope of the agreement, liaison should be conducted through the SEF and the ARATS.[120] This article again makes it clear that the SEF and the ARATS remain to be the main venue for negotiations between Taiwan and China. Only in those areas where bilateral agreements have been concluded, relevant competent authorities may directly contact each other or continue to make specific arrangements.

2. *The Agricultural Products Agreement*

The regulatory design of the Agricultural Products Agreement largely mirrors the Financial Cooperation Agreement, covering principles and objectives; mutual exchanges and information inquiries; notification, handling of emergencies and

[117] The Financial Cooperation Agreement, Art. 4, para. 1.

[118] The Financial Cooperation Agreement, Art. 4, para. 2.

[119] The Financial Cooperation Agreement, Art. 8, para. 1.

[120] The Financial Cooperation Agreement, Art. 8, para. 2. The same spirit is also evident in Article 11 of the agreement.

observation visit and verification; and liaison, implementation and dispute settlement.

Article 1 of the Agricultural Products Agreement sets out of its objectives: for the prevention of the transmission and the spread of harmful organisms of animals and plants and for the assurance of the quality and safety of agricultural products.[121] With a view to facilitating consultations, discussions, exchanges, observational visits and technical exchange, the Parties agreed to establish appropriate mechanisms and, if necessary, working groups on technological cooperation in specialised areas such as quarantines and inspection. The agreement provides little guidance with respect to the mechanisms to be established. The relevant part of the agreement may be liaison. However, the liaison follows the practice of Financial Cooperation Agreement by designating a contact person within the competent authorities in charge of the liaison on the implementation of matters set out in the agreement.[122] In addition to the above mentioned mechanism, the Parties also agreed to provide information on regulations, standards and procedures governing quarantine and inspection[123] and to enhance exchanges on sanitary standards on pesticide and animal drug residues.[124]

The agreement then directs the Parties to promptly notify each other about the incidence of major epidemic situations or sanitary issues affecting agricultural products and to regularly notify each other about intercepted harmful organisms and detected toxic or harmful substances. This notification requirement remains vague in many aspects. First, the terms of 'promptly' or 'regularly' employed in the agreement is of great ambiguity and subject to different interpretation. A clear timeline would be desirable, when compared with the employed language in the agreement. Second, the notification format is to be discussed by the Parties, which may lead to a delay in the implementation of the agreement: implementation deficit remains to be the main factor undermining the effectiveness of these bilateral agreements signed by Taiwan and China.

In cases of emergencies relating to quarantine and inspection, coordinated efforts between the Parties should be achieved; prompt notification, speedy checks, emergent consultations and mutual assistance should be provided.[125] The article is basically cooperative in nature and does not set out for any legal binding obligations. In order to further strengthen agricultural product safety management, the Agricultural Products Agreement set out a tracking system and

[121] The Agricultural Products Agreement, Art. 1.
[122] The Agricultural Products Agreement, Art. 9(1).
[123] The Agricultural Products Agreement, Art. 3(1).
[124] The Agricultural Products Agreement, Art. 3(2).
[125] The Agricultural Products Agreement, Art. 6.

instructs the Parties to provide observation visits to the production and processing sites of agricultural products to each other.[126]

3. *The Intellectual Property Rights Agreement*

At the fifth round of the Chiang-Chen talks, the Parties negotiated on intellectual property rights along with the comprehensive ECFA negotiations. The Intellectual Property Rights Agreement covers patent, trademark, copyright, plant variety rights, and other related intellectual property rights. It deals with priority rights and protection of plant varieties and it sets out implementation mechanisms and authentication procedures.

With respect to priority rights, the Parties agreed to recognise the validity of the first filing date for patent, trademark and variety rights of the other party in accordance with their respective domestic laws and regulations. They also agreed to assertively protect the priority rights through appropriate arrangements.[127] In terms of plant variety rights, the Parties agreed to accept, within its published list of protected plant varieties, applications for variety rights from the other party and to further expand the scope of plant varieties eligible for application.[128] Overall, the Intellectual Property Rights Agreement brings the regulatory regime in line with WTO rules and does not contain many WTO-plus obligations.

The Intellectual Property Rights Agreement nevertheless did advance a bit in terms of intellectual property rights protection between Taiwan and China. It instructs the Parties to establish a cooperative mechanism for copyright authentication which may be processed by relevant associations or specially-designated organisations. This authentication relates mainly to audio-visual products but may also extend to other works such as printed books and software.[129] As this authentication service has formerly been carried out via Hong Kong, this provision helps to reduce transaction costs for intellectual property rights holders when asserting their rights.

The Intellectual Property Rights Agreement also lays down some concrete implementing measures for intellectual property rights protection, with a stress on combating piracy and counterfeits; protecting well-known trademarks, geographical indications or well-known places of origin; and monitoring falsified indications of origin of fruits and other agricultural products.[130] However, the

---

[126] The Agricultural Products Agreement, Art. 7.
[127] The Intellectual Property Rights Agreement, Art. 2.
[128] The Intellectual Property Rights Agreement, Art. 3.
[129] The Intellectual Property Rights Agreement, Art. 6.
[130] The Intellectual Property Rights Agreement, Art. 7(1).

effectiveness of these implementation measures and the Intellectual Property Rights Agreement as a whole relies on China's willingness and efforts in protecting intellectual property rights; just as any other intellectual property rights protection agreement concluded by China, the result never appears to be promising. That being said, the Intellectual Property Rights Agreement does make a step forward in enhancing the intellectual property rights protection between Taiwan and China: the aforementioned authentication service is a good example.

C. *Economic Cooperation Framework Agreement*

1. *Negotiation History*

Overall, the ECFA has been oscillating between the two models of CEPAs and the China-ASEAN Framework Agreement on Comprehensive Economic Co-Operation (China-ASEAN Framework Agreement). Whereas Taiwan tried to inject the contours of the China-ASEAN Framework Agreement into the ECFA, China made great efforts to couple the ECFA with the CEPAs. In other words, while Taiwan might have referred to the WTO rules on FTAs, China preferred to view the ECFA as an 'internal' arrangement carrying no international implications.

The first point to note on the formality is that the ECFA was signed in both simplified and tradition Chinese; the two versions being authentic carry the same meaning. It is understandable given that Taiwan uses traditional Chinese language and China uses simplified Chinese as their official languages. This practice might also have political implications since China has clearly preferred not to internationalise the ECFA and would not have been happy to see the text of the ECFA in English. Apart from political implications, the usage of Chinese has practical and legal implications. The interpretation of the commitments and obligations as contained in the ECFA will greatly depend on the translation efforts should a judicialised dispute settlement mechanism be introduced in future agreements and should a panel composed of non-nationals be established. This difficulty is evident in those previous WTO complaints brought against China.

In terms of the format of the agreement, following the pattern of the direct-transportation agreements, Chiang Pin-Kung, the President of the SEF, and Chen Yunlin, the President of the ARTAS signed the ECFA. The Ma administration, notably the Mainland Affairs Council (the MAC) that has been in charge of China affairs, had delegated negotiation to the SEF to initiate and to conclude the ECFA negotiations. The ECFA was finally inked on 29 June 2010 by the SEF and ARATS and became the first FTA signed by private organisations on behalf of the government. After the signing of the ECFA, it was subsequently sent to the Legislative Yuan for deliberation. The Legislative Yuan finally approved it on 17 August 2010, after the withdrawal of the opposition party (the DPP) from the deliberation process.[131] After the Parties' notifying each other as set out under Article 15 of the ECFA, the ECFA came into force on 12 September 2010.[132]

2. *One Main Text and Five Annexes*

The ECFA is comprised of one main legal text and five annexes that regulate products list and tariffs reduction;[133] provisional rules of origin;[134] safeguard measures;[135] sectors and liberalisation measures;[136] and the definition of services supplier.[137] Similar to the CEPAs concluded between China and Hong Kong and Macau, the main text of the ECFA is relatively short and premature. There are five chapters covering general principles,[138] trade and investment,[139] economic cooperation,[140] Early Harvest Programme,[141] and other provisions relating to the institutional arrangement and dispute settlement.[142]

Article 1 announces of the objective of the ECFA: to 'strengthen and advance the economic, trade and investment cooperation';[143] to 'promote further liberalisation of trade in goods and services';[144] to 'gradually establish fair, transparent and facilitative investment and investment protection mechanisms'; and to 'expand areas of economic cooperation and establish a cooperation mechanism'.[145] In view of the objectives, the envisioned scope of the ECFA is rather limited, compared to other FTAs or partnerships and cooperation agreements. The objectives as set out in the ECFA have been purely economic provisions so it does not cover topics such as sustainable development. During the course of the negotiation, some scholars had advocated for the inclusion of a human rights clause.[146] Doubtlessly, their efforts had resulted in vain.

---

131 Taiwan-China Trade Deal Passed by Taipei Legislators <http://www.bbc.co.uk/news/world-asia-pacific-11008076> accessed 1 September 2011.

132 ECFA Becomes Effective on September 12 <http://www.chinaipr.gov.cn/newsarticle/news/government/201009/947875_1.html> accessed 1 September 2011.

133 The ECFA, Annex I.

134 The ECFA, Annex.

135 The ECFA, Annex.

136 The ECFA, Annex.

137 The ECFA, Annex V.

138 The ECFA, Chapter 1.

139 The ECFA, Chapter 2.

140 The ECFA, Chapter 3.

141 The ECFA, Chapter 4.

142 The ECFA, Chapter 5.

143 The ECFA, Art. 1.1.

144 The ECFA, Art. 1.2.

145 The ECFA, Art. 1.2.

146 Tseng and Wu, ECFA Should Benefit Human Rights, *Taipei Times* (Taipei, 17 July 2010) <http://www.taipeitimes.com/News/editorials/archives/2010/07/17/2003478124> accessed 1 September 2011.

Article 2 then specifies a number of cooperation measures including 'gradually reducing tariff and non-tariff barriers to trade in a substantial majority of goods'[147] and 'restrictions on a large number of sectors in trade in services';[148] and providing investment protection and promoting and facilitating trade, investment and industry cooperation.[149] The pertinent point here has been the terms of 'in a substantial majority of goods' and 'a large number of sectors in trade in services' which clearly deviated from the requirement of 'substantially all the trade'/'substantial sectoral coverage' as seen in the CEPAs. The terminology employed may pose the question whether the ECFA is WTO-compatible.

Chapter 2 of the ECFA then regulates trade in goods, and trade in services and investment. The common feature of the three articles contained in this Chapter is that the Parties are instructed to initiate negotiations with the aim to conclude agreements on trade in goods, trade in services and investment within six months after the entry into force of the ECFA.[150] In addition, the ECFA then provides a list of issues to be dealt with during the envisaged negotiations.[151] The negotiations on trade in goods and trade in services should follow the basis established in the Early Harvest Programme.[152] Based on commitments under the envisaged agreements, the Parties might choose, at their own discretions, to accelerate the tariff reduction or liberalise restrictive measures on the services trade.[153] Regarding the tariff reduction for goods, the ECFA has classified the goods into the following categories: goods subject to immediate tariff elimination, goods subject to phased tariff reduction, and exceptions or others. This implies that, under the envisaged agreement for trade in goods, the speed of liberalisation would vary depending on the sensitivity of the products.[154] Some categories of products may be *a priori* excluded from the liberalisation schedules.

The Early Harvest Programme is provided within Chapter 4, which contains two articles regulating Early Harvest for trade in goods[155] and trade in services.[156] This Early Harvest Programme, modelled from the China-ASEAN Framework Agreement, aims at the fast realisation of the objectives of the ECFA. The Early Harvest Programme for trade in goods should be implemented within six months after the enactment of the ECFA whereas there is no specific timeframe for the

[147] The ECFA, Art. 2.1.

[148] The ECFA, Art. 2.2.

[149] The ECFA, Art. 2.3-2.4.

[150] The ECFA, Arts. 3.1, 4.1, 5.1.

[151] The ECFA, Arts. 3.2, 4.2, 5.2.

[152] The ECFA, Arts. 3.1, 4.1. The designation of the Early Harvest Programme is aimed to reap the fruit of the liberalisation before the negotiations on trade in goods and trade in services really commence.

[153] The ECFA, Arts. 3.4, 4.3.

[154] The ECFA, Art. 3.3.

[155] The ECFA, Art. 7.

[156] The ECFA, Art. 8.

Early Harvest for services trade. The ECFA simply directs the Parties to implement the services trade Early Harvest Programme expeditiously.[157]

The ECFA, in Article 7.2, directs the Parties to implement the Early Harvest Programme in goods trade in accordance with the tariff reduction schedules as set out in Annex I[158] while provisional rules of origin as set out in Annex II and trade remedy measures as set out in Annex III.[159] Products that satisfy the requirements as set out in the Provisional Rule of Origin should be accordingly conferred upon the assigned preferential treatment.[160] The provisional rules of origin and trade remedy measures regulation would cease to apply when the envisaged agreement on trade in good comes into force.[161] With respect to services trade, the Parties have agreed to reduce or to eliminate restrictive measures that might have affected services and services suppliers from the other Party.[162] The definition of a service supplier as provided in Annex V would cease to apply after the commencement of the envisaged agreement on trade in services.[163] Article 8.2(3) then regulates the safeguard measures of services trade. In the case of 'a material adverse impact on the services sectors' arising from the implementation of the Early Harvest Programme for trade in services, the affected Party can request for consultations with the other Party to reach a solution. The solution here referred to seemed to be mutually-agreed or mutually-satisfactory in nature since no further guidance on unilateral measures has been provided under the Early Harvest Programme.

Regarding the institutional arrangement, a Cross-Straits Economic Cooperation Committee (hereinafter, the ECFA Committee), composed of representatives from both Parties, is to be established under the ECFA. The tasks of this ECFA Committee include concluding negotiations necessary for the attainment of the objectives of the ECFA; monitoring and evaluating its implementation; interpreting the ECFA to resolve disputes and notifying each other of important information on trade and economic.[164] The ECFA Committee should convene regularly on semi-annual basis with the possibility of *ad hoc* meetings if agreed by both Parties.[165] It can also establish working groups for specific subject matters under its supervision.[166] With regard to the dispute settlement mechanism, it is consensus-based without any litigation features.[167]

157 The ECFA, Art. 8.1.
158 The ECFA, Art. 7.2(1).
159 The ECFA, Art. 7.2(2), 7.2(3).
160 The ECFA, Art. 7.2(2).
161 The ECFA, Art. 7.3.
162 The ECFA, Art. 8.2(1).
163 The ECFA, Art. 8.2(2), 8.2(3).
164 The ECFA, Art. 11.1.
165 The ECFA, Art. 11.3.
166 The ECFA, Art. 11.2.
167 *See* further text to (n 182) *et seq.*

3. *The Compatibility of ECFA with WTO Rules on FTA*

In determining the compatibility of the ECFA with the WTO rules, there are several questions needed answering first, such as the nature and the legal basis of the ECFA. In other words, the first question would be whether the ECFA is an FTA in itself or merely an interim agreement leading to the formation of a free trade area under Article XXIV:5(b) of the GATT1994. The second question then would follow that in addition to Article XXIV:5 and Article V of the GATS, whether the Enabling Clause can also provide a legal basis for the ECFA. A relevant question would be if the ECFA is an interim agreement, does Article V of the GATS envisage such interim agreement? It appears that the same procedural notification requirement would apply regardless of the answers to the named questions. Article XXIV:7 of the GATT 1994 obliges the Parties to an FTA or to an interim agreement to promptly notify the WTO and to make available of the relevant information. Similarly, paragraph 4 of the Enabling Clause also directs the Parties to differential and more favourable arrangements to notify the GATT Contracting Parties, provide relevant information and offer opportunities for consultation upon request.

Regarding the procedural requirement, Taiwan informed the WTO of the conclusion of the ECFA in accordance with the General Council Decision on the Transparency Mechanism for the Regional Trade Agreements. However, this initiative is part of early announcement under this General Council Decision instead Article XXIV of the GATT 1994. One may wonder why the Parties hesitated in fulfilling this mere procedural requirement and risk the ECFA's WTO-compatibility and their reputations within the WTO. A potential answer to this phenomenon again could be concluded from domestic politics concerns: both Parties, particularly China, possibly preferred to keep the ECFA within the realm of 'internal affairs' instead of internationalising it.

On the nature of the ECFA, based on the following reasons it may be argued that the ECFA would only be an interim agreement leading to the formation of a free trade area. Firstly, the first preambular and Article 1.1 the ECFA speaks of its aim to strengthen trade and economic relations between China and Taiwan.[168] The ECFA then further clarifies that its objective is to promote further liberalisation of trade in goods and services between the Parties,[169] which implied that the liberalisation processes would be implemented in accordance with further developments. In Chapter 2, the ECFA explicitly instructs the Parties to enter into negotiations with the aim to conclude agreements on trade in goods and services within six months after the entry into force.[170] In addition, the inclusion of an Early

[168] The ECFA, 1st preambular, Art. 1.1.
[169] The ECFA, Art. 1.2.
[170] The ECFA, Arts. 3.1, 4.1.

Harvest Programme suggests that the main obligations and commitments of tariff-reduction and liberalisation should be based upon the envisaged agreements on trade in goods and services. Tariff-reduction and liberalisation measures under the Early Harvest Programme were meant to be adopted prior to the entry into force of these two envisaged agreements of trade in goods and trade in services. Consequently, the ECFA could only be an interim agreement leading to the formation of a free trade area and, consequently, those tariff-reduction and other liberalisation measures under the Early Harvest Programme could only rely upon Article XXIV:5(b) for their legal basis. However, it remains unclear whether the Enabling Clause would be relevant.

The WTO Members have the advantage of referring to the Enabling Clause as their legal basis because the requirements as laid out therein are less stringent. The Parties to an agreement concluded on the basis of the Enabling Clause would not be obliged to eliminate duties or other restrictions relating to commerce that could cover 'substantially all the trade'. At the same time, the Parties are not required to provide a plan or schedule when forming a free trade area 'within a reasonable length of time'. While agreements concluded under the Enabling Clause should also be notified to the WTO, the review and consultation process is conducted by the Committee on the Trade and Development which tends to be more lenient than the Committee on Regional Trade Agreements (the CRTA). Nonetheless, the Enabling Clause is only applicable to trade in goods and not to trade in services and it can only be relied upon should there not be two or more developing countries Members.

The pertinent point here would be when Taiwan acceded to the WTO, whether it had renounced its rights stemming from the status of a developing country. Paragraph 6 of the Taiwan's Working Party Report reads that '[t]he representative of Chinese Taipei stated that his government would not claim any right granted under WTO Agreements to developing country Members'.[171] Additionally, some Members of the Working Party also noted that 'Chinese Taipei should assume a level of obligations commensurate to that of the developed economy original Members of the WTO'.[172] One might wish to argue that Taiwan had acceded to the WTO as a developed country and therefore cannot refer to the Enabling Clause for the legal basis of the ECFA. Nonetheless, a closer look would prove this argument groundless given that these two paragraphs relating Taiwan's statement as not to rely upon rights of a developing country are not referred to in paragraph 224 of Taiwan's Working Party Report, which according to Taiwan's Accession Protocol,

[171] WTO, *Working Party on the Accession of Chinese Taipei - Report of the Working Party on the Accession of the Separate Customs Territory of Taiwan, Penghu, Kinmen and Matsu* (hereinafter, Taiwan's Working Party Report) (5 October 2001) WT/ACC/TPKM/18, para. 6.

[172] Taiwan's Working Party Report, para. 7.

constitutes as an integral part of Taiwan's WTO obligations under its accession package. Therefore, the statement that Taiwan would not 'claim any rights granted under WTO Agreements to developing country Members' does not constitute as a part of the obligations or commitments under Taiwan's Accession Protocol. As a result, it appears, from a legal perspective, Taiwan and China could rely upon the Enabling Clause as the legal basis for the ECFA but whether this would be a wise approach remains to be seen. Nevertheless, even if Taiwan and China refer to the Enabling Clause for the legal basis for the ECFA, the Enabling Clause does not cover trade in services as such recourse should be eventually guided by Article V of the GATS.

An application of Article V of the GATS would lead to similar difficulties arising from Taiwan's status; this is because Article V:3(a) provides some flexibility for an FTA to which developing countries are the Parties. According to Article V:1, WTO Members are not prevented from being a party or entering into agreement on liberalising services trade, provided that such agreement has 'substantial sectoral coverage',[173] and contains no discrimination as set out in Article XVII or has eliminated substantially all discrimination through 'the elimination of existing discriminatory measures'[174] and/or 'the prohibition of new or more discriminatory measures'.[175] Article V:3(a) then provides some flexibility for developing countries when they wish to enter into such an agreement. In addition to the leniency on 'substantial sectoral coverage', this subparagraph also lessens the stringency on the elimination of discriminatory measures in accordance with the level of the development within the countries concerned.[176] Therefore, if Taiwan could be deemed as a developing country, the ECFA and the envisaged agreement on services trade would not necessarily need to cover 'substantial sectoral coverage' and might not be obliged to eliminate all discriminatory measures within a reasonable time-frame.

However, one issue remains unsettled even if the Parties to the ECFA could rely on the flexibility provided within V:3(a) of the GATS: the WTO-compatibility of the Early Harvest Programme on trade in services, since the ECFA could only be deemed as an interim agreement leading to the formation of a free trade area. The Early Harvest Programme for trade in goods, depending on whether Taiwan could be classified as a developing country within the WTO and therefore rely upon Article XXIV:5(b) of the GATT 1994 or the Enabling Clause for its legal basis, but neither would be applicable to trade in services. However, in contrast to the designation XXIV:5 of the GATT 1994, the GATS does not explicitly refer to interim

173 The GATS, Art. V:1(a).
174 The GATS, Art. V:1(b)(i).
175 The GATS, Art. V:1(b)(ii).
176 The GATS, Art. V:3(a).

agreement. Controversies then arise as to whether such an Early Harvest Programme is permissible under the WTO law. In reading provisions governing economic integration within the context of Article V of the GATS, Article XXIV of the GATT 1994 and subsequent practice of the WTO, Lo argues that a transitional arrangement under a free trade area and an interim agreement leading to the formation of a free trade area should be differentiated. According to Lo, an interim agreement leading to the formation of a free trade area is not permissible under the GATS. It is thus questionable whether the Early Harvest Programme on trade in services under the ECFA is WTO-compatible since it contains only a plan or schedule to liberalise services trade but not completing of the services trade negotiations.[177]

4. *The Political Implication of the ECFA*

The inking of the ECFA has a number of political implications. According to Lo, the ECFA appeared to have an international nature similar to a treaty hence it should be subject to WTO review.[178] Additionally, the ECFA could be interpreted as China's recognition of Taiwan's legal capacity to enter into FTA talks and to conclude FTAs.[179] Legally, as a WTO member, Taiwan has its own right to initiate FTA negotiations with other WTO Members, but in practice Taiwan has only concluded FTAs with those countries with which it has maintained diplomatic ties. However, the economic interests covered by those FTAs have been quite limited.[180] Taiwan's major trading partners have been reluctant to enter into FTA negotiations with Taiwan due to political concerns. The conclusion of the ECFA may thus contribute to an expansion of Asian economic integration from which Taiwan might be able to benefit.[181] Since China itself has entered into an FTA with Taiwan, other WTO Members may then feel more comfortable in initiating FTA negotiations with Taiwan.

From a geopolitical perspective, the ECFA has to the ability to ease potential conflicts between China and Taiwan, as the ECFA is not a single instrument in itself. It is a framework of agreements aiming to initiate further agreements on trade in goods, trade in services, investments and dispute settlement mechanisms between the Parties. Establishing a close economic integration, it is reasonable to

177 C-F Lo, 'Can There Be an Interim Agreement for Economic Integration in GATS', paper presented in Conference on Trade Remedy, Financial Crisis and the Challenge to the WTO, 29 October 2010, 17-21.

178 Ibid 6-7.

179 Ibid 9.

180 Even in the case of Hong Kong and Macau, they also conclude FTAs which have been notified to the WTO. In addition to the CEPA, Hong Kong has also concluded an FTA with New Zealand.

181 Lo (n 177) 9.

believe the possibility of military conflicts between China and Taiwan would thus be substantially reduced. Finally, from Taiwan's domestic political perspective, whether or not to accelerate economic integration with China is still highly debated. There have been some attempts to have a referendum on the ECFA but these attempts failed due to the ruling party's block-out. Whether it is feasible to decide such a major and highly controversial issue through a referendum remains contested, depicting Taiwan's divided domestic landscape and its legitimacy crisis arising from Taiwan's trade policy with China.

D. *Dispute Settlement Mechanisms in Taiwan-China Bilateral Agreements*

The Taiwan-China bilateral agreements, either the sectoral agreements or the comprehensive ECFA, provide a very primitive dispute resolution mechanism. The Parties are directed to enter into negotiations promptly in case of differences or disputes arising from the application of the agreements. For example, Article 11 of the Air Transport Agreement regulating dispute settlement provides that any dispute arising from its application shall be resolved by prompt negotiation. Nothing else is offered with regard to this 'prompt negotiation' obligation. Similar language reflecting the same spirit can be found in all these 15 agreements concluded between Taiwan and China.

Strictly speaking, this 'prompt negotiation' virtually entails no legal obligations and thus provides no legal/judicial protection for Parties and international economic actors. The prompt negotiation relies mainly upon the attitude of the government, especially the Chinese government. Two cases reveal the weaknesses or the uselessness of this mechanism. After the signature of the Sea Transport Agreement, Taiwanese enterprises, which previously operated between Taiwan and China for gravel shipment, were not able to acquire the permit from China to continue their business. In the absence of a well-developed dispute resolution mechanism in the Sea Transport Agreement, the operators were forced to stage a protest in front of Taiwan Democracy Memorial Hall.[182] The second case related to the allocation of flights during the Lunar New Year 2009 - Taiwanese airlines were not able to obtain the approval from Chinese authorities on their scheduled 36 flights while the tickets had already been sold out. Due the weak dispute settlement mechanism provided in the Air Transport Agreement, all the SEF could do was to ask the ARATS to look into the possibilities to increase the charter flights.[183]

---

[182] S-L Kuo, 'Gravel Shippers to Stage Protest' *Taipei News* (Taipei 19 January 2009) 3 <http://www.taipeitimes.com/News/taiwan/archives/2009/01/19/2003434117> accessed 1 September 2011.

[183] China Post news staff, 'China Asked to Boost direct Flights for Lunar New Year Holiday' *China Post* (Taipei 10 January 2009) <http://www.chinapost.com.tw/taiwan/china-taiwan-relations/2009/01/10/191357/China-asked.htm> accessed 1 September 2011.

These two examples expose the ineffectiveness of the dispute settlement mechanisms provided in these agreements. The fatal point nevertheless lies in the State-centred approach. Under these agreements, private individuals and enterprises have no enforceable rights. In case of any dispute, they have to rely on the governments to negotiate on the subject matters they concerned. Whether the governments are willing to negotiate for the interests of these injured private economic actors depends solely on their discretionary power. Therefore, the protection provided in these agreements is extremely insufficient.

The same flaws are also visible in the ECFA. First, the ECFA directs the Parties to enter into negotiations with a view to establishing an appropriate dispute settlement mechanism within six months after the enactment of the ECFA.[184] At the same time, it also instructs the Parties to reach an agreement expeditiously should the case involved disputes resulting from its interpretation, implementation and application.[185] The second paragraph then provides that where a dispute arises prior to the entry into force of the envisaged agreement on dispute settlement mechanisms, it should be resolved through consultations or the ECFA Committee in an appropriate manner.[186]

Although the ECFA has directed the Parties to enter into negotiations with the aim to reach an agreement on the type of dispute settlement mechanism to be employed, it remains unclear whether the Parties would be able to successfully conclude such agreement. Judging from the legal text of the ECFA, one might claim that the dispute settlement mechanism as provided in the ECFA does not differ significantly from the Air Transport Agreement. The only pertinent element as contained in the ECFA relating to dispute settlement is to resolve the dispute 'in an appropriate manner' which undoubtedly is extremely vague. It appears that the dispute settlement mechanism in the present form as set out in the ECFA relies heavily upon political or diplomatic negotiations. In light of the high degree of economic interdependence and potential economic conflicts, the capacity of this premature dispute settlement mechanism as contained in the ECFA could only cast more concerns between the Parties.

E. *Short Conclusion*

This section examines various bilateral agreements signed between Taiwan and China. It starts with the direct-transportation agreements allowing direct sea and air transport without transhipment via third ports. It also touches upon some sectoral agreements dealing with financial supervision and monetary management,

---

[184] The ECFA, Art. 10.1.
[185] The ECFA, Art. 10.1.
[186] The ECFA, Art. 10.2.

agricultural products and cooperation and their related intellectual property rights protection. It then examines the ECFA that has attracted the most attention by assessing its compatibility with the WTO rules. Regarding the dispute settlement mechanism as set out in these agreements, it is very primitive, providing only 'prompt negotiation' obligations without any further detail. The dispute settlement mechanism will thus rely heavily on the attitude of the Parties and the political climate across the Taiwan Strait.

IV. Trade Disputes between China and Taiwan at the National Level

Since its accession to the WTO, China had initiated many investigations procedures against Taiwanese products, including unbleached kraft liner/linerboard, Polyurethane, polybutylene, terphthalate resin, nonyl phenol, phenol, bisphenol-A (BPA), cold rolled steel products, and nylon 6,66 filament yarn.[187] As of 30 June 2010, definite anti-dumping duties were imposed upon polyvinyl chloride, phenol, ethanolamine (monoethanolamine diethanolamine), polybutylene terphthalate resin, polyurethane, nonyl phenol, bisphenol-A, methyl ethyl ketone, acetone, 1,4-butanediol, and polyamide-6. On the other hand, Taiwan had also taken several anti-dumping measures against Chinese products. It has initiated three investigations procedures against towelling products, footwear, uncoated printing and writing papers.[188] As of 25 February 2011, definite anti-dumping duties were imposed upon benzoyl peroxide (BPO) and sodium formaldehyde sulfoxylate (SFS).[189] Very few of these trade defence measures have been subject to administrative review or judicial review. The proceedings normally end up with a final decision from the competent authorities.

This section thus aims to examine the WTO-compatibility of these trade defence measures and explores the (limited) role of administrative/judicial review in the external trade measures. This section will also touch upon the domestic regulatory regime of China and Taiwan. The analysis will start with an introduction of the relevant regulatory framework, followed by an analysis of the existing practice through a case study. Given that China had filed a complaint against the US on steel safeguards, it offers a good comparison to explore China's domestic

[187] WTO, *Committee on Anti-Dumping Practices - Semi-Annual Report under Article 16.4 of the Agreement - China* (1October 2010) G/ADP/N/202/CHN, 12; *see* also other previous semi-annual reports of Anti-dumping committee.

[188] International Trade Commission, Ministry of Economic Affairs of Taiwan <http://portal.moeaitc.gov.tw/icweb/default.aspx> accessed 1 September 2011, in Chinese.

[189] WTO, *Committee on Anti-Dumping Practices - Semi-annual report under article 16.4 of the Agreement - The Separate Customs Territory of Taiwan, Penghu, Kinmen and Matsu - Revision* (25February 2011) G/ADP/N209/TPKM/rev.1.

trade defence measures against Taiwanese steel products and its attitude in the WTO and domestic setting. Therefore, this section chooses to examine China's anti-dumping and safeguard measures against Taiwanese steel products. As for Taiwan, it initiated a product-specific safeguard investigation, in response to petitions from Yunlin County Towelling Producers' Technology Development Association (the YCTPA) and an anti-dumping investigation on its own initiative against Chinese towelling products. These two investigations are amongst the first investigations initiated by Taiwan and touch upon the special safeguard measures provided in Section 16 of China's Accession Protocol and paragraph 242 of China's Working Party Report. Therefore, they provide a good basis for exploring the impact of China's accession to the WTO on Taiwan's trade regulatory regime and its response. This section will thus focus on these trade defence measures adopted by China and Taiwan against each other.

Before proceeding to the analysis, it is worth briefly to note the legal status of the WTO Agreement in Chinese legal system,[190] which would help to clarify the relevance of the WTO Agreement in domestic administrative and judicial proceedings. Following the pattern of Chapter VI, this section focuses on direct effects and legal hierarchy by examining relevant constitutional provisions and national legislation. A helpful starting point for this examination would be China's statement during its ratification procedure and its WTO Agreement implementing approach as included in the Working Party Report:

> The representative of China stated that China had been consistently performing its international treaty obligations in good faith. According to the Constitution and the Law on the Procedures of Conclusion of Treaties, the WTO Agreement fell within the category of 'important international agreements' subject to the ratification by the Standing Committee of the National People's Congress. China would ensure that its laws and regulations pertaining to or affecting trade were in conformity with the WTO Agreement and with its commitments so as to fully perform its international obligations. For this purpose, China had commenced a plan to systematically revise its relevant domestic laws. Therefore, the WTO Agreement would be implemented by China in an effective and uniform manner through revising its existing domestic laws and enacting new ones fully in compliance with the WTO Agreement.[191]

Several elements are identifiable in this statement: the nature of WTO Agreement in China's domestic legal system; the legal bases for the conclusion of international agreements; and an implementing approach. The statement clarifies that the WTO Agreement falls within the scope of 'important international agreements' and it points to two major instruments that govern the concluding of

[190] For the legal status of the WTO Agreement in Taiwanese domestic legal system, *see supra* Chapter VI, text to (n 10) *et seq.*

[191] China's Working Party Report, para. 57.

international agreements: the Constitution and the *Law on the Procedures of Conclusion of Treaties* (hereinafter the '*Treaty Conclusion Law*').

Article 67 of the Constitution prescribes the powers and functions of the NPCSC, including the ratification and abrogation of treaties and important agreements. The *Treaty Conclusion Law* further regulates the procedures for concluding international agreements. Article 2 defines the scope of the application of this law to bilateral and multilateral treaties; it also covers agreements or any other instruments possessing the nature of a treaty or an agreement. Without offering a definition for 'treaty' or 'agreement', the *Treaty Conclusion Law* directly defines the scope of 'treaties and important agreements' by listing three subject matters: friendship and cooperation, peace and similar treaties of a political nature; territory and delimitation of boundary lines; and judicial assistance and extradition.[192] Treaties and agreements containing provisions inconsistent with Chinese domestic laws and those still subject to ratification fall within the scope of 'treaties and important agreements' as defined by the *Treaty Conclusion Law*.[193] While acceding to a multilateral treaty or an important multilateral agreement, the State Council, after examination and verification, should refer it to the NPCSC to decide on accession.[194] The President of the People's Republic of China shall ratify the multilateral treaty or important multilateral agreement in accordance with the NPCSC's decision.[195]

China's accession to the WTO basically follows the procedures laid down by the Constitution and the *Treaty Conclusion Law*. The NPCSC, prior to the Doha Ministerial Meeting, reached its decision on the issue of WTO accession and authorised the President to ratify the accession protocol. After the Ministerial decision on the adoption of China's accession, Jiang Zemin, the Chinese President, ratified the accession protocol on 11 November 2001. It is also worth noting that the signature of China's Accession Protocol by Shi Guangsheng, the Minister of Foreign Trade and Economic Cooperation, and the ratification by Jiang took place on the same date. The ratified accession protocol was almost immediately deposited with the WTO Secretariat.

The statement also hints how China envisaged its implementing approach. Namely, China would systematically revise its domestic law to meet the WTO Agreement. However, the statement does not fully spell out the direct applicability of the WTO Agreement in the Chinese courts and the way to resolve the conflicts between the WTO Agreement and domestic laws. Views on the judicial enforceability of the WTO Agreement in China differ substantially. The prevailing

[192] The *Treaty Conclusion Law*, Art. 7(2).
[193] The *Treaty Conclusion Law*, Art. 7(2).
[194] The *Treaty Conclusion Law*, Art. 11(2), subparagraph 1.
[195] The *Treaty Conclusion Law*, Art. 7(2).

view seems to deny its direct applicability to the Chinese courts. Yang Linping, former judge of the SPC, argues that the Chinese courts cannot refer to the WTO Agreement. Instead, the Chinese courts are obliged to apply domestic law and regulations while taking due account of the principle of consistent interpretation when resolving conflicts between domestic laws and the WTO Agreement.[196] Apart from Yang's statement, the denial of direct applicability of the WTO Agreement on the Chinese courts may be based on the following reasons. First, in case of non-compliance of the WTO Agreement it is China, the State will resume its state responsibility. While private parties are inevitably affected by these WTO rules, they are *indirectly* affected. The WTO rules are not sufficiently clear and precise and are thus non-justiciable by nature. Therefore, the WTO Agreement cannot be a cause of action for private parties to resort to at the Chinese courts. Additionally, there is no constitutional authority to support the direct application of the WTO Agreement at the Chinese courts. The direct application of treaties or international agreements at the Chinese domestic courts is rare. Moreover, as the WTO Agreement covers extremely complex rules, direct application of these rules may overburden the Chinese courts and result in inconsistency in the interpretation that would undermine the uniformity of the Chinese legal system. Above all, China may be prejudiced in its future negotiation if it recognises direct applicability of the WTO Agreement since most WTO Members do not.[197]

By contrast, some argue that direct application of the WTO Agreement helps to fill the lacuna in those areas where China has not revised or enacted WTO-consistent laws and regulations. Direct application of the WTO Agreement, particularly in the area of intellectual property rights protection, can contribute to the establishment of a well-functioning legal regime. Furthermore, direct application will contribute to the rule of law in China, notably the transparency of its judicial review. Based on these arguments, Chen argues that direct application of the WTO Agreement meets China's real needs and is thus a more practical approach. Following this direct application approach, Chen further argues that, as the WTO Agreement was ratified by the President in accordance with the decision of the NPCSC, it enjoys the same legal status of national legislation and shall prevail over local legislation, autonomous decrees, special decrees, and administrative decrees.[198]

---

196 L Yang, 'Some Issues on China's Judicial Review (Zhongguo sifa shencha zhidu xu guanzhu de ji ge wenti)' (2004) Justice in China (Zhongguo sifa) 70, 70-72, in Chinese.

197 L Zhou, *WTO Rules and Theoretical Innovation of Chinese Economic Law* (*WTO guize yu zhongguo jingji fa lilun chuangxin*) (China University of Political Science and Law Press, Beijing 2003) 160-167.

198 L Xue, 'The Application of the WTO Agreement in China (WTO xieding zai zhongguo guonei de shiyong)' (2002) <http://www.wtolaw.gov.cn/display/displayInfo.asp?IID=200207071511263073> accessed 1 September 2011, in Chinese.

However, debates on direct applicability of the WTO Agreement are largely had amongst the academics and do not seep into the Chinese domestic courts, except for the SPC. In a case before Guangdong Higher Court, the Court was called upon to examine whether the administrative permit for the publication and reproduction of audiovisual products was indispensable for the protection of intellectual property rights. The Court repealed the ruling of the lower court, holding that copyrights are rights protected by national legislation. The Court further declared that these rights will not be affected even though the right holders are not able to obtain an administrative permit for publication and reproduction. Based on these arguments, the Court found that audio-visual products without administrative permit for publication and reproductions did not fall within the scope of subject 'against the prohibitive rules of Chinese administrative rules'. These audio-visual products should also enjoy intellectual property rights protection.[199] Although this case reflects one of the main issues in *China – Intellectual Property Rights*, neither the parties nor the court raised the issue of WTO-inconsistency.

In contrast, the SPC is relatively responsive to concerns of the other WTO Members and the sensitivity of WTO-compatibility of Chinese domestic laws. In response to the political pressure from the US, the SPC issued its second *Judicial Interpretation* on the criminal thresholds of 'serious' or 'extremely serious' as prescribed in Articles 213-217 of *China's Criminal Law* that turned out to be a major issue in *China – Intellectual Property Rights*. Regardless of its responsiveness and sensitivity, the SPC did not refer to in its *Judicial Interpretation*. In its judicial interpretation on the *Regulation Several Problems in the Trial of Trade-Related Administrative Litigation Cases* (the '*Trade-Related Administrative Litigation Regulation*'), the Court made it clear that the applicable laws for the Chinese courts in hearing trade-related administrative cases are national legislation and relevant regulations and decrees.[200] The SPC instructed lower courts to rule on trade-related administrative litigation cases according to Chinese domestic laws and regulations. In case of two reasonable interpretations of national laws and administrative regulations, the SPC added Article 9 of the Regulation to the analysis and expressed that a WTO-compatible interpretation should be preferred. According to the Regulation, the SPC did not envisage a direct application of the WTO Agreement at the Chinese courts. The relevance of the WTO Agreement is limited to the consistent-interpretation approach. The Court did not clarify the

[199] *UFO v. Wumuzhao*, reported as Yue-Kau-Fa-Min-Zhong-San-Zhi No. 210 Ruling (2005) <http://ipr.chinacourt.org/public/detail_sfws.php?id=3275> accessed 1 September 2011, in Chinese. This case precisely corresponds to the first claim of the United States in *China – Intellectual Property Rights, see supra* text to (n 117), *et seq.*

[200] *Regulationon on Several Problems in the Trial of Trade-Related Administrative Litigation Cases*, Art. 7, 8.

issue of legal hierarchy, but it is safe to say that this issue has little importance for the Chinese courts since the WTO Agreement has been excluded from the list of applicable laws at the Chinese courts when hearing trade-related administrative litigation cases. There is thus no need for the SPC to deal with this issue.[201]

A. *China's Trade Defence Measures against Taiwanese Products*

1. *Anti-Dumping Measures*

a. *General Regulatory Framework*

The regulation on anti-dumping practices dates back to Article 30 of the *Foreign Trade Act of People's Republic of China* enacted in 1994 (hereinafter *1994 Foreign Trade Act*).[202] As China strived to accede to the GATT and hoped it could become a founding Member of the WTO, this *1994 Foreign Trade Act* was part of the legislative package that tried to ensure that China's foreign trade regulatory regime was compatible with the GATT/WTO. After the enactment of *1994 Foreign Trade Act,* the State Council issued *Anti-Dumping and Countervailing Regulation of People's Republic of China* in 1997. In connection with China's accession to the WTO, this *Anti-Dumping and Countervailing Regulation* was subsequently repealed in 2001 as a new *Anti-Dumping Regulation of People's Republic of China* was adopted on 31 October 2001. Furthermore, in relation to the amendment of the *1994 Foreign Trade Act* on 6 April 2004, this anti-dumping regulation was also amended on 31 March 2004. Consequently, the *2004 Foreign Trade Act* and *2004 Anti-Dumping Regulation* govern the existing framework for anti-dumping measures.

Chapter 8 of the *2004 Foreign Trade Act,* covering from Articles 40 to 50, regulates trade remedy measures. Article 41 authorises the state to take anti-dumping measures in case 'a product from other countries or regions is dumped into the

[201] An interesting contrast can be drawn in regard to private international law. Chinese statutory designation honors international agreements to which China is a party. Article 142(2) of the *General Principles of Civil Law of People's Republic of China* provides that, regarding civil relations with foreigners, the international treaty concluded or acceded to by China shall apply where conflicts arise between the international treaty concerned and domestic laws. Article 236 of Civil Procedure Law of the People's Republic of China regulates in a similar way. In civil proceedings involving foreign elements, when any international treaty concluded or acceded to by China contains provisions differing from those of the Civil Procedure Law, the provisions of the international treaty shall apply, except those on which China has announced reservations. Nonetheless, these two provisions govern mainly procedural aspect of private international law and of little relevance of the WTO Agreement. China's statutory designation on the legal status and legal hierarchy of international agreements to which it is a party is extremely inconsistent and incoherent.

[202] An unofficial English version <http://www.lawinfochina.com/law/display.asp?id=664> accessed 1 September 2011. Article 30 of *1994 Foreign Trade Act* provides, 'should a well established or fledgling industry at home be in substantial harm or under threat of such harm due to the import of relative goods in under normal value, the State may take any countermeasures to expel or mitigate such harm or threat.'

domestic market at a price less than its normal value and under such conditions as to cause or threaten to cause material injury to the established domestic industries, or materially retards the establishment of domestic industries'. The aim of these anti-dumping measures is to 'eliminate or mitigate such injury, threat of injury or retardation'.[203] In respect of the *2001 Anti-Dumping Regulation,* it consists of six chapters. The first and last chapter are general and supplementary provisions respectively. Chapters 2 to 5 deal with the substantial elements: dumping and injury; anti-dumping measures; and the time limit for and the review of anti-dumping duties and price-undertaking.

Article 66 of the *2004 Foreign Trade Act* regulates administrative review and judicial review of foreign trade measures. Private parties engaging in foreign trade activities may refer to administrative review or resort to people's courts for judicial review when dissatisfied with these measures. Article 53 of the *2001 Anti-Dumping Regulation* offers the same opportunity for administrative review and judicial review. Private parties may refer to administrative review or judicial review for the following three categories of decisions: a final determination on the anti-dumping investigation according to Article 25 of the regulation; an interim review decision; a decision made in accordance with Chapter 4 of the *Anti-Dumping Regulation.* Chapter 4 of the Regulation then cover three types of decisions: whether to levy anti-dumping duties; whether to impose a retrospective levy: whether to levy or refund or not the duties against a new export business operator.

In addition to the *2004 Foreign Trade Act* and *Anti-Dumping Regulation,* the Ministry of Commerce (the MOFCOM, the successor to Ministry of Foreign Trade and Economic Cooperation, the MOFTEC) and State Economic and Trade Commission (SETC) issued a number of ministerial level implementing rules. These rules regulate petition, questionnaire, the disclosure of information, on-site investigation, price-undertaking, interim review, determination of injury, the adjustment of the scope of products, hearing, and so on. In addition, the SPC also issued *Regulation on the Application of Law in the Trial of Anti-Dumping Administrative Litigation Cases* to guide lower courts in the administrative litigation on anti-dumping measures. As noted in Chapter V, this *Regulation on the Application of Law in the Trial of Anti-Dumping Administrative Litigation* can be situated in a broader context of the *Regulation on Several Problems in the Trial of Trade-Related Administrative Litigation Cases* of the SPC.[204]

---

[203] Article 42 instructs the competent authority, notably MOFCOM to consult with governments of exporting countries or regions, where the export of a product, at a price less than its normal value from these countries or regions to the market of a third country causes or threatens to cause material injury to the established domestic industries, or materially retards the establishment of domestic industries.

[204] For the regulatory framework of China's anti-dumping regime, *see* Z Wang and M Yu, *China Foreign Trade Law* (*Zhongguo waimao fa*) (Wuhan University Press, Wuchang 2006) For an overview

b. *Anti-Dumping Measures on Certain Steel Products*

On 23 March 2002, China decided to initiate an anti-dumping investigation against Taiwanese cold-rolled steel products. This initiative, situated in the context of the US safeguard measures against steel products, is the first trade defence measures taken by China against Taiwanese products since their accessions to the WTO.[205] The MOFCOM released its preliminary and final reports on 20 May 2003 and 23 September 2003 respectively. Surprisingly, the MOFCOM in its preliminary report stated that whereas it found a dumping margin and a causal link between dumping and material injury to domestic industry, and whereas it would continue to publish the final report, given the 'particular market condition of the investigated products', it would not impose provisional anti-dumping measures against the products concerned.[206]

In the final report, it found that there were dumped imports, material injury to domestic industry and a causal link between these two factors. Similarly, in light of the 'particular market condition' mentioned in the preliminary report, the MOFCOM in its final report decided not to take anti-dumping measures. Nevertheless, when the US decided to stop the safeguard measure consequently of the WTO-inconsistency finding by the Panel and the Appellate Body, Chinese safeguard measures against Taiwanese steel products were also lifted. As a result, the decision not to impose anti-dumping duties was repealed; a definitive anti-dumping duty was thus imposed upon Taiwanese steel products.[207] In this case, several issues deserve further examination: normal value and export price; injury; causation between dumping and injury; and the relevance of the safeguard investigation to anti-dumping investigation. These aspects will be examined in connection with the obligation to provide sufficiently detailed explanations in its determinations as set out in Article 12 of the Anti-Dumping Agreement (the ADA). Administrative review and judicial review is also to be covered.

---

of China's Foreign Trade Act and its commentary, *see* D Huang and Z Wang, *Understanding Foreign Trade Law of PRC and Related International Rules* (Zhonghua renmin gongheguo duiwai maoyi fa: Tiaowen jing shi ji guoji guize) (Law Press, Beijing 2004). For Literature in English, *see* T W Huang, 'The Gathering Storm of Antidumping Enforcement in China' (2002) 36 Journal of World Trade 255; K W Almstedt and P M Norton, 'China's Antidumping Laws and the WTO Antidumping Agreement' (2000) 34 Journal of World Trade 75. *See* also M U Killion, 'Quest for Legal Safeguards for Foreign Exporters Under China's Anti-Dumping Regime' (2003-2004) 29 North Carolina Journal of Law & Commercial Regulation 417.

[205] This investigation also covers products originating from Russia, Korea, Ukraine, and Kazakhstan. *See* MOFTEC Notice No. 14 (2002) <http://gpj.mofcom.gov.cn/aarticle/cs/200208/20020800035528.html> accessed 1 September 2011.

[206] MOFTEC Notice No. 17 (2002) <http://gpj.mofcom.gov.cn/index.shtml> accessed 1 September 2011. The reason why MOFCOM chose not to impose anti-dumping measure was mainly because a parallel safeguard investigation on certain steel products was undergoing. See *infra*. IIIA(b) Safeguard measures on certain steel products.

[207] MOFCOM Notice 75 (2003) <http://gpj.mofcom.gov.cn/aarticle/cs/200401/20040100170507.html> accessed 1 September 2011.

i. *Fair Comparison between Normal Value and Export Price.* In order to conduct a fair comparison between normal value and export price, the MOFCOM established the normal value by examining whether domestic transactions of Taiwanese producers amounts to five percent of their exports to China, as set out in Article 2.2 and footnote 2 of the ADA. In accordance with Article 2.1 of the ADA, the MOFCOM then excluded below cost sales and related-party sales on the ground that these sales are not 'in the ordinary course of trade'.[208]

In the case of Shang Shing Industrial Co. Ltd, the MOFCOM indicated that Shang Shing's domestic sales in Taiwan is more than 5 percent of its exports to China and was thus eligible for the basis of normal value determination. The MOFCOM then excluded below cost sales for one of the items as it accounted to more than 20 percent of its domestic sales. The rest of domestic sales of this item constituted as the basis for the determination of normal value. In other items where domestic sales were all below cost sales, the MOFCOM decided to adopt a constructed value as the normal value since these sales were not in the ordinary course of trade and could not serve as the basis for normal value determination.[209] In relation to export price, the MOFCOM stated that given Shang Shing Industrial Co. Ltd exported products either directly to China or through a non-related trader, these two prices could thus be adopted as the export price when performing a price comparison. The MOFCOM, arguably, had provided sufficient detail with regard to its decision to exclude below cost sales and to adopt constructed value and export price.

ii. *Material Injury.* With regard to material injury on the domestic industry, the MOFCOM began its decision on accumulation with Article 9 of the *Anti-Dumping Regulation.* Then the MOFCOM justified its decision based upon two reasons. First, each country's dumping margin of the named products is no less than two percent and should be ignored. Second, the dumped imports were competitors to the domestic like products. Thus the injury caused by the dumped imported from different countries could be accumulated. The MOFCOM then established the existence of material injury on the domestic industry based on the following reasons. Firstly, the MOFCOM examined the volume of dumped imports of products and their market share in China. Then, the MOFCOM analyzed the price of dumped imports and their impact on price of domestic like products and on the domestic industry. Finally, the MOFCOM evaluated other economic factors and indices.[210]

---

208 ADA Final report, Section 3.1, normal value and export price, the Taiwan section.
209 Ibid.
210 ADA Final Report, Section 4, Injury.

The injury assessment appeared to comply with Article 3 of the ADA. Nevertheless, the MOFCOM failed to base its determination on an objective examination of the positive evidence as set out in Article 3.1 of the ADA. An objective 'examination of the impact of the dumped imports on the domestic industry,' through an 'evaluation of all relevant economic factors and indices having a bearing on the state of the industry' as mandated by Article 4.4, read in connection with the overarching Article 3.1 of the ADA was lacking. An explanation with sufficient detail as required by Article 12.2.2 of the ADA was also not provided in the final report.

As held by the Appellate Body, the term 'positive evidence' focused on the facts underpinning and justifying the injury determination, and the term 'objective examination' was concerned with the investigation process itself.[211] Article 3.1 of the ADA sets out the general guidance for interpreting the other provisions. According to the Panel in *Thailand – H-Beams,* Article 3.4 of the ADA when read together with Article 3.1 requires the investigation authorities to support its finding on injury with positive factual evidence through a well-reasoned and meaningful analysis of the industry's status. A mere characterisation of every relevance and irrelevance of economic factors would not satisfy this obligation; a thorough evaluation of the state of industry, in light of those factors set out in the last sentence of Article 3.4, is essential. Above all, a persuasive explanation in relation to these factors leading to finding of injury should be offered.[212] Such objective examination on the objective evidence through thorough evaluation of the state of the industry did not exist in the investigation report.

For example, while the MOFCOM argued that imports of products had increased sharply, the imports during 2000 and 2001 increased only 9.84 and 8.32 per cent respectively.[213] From 1999 to 2001, the market share of imported products accounted for 36.17, 35.06, and 37.91 per cent,[214] which was a rather levelled trend instead of an upward trend. With regard to the price of imported products and its impact on the like products in the domestic industry, the average imported price increased from 327.73 (US dollar per ton) to 362.46 from 1999 to 2000, which contradicted conclusion of the MOFCOM that the price was in a downward trend.[215] Furthermore, as

---

211 Appellate Body Report on Appellate Body Report, *United States – Anti-Dumping Measures on Certain Hot-Rolled Steel Products from Japan* (*US – Hot-Rolled Steel*), WT/DS184/AB/R, adopted 23 August2001, DSR 2001:X, 4697, para. 193.

212 Panel Report on *Thailand – Anti-Dumping Duties on Angles, Shapes and Sections of Iron or Non-Alloy Steel and H-Beams from Poland* (*Thailand – H-Beams*), WT/DS122/R, adopted 5 April 2001, as modified by Appellate Body Report, WT/DS122/AB/R, DSR 2001:VII, 2741, para. 7.236

213 ADA Final Report, Section 4, Injury.

214 Ibid.

215 Ibid.

the MOFCOM noted, the average price of like products in domestic industry lowered 1.3 per cent from 1999 to 2001;[216] outcome could not be named as a material injury. Thirdly, concerning other economic factors or indices, the MOFCOM merely referred to them in a checklist. Explanation with sufficient detail for each factor and the overall impact of these factors had not been provided. Take market share for example: the MOFCOM argued that the market share of like products in the domestic industry decreased from 1999 to 2001, accounting for 44.9, 41.70, and 43.94 per cent respectively. Nevertheless, comparing these to the market share of the imported products, which accounts for 36.17, 35.06, and 37.91 per cent respectively, it the market share of like products of Chinese domestic industry in relation to imported products remained to be stable and hardly affected. Thus, the MOFCOM did not draw its conclusion of a decrease of market share of domestic industry from positive evidence and objective examination. More importantly, the analysis of the MOFCOM was not objective and unbiased in that, depending on the results, the MOFCOM focused on the difference between every single consecutive year investigation period, namely from 1999 to 2001.

iii. *Causation between Dumping and Material Injury.* With regard to the causation issue, the MOFCOM established its finding on a causal link between dumping and material injury to domestic injury. It noted that in the final report there was coincidence in the trends between the price and the market share of the imported products and domestic like products. Imported products were the substantial cause of material injury to the domestic industry. The MOFCOM then conducted its non-attribution analysis, excluding such factors indicated in the final sentence of Article 3.5 of the ADA from being injurious factors to domestic industry.[217] Two of these factors should be further elaborated.

First, the MOFCOM noted that the impact of imported products from countries other than the investigated countries was less significant since their market shares altogether accounted for less than 30 per cent of the Chinese market. This non-attribution analysis was not consistent with Article 3.5 of the ADA as the MOFCOM did not go further to identify and distinguish the injurious effects of imports from other countries from the injurious effects of the dumped imports. The MOFCOM thus had no rational basis to determine the degree of injury to be ascribed to dumped imports.[218]

More importantly, the MOFCOM failed to offer a persuasive explanation as to why the injury of Chinese domestic industry was not caused by the change of

[216] Ibid.
[217] ADA Final Report, Section 5, Causation.
[218] *See* Appellate Body Report on *US – Hot-Rolled Steel*, paras. 223-224, 226.

international steel market. The MOFCOM asserted that 15 major steel exporting countries accounted substantially for the market share of the international steel industry, and that the investigated countries were also major exporters at the international steel market and constituted as an important element in affecting the change in steel market. While the price of cold-rolled steel products in different markets could possibly affect one another, only products competing in the same market would be the direct factor. Since those countries' products accounted for 70 per cent of the Chinese market share and continued to increase in volume and market share, they had a more direct impact on the price of like products in China's domestic industry. Therefore, the products of those countries were deemed to be the main cause. Through these imports, the international steel market could affect the price of like products in China's domestic industry and the entire domestic industry as a whole.[219]

The MOFCOM's argument in relation to the change of international steel market was flawed and unfounded. It failed to delineate the international steel market from those countries whose products are under investigation. The MOFCOM's assertion that, even if Chinese industry was affected by the international steel market, the international market injured Chinese market through those investigated countries was inconsistent with Article 3.5 of the ADA, particularly in light of the jurisprudence of the WTO panel/Appellate Body. The MOFCOM did not identify and distinguish the factor of international steel market from the dumped imports; to the contrary, it mingled these two factors, attributing the injurious effects of change in the international steel market to the dumped imports. In addition, the MOFCOM failed to provide a persuasive explanation as to why the reverse could not be true: it is the changes in the international steel market, rather than the imported products, that caused the serious injury to the domestic industry.

iv. *Relevance of Safeguard Measures.* As noted both in the preliminary and final reports, given the 'particular market condition of the investigated products,' the MOFCOM decided to suspend its anti-dumping measure. This unuttered particular market condition is believed to be situated in the context to safeguard measures against steel products adopted by major actors in the international trading system. During its anti-dumping investigation on cold-rolled steel products, the MOFCOM was conducting a concurrent anti-dumping investigation against steel products with wider coverage. On the one hand, these two investigations contradicted with each other in that it is generally held that the anti-dumping measures are trade remedies against unfair trade practice whereas safeguard measures are against fair trade practice. The concerned products cannot

[219] Ibid.

possess fair trade practices and unfair trade practices at the same time. Alternatively, even if one holds that safeguard measures are not necessarily trade remedies against unfair trade practices, and that safeguard measures are merely a less stringent trade remedy provided for in the WTO Agreement, two concurrent investigations may suffer from the problem of 'double remedies'. In other words, the same injury may be remedied by two trade remedy measures. This may explain why the MOFCOM chose to halt the imposition of anti-dumping measures until the lift of safeguard measures against steel products.

v. *Administrative Review/Judicial Review.* In section 7 of the MOFCOM's final decision, it provides that, according to Article 53 of *Anti-dumping Regulation*, administrative review and judicial review can be resorted to as the final determination for anti-dumping measures. This is in line with China's obligation to provide an independent and impartial judicial review, which includes the obligation to inform the applicants of the opportunity for appeal on foreign trade measures. Nevertheless, exporters, traders of the concerned products or petitioners did not seek to administrative review or judicial review in this present case.[220]

2. *Safeguard Measures*

a. *General Regulatory Framework*

Like anti-dumping measures, China's safeguard regulatory regime is also one of the outlined remedies measures in the *1994 Foreign Trade Act*. Article 29 of the *1994 Foreign Trade Act* provides the legal basis for safeguard measures and directs the State to take the necessary protective measures to eliminate or reduce injury or threat of injury on domestic like product producers or on directly competitive products which suffer from material injury or threat of material injury due to the increase of imported products. Nevertheless, it was not until 31 October 2001 that the State Council adopted the *Safeguard Measures Regulation of People's Republic of China* and became effective on 1 January 2002. This regulation was subsequently amended in 2004 because the *Foreign Trade Act* was revised in 2004. The *2004 Safeguard Regulation* also consists of five chapters: general provisions; investigations; safeguard measures; the time limit for and review of safeguard measures;

[220] As noted above, Taiwanese unbleached kraft liner/linerboard had also been previously imposed with anti-dumping duties on 30 September 2005, but this measure was subsequently repealed, on 9 January 2006, by administrative review with the decision of Shang-Fa-Han No. 1 (2006). While the MOFCOM in its Notice No 8 (2006) refers to this decision, and decided to terminate the levy of anti-dumping duties. This decision of administrative review has not been made public available. This points to the weakness of administrative review/judicial review in China, and lack of transparency in this regard.

and supplementary provisions. Moreover, paralleling the anti-dumping measures, several ministerial level implementation rules are issued by the MOFCOM and the SETC. These implementation rules further define and clarify issues on petition, hearing, safeguard measures and the determination of injury, and the adjustment of the scope of the products.[221]

b. *Safeguard Measures on Certain Steel Products*

On 20 May 2002, the MOFTEC initiated a safeguard investigation on certain Taiwanese steel products in response to the petition from China Steel Industry Association, Shanghai Baoshan Steel and Iron Group Corporation, Anshan Steel and Iron Group Corporation, Wuhan Steel and Iron Corporation (Group), Capital Steel and Iron Corporation, and Handan Steel and Iron Company Ltd.[222] Immediately after the investigation, China imposed provisional safeguard measures on the investigated products. On 19 November 2002, the MOFTEC and the SETC co-issued a final report and decided to impose definitive safeguard measures on five steel products: non-alloy hot rolled sheets and coils; non-alloy cold rolled sheets and coils; organic coated sheets; non grain-oriented electrical sheets; and stainless non-alloy cold rolled sheets and coils.[223] Apart from this final report, the SETC also issued a final report on the determination of injury.[224]

China's safeguard measure against Taiwanese steel products should be examined in the context of a series of steel safeguard measures taken by other WTO Members. There is a clear link between proceedings in the WTO Dispute Settlement Mechanism and Members' domestic investigation proceedings.

---

[221] Wang and Yu (n 204) 253-254. For the literature in English on China's safeguard regime, *see* L Chen and Y Gu, 'China's Safeguard Measures Under the New WTO Framework' (2001-2002) 25 Fordham International Law Journal 1169; T W Huang, 'China Launches its Safeguard Enforcement: A Critical Assessment' (2003) 37 Journal of World Trade 329.

[222] MOFTEC Notice No. 29 (2002) <http://gpj.mofcom.gov.cn/aarticle/cs/200211/20021100048869.html>accessed 1 September 2011. This investigation covered products originating from, *inter alia*, Japan, Republic of Korea, the European Communities and Malaysia. *See* also WTO, *Committee on Safeguards - Notification under Article 12.1(a) of the Agreement on Safeguards on Initiation of an Investigation and the Reasons for it – Notification under Article 12.4 of the Agreement on Safeguards before Taking a Provisional Safeguard Measures referred to in Article 6, The People's Republic of China* (23 May 2002) G/SG/N/6/CHN/1, G/SG/N/7/CHN/1, G/SG/N/11/CHN/1.

[223] MOFTEC Notice No. 29, in particular the final report in attachment 2, available at <http://gpj.mofcom.gov.cn/aarticle/cs/200211/20021100048869.html> accessed 1 September 2011. *See* also WTO, *Committee on Safeguards - Notification under Article 12.1(c) of the Agreement on Safeguards on Finding a Serious Injury or Threat Thereof Caused by Increased Imports Notification pursuant to Article 12.1(c) of the Agreement of Safeguards, the People's Republic of China* (5 November 2002) G/SG/N/8/CHN/1, G/SG/N/10/CHN/1. In this notification, it is stated that a copy of the notification has been sent to the permanent missions of the aforementioned WTO Members. Nevertheless, China did not notify Taiwan, which was already a Member of the WTO at that point.

[224] SETC Notice No. 829 (2002) <http://www.cacs.gov.cn/cacs/anjian/anjianshow.aspx?str1=1&articleId=38849> accessed 1 September 2011.

As noted in Section II, it is worth exploring whether Taiwan's (or even China's) arguments as a third party in *US – Steel Safeguards* during the WTO Dispute Settlement Mechanism may be seen as a gesture to argue against the WTO-consistency of Chinese steel safeguard measures.

i. *Unforeseen Development.* 'Unforeseen development' is one of the major issues that attract much of the Panel's attention during the *US – Steel Safeguards* proceeding. Ironically, China seemed to pay insufficient attention to this issue in its safeguard investigation. In its notification to the Committee on Safeguards, China identified the safeguard measures against steel products imposed by the US and the EU as unforeseen developments. Some explanations, though not adequate and reasoned, were provided in the SETC report on the determination of injury. The SETC asserted that a comprehensive and stringent safeguard measure with great magnitude against steel products imposed by the US was unforeseeable even if it was aware of the safeguard investigation conducted by the US. The chain reaction of safeguard measures by other Members and the impact of these safeguard measures on the increase in steel export to China was also unforeseeable.[225] On the one hand, China seems to confuse 'unforeseen developments' with 'unforeseeable developments'. In its final injury report, it tried to justify these developments as 'unforeseeable' rather than 'unforeseen'. On the other hand, China did not address the issue of 'logical connection' as dictated by the phrasing of the requirement. More specifically, China failed to provide an adequate and reasoned explanation on the logical connection between its incurring of the WTO treaty obligation, the alleged unforeseen developments, increased import and serious injury or threat of serious injury to its domestic industries. Furthermore in the report co-issued by the MOFCOM and the SETC, the issue of 'unforeseen developments' is dealt with only after the determination of increased imports; serious injury and causation have been established. This implies that China simply singled out several events and labelled them as 'unforeseen developments'. Therefore, there is no examination on the 'logical connection' requirement.

ii. *Causation.* In relation to causation, China argued in *US – Steel Safeguards* that the causal link between increased imports and serious injury is 'a genuine and substantial relationship of cause and effect;' this causal link requires a coincidence between an increased imports and a serious injury and should also meet with criteria of non-attribution criteria. An examination based on these criteria cannot be found in China's final report on steel safeguard measures. Several issues are

[225] Ibid Chapter 3.

relevant here. When determining the coincidence between an increased imports and a serious injury, China included an investigation period from 1997 to the first quarter of 2002. This methodology is problematic since China did not accede to the WTO until 11 December 2001. China tried to justify its finding on the increased imports with pre-WTO figures and subsequently establishing a causal link between the increased imports and the serious injury by emphasising even greater increase in imports from 2001 to the first quarter of 2002.[226] However, this does not cure it of its methodological defect on its finding of the coincidence between increased imports and serious injury. Assuming that China's claim that safeguard measures against steel products imposed by the US and the EU constitute unforeseen developments, coincidence between increased imports and serious injury should thus be established during the period starting from the point of the unforeseen developments occurred. More importantly, China did not exclude these alleged increased imports before its accession when conducting its causation analysis. While China stated that factors such as domestic consumption, intra-industry competition, and technological innovation had no causal link to the serious injury experienced by the domestic industry – which appears to be a non-attribution analysis – the pre-existent injury prior to its accession to the WTO had not been excluded. This also corresponds to Taiwan's argument on proportionality of safeguard measures. China's safeguard measures should not be used to redress all injury felt by its domestic industry; instead, the safeguard measures can only be imposed to remedy the serious injury caused by increased *imports because of unforeseen developments, and in this case it would be the steel safeguard measures imposed by the US and the EU.*

In light of Taiwan's argument in *US – Steel Safeguards*, the terminology of 'substantial cause' employed by China in its final report is of great significance.[227] This is not surprising since China's trade remedy regulatory regime is highly influenced, if not designed, by the US. In this vein, Taiwan's argument that the 'substantial cause' test is WTO-inconsistent may be also used against China's safeguard measures. While the Panel did not require the increased imports to be the only factor causing the serious injury to domestic industry, it nevertheless stressed the significance of the increased imports when compared to other factors as a whole. A reasoned and adequate explanation should be offered on this point. China, in its final report claimed that the increased imports were the 'substantial cause' of serious injury to domestic industry. At the same time, it also pointed to the domestic

---

226 *See, e.g.*, Final Report by MOFTEC and SETC, paras. 68-70.

227 The term of 'substantial cause' is not used in ASG. For a critic of this terminology, *see* Huang (n 221) 344-345.

industry's increased productivity as another factor causing injury to the domestic industry.[228] Nevertheless, China noted that, due to the increase in domestic consumption and decrease in productivity in 2001, the adverse effect of the increased productivity on the domestic industry is lessened.[229] This explanation is far from being reasoned and adequate.

iii *Definition of Domestic Industry.* On the definition of domestic industry, taking Taiwan's argument in *US – Steel Safeguards* into account, it is interesting to note that the same terminology of 'major proportion' of the domestic industry is also used by China. The final report stated that the SETC conducted an investigation amongst the domestic producers, whose production constituted as a major proportion of the total volume of domestic production and could thus represent the domestic industry.[230] Nevertheless, China did not provide further information about these producers, in particular the percentage of their production. It is thus difficult to ascertain whether these producers could constitute a major proportion of total volume of domestic production and whether these producers could represent the domestic industry. As Taiwan argues in *US – Steel Safeguards,* since the determination of domestic industry is among 'all pertinent issues of fact and law' as set out in Article 3.1 of the ASG, China is thus obliged to provide an adequate and reasoned explanation on the determination of domestic industry. China's failure to provide an adequate and reasoned explanation on its definition of 'domestic industry' breaches its WTO obligation under the ASG.

B. *Taiwan's Trade Defence Measures against Chinese Products*

1. *Safeguard Measures*

a. *General Regulatory Framework*

When pursuing its GATT membership, Taiwan substantially reformed its trade regulatory regime. One of the most significant efforts was the enactment of *Foreign Trade Act* in 1993, where it laid down the regulatory framework for Taiwan's foreign trade regime. Since its first enactment in 1993, this *Foreign Trade Act* has been subsequently amended in 1997, 1999, 2002, and 2007. According to Article 18 of the latest amended *Foreign Trade Act,* safeguard measures are termed as 'import relief (*jinkou jiuji*)'. As provided, in case of an increase in imports and thereby causing or threatening to cause serious injury to the domestic industry which produces like or directly competitive products, the said industry, its responsible authority or its

[228] Ibid, paras. 67,107,148,188,230.
[229] Ibid.
[230] SETC Final report, paras. 50, 91, 132, 171, 214.

associations, or related organisations can apply for an investigation into the injury and apply for import relief.[231] Little hint has been offered on in this provision. Whether 'unforeseen developments' would be a condition for the imposition of safeguard measures is not dealt with in, nor is the quantity of increased imports and the extent of this increase.

Article 18(3) of the *Foreign Trade Act* thus delegated the Ministry of Economic Affairs (the MOEA) to draft an implementing regulation governing injury investigation and corresponding import relief. With this delegation, a regulation, entitled *Regulation on Import Relief* was issued by the MOEA in 1995 to further define regulatory framework on safeguard measures. Rules governing the conditions for the imposition of safeguard measures and for the investigation procedures were also provided with more details. This *Regulation on Import Relief* has also been often revised. The most significant revision relates to a parallel domestic special safeguard measures and textile safeguard measures, as set out for in Section 16 of China's Accession Protocol and the Chinese textile safeguard measures under paragraph 242 of China's Working Party Report. Chapter 4 *bis* regulates special safeguard measures against Chinese non-textile products and chapter 4 *ter* regulates special safeguard measures against Chinese textile products.

b. *Safeguard Investigations on Certain Towelling Products*

On 24 August 2005, the YCTPA applied for a safeguard measure investigation against Chinese towelling products. While the International Trade Commission of the MOEA (the ITC of the MOEA) denied the request for provisional safeguard measures, its investigation found market disruption due to the increased imports of Chinese towelling products.[232] Before finishing its final report, the ITC of the MOEA carried out several on-site investigations on the domestic producers. It also held a series of public hearings where delegates from the Chinese towelling industry were present.[233] This was the first time that Chinese producers participated in Taiwan's investigation proceedings of trade defence measures. During the investigation, the ITC of the MOEA also found evidence of dumping of Chinese towelling products, and thus referred the matter to the Ministry of Finance (the MOF) for an anti-dumping investigation as required by Article 28 of this *Regulation on Import Relief*.[234] Consequently, a concurrently anti-dumping investigation was initiated by the MOF. In the end, anti-dumping measures, instead of safeguard measures were imposed against Chinese towelling products.[235]

---

[231] *Foreign Trade Act* (Taiwan), Art. 18.1.

[232] ITC, *Final report on injury investigation of import relief measures against Chinese towelling products* (17 March 2006) 1.

[233] Ibid 3-4.

[234] *See infra* Subsection (b) anti-dumping measures, text to (n 165) *et seq.*

[235] Taiwan's choice of anti-dumping measures instead of safeguard measures can be contrasted with China's preference on safeguard measures over anti-dumping measures. In the case of

Apart from its symbolic significance, this safeguard measure investigation has great legal importance in several aspects. Firstly, this investigation points to the unsettled relationship between the ASG and Section 16 of China's Accession Protocol and paragraph 242 of China's Working Party Report. Explanations provided in this final report on market disruption include increased imports, material injury to domestic industry and the causal link between them, and these should be carefully examined in light of their WTO-consistency.

i. *Legal Status of Section 16 of China's Accession Protocol and Paragraph 242 of China's Working Party Report.* Existing WTO rules on safeguard measures are mainly laid down in Article XIX of the GATT 1994 and the ASG. Section 16 of China's Accession Protocol and paragraph 242 of its Working Party Report provide additional rules on the imposition of safeguard measures against Chinese products. How to interpret these rules in the context of existing WTO agreements should thus be addressed.

Section 16.1 of China's Accession Protocol provides, 'in cases where products of Chinese origin are being imported into the territory of any WTO Member in such increased quantities or under such conditions as to cause or threaten to cause market disruption to the domestic producers of like or directly competitive products, the WTO Member so affected may request consultations with China with a view to seeking a mutually satisfactory solution'. If the requesting Member and China reach the conclusion that Chinese products are the cause for market disruption, China is obliged to take actions to remedy this market disruption.[236] If a mutual agreement has not been reached within 60 days after the request for consultation, the affected Member may withdraw concession or limit the imports only to the extent necessary to prevent or to remedy the market disruption.[237] Under Section 16.4, market disruption is found to exist when 'imports of an article, like or directly competitive with an article produced by the domestic industry, [being] increasing rapidly, either absolutely or relatively, to be a significant cause of material injury, or threat of material injury to the domestic industry.' Other procedural requirements, such as notification to the Committee on Safeguards,[238] decision-making based on objective factors,[239] public notice and opportunities to

safeguard measures against Chinese products, China's Accession Protocol provides a less stringent condition for their imposition. It is thus difficult to understand why Taiwan's agency chose to impose anti-dumping measures with the objection of petitioners in safeguard measures investigation. Moreover, there is no petitioner in the anti-dumping investigation. The MOF self-initiated the anti-dumping investigation.

236 China's Accession Protocol, S. 16.2.

237 China's Accession Protocol, S. 16.3.

238 *See, e.g.*, China's Accession Protocol, S. 16.1, last sentence, S. 16.2, last sentence.

239 China's Accession Protocol, S. 16.4, second sentence.

comment,[240] and proportionality of safeguard measures[241] are also provided in relation to the imposition of product-specific safeguard measures against Chinese products. In critical circumstances, provisional safeguard measures may also be taken under this product-specific safeguard measure mechanism.[242]

The first issue that should be addressed is the applicability of those conditions set out in the WTO agreements, notably the requirement of 'unforeseen developments.' As noted in the Section II of this chapter, it is the settled jurisprudence of the WTO panel/Appellate Body that demands the requirement of 'unforeseen developments', as set out in Article XVI:1(a) of the GATT 1994; it now constitutes as one of the conditions that WTO Members have to fulfil with when imposing safeguard measures. Nevertheless, it is not entirely clear as to whether this requirement of 'unforeseen developments' is also applicable in the case of product-specific safeguard measures against Chinese products. It may be argued that Article XIX of the GATT 1994 and/or the ASG merely serve as a context for the interpretation this product-specific safeguard measure mechanism. Thus, this product-specific safeguard mechanism should be interpreted, to the most possible extent, in a manner that is compatible with existent WTO rules on safeguard measures. In other words, it should be read as in line with, instead of a deviation from, the existing WTO agreements. The requirement of 'unforeseen developments' should be applicable when appropriate.

Nevertheless, this interpretation seems to be ill-fitted on the 'objective and purpose' of this product-specific safeguard mechanism, which was intended to lower the threshold for the imposition of safeguard measures against Chinese products. The effectiveness of this product-specific safeguard mechanism would be undermined if other conditions laid down in the existing WTO agreements are simultaneously applicable. As Huang correctly points out, it is precisely because an increased imports in other Members' territories are foreseeable that the Working Party on China's accession drafted this product-specific safeguard mechanism. Compromising this product-specific safeguard mechanism with the requirement of 'unforeseen developments' is to 'force Members to forget what they clearly foresaw and create unnecessary legal fiction to circumvent the non-applicable standard of unforeseen developments.'[243]

In addition, in the investigation concerning Chinese towelling products, it also triggered another special safeguard mechanism lasted until 31 December 2008

[240] China's Accession Protocol, S. 16.5.
[241] China's Accession Protocol, S. 16.6.
[242] China's Accession Protocol, S. 16.7.
[243] T W Huang, 'Taiwan's Protocol 16 Special Safeguard and Anti-dumping Enforcement on Imports from China' (2007) 41 Journal of World Trade 371, 390.

against Chinese textiles as provided for in paragraph 242 of China's Working Party Report. This paragraph is referred to in paragraph 342 of the Working Party Report, and subsequently incorporated into China's Accession Protocol. It is designed to prevent or remedy market disruption caused by Chinese textile and apparel products. It covers all textiles and apparel products covered by the Agreement of Textile and Clothing when the WTO Agreement entered into force. In the case that a WTO Member believes that, due to market disruption, Chinese textile and apparel products are threatening to 'impede the orderly development of trade in these products,' the affected Member can request for consultation with a view to easing or avoiding such market disruption.[244]

After the request of consultation, a factual statement on the reasons and justifications for the request should be provided, in particular, data in relation to the existence or threat of market disruption and the role of Chinese products in that disruption.[245] Upon receiving the request, China should restrict its exports of the concerned products to a level 'no greater than 7.5 per cent (6 per cent for wool product categories) above the amount entered during the first 12 months of the most recent 14 months preceding the month in which the request for consultations was made.'[246] If a mutual agreement cannot be reached within 90 days as set out in subparagraph(b) of 242, the affected Member may continue the limit, i.e., quantitative restrictions, while the consultation continues.[247] Additionally, measures under this paragraph and under Section 16 of China's Accession Protocol cannot be applied to the same product at the same time.[248]

Paragraph 242 of China's Working Party Report adds more complexities to Taiwan's safeguard investigation against Chinese towelling products. While paragraph 242(g) prohibits the concurrent imposition of safeguard measures against Chinese textile and apparel products under Section 16 of China's Accession Protocol and under paragraph 242 of China's Working Party Report, it provides no guidance on the relationship between these two special safeguard measures. One may be tempted to argue that the rule of *lex specialis* applies here.[249] In this instance, paragraph 242 of China's Working Party Report is designated to safeguard measures against Chinese textile and apparel products in particular. In this

---

[244] China's Working Party Report, para. 242(a), first sentence.
[245] China's Working Party Report, para. 242(a), last sentence.
[246] China's Working Party Report, para. 242(c).
[247] China's Working Party Report, para. 242(d).
[248] China's Working Party Report, para. 242(g).
[249] *See, e.g.*, D Huang, 'Legal Interpretation of Paragraph 242 of the Report of the Working Party on the Accession of China under the World Trade Organisation Legal Framework' (2006) 40 Journal of World Trade 137, 147-148. While Huang does not explicitly refer to *lex specialis*, he argues that textile and apparel products are singled out as a special category.

case, paragraph 242 should be thus applicable, and the application of Section 16 of China's Accession Protocol should be excluded.

Nevertheless, this reading may be problematic. Firstly, paragraph 242(g) reads as follows: 'measures could not be applied to the same product at the same time under this provision and the provisions of Section 16 of the Protocol.' As this subparagraph (g) is situated in the context of special safeguard measures against Chinese textile and apparel products, 'the product' therein is thus referred to as those products covered by the ATC on the date that the WTO Agreement entered into force. Thus, it suggests that textile and apparel products may also be subject to the special safeguard measures as provided in Section 16 of China's Accession Protocol. Besides, the procedure, remedy and most importantly the phasing out period of these two safeguard measures are different. Since special safeguard measures against Chinese textile and apparel products under paragraph 242 of China's Working Party Report expires on 31 December 2008, the *lex specialis* approach may lead to a conclusion that special safeguard measures against Chinese product as provided in Section 16 of China's Accession Protocol cannot be applicable to Chinese textile and apparel products.[250] This interpretation counters the legal text of paragraph 242 of China's Working Party Report.

In the safeguard investigation against Chinese towelling products, the domestic legal basis for safeguard measures against Chinese products in general and against Chinese textile products differed. Nevertheless, the ITC of the MOEA barely touched upon the issues of legal basis and applicability of other requirements provided in existing WTO agreements in relation to the imposition of safeguard measures. In its final report, the ITC of the MOEA found its domestic legal basis stemming from chapter 4 *bis*, import relief against products from China. It also referred to Section 16.4 of China's Accession Protocol for the determination of 'market disruption.'[251] The ITC of the MOEA did not provide further explanation in relation to its determination of legal basis. Nevertheless, one may guess that procedural requirement laid down by paragraph 242 of China's Working Party Report prevents the ITC of the MOEA from adopting a special safeguard measures under this paragraph against Chinese towelling product, as the ITC of the MOEA would have been obliged to request for consultation with China in this regard. Regarding the requirements as set out in Article XIX of the GATT 1994 and the ASG, the ITC of the MOEA did not spend much effort as well. Taking the requirement of 'unforeseen development' for example, while it is argued by Chinese producers that this

[250] Huang argues that after the expiry of paragraph, special safeguard measures provided for in Section 16 of China's Accession Protocol. Read otherwise, it would be 'abusive' application of safeguard measures against Chinese products. Ibid.

[251] ITC (n 232) 2.

requirement should also be applied to the investigation, the ITC of the MOEA rejected this argument in a brief note. The ITC of the MOEA stated that the requirement of 'unforeseen development' was not referred to in Section 16 of China's Accession Protocol and that practices of other WTO Members also supported this interpretation.[252] This requirement becomes thus irrelevant to the present case. While the ITC of the MOEA's decision on the legal basis and applicability of the requirement of 'unforeseen developments' could be acceptable, its reasoning was nevertheless insufficient and flawed.

ii. *Market Disruption.* In respect to the substantive issue, emphasis should be placed on the definition of 'market disruption.' Admittedly, Section 16.4 of China's Accession Protocol provides some guidance on the determination of market disruption. Nevertheless, divergent views arise as to whether market disruption exists if and *only if* 'imports of an article, like or directly competitive with an article produced by the domestic industry, are increasing rapidly, either absolutely or relatively, so as to be a significant cause of material injury, or threat of material injury to the domestic industry'. The ITC of the MOEA apparently equated market disruption with the criteria provided in Section 16.4, as it explicitly refers to these criteria in its definition of 'market disruption.'[253] However, this interpretation is not unquestionable as the legal text reads 'market disruption shall exist *whenever* imports of an article, like or directly competitive with an article produced by the domestic industry, are increasing rapidly, either absolutely or relatively, to be a significant cause of material injury, or threat of material injury to the domestic industry.' As suggested, while the rapidly increased Chinese imports had caused or threatened to cause material injury to the domestic industry could be market disruption, market disruption is not exclusively defined by it.[254]

Even if taking the ITC of the MOEA's interpretation, one should also be cautioned against the usage of 'material injury' in this special safeguard mechanism. 'Material injury' is not the criterion prescribed in Article XIX of the GATT 1994 and the ASG, but in Article VI of the GATT 1994 and the ADA instead. While there is no clear-cut definition for 'material injury,' it is nevertheless settled that 'material injury' sets a lower bar for injury determination than 'serious injury.' Section 16 covers both like products and directly competitive products, which is in line with

[252] Ibid 18.

[253] Final Injury Report on the Safeguard Measure Investigation on Chinese Toweling Products (the ITC of the MOEA, 29 August 2006, hereinafter 'Safeguard Final Injury Report') <http://portal.moeaitc.gov.tw/icweb/webform/wFrmWebDownload.aspx?kind=report&id=247>accessed 1 September 2011. This interpretation is in line with other Members'practice, *see, e.g.*, USITC Report on Steel Wire Garment Hangers from China, Inv. No. TA-421-3 (29 July 2003) <http://www.usitc.gov/trade_remedy/731_ad_701_cvd/investigations/2002/421_garment_hangers/safeguard.htm> accessed 1 September 2011.

[254] Huang (n 243) 390.

Article XIX of the GATT 1994 and the ASG. The imported article is not limited to a like product to the product produced by domestic industry; an article directly competitive with the domestic product can also be taken into account in the injury determination process.

Finally, Section 16.4 regulates the causal link with the threshold of 'a significant cause of material injury, or threat of material injury to the domestic industry.' As noted in Section II of this chapter, it is settled in the WTO jurisprudence that in a safeguard measure investigation, the increased imports need not to be the only cause contributing to serious injury to the domestic industry. In Members' practice, 'a significant cause' is normally defined as in respect of a material injury or threat thereof, an important cause that need not be equal to, or more important than, any other cause of the material injury or threat.[255] In sum, when comparing to the existing WTO rules on safeguard measures, the special safeguard mechanism provided in Section 16 of China's Accession Protocol is looser in the extent of injury but wider in the coverage of products concerned; the requirement of causal link is nevertheless unclear.

Examining the explanation provided in the ITC of the MOEA's final report in light of the forgoing analysis, one is safe to say that the ITC of the MOEA paid little attention to these elements and their deviation from existing WTO rules. The ITC of the MOEA noted that since the liberalisation of its market on towelling products to Chinese products in 2002, Chinese products accounted for 69.3 per cent of its market share at the time of its investigation in 2005. The market share of Taiwanese towelling products decreased from 16.6 per cent to 8.2 per cent, while the market share of towelling products from other origins decrease from 83.4 per cent to 22.5 per cent during the period of 2001 to the first three quarter of 2005.[256] Based on this, the ITC of the MOEA found the rapid increase of imports of Chinese towelling products.

While there was an evidently rapid increase of imports of Chinese towelling products, material injury to domestic industry was not so evident, in particular in terms of the decrease of market share of Taiwanese towelling products. As Chinese producers argued, the decrease of market share of Taiwanese towelling products was a result from the transformation and upgrading of Taiwanese industrial structure. Taiwanese towelling industry has moved out to China or Viet Nam and a large proportion to Chinese towelling products sold back to Taiwan are actually made by Taiwan-invested enterprises in China. The material injury in Taiwan's towelling industry does not exist.[257] The ITC of the MOEA failed to rebut this argument in a satisfactory and convincing manner. Taking into account

[255] *See, e.g.*, US Trade Act of 1974, Section 421(c)(2); Canadian International Tribunal Act, Section 30.2.

[256] Safeguard Final Injury Report, 9-10.

the fact that Chinese towelling products are aimed at mainly low-price market and the fact that the average price of Taiwanese towelling products increase, the determination of material injury in Taiwanese towelling industry seems to be unfounded. In addition, the ITC of the MOEA did offer any explanation as to whether Chinese towelling products constituted a significant cause of material injury.

2. *Anti-Dumping Measures*

a. *General Regulatory Framework*

Taiwan's anti-dumping regulatory regime was first laid down in 1967, albeit loosely drafted, in its *Customs Act*. Later, a more detailed implementing rule, *Regulation on Anti-Dumping Duties and Countervailing Duties* was issued by the MOF under the authorisation of the *Customs Act* in 1984. Since Taiwan's application for its GATT membership in the earlier 1990's, the *Customs Act* was substantially amended. The last revision of this act was in May 2010. Chapter 4 of the existing *Customs Act* regulates anti-dumping duties, countervailing duties and safeguard measures.

Article 68 authorises the imposition of anti-dumping duties where imported goods are found to be imported at a price less than the normal value of its like product, thereby causing injury to the domestic industry.[258] 'Normal value' is defined in the second paragraph as 'the comparable domestic selling price in the country of exportation or origin in the ordinary course of trade.' This paragraph further elaborates that, in the absence of such a domestic selling price, the comparable selling price exported to an appropriate third country or the constructed price can be used to determine the normal value. Article 69, in the first paragraph, defines the term 'causing injury to domestic industry' as 'material injury', 'threat of material injury to the industry', or 'material retardation of the establishment of such an industry' in Taiwan. Article 69(4) authorises the MOF to issue regulations governing the qualification of applicants, application contents, investigations, determination, public comments, and relevant procedures after the approval of the Executive Yuan, the highest administrative organ in Taiwan. Additionally, in Article 72, it provides the possibility to increase duty rate, adopt tariff quota, or to impose additional duties where import relief or special safeguard measures are adopted in accordance with Article 18 of the *Foreign Trade Act*.[259]

---

[257] Safeguard Final Injury Report, 19. *See infra* text to (n 261) *et seq.*

[258] Further guidance on the definition of 'like products' is provided in Article 5 of *Anti-Dumping and Countervailing Duties*. Nevertheless, conflicts arise in relation to the scope of domestic products between *Foreign Trade Act* and *Customs Act*. Foreign Trade Act refers to 'domestically produced products competing with the said (imported) goods' whereas *Customs Act* uses the term 'like products'.

This *Foreign Trade Act*, firstly legislated in 1993, is part of Taiwan's bidding package for GATT membership. As a consequence of this enactment, and in view of the Anti-Dumping Code after the Tokyo Round, the *Regulation on Anti-Dumping Duties and Countervailing Duties* has thus been amended and further defined in 1994. It clarifies petitions, investigation procedures, and the time limit for the investigations. On 19 December 2001, the eve before Taiwan's accession to the WTO, this regulation was once again amended to ensure it is WTO-compatible, notably with the ADA and the ASCM. It includes the requirements of, *inter alia*, consultation with exporting countries, public notice and comments, disclosure of information to interested parties, and overall evaluation of domestic industry including public interest.

Article 19 of the *Foreign Trade Act* regulates trade remedies against dumping and subsidies, providing that anti-dumping duties and countervailing duties may be imposed by the MOF after the MOEA investigation where material injury to the domestic industry has been verified. This article loosely prescribes the condition for the imposition of anti-dumping duties: the existence of dumping; a material injury or threat thereof to the domestic industry or a substantial hindrance to its establishment; and causation.[260] The injury investigation is carried out by the ITC of the MOEA, while the final anti-dumping determination and the decisions on anti-dumping measures are carried out by the MOF. With a view to avoiding the conflict and disparity between determinations conducted by the ITC of the MOEA and the MOF, especially injury determinations, Article 14 of the *Implementation*

---

[259] *See* further subsection (b) (n 231) *et seq.*

[260] Article 19 of the *Foreign Trade Act* deviates significantly from the WTO rules on anti-dumping and anti-subsidy measures. The official English transition of this article reads, 'in the event that a foreign country exports any goods to this country by way of subsidising or dumping thereby causing or threatening to cause substantial injury to domestically produced products competing with the said goods or creating substantial hindrance to the establishment of the domestic industry concerned, and the injury has been verified after investigation by the MOEA, the Ministry of Finance may impose, by law, countervailing or anti-dumping duties.' Firstly, the provision does not mention like products; it refers to domestic products competing with the exported products instead. In contrast to Article 18 of the same Act, which regulates safeguard measures, it term 'like or directly competitive products' is employed. As is clarified by the Appellate Body in *Korea—Alcoholic Beverages*, 'Like' products area subset of directly competitive or substitutable products: all like products are, by definition, directly competitive or substitutable products, whereas not all 'directly competitive or substitutable' products are 'like'. The notion of like products must be construed narrowly but the category of directly competitive or substitutable products is broader.' *See* WTO, 'Korea - Taxes on Alcoholic Beverages - AB-1998-7 - Report of the Appellate Body' (18 January1999) WT/DS75/AB/R, WT/DS84/AB/R, para. 118). The act fails to clearly distinguish different requirements laid down by ADA (and SCMA) and ASG in relation to the scope of products under consideration. Besides, Article 19 dictates the finding of 'injury' to be verified by MOEA; nevertheless, material injury to domestic industry, threat of material injury to domestic industry and the material retardation to its establishment are all conditions eligible for the imposition of anti-dumping measures. Article 19 is still unclear as to the scope of 'injury' determination to be carried out by MOEA, notwithstanding the clarification of Article 14 of *Implementation Rules of the Foreign Trade Act*.

Rules of the Foreign Trade Act instructs the injury investigating authority to make a determination of material injury, threat of material injury, or material hindrance to the establishment of domestic industry based on the same criteria as the MOF does under Article 69 of the *Customs Act* in relation to its injury determination in anti-dumping and countervailing duties. Nevertheless, this provision does not offer much help as the injury determination, even in the case of anti-dumping and anti-subsidy investigation, is carried out by the ITC of the MOEA. The MOF is obliged to accept the determination made the ITC of the MOEA and is in no position to alter this determination.

In respect of judicial/administrative review, the *Foreign Trade Act* or *Customs Act* does not regulate specifically this issue. Therefore, administrative review and judicial review need be referred to the general legal framework governing administrative review and judicial review laid down by the *Administrative Litigation Act* and its accompanying legislation.

b. *Definitive Anti-Dumping Measures on Certain Towelling Products*

Under Article 2 of the *Regulation on Anti-dumping Duties and Countervailing Duties*, the competent authority can self-initiate an anti-dumping investigation even in the absence of petition. During its safeguard measure investigation, the ITC of the MOEA, as required by Article 28 of *Regulation on Import Relief*,[261] referred to the MOF on 3 January 2006 for anti-dumping investigation as the ITC of the MOEA found that, according to its data collected, there was evidence of dumping by Chinese towelling producers.[262] Based on this referral, the MOF self-initiated its anti-dumping investigation against Chinese towelling products on 1 March 2006. The MOF subsequently referred to the ITC of the MOEA for the injury investigation under anti-dumping proceedings. A preliminary determination on injury to domestic towelling industry was made and notified to the MOF by the ITC of the MOEA on 22 March 2006; based on this injury determination, provisional anti-dumping duties were imposed against certain Chinese products on 1 June 2006. On-site investigations to two Chinese producers were carried out from 13 June 2006 to 22 June 2006.[263] The final report on anti-dumping investigation was released on 28 July 2006.[264] Based on the finding, the BOF referred to the ITC of the MOEA for the final determination of material injury to the domestic industry. The

[261] Article 28 of *Regulation on Import Relief* provides that in cases that MOEA, during its injury investigation, find that subsidisation or dumping as provided for under Article 67 or Article 68 of the Customs Act is involved, it shall promptly notify the MOF and the petitioner. *See* further subsection (b) (n 183) *et seq.*

[262] BOF, Final Report on Anti-dumping Investigation on Chinese Toweling Products (24 July 2006, declassified version, hereinafter, Anti-dumping Final Report), 1 <http://doca.mof.gov.tw/ct.asp?xItem=31384&ctNode=60&mp=1> accessed1 September 2011.

[263] Ibid 2.

final report on material injury to the domestic industry was released on 29 August 2006. Consequently, the MOF on 19 September 2006 decided to impose definitive anti-dumping duties upon Chinese towelling products, except the products of the six producers whom accepted price-undertaking.[265]

i. *Non-market Economy*. The first issue to be examined in this anti-dumping investigation is Taiwan's decision on China's status of non-market economy. Before China's accession to the WTO, legal basis for non-market economy derives mainly from Ad Article VI:1 of the GATT 1994. Moreover, Section 15 of China's Accession Protocol provides additional rules for other Members to treat China as a non-market economy. Section 15(a) reads that a Member, when conducting an anti-dumping investigation against Chinese products, can use either prices or costs provided by Chinese producers, or base on a methodology not strictly based on comparison with prices or costs in China. In the case that a producer under investigation cannot clearly show that the market economy conditions set out that manufacture, production and sale of the product should prevail, Members may use a methodology not strictly based on comparison with prices or costs in China.[266] According to this provision, Chinese producers bear the burden of proof to show that their business practices are in accordance with market economy conditions. Otherwise, Members may be free to adopt a methodology that is not strictly based on comparison with prices or costs in China. Market economy status may be granted to China or a particular industry or sector if Members view that China has satisfied the requirements for market economy according to their national law.[267]

Before this investigation, Taiwan's foreign trade regulatory regime provided nothing on non-market economy. After the initiation of this anti-dumping investigation, the MOF on 29 May 2006 issued its criteria for the determination of a non-market economy. With the same notice, it was decided that China should be viewed as a non-market economy.[268] The standard set out by the MOF for the determination of the non-market economy status of a country during its anti-dumping investigation covers the following factors:

(1) The flexibility of foreign exchange;
(2) The extent under which collective bargaining is practiced;

---

[264] Ibid 2-3.

[265] Notice of MOF, Tai-Cai-Guan-Zhi No. 09505505100 (2006) <http://www.mof.gov.tw/fp.asp?xItem=32014&ctNode=656> accessed 1 September 2011.

[266] China's Accession Protocol, S. 15(a)(ii).

[267] China's Accession Protocol, S. 15(d).

[268] BOF Notice, No. Tai-Cai-Guan-Zhi No. 09505502880 (2006) <http://www.mof.gov.tw/ct.asp?xItem=30158&ctNode=656&mp=1> accessed 1 September 2011.

(3) The extent that foreign investment is restricted in joint ventures or local investment;
(4) State ownership or control of factors of production;
(5) State control of resources;
(6) The extent to which price and production is determined by enterprises;
(7) The extent of legal protection of business operations;
(8) The conformity of business accounting practices to international standards.

Based upon those criteria, the MOF then stated that China should be treated as a non-market economy in light of the following factors: China's strict controls of its foreign exchange and financial policy and national resource; maintenance of macro-economic control; state intervention in the operation of state owned enterprises, notably the state owned banks; lack of significant progress in liberalisation of production factors and its bankruptcy regime; and a large number of restrictions on imports, exports and foreign investments.[269] Thus, when conducting anti-dumping investigations against Chinese products, an analogue country should be chosen for the determination of the normal value according to the market scale and economic/social development of third countries.

Factors referred to in this determination of China's non-market economy status in Taiwan's domestic legal system are mostly irrelevant in this towelling investigation, as those factors have of little importance in the Chinese towelling industry. Specific links between those factors and Chinese towelling industry had not been provided. While the ITC of the MOEA examined whether market economy treatment for individual producers was to be granted, little has been said on its negative decision. The ITC of the MOEA stated that two producers requesting market economy treatment but was unable to provide evidence to prove that their prices and costs had not been affected by China's non-market economy; since they accept price-undertaking, they refused on-site investigations.[270]

ii *Self-elicited Injury, Injury, Causation*

After the final determination on dumping, the MOF referred to the ITC of the MOEA to conduct further investigation on the material injury to the domestic industry. Some issues should be discussed in relation to injury determination. First, the organisational arrangement may be problematic. While it is not against the WTO rules to issue separate reports by different agencies in a single anti-dumping investigation, this may lead to inconsistency and incoherence in the final reports compiled by these agencies. In this present case, the initiation of investigation resulted from the referral of the ITC of the MOEA. In the absence of petitioners, the MOF decided to self-initiate the anti-dumping investigation, and subsequently referred back to the ITC of the MOEA for the injury investigation.

[269] Ibid.
[270] Anti-Dumping Final Report, 6-7.

The impartiality and objectivity of the ITC of the MOEA may thus be questionable. The reason why the MOF chose to self-initiate the anti-dumping investigation has not been clearly explained. The MOF did not even participate in the injury hearing during anti-dumping investigation by the ITC of the MOEA, which attracted server criticism by one of the participants.[271] Furthermore, the ITC of the MOEA notes in its final report that given that the scope of products under investigation (alleged dumped imports and like products), the domestic industry, and the fact that anti-dumping and special safeguard investigation criteria are identical, it based its finding of material injury in domestic industry had mainly been based on the data and information collected in the special safeguard investigation.[272] Notwithstanding the difference of scope of products, The ITC of the MOEA failed to distinguish between anti-dumping investigation and product-specific safeguard investigation. The special safeguard measures cover 'like products' and 'directly competitive products' whereas the anti-dumping measures only cover 'like products'.

Second, a very interesting point to note is that one major Chinese producer, Yuanfu Fangzhi Co. Ltd., was actually a Taiwan-invested enterprise, previously located in the same region as petitioners in the special safeguard investigation, before it decided to uproot its main sectors to China. While products by this producer can certainly be treated as Chinese products under the Agreement of Rules on Origin just as the ITC of the MOEA had noted in its response to the arguments put forward by the Chinese producers, it added difficulties to the assessment of injury. As argued by Taiwan Chungda Co. Ltd, the Taiwanese investor of Yuanfu Fangzhi Co. Ltd., at the anti-dumping investigation's injury hearing, that Taiwanese towelling industry's injury was not caused by Chinese products. Instead, the injury of Taiwan's domestic towelling industry existed before the importation of Chinese products.[273]

The argument of Chunda Co. Ltd. has two implications. As far as this anti-dumping investigation is concerned, this argument points to the ambiguity in determining the scope of domestic industry. Article 4.1 of ADA authorises competent authorities to exclude domestic producers from the definition of domestic industry when 'producers are related to the exporters or importers or are themselves importers of the alleged dumped product.' Footnote 11 to the ADA provides

[271] Record of the hearing on injury to domestic industry in anti-dumping investigation (21 August 2006) 12 <http://portal.moeaitc.gov.tw/icweb/webform/wFrmSearchDetail.aspx?caseid=57#base> accessed 1 September 2011 (hereinafter the 'Hearing Record').

[272] ITC of the MOEA, Final Injury Report on Anti-dumping Investigation on Chinese Towelling Products (hereinafter, the Anti-dumping Final Injury Report) (17 March 2006) 8 <http://portal.moeaitc.gov.tw/icweb/webform/wFrmWebDownload.aspx?kind=report&id=245> accessed 1 September 2011.

[273] The Hearing Record, 17-18.

further guidance for the interpretation of 'related' producers to be excluded from domestic industry. Producers may be deemed related to exporters or importers only if these producer fall into one of these three categories: (a) one of them directly or indirectly controls the other; or (b) both of them are directly or indirectly controlled by a third person; or (c) together they directly or indirectly control a third person. Otherwise, there must be grounds for the competent authorities to believe or to suspect the producers concerned, such as their relationships with others and their behaviours if those different substantially from other non-related producers. The final report on injury determination refers to Article 5.2 of the *Regulation on Anti-Dumping and Countervailing Duties* for the definition of domestic industry, which similarly provides the exclusion of related producers. Nevertheless, the ITC of the MOEA does not clarify whether these related producers are excluded.

iv. *Administrative Review/Judicial Review.* In this present case, the petitioner, the YCTPA, referred the MOEA's decision of not to impose additional duties on Chinese products, and considered other possible provisional safeguard measures to the Administrative Appeal Review Committee of the Executive Yuan. With regard to the MOEA's decision not to impose additional duties on the Chinese products, the Administrative Appeal Review Committee of the Executive Yuan dismissed the appeal on procedural grounds because the attorney in this appeal failed to provide an authentic written form of authorisation within the expiry of the period for amendment.[274] With regard to the ITC of the MOEA's decision to consider other possible provisional safeguard measures, the Administrative Appeal Review Committee of the Executive Yuan held that, as it was the decision of the ITC of the MOEA, it fell into the jurisdiction of the Administrative Appeal Review Committee of the MOEA. The Administrative Appeal Review Committee of the Executive Yuan thus referred this decision to the Administrative Appeal Review Committee of the MOEA. However, according to the Administrative Appeal Committee of the MOEA, in its decision to consider other possible provisional measures, the ITC of the MOEA merely referred to those available measures provided for in Article 4 of the *Regulation on Import Relief*.[275] It is intended to notice the petitioner that the ITC of the MOEA duly received the petitioner's request to impose other possible provisional safeguard measures, and that the ITC of the MOEA would consider possible measures provided for by

[274] Department of Customs Administration, Ministry of Finance, R.O.C., Tai-Tsai-Zhi No. 09505505100 <http://doca.mof.gov.tw/ct.asp?xItem=32014&ctNode=60&mp=1> accessed 1 September 2011.

[275] Article 41 of the Regulation on Import Relief provides, 'for those import relief cases in which the existence of injury or threat thereof has been established pursuant to these Rules, the Ministry of Economic Affairs may adopt the following relief measures:1.adjusting the tariffs,2. imposing import quotas,3.providing financing guarantee, subsidy for technological research and

relevant rules. This is not an administrative action (Verwaltungsakte), which could be subject to administrative review. The Administrative Appeal Review Committee of the MOEA thus dismissed the appeal.

The YCTPA again referred the final decision of the MOF's anti-dumping investigation, including the choice of analogue country and the determination of dumping margin, the anti-dumping measures and the acceptance of price-undertaking to the Administrative Appeal Review Committee of the Executive Yuan for administrative review. Nevertheless, this appeal was rejected based on the lack of standing. The Administrative Appeal Review Committee held that, the MOF decisions are aimed at imposing anti-dumping measures against Taiwanese importers or agents and Chinese producers or exporters. As the YCTPA is an association and is not engaged in economic activities, and it was not even the petitioner in this present investigation, the rights and legal interests of the YCTPA would thus not be able to affect this decision. Based on this reasoning, the Administrative Appeal Review Committee then concluded that the YCTPA was not 'an interested party' in terms of the first sentence Article 1.1[276] and Article 18[277] of the *Administrative Appeal Act*, and that the appeal should be rejected.

The decision of the Administrative Appeal Review Committee is inconceivable. It ignored the purpose of the whole investigation proceedings when it notes that the YCTPA was not an interested party as defined in the first sentence Article 1.1 and Article 18 of the *Administrative Appeal Act* since its rights and legal interests had not been affected. The YCTPA is an association composed of Taiwanese towelling producers, whose rights and legal interests were the rights and interests that this anti-dumping investigation was aimed to protect. The objective and purpose of the *Regulation on Anti-Dumping and Countervailing Duties* is to prevent and remedy injury to the domestic industry. In this case, the YCTPA constitutes the major proportion of the domestic industry, which can be clearly seen by the final report by the MOF and the ITC of the MOEA. More precisely, Article 10 of this regulation classifies interested parties in four categories, one of which is domestic producers of like products and associations of commerce, industry, or agriculture mainly composed of these producers. Moreover, this anti-dumping investigation was concluded from a concurrent special safeguard investigation where the YCTPA was the petitioner. Since the MOF initiated the anti-dumping investigation on its

development, assistance for changing the line of business, professional training or other adjustment measures or assistance'.

[276] The first sentence of Article 1.1 provides, 'anyone who's right or interest was unlawfully or improperly injured by a centre or local government agency's administrative action is entitled to file an administrative appeal according to this Act.'

[277] Article 18 of Administrative Appeal Act provides, 'any individual, legal entity or organisation or anyone whom an administrative action is issued to as well a third party with interest at stake may file an administrative appeal.

own initiative to which the petitioner objected, one could not reasonably expect that the YCTPA was not an interested party in this anti-dumping investigation.

C. *Short Conclusion*

This section examines trade dispute resolution between Taiwan and China at the national level, focusing on trade defence regulatory regime. It emphasises the obligation to provide an adequate and reasoned explanation when a Member adopts a trade defence measure. By using China's anti-dumping and safeguard measures against Taiwanese steel products, and Taiwan's anti-dumping and product-specific safeguard measures against Chinese towelling products as case studies, this section explores their interaction in these investigation proceedings and to examine the WTO-consistency of these trade defence measures.

V. Short Conclusion

This chapter examines dispute resolution between China and Taiwan at the multilateral, bilateral and domestic levels. In the multilateral WTO Dispute Settlement Mechanism, given that there is no direct complaint against each other, this chapter explores the interaction between China and Taiwan by examining their interventions in complaints related to each other. In terms of the intensities of their third party participation, three different categories can be found: a passive observer; a active third party participant; and a third party requesting enhanced third party rights. In complaints brought about by China, Taiwan might cooperate with China in arguing against the responding Members. When China is the responding Member, Taiwan might argue against China. In the complaint brought by Taiwan, China had stood in line with Taiwan arguing against the EU. Through the lens of third party intervention, this delicate interaction between China and Taiwan and the nuanced differences in different complaints is detected.

With respect to the bilateral dispute settlement mechanism, it remains to be in an immature form providing only 'prompt negotiation' obligation. No legal or judicial protection is available under the bilateral agreements signed between China and Taiwan. In view of the high degree of economic interdependence between China and Taiwan and the potential economic conflicts, such a thin form of dispute settlement mechanism is far from sufficient or being effective.

Domestically, this chapter examines Chinese trade defence measures against Taiwanese products and vice versa. It chooses to focus on China's anti-dumping and safeguard measures against Taiwanese steel products since China is a complaining Member in the *US – Steel Safeguards* where Taiwan has participated as a third party. It also examines Taiwanese trade defence measures against Chinese towelling products. As Taiwan initiated both anti-dumping and product-specific safeguard investigations against these products, these two investigations also illustrate the complexities added by China's 'WTO-plus' obligations. This chapter also examines the domestic administrative/judicial review of these trade defence measures, which again points to the significance of China's obligation to provide an independent and impartial judicial review. However, although the possibility to seek administrative review/judicial review is provided in China's trade defence regulatory regime, it is hardly used. This chapter also argues that the Administrative Review Committee of the Executive Yuan in Taiwan, in interpreting the 'interested parties' technically and excluding the petitioner from the scope of interested parties, failed to correctly perceive its role as a review body to protect the rights and interests enjoyed by the petitioner.

CHAPTER EIGHT

ONE COUNTRY, TWO SYSTEMS, AND THREE MEMBERSHIPS: TRADE DISPUTE RESOLUTION BETWEEN CHINA AND HONG KONG AND MACAU

I. Introduction

As People's Republic of China resumed its sovereignty over Hong Kong in 1997, and subsequently over Macau in 1999, the idea of 'One Country, Two Systems' as advocated by Deng Xiao-ping has been applied to these two areas. China amended its constitution to provide the legal basis for the establishment of the Special Administrative Region (the SAR) and thus made the Hong Kong Special Administrative Region (the HKSAR) and the Macau Special Administrative Region (the MASAR) possible. Hong Kong Basic Law (the HKBL) and Macau Basic Law (the MABL) were promulgated by the National People's Congress (the NPC) in order to ensure a high degree of autonomy in these two SARs to remain unchanged in fifty years after their return to China. These two sets of Basic Laws are not only national laws of China, but they are also mini-constitutions of these two SARs.

The diversity of legal cultures in these three areas provides a variety of materials for comparative lawyers. Hong Kong, formerly a British colony, has been deeply influenced by the common law tradition while Macau, albeit to a lesser extent, has been influenced by the Portuguese legal order. Apart from these two legal traditions, there is China's legal system, the so-called 'socialist rule of law with Chinese characteristics', which is a genre of its own. The integration of different legal cultures in these three areas yields great particularity. Thus, interactions between these three areas also attract the interests of international trade lawyers. As Hong Kong and Macau are full Members of the WTO just like China, their autonomy in external trade is ensured by the two Basic Laws and the Sino-British and Sin-Portuguese Joint Declarations. Thus, their interactions with the WTO forum appear to be unique. In addition, China signed a Closer Economic Partnership Arrangement (the 'CEPA') with Hong Kong on 29 June 2003, and subsequently another with Macau on 17 October 2003. These two CEPAs can be seen as Free Trade Agreement ('FTAs'), though not the name. Legal and economic integration through the WTO and the CEPAs between China and its two SARs offer a lot for international trade lawyers to explore.

This chapter focuses on dispute resolution mechanisms between China and its two SARs, which encompass the domestic courts under the constitutional/

national law framework and the dispute settlement mechanisms provided under the CEPAs and the WTO. This chapter thus aims to examine whether, and how, the Court of Final Appeal (the 'CFA') of these two SARs guard their economic autonomies, and to explore whether, and how, different legal cultures influence each other. With regard to the perspective of international trade law, this chapter will focus on the potential use, though highly improbable, of the WTO forum, as well as the dispute settlement mechanisms provided in these two CEPAs.

Following this introduction, Section II will examine dispute resolution on the constitutional and national levels. Vertical and horizontal interactions between the Standing Committee of the NPC (the NPCSC and the two SARs will be examined. Vertical interaction includes competence to interpret the Basic Laws of the NPCSC and the allocation of competence between China's Central Authority and the two SARs; horizontal interaction focuses on the competition for competence between the different state organs. Section III will analyse the trade dispute settlement mechanisms under the WTO and the CEPAs from the perspective of international trade law. A short concluding remark will then be offered in the final section of this chapter.

II. Constitutional/National Law Framework

A. *Diversity of Legal Cultures*

As mentioned in the introductory section, China and its two SARs present a diversity of legal cultures. The scope of this diversity goes beyond the coverage of this chapter. Some background knowledge will be helpful to better understand the particular legal context in which the following discussions will take place. As this chapter focuses mainly on trade dispute resolution, it will thus analyse the judicial review systems in China and its two SARs. However, judicial review in China should also be dealt together with an examination on the competence of the NPCSC. Although the NPC and the NPCSC are legislative organs by nature, they exercise the competence of reviewing the constitutionality of Chinese laws and regulations. These organs are also in charge of the interpretation of the Basic Laws. It is thus feasible to examine the NPC and the NPCSC together with the Supreme People's Court (the SPC) when dealing with trade dispute resolution between China and Hong Kong and Macau. Therefore, this section will firstly examine the interactions between the SPC and the NPC and NPCSC. It will then examine how the CFAs in Hong Kong and Macau exercise their competence in the judicial review, which lays a sound basis for the discussion in the following subsection which is devoted to the interactions between the NPCSC and these two CFAs.

1. *Legislative Interpretation/Judicial Interpretation: the Relationship between the SPC and the NPC and NPCSC*

As noted in Chapter V, one of the important features of Chinese legal system is the distinction between legislative interpretations and judicial interpretations.[1] According to the 1982 Constitution, the power to interpret national legislations and the constitution has been conferred upon the NPC and NPCSC, whereas the SPC enjoys a limited competence in delivering judicial interpretations on questions involving specific application of laws and decrees during the judicial proceedings. According to a decision of the NPCSC on 10 June 1981, which predated China's 1982 Constitution, the NPC and the NPCSC shall have the competence to further define or stipulate additionally laws and decrees while the SPC may provide interpretations on questions involving their specific application. In reality, the NPC and NPCSC have rarely delivered legislative interpretations, except the interpretation of the HKBL. In contrast, the SPC has continuously laid down judicial interpretations to complement national laws or decrees.

As the line between 'further definition', 'additional stipulation' and 'the specific application of laws and decrees' has never been clear-cut, the distribution of competence under legislative interpretations and judicial interpretations need further clarification. The enactment of *Law on Legislation* on 7 January 2000 is an important step made by the NPC attempting to clearly define the allocation of competence between the NPC and SPC.[2] The *Law on Legislation* mainly aims to standardise the legislative process, which lays down procedural requirements for central, provincial and regional legislation. It also addresses which bodies have the competence to interpret laws and regulations and provides a mechanism to review the legal validity of the legal instruments. Similar to the NPCSC decision on 10 June 1981, the *Law on Legislation* reserves the competence to interpret national laws for the NPC and the NPCSC. Wherever '(a) the specific meaning of a provision of such legislation requires further clarification or (b) a new situation arises after enactment of such legislation, thereby requiring clarification of the basis of its application,'[3] the NPC or the NPCSC should deliver legislative interpretations either on its own initiative or upon the request of the State Council, SPC and other state organs.[4] Legislative interpretations delivered by the NPC and the NPCSC enjoy the same binding effect of statutes.[5]

---

[1] Cf. Chapter V, text to (n 122) *et seq.*

[2] An official English version is available at <http://www.novexcn.com/legislat_law_00.html> accessed 1 September 2011.

[3] Law on Legislation, Art. 41.

[4] Law on Legislation, Art. 43.

[5] Law on Legislation, Art. 47.

In order to ensure the legal hierarchy between the Constitution, national legislation and provincial decrees to be respected, the *Law on Legislation* also authorises the NPC, the NPCSC and the Local People's Congress to amend or repeal contradicting legislation or decrees.[6] Article 90 further provides that the State Council, the SPC and other state organs can make a request for constitutional review. Social groups, enterprises or non-enterprise institutions or citizens can also make a written proposal for such review. The *Law on Legislation* aims to remedy the conflicts and incoherence among various central and local legislation, regulations and decrees. This review mechanism aims to establish a clearer legal hierarchy and to correct the local protectionism. It also indicates the NPC's and the NPCSC's uneasiness towards the encroachment of the judicial organs. The passage of the *Law on Legislation* may be also viewed as a gesture made by the NPCSC to respond toward the public's demand for a stronger constitutional review mechanism.[7]

Another effort made to clarify the relationship between judicial interpretations and legislative interpretations and to ensure a coherent legal hierarchy is the adoption of two working procedures on 19 December 2005: the *Working Procedures Governing Notification and Review of Administrative Regulations, Regional Laws, Autonomous Decrees and Special Decrees, Regulations of Special Economic Zones* and the *Working Procedures Governing Notification and Review of Judicial Interpretations*. These working procedures list three types of review. The NPCSC can review relevant regulations and decrees either on its own initative or upon the request by governmental agencies, citizens or legal persons. Whenever the NPCSC finds a conflict between different legal sources, it should invite relevant state organs to harmonise these contradictory legal texts and ask them to enact a new decree. The NPCSC may also repeal the conflicting decrees by itself. The working procedures also stipulate that the SPC should notify its judicial interpretations within 30 days after their issuance. Similar review mechanisms are also available to judicial interpretations. Hence, governmental agencies, social groups, enterprises, non-enterprise institutions and citizens may also request the NPCSC to review judicial interpretations.

2. *The Formation and Legal Status of Judicial Interpretations*

In order to present a clear picture on how the SPC interacts with the NPC and the NPCSC, it is essential to further explore how these judicial interpretations are delivered and what legal status they should enjoy. One of the most important

[6] Law on Legislation, Art. 89.

[7] For constitutional review in China, *see generally* Z Wang, *Constitutional Review in China* (*Zhongguo weixian shencha zhidu*) (China University of Politic Science and Law Press, Beijing 2004).

features of the Chinese judicial system is the existence of adjudicative committees which have their legal basis in the *Organic Law of People's Courts*. The main task of the adjudicative committees is to 'sum up judicial experiences and to discuss important or difficult cases and other issues related to judicial work'.[8] As the constitution requires the SPC to supervise the lower courts,[9] the SPC adjudicative committee uses this competence of 'summing up judicial experiences and discussing important or difficult cases and other issues relating to judicial work' to issue a variety of 'decisions'. These decisions range from opinions, legal instructions to official replies to the lower courts. These decisions may also take the form of official opinions, letters, notices and explanations. Some of the given decisions are merely on judicial administrative affairs whereas some fall squarely within the scope of judicial interpretations as defined in the NPCSC's decision on 10 June 1981.[10]

Since 1985, the SPC has also continuously published some of its decisions, those which it deems as of significant legal importance, in the Gazette. Cases reported in the Gazette should be 'mature' enough for the SPC to give its own opinion on the issues within in cases and should be 'representative' enough to warrant for such publicity or uniformity.[11] With regard to the legal effects of these decisions, the SPC used to hold position that such publications were merely meant to serve as guidance for the lower courts and should not be cited as legal authority in judgments.[12] Liu, a former professor in Hong Kong University nevertheless argues that these case reports in the Gazette function as precedents in the Chinese legal system.[13] However, with the passage of the *Stipulation Concerning the Duty of Judicial Interpretation in Supreme People's Court* in 1997,[14] the legal status of judicial interpretations has been officially acknowledged and recognised. Judicial interpretations delivered by the SPC in the forms of replies, explanations and regulations[15]

---

[8] Organic law of People's Court (China), Art. 11.

[9] Constitution (China), Art. 127(2).

[10] R C Brown, *Understanding Chinese Courts and Legal Process: Law with Chinese Characteristics* (Kluwer Law International, The Hague; Boston 1997) 75–78.

[11] N Liu, 'Legal Precedents with Chinese Characteristics: Published Cases in the Gazette of Supreme People's Court' (1991) 5 Journal of Chinese Law 107, 116.

[12] People's Supreme Court's Reply on People's Courts Using Standardised Legal Documents When Making Judgments <http://www.cecc.gov/pages/newLaws/standardLegalDocs.php> accessed 1 September 2011.

[13] Liu, (n 11), 118–122. For further discussion on the importance of the guidance reported in the Gazette, *see* also N Liu, 'An Ignored Source of Chinese Law: the Gazette of Supreme People's Court' (1989) 5 Connecticut Journal of International Law 271.

[14] The legal text is available at <http://www.court.gov.cn/lawdata/explain/main/200304040012.htm> last accessed 25 June 2007.

[15] The Stipulation Concerning the Duty of Judicial Interpretation in People's Supreme Court (the *Stipulation*), Art. 9.

can enjoy the same binding effects as national legislations.[16] When referred to in judgments, judicial interpretations should be cited after the relevant laws.[17]

Paradoxically, it appears that it is difficult for the SPC to justify its decisions that judicial interpretations have the same legal effect as national laws. Although it has tried to derive its legal basis from the NPCSC's decision on 10 June 1981 and from the *Organic Law of People's Court*, these two authorities provide no foundation to justify this claim, since the SPC is merely granted a limited competence of judicial interpretations when adjudicating a s specific cases. Even in the case of judicial interpretation, it did not constitute a legal instrument with a legal binding effect. Along this line, it is a forthright step for the SPC to define, by itself, the legal status of its judicial interpretations.[18] It is worth exploring whether the SPC could derive its competence in constitutional interpretation based on the same approach.[19]

3. *Judicial Review in Hong Kong*

Hong Kong commenced its constitutional reform journey with the Joint Sino-British Joint Declaration in 1984. The passage of the Bill of Rights in 1991 and the entry into force of the HKBL are seen as two constitutional revolutions of the *Grundnorm*.[20] The Bill of Rights was introduced in Hong Kong and the Ordinance of Bills of Rights was enacted in 1991. It incorporated the main provisions of the International Covenant on Civil and Political Rights (ICCPR) which had already been applied to Hong Kong by the United Kingdom (the UK) as a source of international law since 1976. This Ordinance explicitly repealed all pre-existing conflicting legislation and the Letters Patent had been amended with the aim to give primacy to the ICCPR over future ordinances from the colonial legislature.[21]

In 1994 the Court of Appeal held as followed:

> The Letters Patent entrench the Bill of Rights by prohibiting any legislative inroad into the International Covenant on Civil and Political Rights as applied to Hong Kong. The Bill is the embodiment of the covenant as applied here. Any legislative

---

[16] The *Stipulation*, Art. 4.

[17] The *Stipulation*, Art. 14.

[18] An interesting comparison to this is the *Judicial Yuan Interpretation* No 185 of Constitutional Court in Taiwan, where the constitutional court declares that its interpretations shall enjoy the same legal hierarchy as the Constitution. An English version is available at <http://www.judicial.gov.tw/constitutionalcourt/en/p03_01.asp?expno=185> accessed 1 September 2011

[19] Litigation based on constitutional rights and constitutional arguments has been occasionally reported by the Chinese courts. For Literature in English, *see* S Balme, 'The Judicialsation of Politics and the Politicisation of Judiciary in China (1978–2005)' (2005) 5 Global Jurist <http://www. bepress .com/gj/frontiers/vol5/iss1/art1> accessed 1 September 2011.

[20] A H Chen, 'The Interpretation of the Basic Law – Common Law and Mainland Chinese Perspectives' (2000) 30 Hong Kong Law Journal 380, 418.

[21] Ibid.

[22] *R v Chan Chak Fan* [1994] 3 H.K.C 145, 153.

> inroad into the Bill is therefore, unconstitutional, and will be struck down by the courts as the guardians of the constitution.[22]

Accordingly, the Bill of Rights had two functions. On the one hand, it confers constitutional protection to Hong Kong citizens shielding them against unconstitutional infringements on human rights; on the other hand, it provided the judiciary legal basis and a well-defined standard of review to review and to invalidate conflicting local legislations. According to Chen, a professor in Hong Kong University, at the point of the reversion on Chinese rules in 1997, the Hong Kong judiciary had developed a well-functioned and experienced judicial review mechanism to control the constitutionality of legislation, based on the principle of rationality and proportionality. The Hong Kong judiciary had also adopted a generous and purposive constitutional approach with regard to the interpretation of human rights.[23]

However, such approach employed by the Hong Kong courts was soon challenged when China resumed its sovereignty. Hills, an Australian legal scholar argues that an unsolvable conflict exists between British liberalism and Chinese Socialism.[24] Specifically, such conflicts can be identified as the separation between interpretation and adjudication in the HKBL,[25] which bridges the two legal systems. Nevertheless, the intermingling of the two legal systems in the HKBL has brought about conflicting understandings in legal terms such as 'judicial independence', 'interpretation' and 'adjudication'.[26] As previously noted, in Chinese legal system, the NPC and the NPCSC have the competence to interpret the laws. Only certain interpretative competence related to the specific application of laws during the judicial proceedings have been assigned to the judicial organs. Chinese legal system considers that the interpretation and adjudication roles are severable but not so in the British legal system. Therefore, how the Hong Kong judiciary adjudicates with its limited interpretative competence in the HKBL turns out to be the crucial issue. Concerns have also been voiced in light of the intervention of the NPCSC when exercising its competence in the interpretation of the HKBL. This may menace the finality of judgments relating to the CFA in Hong Kong.[27]

---

[23] Chen (n 20) 419.

[24] M Hills, 'The Rule of Law and Democracy in Hong Kong – Comparative analysis of British Liberalism and Chinese Socialism' (1994) 1 Murdoch University Electronic Journal of Law <http://www.murdoch.edu.au/elaw/indices/title/mhills_abstract.html> accessed 1 September 2011.

[25] M L E Estanislao, 'Right of Final Adjudication in Hong Kong: Establishing Procedures of Constitutional Interpretation' (2000) 1 Asian – Pacific Law & Policy Journal 10 (case note), 12.

[26] A D Jordan, 'Lost in the Translation: Two Legal Cultures, the Common Law Judiciary and the Basic Law of the Hong Kong Special Administrative Region' (1997) 30 Cornell International Law Journal 335, 339–341, 353–354, 358–359.

[27] *See, e.g.*, F Lin, 'The Constitutional Crisis inHong Kong – Is it Over?' (2000) 9 Pacific Rim Law and Policy Journal 281; B Tai, 'Is "Final" Really Final?' (2002) 32 Hong Kong Law Journal 35.

With regard to judicial review, the HKBL is silent as to whether the Hong Kong judiciary has the competence to invalidate local legislation based on the HKBL. According to Chen, the HKBL is meant to serve as the mini-constitution, to maintain its supremacy in Hong Kong, and to provide effective judicial protection on human rights. If the Hong Kong judiciary cannot invalidate local legislation based on the HKBL, then such objectives cannot be materialised.[28] Such argument can also find support from the legal text of the HKBL, which provides that the judicial system previously practised in Hong Kong, shall be maintained except for those consequent changes upon the establishment of the CFA.[29] It can be reasonably assumed that judicial review should be maintained since there was no indication for a change on this point. In addition, judicial review is valued as the one of the most important features of the rule of law in Hong Kong, without which the judicial system previously practised in Hong Kong will be incomplete.

In *HKSAR v Ma Wai-kwan* the Court of Appeal exercised its competence in reviewing the constitutionality of local legislation.[30] This decision remained unchallenged in subsequent litigations and paved the way for the controversial *Na Ka Ling* case[31] on the right of abode. Even though the Interpretation delivered by the NPCSC reads Article 24(2)(iii) of the HKBL differently, it has not touched upon the competence of judicial review in the Hong Kong courts.[32]

4. *Judicial Review in Macau*

Compared to Hong Kong, the judicial review paints a quite different picture in Macau. It can be partly attributed to the dictatorship of Portugal which lasted until 1974. It can also be attributed to the different colonial ruling approaches taken between the UK and Portugal.[33] In the 1976 Constitution, a mixed judicial review was introduced into the Portuguese legal system. The same kind of judicial review system was extended to Macau by incorporating the 1976 Constitution into the *Organic Statute of Macau* through an explicit reference.[34] This Organic Statute served as a kind of mini-constitution until the handover. Since the Portuguese constitution was incorporated by a reference in the Organic Statute and most Portuguese laws and decrees were applicable in Macau, the judiciary in

---

[28] A H Chen, 'The Basic Law and the Protection of Property Rights' (1993) 23 Hong Kong Law Journal 31, 50–55.

[29] HKBL, Arts. 19(2), 81(2).

[30] *HKSAR v Ma Wai-kwan* [1997] 2 HKC 315 351.

[31] *Ng Ka Ling* v *Director of Immigration* [1999] 1 HKLRD 315 (CFA).

[32] Chen (n 20) 425.

[33] *See generally* M K Chan, 'Different Roads to Home: the Retrocession of Hong Kong and Macau to Chinese Sovereignty' (2003) 12 Journal of Contemporary China 493.

[34] The Estatuto Orgânico de Macau (Organic Statute of Macau), Art. 2. <http://www.imprensa.macau.gov.mo/bo/i/76/09/eo/pt/default.asp> accessed 1 September 2011.

Macau constituted a 'sub-judiciary district' of Portugal's judicial framework. All cases appealed from the Macau courts were heard in an appellate court in Lisbon.[35]

The mixed judicial review mechanism as set out in the 1976 Portuguese constitution provides two venues to challenge the unconstitutionality of a national legislation. It may be either preventively reviewed by the Constitutional Court or to be refused to be applied by any othe court whenever the lower court finds it unconstitutional in adjudicating a case.[36] During this period, although the competence of judicial review was granted by the Portuguese constitution and the Organic Statute, the judiciary in Macau did not enjoy the competence of the final adjudication. With the authorisation of the 1989 constitutional amendment, Macau was able to establish a judicial system suitable for its needs. As provided in Article 11 of Lei n° 112/91, *Lei de Bases da Organização Judiciária de Macau,*[37] Macau Higher Court is the final appellate court in Macau. Nevertheless, this provision does not prejudice the jurisdiction of a Supreme Court, a Supreme Administrative Court, and a Constitutional Court.

Compared to the judiciary in Hong Kong, the judiciary in Macau, before the reversion, had limited judicial review experience. At the point of handover, judicial independence was far weaker to safeguard itself from the intervention of a Central Authority.[38]

Following the model of the HKBL, the MABL was promulgated to ensure the policy of 'One Country, Two Systems' and the promise of 'unchanged in fifty years' being fully respected. The MABL also lays down the constitutional framework for the MASAR. A separate judicial organ was established, vested with judicial power as well as the final adjudication. Whether judicial review would extend beyond the handover is uncertain from the legal text. While the HKBL prescribes that the judicial system previously practised in Hong Kong shall be maintained and carried in its entirety, such arrangement is absent in the MABL. Instead, the MABL provides that the structure, powers and functions as well as operation of the courts of the MASAR shall be prescribed by the law.[39]

Although Article 16 of Lei n° 9/1999, *Lei de Bases da Organização Judiciária* (Law of Judicial Organ)[40] lays down the basic principles concerning the interpretations of the MABL, it does not refer to the competence of invalidating local legislation.

---

[35] J R Krebs, 'One Country, Three Systems? Judicial Review in Macau after Ng Ka Ling' (2000) 10 Pacific Rim Law and Policy Journal 111, 134.

[36] Ibid 136.

[37] <http://www.imprensa.macau.gov.mo/bo/i/91/36/leiar112.asp> 1 September 2011.

[38] F M Luke, 'The Imminent Threat of China's Intervention in Macau's Autonomy: Using Hong Kong's Past to Secure Macau's Future' (2000) 15 American University International Law Review 717, 745–747.

[39] MABL, Art. 84.

[40] Lei N. 9/1999, Lei de Bases da Organização Judiciária (The Statute of Judicial Organ) <http://www.imprensa.macau.gov.mo/bo/i/1999/01/lei09.asp> accessed 1 September 2011.

Therefore, whether the Macau judiciary has the competence to invalidate local legislation is subject to dispute. Before the handover, the judicial review system was extended to Macau by a reference to the constitution in the Organic Statute. Such approach is not applicable since judicial review has not been fully developed in China. In the absence of an explicit provision authorising the Macau judiciary to invalidate MASAR legislation, it would be difficult for the Macau judiciary to develop such competence itself.

Wang, a Macau scholar thus argues that as constitutional review was formerly performed by Portuguese constitutional court and as judicial practices prior to the handover did not cover this competence of constitutional court, Macau's courts will not have the competence to invalidate local legislations.[41] The capacity of the Macau judiciary to safeguard legal autonomy and protect individual rights against public authorities is further weakened with the exclusion of 'act of state' from its jurisdiction. Some even proposes to exclude free trade policies from the jurisdiction of the Macau jurisdiction by characterising them as 'political actions'.[42]

Some of these propositions and arguments should be rejected. Article 19(1) provides that the exercise of political functions, regardless if such is action or inaction, does not fall into the jurisdiction of administrative, fiscal, and customs litigations. To rely upon this provision as the legal basis for the 'political question' doctrine is problematic: the objective of this article is to allocate the jurisdiction of the Macau judiciary as can be seen in the paragraph 3 and 4, which exclude criminal proceedings and private disputes from the jurisdiction of administrative courts. However, it does not necessarily entail that the exercise of political functions cannot be reviewed by other courts. Macau courts before the handover might have refused to apply local legislations despite being incompetent to declare it invalid. Consequently, it does not necessarily follow that after the handover, the courts in the MASAR should have no competence in invalidating the local legislations. That being said, the vulnerability of the judiciary in the MASAR should be highlighted. The MABL has a born-defect and the jurisdiction of Macau judiciary may also be removed by amending the *Lei de Bases da Organização Judiciária*.

B. *The Interaction between Central Authority and The SARS*

In dealing with trade dispute resolution mechanisms between China and its two SARs under the constitutional/national law framework, three interconnected

[41] Y Wang, 'An Analysis on the Act of State and Political Question in the Basic Law of Hong Kong and Macau (Lun gang ao jibenfa zhong de guojia xingwei he zhengzhi wenti)' (2005) 30 Journal of Macau Studies (Aomrn yanjiu) 25, 25–26.

[42] Ibid.

issues should be carefully examined: the relationship between the NPCSC and the two CFAs; the allocation of competence; and the competition for jurisdiction. The first two can be seen as a vertical interaction between the Central Authority (the NPCSC) and the two SARs (the CFAs) while the latter can be classified as a horizontal interaction between the various judiciaries.

1. *Vertical Interaction*

a. *CFA/NPCSC*

In China, the NPC and the NPCSC dominate the interpretative competence of Chinese constitution and national legislations. Chinese courts may exercise the competence of 'judicial interpretations' related to specific application of the laws when adjudicating cases. This separating of interpretation and adjudication is also apparent in the HKBL and the MABL. Such approach is seen as an effort to bridge the Chinese legal system and the existing legal systems in Hong Kong and Macau. However, this approach points to the irresolvable conflicts between the Chinese legal system and Hong Kong's and Macau's legal system.[43]

Article 158 of the HKBL and Article 143 of the MABL define what constitutes as an interpretative competence in these two Basic Laws. These two articles are basically identical. In both articles, the first paragraph provides that the power to interpret the Basic Laws shall be vested in the NPCSC. Both fourth paragraphs lay down the procedures to interpret these two Basic Laws. Before delivering its interpretations, the NPCSC should consult the corresponding Basic Law Committees. In both articles, the second paragraph nonetheless provides that the NPCSC 'shall' authorise courts of these two SARs to interpret, on their own, those provisions in the Basic Laws that fall within the scope of their autonomy. The legal texts are unclear as to exactly what have been authorised. Although the English translation of the HKBL chooses to use the term 'shall' instead of 'may', such difference is not visible in the original Chinese legal texts. The Chinese versions of the Basic Laws simply refer to the verb 'authorise'. It is thus unclear whether the NPCSC the NPCSC 'shall' or 'may' authorise courts in the SARs to interpret those provisions falling within the autonomy of the SARs. Besides, the competence of the courts in these SARs to interpret the Basic Laws is incumbent on the adjudication of cases. This does not constitute a real obstacle as adjudication and interpretation was carried out simultaneously in judicial practices before the handover. It should be,

[43] For the conflicting legal cultures between China and Hong Kong, *see* A H Chen, 'Interaction of Legal Systems in Hong Kong and Mainland' (Huigui hou Hong Kong yu neidi fazhi de hudong) in A H Chen (ed), *The World of Legal Theory* (Fa lixue de shijie) (China University of Politics and Law Press Beijing 2002) 396–415.

however, noted that the two Basic Laws do not clearly define the scope of autonomy. In other words, the scope of the autonomy of the SARs or their exclusive competence, if any, has not been defined in the Basic Laws.

The major controversy appears in paragraph 3 of Article 158 of the HKBL and Article 143 of the MABL, which provide two conditions for the courts in these two SARs to seek legislative interpretations from the NPCSC on the two Basic Laws. Although the courts in these two SARs may interpret other provisions of the Basic Laws beyond the limit of their autonomy, they may refer to the NPCSC on the interpretation of the Basic Laws where: (a) the subject matter concerns affairs which are within the responsibility of the Central People's Government, or concerns the relationship between the Central Authority and the special administrative region, and (b) the interpretation affects the result of the case concerned. Courts in the HKSAR and MASAR whose decisions not appealable, are nonetheless obliged to refer to the NPCSC for the interpretation on relevant provisions of the Basic Laws before delivering their own judgments, when the aforementioned two conditions are satisfied.

Different readings of paragraph 3 of Article 158 of the HKBL have brought about the controversial right of abode case, which is generally referred as the first constitutional crisis in the HKSAR. The CFA establishes a two-step test to determine the condition of a mandatory referral has been met. The first step is to define whether the legal provisions before the courts fall within the scope of the excluded provisions, namely, those concerning (a) affairs which are under the responsibility of Central Authority and (b) the relationship between Central Authority and HKSAR (the classification condition.) The second step is to determine whether the NPCSC's interpretation would affect the judgment of the case, which necessitates such interpretation (the necessity condition). The CFA emphasised that *it is for the Court of Final Appeal and for it alone* to decide whether these two conditions have been satisfied.[44] The Court then concluded that the two conditions were not satisfied and, therefore, a referral is not required.

However, this provocative approach is not supported by the NPCSC. In the preamble of its *Interpretation by the Standing Committee of the National People's Congress of Articles 22(4) and 24(2) (3) of the Basic Law of the Hong Kong Special Administrative Region of the People's Republic of China* (the *Interpretation*),[45] the NPCSC states that Article 22(4) and 24(2)(iii) of the HKBL set out the responsibilities of the Central Authority and concern the relationship between the Central

[44] *Ng Ka Ling*, 342 (emphasis added).

[45] <http://www.info.gov.hk/basic_law/fulltext/> accessed 1 September 2011.

Authority and the HKSAR. As the judgements of the CFA in the HKSAR are not appealable, the CFA is required to request for an interpretation from the NPCSC.[46]

After the interpretation of the NPCSC on Article 24(2), (3) of the HKBL was delivered, the case series continued. In *Lau Kong Yung*,[47] the CFA had to determine the scope within which the Court is bound by the *Interpretation* and the requirement, if any, for the NPCSC to deliver its interpretation on HKBL. In this case, the Court explicitly declared it would revisit the test laid down in *Ng Ka Ling*.[48] Those who embraced and applauded for the *Ng Ka Ling* case were disappointed that in *Lau Kong Yung* the CFA perceived the HKBL more as a Chinese national legislation than as the mini-constitution of the HKSAR. The CFA thus arrived at the conclusion that the NPCSC has the plenary competence to interpret the HKBL.

After the *Ng Ka Ling* case, in 2010 the CFA was again faced with the dilemma to balance its duty to secure the finality of its decision and judicial independence in the HKSAR and its obligation to refer to the NPCSC for the interpretation of the HKBL when dealing with cases relating to the responsibilities of the Central Authority or cases concerning the relationship between the Central Authority and the HKSAR. In deciding whether to enforce two arbitral awards to which the Democratic Republic of Congo is a party, the CFA was called upon to examine the scope of state immunity and its applicability in commercial transactions. This case is derived from a cooperation agreement between Congo and China Railway Group Ltd, a state-owned enterprise incorporated in China. It is listed both in Hong Kong and Shanghai which has three subsidiaries in Hong Kong. Under this cooperation agreement, the three subsidiaries would pay a sum of 221 million US Dollars to Congo as an entry fee for a mining project in Congo. FG Hemisphere Associates LLC thus applied to the Court of First Instance (the CFI) in the HKSAR for the execution of these arbitral awards by seizing the sum payable to Congo.[49]

During the proceedings before the lower courts and the CFA, the Office of the Commissioner of the Ministry of Foreign Affairs (the 'OCMFA') addressed to the Constitutional and Mainland Affairs Bureau of the HKSAR through three letters which were subsequently placed before the court through the Secretary of Justice of the HKSAR. In these letters, they emphasised that China has consistently adopted the doctrine of strict state immunity to which the pertinent case relates. Thus, the Chinese courts have no jurisdiction over any case where a foreign state or its government is the defendant, nor does it have jurisdiction over any claim

[46] *See* preamble of the *Interpretation*.

[47] *Lau Kong Yung & others v. Director of Immigration* [1999] 3 HKLARD 778.

[48] Ibid 800.

[49] *Democratic Republic of Congo & Ors* v. *FG Hemisphere Associates LLC* (hereinafter, '*Congo*'), CFA FACV 5/2010, [2011] HKCU 1049, paras. 185–193.

that involves properties of a foreign state or its government.[50] The OCMFA also stressed that state immunity is an important component of the foreign affairs, a competence for which the Central Authority is responsible. If the HKSAR adopts a position that is inconsistent with that of China, it would seriously prejudice the sovereignty of China and undermine its interests.[51]

The CFA had to decide, upon China's resumption of the sovereignty over Hong Kong, whether the restrictive immunity could still be upheld in the HKSAR, even though the pertinent British legislation, State Immunity Act, was no longer applicable. In answering this question, the CFA had to clarify whether, in accordance with the constitutional and legal principles, the HKSAR would be in a position to maintain a state immunity regime other than that of the Central Authority. The applicant argued that the HKSAR may maintain a restrictive immunity through the common law approach and this position is not incompatible with China's state immunity policy. By a three-to-two majority, the CFA held that 'the HKSAR cannot, as a matter of legal and constitutional principle, adhere to a doctrine of state immunity which differs from that adopted by the PRC. The doctrine of state immunity practised in the HKSAR, as in the rest of China, is accordingly a doctrine of absolute immunity.'[52]

After declaring that the HKSAR has to adopt the same position as the Central Authority on state immunity, the CFA then had to decide whether a reference to the NPCSC would be necessary. In reviewing its case-laws relating to the duty to refer to the NPCSC for the interpretation of the HKBL, the CFA considered that the present case is not an appropriate case to revisit the test laid down in *Ng Ka Ling*.[53] Nonetheless the pertinent case was related to Articles 13 and 19 of the HKBL. The CFA was thus under a duty to refer to the NPCSC for an interpretation as set out in Article 158(3) of the HKBL.[54]

This holding has both political and economic implications. Firstly, given this is the CFA's first decision to refer to the NPCSC for the interpretation of the HKBL, there is a deep concern towards the judicial dependence of the HKSAR. In light of the repeated statements from the OCMFA, one may wonder whether the CFA had yielded to its pressure. This decision also has practical or economic significance. Hong Kong has long been a hub for arbitration services. The extension of state immunity to commercial arbitrations would definitely undermine the development of arbitration services in the HKSAR, since the arbitral awards to which a state is a party would not be enforceable in the HKSAR.

---

[50] *Congo* para. 197.
[51] *Congo*, para. 211.
[52] Ibid.
[53] *Congo* paras. 396–406.
[54] *Congo*, para. 183.

b. *Exclusive Competence/Residual Competence*

The question as to who can decide whether the two conditions for the referral have been satisfied is closely related to the allocation of competence. Although the two CFAs can arguably determine on the 'necessity condition' of such referral, whether the court can define the 'classification condition' deserves further examination. The ambiguity in the Basic Laws as to the autonomy or exclusive competence of the SARs adds even more complexities to this issue. Whereas the Basic Laws clearly identity the exclusive competence of the Central Authority, the autonomy or exclusive competence of the SARs is not as apparent. The exclusive competence of these two SARs, if any, is not secured since the NPCSC, by exercising the competence of interpretation, might substantially reformulate the allocation of competence between the Central Authority and the two SARs.

With regard to the exclusive competence, the clearest examples are foreign affairs and defence.[55] It is explicitly prescribed that the Central Authority is responsible for the foreign affairs and defence. However, as the Basic Laws also provide that with the authorisation of Central Authority the SARs can conduct relevant 'external affairs' on their own,[56] some confusions exist. The line between 'foreign affairs' and 'external affairs' is in fact anything but clear-cut. Nevertheless, since these two SARs may conduct relevant external affairs only within the scope authorised by the Central Authority, it seems clear that external affairs cannot be considered as one of exclusive competence of these two SARs. In addition, the Basic Laws explicitly remove the jurisdiction of judiciary in these two SARs on 'acts of state such as defence and foreign affairs',[57] even though such falls within the scope of acts of state is not entirely clear, because it would depend on the interpretation of the NPCSC.

That being said, to remove all external relations competence from the exclusive competence of these two SARs is also problematic. With regard to the exclusive competence of these two SARs, although the Basic Laws do not explicitly provide which competence falls within the exclusive competence of the SARs, they have indicators such as 'within the limits of autonomy'[58] and 'outside the limits of autonomy'.[59] It implies the existence of exclusive competence available to these two SARs. While autonomy does not necessarily equal to exclusive competence, autonomy can be best safeguarded by a clear definition of exclusive competence. In addition, in light of the purpose and objective of the Basic Laws, namely to ensure the high degree of autonomy, exclusive competence seems indispensable

[55] HKBL, Art. 13(1), 14(1), MABL, Art. 13(1), 14(1).
[56] HKBL, Art. 13(3); MABL, Art. 13(3).
[57] HKBL, Art. 19(3).
[58] HKBL, Art. 158(2); MABL, Art. 143(2).
[59] HKBL, Art. 18(3); MABL, Art. 18(3).

for these two SARs. One may argue that the two Basic Laws implicitly assign various subject matters as exclusive competence of the SARs.

A good example is the maintenance of public order in these two SARs. Article 14(2) of these two Basic Laws provides that the government of the SARs is responsible for the maintenance of public order. The third paragraph under the same article in the HKBL provides that any military force stationed in Hong Kong shall not interfere with local affairs and that only upon the request of the HKSAR government may the military force assist with the maintenance of public order. It is thus made clear that the maintenance of public order constitutes an exclusive competence of the SARs, where the stationed military force and the Central Authority should not intervene.

Taxation and monetary system are also good examples. It is also clearly provided that the Central Authority shall not levy taxes in these two SARs,[60] and that these two SARs shall maintain independent taxation systems.[61] With regard to the monetary competence, it is again explicitly provided that the authority to issue Hong Kong Dollar and Macau Pataca is vested in the governments of the SARs.[62]

After ascertaining the existence of exclusive competence of these two SARs, it is then feasible and indispensable to examine whether all external relations fall within the exclusive competence of the Central Authority. The competence of Hong Kong and Macau, as separate customs territories, to participate in international trading regime is not only ensured both by these two Basic Laws but also by the Sino-British and Sino-Portuguese Joint Declarations.[63] Furthermore, the legal basis for these two SARs to participate in the WTO is laid down in paragraph 1 of Article XII of WTO, which reads as follows:

> Any State or separate customs territory possessing full autonomy in the conduct of its external commercial relations and of the other matters provided for in this Agreement and the Multilateral Trade Agreements may accede to this Agreement, on terms to be agreed between it and the WTO.

The requirement for these two SARs, as separate customs territories, to participate in the WTO, is to possess of 'full autonomy in the conduct of its external commercial relations and of the other matters provided for in this [WTO] Agreement and the Multilateral Trade Agreements'. Full autonomy may be here read as a synonym for exclusive competence. It is also against the purpose and objective of the Sino-British and Sino-Portuguese Joint Declarations to assign the entire foreign affairs as an the exclusive competence of the Central Authority, particularly in

[60] HKBL, Art. 106(3); MABL, Art. 104(3).
[61] HKBL, Art. 108(1); MABL, Art. 106(1).
[62] HKBL, Art. 112(2); MABL, Art. 108(2).
[63] HKBL, Art. 116; MABL, Art. 112.

terms of external commercial relations. A different interpretation will undermine the autonomy of these two SARs as separate customs territories and threat the basis of their participation in the WTO. This runs counter to the purpose and objective of the two aforementioned declarations and the two Basic Laws. In order to ensure the capacity of these two SARs to participate in the WTO, external commercial relations should be read as exclusive competence of these two SARs.

Along the same line, the characterisation of external commercial relations as an exclusive competence of these two SARs may also prevent any direct or indirect intervention from the Central Authority through administrative measures.[64] Consequently, external commercial relations would consequently not fall within the scope of 'acts of state' over which the CFA has no jurisdiction. In addition, external commercial relations, with this reading would fall clearly beyond the scope of excluded provisions. The CFA's referral to the NPCSC is thus not obligatory. This ensures the finality of the decisions given by the CFA on external commercial relations. Nevertheless, it should be pointed out that the jurisprudence of the CFA may still be affected by the NPCSC through the interpretation of these two Basic Laws.

Residual competence is another major issue in the allocation of competence. It is argued that only residual competence should be vested in the Central Authority as Article 2 of both Basic Laws, provide that the high degree of autonomy in these two SARs has been authorised by the NPC. Since their autonomy is authorised by the Central Authority through its NPCSC, the Central Authority should therefore retain the residual competence.[65] However, this argument may be problematic.

In examining this issue, one has to correctly define the nature of these two Basic Laws. Although these two Basic Laws are undoubtedly national legislations enacted by the NPC, they are also constitutional instruments of these two SARs aiming to ensure their highest degree of autonomy remains unchanged in the next fifty years. In some sense these two Basic Laws can be perceived as contracts between the Central Authority and these two SARs. Therefore, it is against the purpose and objective of these two Basic Laws to base solely upon the reference

[64] This view of preventing intervention from the Central Authority on the autonomy and exclusive competence of the SARs is also shared by some Chinese lawyers. *See, e.g.*, Z Wang, *The Relationship between Central Authority and the Special Administrative Regions: An Analysis of Legal Structure* (*Zhongyang yu tebie xingzhengqu guanxi: yi zhong fazhi jiegou de jiexi*) (Tsinghua University Press, Beijing 2002) 118–119. Wang argues that 'a high degree of autonomy' means: (a) the Central Authority shall not intervene the sphere of autonomy of the SARs; (b) the decisions taken by the SARs within the limits of their autonomy are 'final', whereby the approval of the Central Authorities are not necessary; (c) the SARs enjoy discretionary power in decision-making within their autonomy; and (d) the governments of the SARs, in exercising their competence within the limit of autonomy, can freely choose measures they deem appropriate.

[65] Ibid 173–176.

to Article 2 and to hold that residual competence is reserved to the Central Authority. To put it more precisely, this issue relates to the competing value between 'One Country' and 'Two Systems'. In other words, in order to correctly define residual competence, one needs to answer whether the objective and purpose of these two Basic Laws have placed the emphasis on 'One Country' or on 'Two Systems'. One may be tempted to answer that they are equally valued in the Basic Laws. Nevertheless, this does not help to resolve the conflict between the competing values. Between these conflicting and competing values, the term 'a high degree of autonomy' is of decisive importance. A high degree of autonomy is the key that links 'One Country' to 'Two Systems'. In light of this high degree of autonomy, any residual competence should be thus interpreted as vested in these two SARs in order to maximise and effectuate their highest degree of autonomy.

2. *Horizontal Interaction: Competition of Jurisdiction*

Under the constitutional/national law framework, another issue related to trade disputes between China and its two SARs is the competition of jurisdiction. Prior to their reversion to China, the competition of jurisdiction between China, Hong Kong, and Macau is governed by the rules of private international law. After the establishment of these two SARs, these rules become inapplicable since China and its two SARs are one country. However, closer economic relationships and trade disputes have demanded for a set of rules that clearly regulate the competition of jurisdiction, since the quality and training of judges in these three areas differs substantially and may thus eventually influence the decision of a dispute.

The competition of jurisdiction may exist in both criminal and civil proceedings. With regard to trade disputes, the intellectual property rights serve as the best example as both criminal and civil proceedings are provided in the Agreement on the Trade-related Aspects of Intellectual Property Rights (TRIPS Agreement). As Chinese criminal law does not apply to Hong Kong and Macau, and cross-border criminal offenses infringing intellectual property rights may be charged in any of these three jurisdictions, the choice of forum where the criminal offences are charged largely determines the result of the judgements.[66] Civil procedures face the same, if not more serious, difficulties in competition of jurisdiction. With the ever-closer economic interdependence between China and its

[66] The importance of this issue is exemplified in the Zhang Zhiciang case. The most severe punishment for Chinese criminal court is capital punishment, whereas such does not exist in HKSAR. If this case were tried in HKSAR, the decision would be completely different. Ibid 296–302.

two SARs and ever-growing number of transnational litigations, private economic actors are conscious of the competition of courts and the choice of the laws and the resultant economic impacts that they need to face. As the judiciary of China, Hong Kong and Macau differ much from one another and as litigation procedures in Hong Kong are more developed and advanced than those in China and in Macau, a better strategy for litigants may be to refer disputes to the courts in Hong Kong and subsequently to enforce the judgments in China, after these judgments have been made.

With regard to the competition of jurisdiction, it is normally settled through the rules of private international law. However, this approach is apparently not acceptable to China as both Hong Kong and Macau are SARs of China. Private international law has no role in national affairs. In practices, this issue is normally settled after agreements have been reached between the SPC and the Department of Justice of Hong Kong and Macau. The SPC would then deliver guidance and interpretations governing the competition of jurisdiction, sometimes including the recognition of judgments. The two SARs would also enact local legislations prescribing the same content.

III. The WTO/CEPA Framework: One Country, Two Systems, Three Memberships

Trade disputes resolution between China and its two SARs may also be examined from another perspective: the perspective of international trade law. As separate customs territories, Hong Kong and Macau enjoy full WTO memberships. With the signing of the CEPAs, trade dispute resolution between China and its two SARs may also be examined under the CEPA framework. Therefore, this section will firstly analyse the legal status of the CEPAs under the WTO Agreement, covering the negotiating history, the main content of these legal document and their compatibility with WTO law governing FTAs. It will then examines the dispute settlement mechanism provided within the CEPAs and explore the possibility of complaints under the WTO Dispute Settlement Mechanism.

A. *Legal Status of CEPA under WTO law*

1. *The Negotiation History*

As characterised by the Parties to the China-Hong Kong CEPA in their joint notification to the Committee on Regional Trade Agreements (the CRTA), the China-Hong Kong CEPA 'establishes a free-trade area within the meaning of Article XXIV of the GATT 1994 and provides for the liberalisation of trade in services within the meaning of Article V of the GATS.'[67] It is the first FTA signed by both China and Hong Kong.[68] This model was soon copied: the China-Macau CEPA was subsequently signed on 17 October 2003 entering into effect on 1 January 2004.[69] The China-Macau CEPA is also the first FTA ever signed by Macau.[70]

As the economy of Hong Kong has long relied much on its role as an 'intermediary' between China and the 'outside' economies, its economic growth was negatively affected when China started its 'open-up' policy in 1980's. The fear that its economic growth would be further undermined was deepened by China's accession to the WTO, as Hong Kong feared that it might not be able to continue to enjoy preferential treatments from China since such would contradict the Most-Favoured-Nation principle. A WTO-consistent FTA between China and Hong Kong was thus proposed by Hong Kong General Chamber of Commerce (the HKGCC).[71] After a written request and meeting with the Chief Executive of the HKSAR on 22 November 2001, this proposal for the FTA was carried out after consensus was obtained between the HKSAR and the Central Authority. Consultations with regard to the coverage and the form of this FTA lasted roughly 18 months, when the final agreement on the main parts of the CEPA was reached late in June 2003.[72]

However, a 'Free Trade Agreement' carrying sovereignty implications and normally signed by two States was rejected by China. The term 'arrangement' was thus introduced to differentiate this legal text from other FTAs. After the CEPA between China and Hong Kong was successfully concluded, this model was immediately introduced to Macau. Most provisions in the China-Macau CEPA are identical to those provided in the China-Hong Kong CEPA. The coverage of the two CEPAs has since been gradually expanded; seven supplements have subsequently been added to the original texts. Since 1 January 2006 with the entering into force

---

[67] WTO, *Committee on Regional Trade Agreements – Council for Trade in Services – Closer Economic Partnership Arrangement between China and Hong Kong, China – Notification from the Parties* (12 January 2004) WT/REG162/N/1; S/C/N/264.

[68] WTO, *Committee on Regional Trade Agreements – Thirty-Ninth Session – Examination of the Closer Economic Partnership Arrangement between China and Hong Kong, China, Note on the Meeting of 18 February 2005* (21 March 2005) WT/REG162/M/1, paras 4, 6.

[69] WTO (n 67).

[70] WTO (n 68) para. 6.

[71] This is also an illustrative example of the influences of private enterprises in initiating and shaping the contents of an FTA.

[72] H S Gao, 'The Closer Economic Partnership Arrangement (CEPA) between Mainland China and Hong Kong ?Legal and Economic Analyses' in P J Davidson (ed), *Trading Arrangements in the Pacific Rim: ASEAN and APEC* (Oxford University Press, New York 2004) <http://ssrn.com/paper=752785> accessed 1 September 2011, 1. *See* also, W Wang, 'Regional Integration: Comparative Experiences: A Lawful Free Trade Agreement under "One Country, Two Customs Territories' (2004) 10 Law and Business Review of the America 647.

of Supplement II, China applied zero tariffs to all imported goods from Hong Kong and Macau as long as these goods satisfied the requirements of rules of origin laid down in the CEPAs. In 2004, when the CEPAs firstly came into force, 95 and 94 percent of imported goods, in value terms, into China from Hong Kong and Macau respectively enjoyed zero tariffs.[73] It was also claimed by the Parties to these two CEPAs that those imported goods which did not enjoyed zero-tariff treatment are mainly due to the exclusion of 'imported goods' under the CEPAs because of China's laws and regulations and its international obligations, and due to the unavailability of rules of origin under the existing tariff lines.[74]

2. *One Main Text, Six Annexes,*[75] *and Seven Supplements*[76]

In both CEPAs, the main text contains 23 articles and accompanies by six annexes. Annex 1 provides the schedules for the zero-tariff treatment on imported goods from Hong Kong and Macau. It also sets out the procedures for the producers in Hong Kong and Macau to include their products under the zero-tariff schedules. Annex 2 governs the rules of origin in respect of trade in goods. In addition to goods wholly obtained in either party, goods undergone 'substantial transformation' can also be qualified as goods originating from the Parties. Article 3 and 5 of Annex 2 define the terms of 'wholly obtained' in either party and of 'substantial transformation' respectively. Annex 3 lays down the procedures for the issuance and verification of certificates of origin. Annex 4 provides specific commitments with regard to the liberalisation of trade in services. Annex 5 defines the term 'service supplier' as set out in the CEPA and clarifies the types of service suppliers that are entitled to benefit from this arrangement. As the services professions constitute a major proportion of Hong Kong's economy, Hong Kong devoted great importance to the services trade during the CEPA negotiation, and such is thus laid down in detail with rules regulating the eligibility of being a service supplier under the CEPA. Lastly, Annex 6 stipulates the scope of trade and investment facilitation and puts forward a set of implementing measures.

---

[73] *See* WTO (n 68), para. 9; WTO, *Committee on Regional Trade Agreements – Thirty-Fifth Session – Examination of the Closer Economic Partnership Arrangement between China and Macao, China – Note on the Meeting of 18 February 2005* (21 March 2005) WT/REG163/M/1, para. 10.

[74] WTO, *Committee on Regional Trade Agreements – Closer Economic Partnership Arrangement between China and Hong Kong, China – Questions and Replies* (30 May 2006) WT/REG162/7.

[75] The main text of the two CEPAs has been notified to the CRTA. The main text and its annexes and supplements are all available at <http://www.tid.gov.hk/english/cepa/legaltext/fulltext.html> (China-Hong Kong CEPA) accessed 1 September 2011 and at <http://www.cepa.gov.mo> (China-Macau CEPA) accessed 1 September 2011.

[76] *See* WTO, *Committee on Regional Trade Agreements – Closer Economic Partnership Arrangement between China and Hong Kong, China – Addendum* (21 January 2005; 13 January 2006; 06 December 2006) WT/REG162/1/Add.1–3, WT/REG163/1/Add.1–3 for the Supplement I – III.

With regard to the coverage, the CEPAs cover three elements: trade in goods, trade in services and trade and investment facilitation. The six annexes duly correspond to such coverage. As Hong Kong and Macau are both free ports, only China had to adjust to the zero-tariff treatment on imported goods; Hong Kong and Macau were merely required to maintain their zero-tariff policy. The Parties to the two CEPAs undertake not to take anti-dumping and anti-subsidy measures.[77] Since Hong Kong and Macau have never taken any of these two measures (Hong Kong does not even has such legislations), it is clear that this obligation is designated solely for China. Nevertheless, due to the small trade volume of imported goods from Hong Kong and Macau, this article is more of symbolic significance than of economic importance. Article 9 of both CEPAs regulates safeguard measures. As transitional product-specific safeguard measures and safeguard measures in textile products have been excluded from the CEPAs, such should be referred back to the Agreement on Safeguards (the ASG) when imposing safeguard measures. Importantly, the safeguard provisions in the CEPAs lay down different rules, which according to some Members have deviated from the existing ASG.[78]

Article 9 also refers to Article 19 of the CEPAs: consultations in case of 'sharp increase' of imported goods. Whereas the affected Party may suspend preferential treatments or concessions, upon request, it should promptly commence consultations under Article 19 with a view to reaching a mutually satisfactory agreement. This is the sole provision in the CEPAs which explicitly refers to the consultation procedures in the case of trade disputes. In view of the limited trade volume of imported goods into the Chinese market from Hong Kong and Macau, it is unlikely to cause or threaten to cause 'serious injury' to the Chinese domestic industry. On the other hand, given Hong Kong and Macau's free-port status, it is also difficult to imagine a sharp increase in imported goods due to the liberalisation of this market access.

Article 10 governs general rules of origin, which are further elaborated in Annex 2, defines the scope of imported goods eligible for preferential treatments. In respect of trade in services, Article 11 deals with market access, which is supplemented by Annex 4. The scope and criteria for the 'service supplier', a key issue for

---

[77] The CEPA, Arts. 7, 8.

[78] Concerns have been voiced during the process of the CRTA examination. It is pointed out that the safeguard provision as set out in the CEPA derogates considerably from the WTO Safeguard Agreement. However, in response to these doubts, Hong Kong reiterates its long-established free trade policy and states that there are no rules governing global safeguard measure in Hong Kong and that it has never adopted any safeguard measures in the past. Therefore, this safeguard measure provided within the CEPA appears to design solely for China, which is nevertheless unlikely to use it. *See* WTO, *Committee on Regional Trade Agreements – Closer Economic Partnership Arrangement between China and Hong Kong, China – Questions and Replies* (13 March 2006) WT/REG162/6, 3.

services trade, is defined in Article 12 and further elaborated in Annex 5. Articles 13–15 then regulate cooperation in the financial and tourism sectors; and mutual recognition of professional qualifications. Cooperation in the financial sector, namely banking, insurance and securities, are of great importance from the policy perspective, as financial professions in Hong Kong may be of great help during the Chinese financial reform and may contribute to the competitiveness of financial sectors in China. Funding coming from China may also contribute to the prosperity of the financial market in Hong Kong. Chinese tourists in Hong Kong and Macau can contribute greatly to the economic growth of these two separate customs territories. With regard to the qualification, the Parties opt to 'mutual recognition' approach, as it would unpractical to establish 'common rules on professional qualifications' due to their disparity in development and quality in these three areas.

Article 16 and 17 govern the trade and investment facilitation. Greater transparency, standard conformity and enhanced information exchange are 'measures' to be taken to facilitate trade and investment. Article 17 defines the scope of cooperation covering 'trade and investment promotion; customs clearance facilitation; commodities inspection, inspection and quarantine of animals and plants, food safety, sanitary quarantine, certification, accreditation and standardisation management; electronic business; transparency in laws and regulations; cooperation of small and medium sized enterprises; and industries cooperation.' The Parties may also include other subjects through consultations.

Lastly, since the signing of the original CEPAs, seven supplements have so far been signed between China and Hong Kong and Macau: in 2004, 2005, 2006, 2007, 2008, 2009, and 2010.It seems the Parties add supplements to the original text on an annual basis. The purpose of these seven supplements is to further liberalise access to the Chinese market and to redefine service suppliers and rules of origin.

3. *The Compatibility of CEPA with WTO Rules on FTA*

Procedural and substantial requirements governing the compatibility of FTAs to the WTO rules are laid down in Article XXIV of the GATT 1994 and Article V of the GATS. The Appellate Body has also dealt with this issue in *Turkey – Restrictions on Imports of Textile and Clothing Products* (*Turkey - Textiles*).[79] For an FTA to be WTO-compatible, firstly it has to satisfy the 'neutrality' requirement, which dictates that the overall effects of the FTA may not to be more trade-restrictive than

[79] Appellate Body Report, *Turkey – Restrictions on Imports of Textile and Clothing Products* (*Turkey – Textiles*), WT/DS34/AB/R, adopted 19 November 1999, DSR 1999:VI, 2345.

the previous existing trade policies between the Parties.[80] Secondly, the FTA has also to meet the procedural requirements and substantial coverage.

With regard to the procedural requirement, both CEPAs have been notified to the CRTA and been examined by the Committee. Although the Committee did not arrive at any decision on the compatibility of these two CEPAs with Article XXIV of the GATT 1994 and Article V of the GATS, the Parties to the CEPAs did discharge their notification obligation. In respect of the coverage of the FTA, the legal text prescribes for the criteria of 'substantially all the trade' for trade in goods and 'substantial sectoral coverage' to trade in services. The Appellate Body has also slightly addressed this issue. According to the Appellate Body, "substantially all the trade' is not the same as *all* the trade and 'substantially all the trade' is something considerably more than merely *some* of the trade."[81] Nonetheless, this passage offers little guidance on the line between 'some,' 'substantially all' and 'all'.

In assessing the WTO-consistency of the China-Hong Kong CEPA, Cao, a Chinese legal scholar, argued that the main text of China-Hong Kong CEPA and its six annexes have already covered 90 per cent of total exported trade to China from Hong Kong and have fully liberalised five sectors (construction and related engineering service; distribution services; financial services; tourism and travel related services; and transport services) while partially liberalised two sectors (business services and communication services). No mode of services supply is *a priori* excluded. Those commitments made in the China-Hong Kong CEPA, read together with China's WTO accession commitments, cover 'substantially all the trade' and have 'substantial sectoral coverage'.[82] However, this view is not shared by some WTO Members. For example, the European Union had repeatedly emphasised its position that the China-Hong Kong CEPA cannot be qualified as covering 'substantially all the trade'. The European Union views the China-Hong Kong CEPA "more as a framework agreement to provide future liberalisation than an actual liberalisation agreement."[83]

---

[80] The Appellate Body Report addresses this requirement in paragraph 58 and lays down two conditions, which should be fulfilled, so that the regional trade agreement may be WTO-compatible. In the words of the Appellate Body, '[F]irst, the party claiming the benefit of this defence must demonstrate that the measure at issue is introduced upon the formation of a customs union that fully meets the requirements of sub-paragraphs 8(a) and 5(a) of Article XXIV. And, second, that party must demonstrate that the formation of that customs union would be prevented if it were not allowed to introduce the measure at issue'. *See* Appellate Body Report, *Turkey – Textiles*, para. 58. Another relevant issue here is whether the rules of origin as set out in the CEPA can constitute as 'more trade restrictive' measures.

[81] Appellate Report, *Turkey – Textiles*, para. 48 (emphasis original).

[82] Gao (n72) 4–5.

[83] WTO, *Committee on Regional Trade Agreements – Forty-Second Session – Examination of the Closer Economic Partnership Arrangement between China and Hong Kong, China, Goods and Services – Note on the Meeting of 4 April 2006* (15 May 2006) WT/REG162/M3, para 12.

B. *Dispute Resolution in the Closer Economic Partnership Arrangement*

With regard to trade dispute resolution mechanism under the CEPA framework, in Article 19 of both CEPAs provide nearly identical provisions governing institutional arrangements. A Joint Steering Committee, comprised of senior representatives or officials from both China and Hong Kong and Macau is to be established. Under this Steering Committee, liaison offices should be established both within the Central Authority and the governments of these two SARs. Working groups may also be set up under this Steering Committee. Subsequently, three working groups Working Groups on Trade in Goods, Trade in Services and Trade and Investments Facilitation were established at the first Steering Committee meeting.

Paragraph 3 of this Article provides the functions of the Steering Committee, which reads:

> The functions of the Steering Committee include:
>
> 1. Supervising the implementation of the 'CEPA';
> 2. Interpreting the provisions of the 'CEPA';
> 3. Resolving disputes that may arise during the implementation of the 'CEPA';
> 4. Drafting additions and amendments to the content of the 'CEPA';
> 5. Providing steer on the work of the working groups;
> 6. Dealing with any other business relating to the implementation of the 'CEPA.'

This provision defines the competence of the Steering Committee: interpretation and implementation; further additions and amendments; and supervision of working groups. The Steering Committee is also responsible for dispute resolution. The fifth paragraph of the same article lays down the procedural rules governing the interpretation and implementation of the CEPAs. The Parties to the CEPAs shall resolve problems resulting from the interpretation and implementation of the CEPAs 'through consultation in the spirit of friendship and cooperation'. In accordance with this spirit, the Steering Committee shall thus reach its decisions by consensus. However, the legal text is does not provide further guidance should a mutual agreed solution be unattainable.

In its submission on 25 July 2003, the HKGCC thus voiced its concerns on the functioning of the Steering Committee in general, particularly on the substantive content of the dispute settlement mechanism. It questioned the working procedures and private participation in the Steering Committee and the enforcement and appeal procedures of the dispute settlement mechanism.[84] In August 2003, the government of HKSAR released a preliminary response on the implementation of the China-Hong Kong CEPA. However, those questions related to the

[84] 51 Questions on the CEPA, submitted by the General Chamber of Commerce of Hong Kong (25 July 2003) <http://www.chamber.org.hk/en/information/policy_comments.aspx?ID=119> accessed 1 September 2011.

competence, working procedures and substantial content of the dispute resolution have not been answered.[85]

One may have to further reflect on the questions put forward by the HKGCC, especially whether they are hypothetical or real concerns. A passage in the Parties' notification to the CRTA on the dispute resolution procedures is telling on this point:

> The two sides have set up a Joint Steering Committee to, among others, supervise the implementation of the CEPA, interpret the provisions of the CEPA, and resolve disputes that may arise during the implementation of the CEPA. The two sides will resolve any problems arising from the interpretation or implementation of the CEPA through consultation in the spirit of friendship and cooperation. The Joint Steering Committee will make its decisions by consensus.[86]

This passage clarifies on the Parties' perception and characterisation towards the dispute resolution mechanism as provided in the CEPAs and helps toexplain its primitiveness. According to some Macau scholars, the two CEPAs are policy instruments in nature, with the aim to provide preferential treatments to Hong Kong and Macau. The dispute resolution mechanism set out in these CEPAs is thus of political and diplomatic in essence that neither follows the practices of other FTAs nor specifies formalities or working procedures to be taken because it would not be necessary.[87] Any difference arising from the implementation of the CEPAs will be, and have to be resolved, in the spirit of friendship and cooperation.

During the process of examination in the CRTA, this supposition can be supported by the Parties' response to the question whether any arbitration in case of unavailability of consensus. It is reiterated by China and Macau that, 'under Article 19(3) of CEPA, one of the functions of the Steering Committee is to resolve disputes that may arise during the implementation of the China-Macau CEPA.

---

[85] Chamber's Question on CEPA: A Preliminary Update <http://www.chamber.org.hk/wto/content/cepa_papers_rta_main.asp> accessed 25 June 2007.

[86] WTO, *Committee on Regional Trade Agreements – Closer Economic Partnership Arrangement between China and Hong Kong, China – Goods Aspects – Communication from the Parties* (25 January 2005) WT/REG/162/3, 5; WTO, *Committee on Regional Trade Agreements – Closer Economic Partnership Arrangement between China and Macau, China – Goods aspects – Communication from the Parties* (28 January 2005) WT/REG163/3, 5.

[87] L Chen and Y Zhao, 'A Study on the Dispute Resolution Mechanism in Region Trade Agreements: Article 19 of CEPA (Quyu maoyi xieding zhong de zhengduan jiejue jizhi yanjiu——jian xi CEPA di shi jiutiao)' in G Wang (ed), *A Research on the Economic Arrangement among the Cross-Strait Four Areas* (*Liang an si di jingmao anpai yanjiu*) (Beijing University Press, Beijing 2006) 253.

Both Parties believe that any problems arising from the interpretation or implementation of the CEPA will be resolved through consultation in the spirit of friendship and cooperation as well as under the principle of mutual benefits.'[88]

Whereas this approach has its merit from political concerns, this informal dispute resolution mechanism nonetheless constitutes a major defect for these two CEPAs. Although China and Hong Kong and Macau are politically under the same sovereignty, it does not guarantee that no conflict of economic interests among these three areas will ever arise. In light of these inevitable conflicting economic interests arising from close economic integration, the protections provided in the CEPAs is far from adequate or effective.[89] The unavailability of private participation in this dispute resolution mechanism is then another major defect. This concern has also been clearly articulated in the HKGCC's submission on 25 July 2003. Since this dispute resolution mechanism can only be dealt with through the channel of governmental consultation, no opportunity is provided for private actors to participate. The only way for private actors to influence the outcome of a dispute is through lobbying and various informal petitions. So far, there has been no case referred to the Steering Committee, as this ill-designated dispute resolution mechanism has discouraged disputes referrals. This prevents effective resolution of commercial disputes between China and Hong Kong and Macau and the protection economic interests of private actors therein.

C. *Dispute Resolution through the WTO Dispute Settlement Mechanism*

Compulsory jurisdiction and permanent Appellate Body are two major characteristics of the WTO Dispute Settlement Mechanism. In purely legal terms, as two full WTO Members, Hong Kong and Macau may avail themselves of this Dispute Settlement Mechanism. After the panel proceedings, they may also refer to the Appellate Body. However, it is unlikely, or even impossible, to see a case brought about by one against another under this WTO Dispute Settlement Mechanism.[90] This view is also shared by some Hong Kong scholars.[91]

---

[88] WTO, *Committee on Regional Trade Agreements – Closer Economic Partnership Arrangement Between China and Macao, China – Questions and Replies* (24 May 2005) WT/REG163/5, 3.

[89] Ibid 253–254.

[90] Another relevant issue is the potential use of this dispute settlement mechanism between China and Taiwan: *see, e.g.*, Q Kong, 'Can the WTO Dispute Settlement Mechanism Resolve the Trade Disputes Between China and Taiwan?' (2002) 5 Journal of International Economic Law 747; J S Mo, 'Settlement of Disputes between Mainland China and the Separate Territory of Taiwan within the WTO' (2003) 2 Chinese Journal of International Law 145.

[91] *See, e.g.*, Gao (n72) 7.

IV. Short Conclusion

This chapter examines trade disputes resolution mechanisms between China and its two SARs under two frameworks: the constitutional/national law framework and the WTO/CEPA framework. The interaction of China and its two SARs are unique both in their domestic constitutional structures and in their international trading regimes. Firstly this chapter briefly introduces the judicial review in these three areas and examines the vertical and horizontal interactions between China and its two SARs. Emphasis is placed on the interaction between China and the HKSAR, as courts in Hong Kong have more experiences in judicial review. The efforts to characterise free trade policy as 'political action' and subsequently to remove the jurisdiction of judiciary in Macau on this subject demonstrate the constraints faced by the Macau courts and present the weaknesses in Macau's judicial review. This chapter then explores the nature of the CEPAs under the WTO rules and examines existing trade dispute mechanisms in both the WTO and the CEPAs. It points out the unlikeness of these three Members to refer matters to the WTO Dispute Settlement Mechanism. This chapter then illustrates major defects in the dispute resolution mechanism within the two CEPAs and explains why a judicialised dispute settlement mechanism under the CEPA framework is not preferable to the Parties.

CHAPTER NINE

NEITHER NATIONAL NOR INTERNATIONAL: TRADE DISPUTE RESOLUTION BETWEEN TAIWAN AND HONG KONG AND MACAU

I. Introduction

This chapter aims to examine and explore the trade dispute resolution among the three WTO separate-customs-territory Members: Taiwan, Hong Kong and Macau. More precisely, it focuses on Taiwan in relation to Hong Kong and Macau, which are Members of the WTO, but at the same time Special Administrative Regions (SARs) of China.[1] Therefore, while the interaction between Taiwan and Hong Kong and Macau may be subject to WTO law, 'China factors' nevertheless also play a pivotal role in this subject matter.

In this context, this chapter will firstly review the negotiation on the freedom of the air (or the flight rights, or traffic rights) between Taiwan and Hong Kong with the aim to illustrate how 'China factors' affect the progress and result of this negotiation. By this example, it reminds the readers that, when examining economic integration and trade dispute resolution among these three Members in relation to, *inter alia*, the choices of forum and their approaches, one should not neglect the 'invisible hand' of China Central Authority. Besides, this example echoes the negotiations of direct transportation agreements between Taiwan and China and helps to clarify the role of Hong Kong and Macau in the cross-Taiwan-strait trade relations.

Following this example, this chapter, in section III explores the relevance and significance of the WTO Dispute Settlement Mechanism. Given the status of free ports, the role of an 'intermediary' and the main transhipment ports for goods between Taiwan and China prior to the signature of the Taiwan-China direct transportation agreements, it is unlikely that either Taiwan or Hong Kong and Macau would refer to the WTO forum. However, it does not suggest the absence of trade disputes between Taiwan and Hong Kong and Macau. This section points to an alternative dispute resolution – arbitration, and explains why arbitration is

[1] As clarified Chapter I, there may be several confusing terminological issues. To avoid this confusion, 'Hong Kong' will be used when this work tries to refer to it as a geographic indication with neutral political connotation. The 'HKSAR' is to be employed when emphasis is placed upon Hong Kong being a special administrative region of China, while 'Hong Kong, China' will be used when it focuses on its external autonomy in economic and commercial affairs and its WTO membership. This chapter will follow this practice.

appealing to these three Members, or more precisely, to private individuals and enterprises thereof. This section then investigates their domestic legal framework and jurisprudence in relation to the mutual recognition of arbitration awards/ judgments, and finally revisits the role of China on this issue. A short conclusion summarising this chapter will be provided in Section IV

II. The Haunted China Factors: Taiwan-Hong Kong Negotiation on the Freedom of The Air as An Example

As noted in Chapter VIII, the constitutional design of Hong Kong Special Administrative Region (the HKSAR) is governed by its mini-constitution, the Hong Kong Basic Law (the HKBL). The most significant event in Hong Kong's constitutional development is undoubtedly its return to China. As a conventional practice, the agreement on flight rights between Hong Kong and Taiwan lasts for five years. Setting the handover as a time-point, one can separate the negotiation of Taiwan and Hong Kong into three phases: pre-handover, transition period and after the handover. In 2002, when their agreement on flight rights expired, Hong Kong has already been part of China whereas the ruling party in Taiwan was the Democratic Progress Party (the DPP) that advocates for the independence of Taiwan. This added much complexity to the negotiation process. This post-handover negotiation in 2002 projected the prospective negotiation on the direct-transportation between Taiwan and China. It was also during this negotiation that the influence of China Central Authority became even clearer. Therefore, this section will focus on post-handover negotiation while the negotiation in the pre-handover and transition phases will be briefly considered.

A. *Pre-Handover*

The initiation of flights between Taiwan and British Hong Kong dated back to 1957, few years after the official diplomatic relation between Taiwan and the United Kingdom was cut off in 1950. Due to the absence of official diplomatic relation, the negotiation of aviation pact between Taiwan and British Hong Kong was carried out by their major and the only at that time airplane companies: Cathay Pacific Airways and China Airlines.[2] In other words, the negotiation was delegated to the flight operators. The agreement was private commercial contract in nature in order to avoid the issues of sovereign power or public authority. After the agreement was done, the agreement concerned should be reported to and approved by

[2] It should be noted that China Airlines is the airline operated in Republic of China, the official title of Taiwan, while China Airways is the airline operated in People's Republic of China.

their respective flight regulatory agencies. Namely, the public authority stayed behind and was not visible during the negotiation process.[3]

B. *Transition Period*

Taiwan launched its 'open-sky' policy in 1987. Its state-owned airline had been gradually privatised and some other airline companies were allowed to enter into the market. Notwithstanding its liberalisation policy in aviation services, the fact that China Airlines and Cathay Pacific Airways dominated the market remained unchanged until 1995. When the agreement on the flight rights between Hong Kong and Taiwan expired on 29 April 1995, the new agreement, if the conventional practice of five years' term was followed, would cross the transition period. Since this agreement would cover post-handover period, the deal between Taiwan and Hong Kong should thus be subject to the approval of China Central Authority, or precisely speaking, the Sino-British Joint Liaison Group at that time.[4]

At the same time, with China's resumption of sovereign power on Hong Kong, and subsequently the coming into being of the HKSAR, Taiwan would have to decide the status of the HHSAR since the direct transportation between Taiwan and China was prohibited before the signature of Taiwan-China direct transportation agreements on 4 November 2008.[5] To this end, the *Statute on the Relations of Hong Kong and Macau* (the *Hong Kong and Macau Statute*)[6] was enacted on 2 April 1997 in order to regulate differently the relations between Taiwan and Hong Kong and Macau after their handover. According to this *Statute*, air and sea transportation between Taiwan and Hong Kong and Macau is possible even after their return to China.[7] The flight between Taiwan and British Hong Kong is defined as

---

[3] B-S Qiu, *A Study on the Negotiation of Freedom of the Air between Taiwan and Hong Kong* (*Tai gang hang quan tanpan zhi yanjiu*) (National Chung Hsing University, Taipei 2003) 55. The factual aspects of air services negotiation between Taiwan and Hong Kong in this section relies heavily on Chiu's work.

[4] According to Article 4 of the Joint Declaration of the Government of the United Kingdom of Great Britain and Northern Ireland and the Government of the People's Republic of China on the Question of Hong Kong (Sino-British Joint Declaration), a Sino-British Joint Liaison Group should be established to ensure the smooth transfer of Hong Kong. Annex II to the Declaration provides the legal basis and guidelines for the working procedure of the Joint Liaison Group. Wherever an issue is related to the transitional period, it may be referred to this Joint Liaison Group for consultation and discussion. A failure in this procedure might lead to China's refusal to recognise its validity after China's resumption of the sovereignty of Hong Kong. The reform of the Legislative Council introduced by Chris Patten, the 28th and last Governor of Hong Kong.

[5] *Statute Governing the Relations of People in Taiwan Area and Mainland Area* (the *Statute*), Arts. 28-31.

[6] An English translation available at <http://www.mac.gov.tw/ct.asp?xItem=51261&ctNode=5915&mp=3> accessed 1 September 2011.

[7] The *Hong Kong and Macau Statute*, Arts. 24-27.

international route, whereas, after the handover it is deemed as a special route neither international nor domestic.

In this context, Taiwan aimed to enter into a pact effective through the transition period, namely from 1995 to 2000. In addition, other competitors should be allowed to enter into the market of civil aviation services between Taiwan and Hong Kong. Since China Airlines should be no longer the only operator therein, the delegation for the negotiation should include other airlines companies. Thus, during this negotiation, it was Taipei Airline Association (the TAA), composing China Airlines and other airlines companies, delegated to negotiate the flights rights. In contrast to Taiwan, Cathay Pacific Airways was in charge of this negotiation in the beginning.

Nevertheless, 'China factors' eventually became clear in the later stage of this negotiation. Corresponding to Taiwan, the civil aviation services market in Hong Kong was also forced to be liberalised, notably, to Chinese airlines companies.[8] The China National Aviation Corporation, a wholly state-owned enterprise at that time, was registered in Hong Kong in 1995 in order to be eligible for the allocation of flight rights between Taiwan and Hong Kong. As this pact would go through 1997, the approval of China Central Authority was indispensible. When the stance of China became clear, Cathay Pacific Airways found the trend to open the market to other competitors irresistible and inevitable. Cathay Pacific Airways then proposed that Hong Kong Dragon Airlines to be the additional flyer between Taiwan and Hong Kong. This proposal was rejected by China. As an alternative, Cathay Pacific Airways offered to sell its share to the China National Aviation Corporation so that China National Aviation Corporation might indirectly benefit from the liberalisation of civil aviation service between Taiwan and Hong Kong.[9] In this way, the deal that Cathay Pacific Airways and Hong Kong Dragon Airlines operate the flights between Taiwan and Hong Kong was settled.

With regard to the formality of the agreement, it was intended by Taiwan to be signed by association to association. With the opposition of China, it remained to be commercial pact between airline companies and airline companies. The result turned out to be a commercial pact signed by China Airline and Cathay Pacific; the other was signed by Hong Kong Dragon Airline and Evergreen Air, the

[8] At this stage, apart from Cathay Pacific, there were some other airlines who might participate in the allocation of flights rights between Taiwan and Hong Kong: Hong Kong Dragon Airlines, Air Hong Kong, and China National Aviation Corporation. Although Hong Kong Dragon Airlines was originally owned by China International Trust and Investment Company, a state-owned investment company, Cathay Pacific became the major shareholder at the time of negotiation. Air Hong Kong, due to its financial crisis, became a subsidiary company of Cathay Pacific after Cathay Pacific took 75% of its share in 1994 and the rest 25% in 2002.

[9] Qiu (n 3) 86-92.

new operator in Taiwan. With the extension of the 1990 agreement for seven times, the 1995 round negotiation on the flight right was finally settled in April 1996.[10]

C. *Post-Handover and the DPP as Ruling Party in Taiwan*

During this first post-handover negotiation, Taiwan's relations with the HKSAR had also been subject to the new regulatory regime as set out in the *Hong Kong and Macau Statute*. Some experiences might have already been learned. However, a new factor complicated this first post-handover negotiation: the DDP won the presidential election in Taiwan in 2000. It was the first time that Hong Kong, with China sitting behind, had to negotiate with a party favouring the independence of Taiwan. Further, this negotiation was seen as a signal to test the political climate between Taiwan and China, and might be used as a precedent for the negotiation for Taiwan-China direct-transportation agreements. In respect of Hong Kong, the mixture of being a SAR of China and at the same time a Member in the WTO was amplified. At this stage, the HKBL had entered into force for nearly three years. The interaction between China and Hong Kong should thus be governed by the HKBL. Similarly, some patterns might have also already been gradually developed. In the context, a careful legal analysis of the new regulatory framework set out by the HKBL and the *Hong Kong and Macau Statute* governing the civil aviation is essential and beneficial. Therefore, this subsection will start with an analysis of the legal framework on the civil aviation transportation in these two jurisdictions and then examine the interaction of Taiwan, China and Hong Kong during this negotiation.

1. *Statute on the Relations of Hong Kong and Macau*

Article 4 of the *Hong Kong and Macau Statute* lays down the regulatory framework of the transportation and shipping between Taiwan and Hong Kong, covering the

[10] During the course of this negotiation, a negotiation between Taiwan and Macau was also undergoing. The pattern of the negotiation between Taiwan and Hong Kong was followed. Namely, Taiwan delegated the authority to the TAA while Air Macau was in charge of this negation. The flight between Taiwan and Macau was an alternative to that between Taiwan and Hong Kong. In case that the negotiation between Taiwan and Hong Kong could not successfully be concluded, Taiwan might be faced with the difficulties that there were no flight between Taiwan and China and suffered from a great loss of economic interests. Therefore, when the negotiation between Taiwan and Hong Kong seemed not so promising, Taiwan conducted a parallel negation with Macau. The agreement on the flight rights between Taiwan and Macau was done on 1 December 1995. Undoubtedly, Taiwan had to deal with China who sat behind Macau, since the agreement of traffic rights would cross the transition period, 20 December 1999. Nevertheless, one of the factors blocking the negotiation between Taiwan and Hong Kong was the attitude of Chris Patten, the Governor of the Colony at that time. Due to many conflicts between him and China, notably the reform of the Legislative Council, Patten was reluctant to make a deal cross the handover, which would force him to deal directly with China.

vessels and civil aircrafts. While the civil aviation may be subject to restrictions or prohibition in circumstances of threat to national security, civil aircrafts registered in Taiwan or Hong Kong are generally allowed to fly between Taiwan and Hong with the permission from the Ministry of Transportation and Communications (the MOTC).[11] Besides, foreign-registered civil aircrafts may also fly between the Taiwan and Hong Kong in accordance with air traffic rights exchanges and by reference to international air traffic conventions.[12]

2. *Hong Kong Basic Law*

Article 4 of the HKBL regulates the civil aviation of the HKSAR. In order to maintain the status of the HKSAR as a centre of international and regional aviation,[13] the pre-existent regulatory regime of the civil aviation management should continue. The HKSAR should also keep its own aircraft register system. Nonetheless, the practices in civil aviation management and aircraft register system should be in conformity with laws and regulations of China Central Authority pertaining to nationality marks and registration marks of aircrafts.[14] The access of foreign state aircraft to the HKSAR should also obtain the permission from China Central Authority.[15] Article 130 provides that the HKSAR is responsible on its own 'for matters of routine business and technical management of civil aviation.' Arrangements should be made after the consultation between China Central Authority and the HKSAR in respect of the air services between the HKSAR and other parts of China.[16] Then the HKBL assigns the competence to the China Central Authority on agreements relating to air services (a) between China and other states and regions with stops at the HKSAR and (b) the HKSAR and other states and regions with stops in China.[17] These two categories of air services agreements should be concluded by the China Central Authority. In other words, when any part of China is at stake, be it the final destination or a temporary stop, China Central Authority is competent for the conclusion of an agreement with the interests of the HKSAR taken into consideration. The HKSAR may also be included as members of Chinese delegation.[18]

---

[11] The *Statute*, Art. 26(1).
[12] The *Statute*, Art. 27(1).
[13] HKBL, Art. 128.
[14] HKBL, Art. 129(1). Article 135 also provides that 'Airlines incorporated and having their principal place of business in Hong Kong and businesses related to civil aviation functioning there
[15] Regarding the issue of state aircraft, China Airlines decided not to carry Taiwan's national flag in order to avoid the potential sovereignty controversies in 1992.
[16] HKBL, Art. 131.
[17] HKBL, Art. 132(1).
[18] HKBL, Art. 132(2), (3).

Two articles are most relevant here. Article 133(1) provides that, acting under the specific authorisation of China Central Authority, the HKSAR may:

(1) renew or amend air service agreements and arrangements previously in force;
(2) negotiate and conclude new air service agreements providing routes for airlines incorporated in the Hong Kong Special Administrative Region and having their principal place of business in Hong Kong and providing rights for over-flights and technical stops; and
(3) negotiate and conclude provisional arrangements with foreign states or regions with which no air service agreements have been concluded.

Article 134 the prescribes that China Central Authority should give the HKSAR the authority to designate such airlines, to negotiate and conclude relevant arrangements for the implementation of those air services agreements and provisional arrangements as referred to in Article 133.[19] Authority should also be given to issue licenses to airlines incorporated in the HKSAR with principal place of business therein, and to issue permits to foreign airlines for services other than those to, from or through the mainland of China.[20]

To sum up, regardless of the authority given to the HKSAR to regulate its own licensing and permit regime and to negotiate and conclude relevant arrangements a specific authorisation is necessary when the HKSAR intends to renew, amend, negotiate or conclude air service agreements or arrangements. This means that China Central Authority can veto any deal done by Taiwan and Hong Kong. Without the approval of China, the air service agreement between Taiwan and Hong Kong can never be effectuated.

3. *Negotiation Process*

When the 1996 air service agreement expired on 30 June 2001, it was immediately extended for six months till 31 December 2001. This was mainly because China had to take more time to observe and ascertain the attitudes and approaches taken by the DPP. Besides, this negotiation was immediately before the eve of China and Taiwan's accession to the WTO. The linkage between direct-transportation between Taiwan and China and this air service negotiation between Taiwan and Hong Kong was thus inevitable. In fact, it was also hoped in Taiwan at that time that, after its accession to the WTO its trade relations with could be normalised and governed by the WTO framework, which would help to resolve the direct-transportation issue. Nevertheless, as noted in Chapter VI, it was not until on 4 November 2008 when the Kuomintang (the KMT) won again the presidential

[19] HKBL, Art. 133(1), (3).
[20] HKBL, Art. 133(2), (4).

election and restored the executive power that the direct transportation agreements between Taiwan and China were concluded.

However, Taiwan's synergic strategy brought about the first controversy: who should be in charge of this negotiation. As Hong Kong and Macau were returned to China in 1997 and 1999, affairs related to these two SARs are assigned to the competence of the Mainland Affairs Council (the MAC) of Taiwan. Therefore, the MAC made clear that it would dominate this round of negotiation. The prospective negotiation on the direct-transportation between Taiwan and China and national security are major arguments of the MAC. Secondly, Taiwan aimed to change the previous negotiation model, namely, airline to airline and Cathay Pacific Airways to the TAA, commercial agreements in formality. Taiwan demanded that the negotiation should be government to government and that the formality should include a main legal text with annexes as are generally employed by other international agreements of freedom of the air. Doubtlessly, this proposal would not be acceptable to China and was thus soon rejected. Nonetheless, the HKSAR signalled that the Civil Aviation Agency (the CAA) of Taiwan could participate in the negotiation as a consultant. However, the MAC did not accept this proposal. Thus, the 1996 air service agreement was again extended for six months till 30 June 2002.

After the second-time extension of the 1996 air service agreement, the MAC softened: it denounced its government-to-government position, but asked instead that the agreement to be signed by the governmental official of the CAA. But this proposal was still unacceptable to the HKSAR. Instead, the HKSAR reiterated its position that the TAA acted as the main negotiator and the official of the CAA in Taiwan could participate as a consultant. In addition, the HKSAR maintained that, if a new agreement could not be reached before 30 June 2002, the 1996 air service agreement might not be extended. In other words, the flight between Taiwan and the HKSAR might be suspended.

With the threat of suspension of the flight between Taiwan and the HKSAR, the two parties finally entered into substantial negation. Taiwan then proposed that the agreement should be permanently valid in the formality of a main text with annexes. But the HKSAR maintained that the conventional practice should be carried on. No consensus was reached. On 24 May 2002, Taiwan gave up its prior position and accepted the agreement to be in the formality of rights and obligation listed in the agreement. The HKSAR then welcomed this position and agreed that the TAA to be the signatory of Taiwan, while the Cathay Pacific and Hong Kong Dragon Airline were to be the signatories of the HKSAR.

On 29 June 2002, one day before the expiry of the twice-extended air service agreement, a new agreement was settled. At the final stage of this negotiation, on Taiwan's side, only the official of the MAC, the CAA and the Secretary General of the TAA remained on the table. Actually, the government officials dominated this final stage of negotiation. In contrast, the representatives of the airline companies remained to be the main negotiators.

While the final deal was signed by the Secretary General of the TAA, it was indicated that the signature was 'signed under the instruction', which suggested the presence of public authority in Taiwan. This agreement goes beyond a commercial pact, using the title of 'Arrangement Concerning the Transportation between Taiwan and Hong Kong'. It also includes the wording of freedom of the air, exchange of traffic rights. This may be seen a step forward between the inter-governmental interaction between Taiwan and the HKSAR, with China Central Authority standing behind the HKSAR. Finally, it should also be noted that this 2002 arrangements expired in 2007, but still in the status of extension.[21] This again points to the linkage between the air service between Taiwan and Hong Kong and the direct-transportation issue between Taiwan and China.

As the KMT won the presidential election in 20008, direct air and marine transportation agreements between Taiwan and China were signed on 4 November 2008. This development affects and undermines the role of Hong Kong as intermediary in the field of cross-Taiwan-strait trade relations. Besides, these new direct transportation agreements may turn back to affect the course of the negotiation between Taiwan and Hong Kong. In the meantime, Taiwan devotes most efforts on negotiation with China which results the marginalisation of Hong Kong. This also helps to explain why Taiwan is not particularly eager to renegotiate with Hong Kong on a new air service agreement.

D. *Piercing the Veil: the Role of China*

With China's resumption of the sovereignty of Hong Kong in 1997, the negotiation of the flight rights between Taiwan and Hong Kong was virtually dominated by China. The coming into power of the DPP in 2000 added complexities to this issue. While Taiwan aimed to 'upgrade' the negotiation to intergovernmental level, the HKSAR and China insisted it to be commercial pacts between airline and airline. The HKSAR and China tried to prevent the image of two equal governmental entities since China has long regarded Taiwan as its local province. This negotiation might project the subsequent direct-transportation between Taiwan and China. It also reveals different approaches adopted and maintained by Taiwan, Hong Kong and China in the WTO forum. A direct intergovernmental confrontation between Taiwan and China is the last thing that China is delighted to see.

Nevertheless, it does not mean that the interests of the HKSAR and China are always correlative. As Cathay Pacific Airways is mainly a British-invested company, its dominant position in the air transport services market in Hong Kong would inevitably be challenged as the British government left in 1997.

---

[21] In addition to the air service agreements between Taiwan and Hong Kong, the air service agreement between Taiwan and Macau expired in 2005 and has been repeatedly extended.

China-invested airlines are expected to benefit from this air service market between Taiwan and Hong Kong. Furthermore, China-funded airlines may be more competitive and benefit more in this market than Cathay Pacific Airways. For example, the Hong Kong Dragon Airline is allowed to transit in Hong Kong and to continue to fly into China by changing the code of the airline, since, as a conventional practice in the international civil aviation the change of flight code signifies the change of route. It is thus not a direct flight between Taiwan and China. This practice has made the Hong Kong Dragon Airline much more competitive.[22] Moreover, with the Ma administration coming to power in 2008 in Taiwan, economic relations between Taiwan and China highly accelerate. Hong Kong's status of intermediary and its economic benefit from this status is threatened. In response to this development, the Chief Executive of HKSAR, when welcoming the visit of the President of Straits Exchange Foundation in Taiwan, Chiang Pin-kung, proposed to deepen the economic and trade relations between the HKSAR and Taiwan.[23] Therefore, one should not fail to see the relevance of Taiwan-China relations in examining the interaction between Taiwan and Hong Kong. A warmer political climate between Taiwan and China may turn back to feed a closer economic tie between Taiwan and Hong Kong.

Finally, when talking about the economic integration in the Greater China, Macau is usually the missing point. It is mainly because of the economic and industrial structure of Macau, which consists in mainly its gambling services and other related tourism services. However, Macau can also be chosen as a competitor to Hong Kong. When the negotiation of the air service agreement between Taiwan and Hong Kong in 1995 was unpromising, a deal on the traffic rights between Taiwan and Macau were settled in October 1995. Flights between Taiwan and Macau can go 'directly' into China after a temporary stop in Macau with the same flight through a mere change of the flight code. This quasi-direct flight model was actually borrowed by the final deal of 1996 air services agreement between Taiwan and Hong Kong. The quasi-direct flight in the Taiwan-Macau air services agreement predates that in the Taiwan-Hong Kong air service agreement. In this sense, Macau is also competing with its counterpart, Hong Kong. In a word, when thinking about the economic integration and trade dispute resolution in the Greater China, one may be tempted to deem China and its two SARs as a whole and thus fail to appreciate the potential competition and conflict between China and its two SARs, or even between the two SARs. This also points to the

[22] This practice is also seen as 'quasi-direct flight' between Taiwan and China.

[23] AFP, 'Hong Kong, Taiwan Leaders Agree to Strengthen Economic Ties' (19 July 2008) <http://www.channelnewsasia.com/stories/afp_asiapacific_business/view/361258/1/.html> accessed 1 September 2011.

multifaceted nature of Hong Kong and Macau: a SAR of China, but at the same time a full Member in the WTO.

III. Trade Dispute Resolution between Taiwan and Hong Kong and Macau

As dictated by the HKBL and MABL, Hong Kong and Macau, even after their return back to China should maintain their status as a free port. With respect to trade in goods, Hong Kong and Macau mainly maintain a zero-tariff policy, which virtually prevents disputes concerning customs issues. At the same time, Taiwan had heavily relied upon Hong Kong and Macau as an intermediary for its trade and investments into China until May 2008. It is thus unlikely that Taiwan singles out Hong Kong or Macau as a main respondent in the intergovernmental WTO forum. Nevertheless, a close economic relation between Taiwan and Hong Kong and Macau inevitably gives rise to disputes, in particular between Taiwan and Hong Kong. Since the governmental initiative may not be available, disputes should thus be resolved through the private approach. Namely, private enterprises and individuals may have to resolve their disputes through domestic courts or international/national arbitration. In this vein, this section firstly clarify the insignificance and irrelevance of the WTO forum due to the free-port status and zero-tariff policy maintained by Hong Kong and Macau as well as their particular relations with Taiwan. It then investigates the domestic law and regulation in these three Members and explores how and why other forums, namely, domestic courts and arbitration procedures are preferable to private enterprises or individuals to resolve their private disputes. Due to their political concerns, arbitration procedures turn out to be a better alternative for Taiwan, Hong Kong and Macau to respond to their needs deriving from commercial transactions.

A. *The Insignificance of WTO Forum*

From an institutional perspective, as these three WTO Members have full membership in the WTO and enjoy the same rights and obligations as other State Members, they are entitled to refer to the WTO Dispute Settlement Mechanism against one another if they so wish. Nevertheless, as will be shown below, they avoid the WTO forum and opt for other venues as a conventional practice. This can be partly explained by the free-port status and zero-tariff policy of Hong Kong and Macau. Their reliance on one another also contributes to their reluctance for recourse for the WTO forum. As far as the flight between Taiwan and Hong Kong and Macau is concerned, it is not only Taiwan that relies upon the latter two, but the latter also rely upon Taiwan for the economic interests brought about during the transit and transhipment. Further, political consideration also prevents these three Members from going for the WTO forum. As noted above, the least thing China likes to see is the intergovernmental confrontation between Taiwan and Hong Kong and Macau. China's position also prevents these three Members from bringing about a complaint in the WTO against one another. These factors will be examined in detail below.

As stated by the representative of Hong Kong, China during its Trade Policy Review in 2006, Hong Kong, China maintained a long-established policy of free and open trade and investment. The cornerstone of Hong Kong, China's economy rested on free enterprise, free trade and free markets. There were no barriers to trade: no tariffs, no quotas, no exceptions, no restrictions on inward or outward investments, no foreign exchange controls, and no nationality restrictions on corporate or sectoral ownership.[24]

The same applies to Macau, China. According to the Trade Policy Report prepared by the Secretariat of the WTO, Macau, China, being a small and open economy, attaches great importance to international trade and 'continues to maintain the objectives of structural diversification and a market-driven, *laissez-faire* and rules-based trade policy. As one of the most liberal economies in the world that has applied tariffs of zero on all imports, Macau, China is supportive of the multilateral trading system.'[25] Zero-tariff policy is adopted and maintained by Macau in respect of all imports.

Given the long-established policy of free trade and zero-tariff on imports, it is unlikely that Taiwan might recourse to the WTO forum concerning customs matters against Hong Kong and Macau. That being said, with the entering into force of the Closer Economic Partnership Arrangements (CEPAs) between China and its two SARs, rule of origin in Hong Kong and Macau have changed. Taiwan voiced its concerns on this issue, emphasising that the regulatory environment of Macau should not become more restrictive to third countries than before the formation of CEPA.[26]

In addition, in respect of the flight between Taiwan and Macau, Taiwan indicated that there are more than 1.4 million Taiwanese visitors to Macau and through Macau in transit into China. Since Macau is an important market to

---

24 WTO, *Trade Policy Review Body – 13 – 15 December 2006 – Trade Policy Review – Hong Kong, China – Minutes of Meeting* (16 February 2007) WT/TPR/M/173, para. 6.

25 WTO, *Trade Policy Review Body – Trade Policy Review – Report by the Secretariat – Macao, China* (26 March 2007) WT/TPR/S/181, 21-22.

26 WTO, *Trade Policy Review Body – 30 April and 2 May 2007 – Trade Policy Review – Macao, China – Minutes of Meeting* (12 June 2007) WT/TPR/M/181, para. 54. Regarding the potential challenge on the WTO-incompatibility of the rules of origin included in the CEPAs, *see* H S Gao, 'The Closer Economic Partnership Arrangement (CEPA) between Mainland China and Hong Kong ?Legal and Economic Analyses' in P J Davidson (ed), *Trading Arrangements in the Pacific Rim: ASEAN and APEC* (Oxford University Press, New York 2004) 7 <http://ssrn.com/abstract=752785> accessed 1 September 2011.

develop transport and tourism services, fair and equal treatment should thus be granted to Taiwan's airlines making such transit.[27] Although Taiwan voiced its concerns during the Trade Policy Review, the WTO rules offer little help in this regard. While both Taiwan and Macau are Contracting Parties to the Agreement on Trade in Civil Aircraft (the ATCA), this agreement regulates mainly the trade of the following products: civil aircrafts; civil aircraft engines and their parts and components; any other parts, components, and sub-assemblies of civil aircraft; and all ground flight simulators and their parts and components. Therefore, the ATCA is of little relevance on the transit issue. Further, the transit issue is not subject to the regulation of the GATS either since, in respect of air transport services, paragraph 2 of the Annex on Air Transport Services explicitly excludes, except as provided in paragraph 3, the application of the GATS on traffic rights issues or services directly related to traffic rights.

Even if there may be potential inconsistency with WTO law, it is still unlikely for Taiwan to file a complaint against Hong Kong or Macau. These two Members have long played the role of intermediary between Taiwan and China. They are economically complementary. Prior to the entry into force to direct transportation agreements, Taiwan had long relied upon Hong Kong and Macau for their role of an intermediary. Hong Kong and Macau had also greatly benefited from Taiwan's transit or transhipment. In view of these economic concerns, these three Members have no incentive to refer trade disputes to the WTO Dispute Settlement Mechanism against one another. Further, Taiwan's trade relations with Hong Kong and Macau are mainly governed by the *Hong Kong and Macau Statute*. While restriction and limitation may be imposed, Taiwan trade policy and practice toward Hong Kong and Macau is generally in line with the spirit of WTO law. It is also unlikely that Hong Kong or Macau would challenge trade measures adopted or maintained by Taiwan in the WTO Dispute Settlement Mechanism.

Moreover, as a conventional practice, Hong Kong and Macau rarely refer to this WTO Dispute Settlement Mechanism except the *Turkey—Restrictions on Imports of Textile and Clothing Products* (*Turkey – Textiles*).[28] In that case, while Hong Kong, China requested for consultation with Turkey, it eventually did not request the establishment of a panel. Instead, it participated as a third party in the *Turkey – Textile* complained by India.[29] With regard to Macau, China, its recourse to the

[27] WTO, ibid.

[28] WTO, *Turkey – Restrictions on Imports of Textile and Clothing Products – Request for Consultations by Hong Kong* (15 February 1996) WT/DS29/1.

[29] Panel Report, *Turkey – Restrictions on Imports of Textile and Clothing Products*, WT/DS34/R, adopted 19 November 1999, modified by Appellate Body Report, WT/DS34/AB/R, DSR 1999:VI, 2363. Apart from this *Turkey – Textiles* case, Hong Kong, China also participates as a third party in some

WTO Dispute Settlement Mechanism is even rarer. According to the Trade Policy Review Report prepared by the Secretariat, 'Macau, China has never had a trade dispute with Members or non-members of the WTO.'[30] While China participated as a third party in the *United States – Measures Affecting the Cross-Border Supply of Gambling and Betting Services* (*US – Gambling*), Macau, China did not.[31] However, Macau, China did negotiate the United States in relation to the compensation for the withdrawal from its concessions on gambling service.[32] Over all, Hong Kong and Macau do not actively participate in the WTO Dispute Settlement Mechanism. In light of the conventional practice of Hong Kong and Macau, one is safe to say that they tend not to refer to the WTO Dispute Settlement Mechanism in case of trade disputes. In addition, the longstanding attitude of China on the flight negotiation between Taiwan and Hong Kong and Macau is to avoid intergovernmental contact or negotiation. The same attitude is firmly held by China in other subject matters. China would make every possible means to prevent a dispute between Taiwan and Hong Kong and Macau in the WTO forum. In light of these factors, a complaint from Hong Kong or Macau against Taiwan within the WTO is unlikely to come.

B. *Domestic Courts or Arbitration as Alternative Venues*

The above subsection explains why Taiwan and Hong Kong and Macau tend not to refer to the WTO Dispute Settlement Mechanism. It is mainly because trade policy and practice adopted and maintained by Taiwan and Hong Kong and Macau is generally compatible with WTO law. Besides, the role of Hong Kong and Macau as an intermediary between Taiwan and China curtails potential recourse to the WTO Dispute Settlement Mechanism. Further, China's political preference also prevents Hong Kong and Macau from resorting to WTO Dispute Settlement Mechanism. Nevertheless, commercial or trade disputes between private parties among these three Members do not dissolve merely because the governments choose not to resolve these disputes in the intergovernmental WTO forum. While there may be only a few trade disputes derived from governmental

---

other panels, *e.g.*, *United States – Laws, Regulations and Methodology for Calculating Dumping Margins ('Zeroing')* and *European Communities – Selected Customs Matters*. It is also interesting to note that, in these two complaints, Taiwan, China and Hong, Kong, China all participate as a third party. In addition, the attitude of Hong Kong, China can be contrasted to its approach in the GATT era. Hong Kong had acted as a complainant in several panels. *See supra* Chapter I, Section II (D).

[30] WTO (n 25) 25.

[31] Panel Report, *United States – Measures Affecting the Cross-Border Supply of Gambling and Betting Services*, WT/DS285/R, adopted 20 April 2005, modified by Appellate Body Report, WT/DS285/AB/R.

[32] Reuters, '*UPDATE 1-Antigua Seeks WTO Arbitration in US Gambling Dispute*' (31 January 2008) <http://uk.reuters.com/article/mediaNews/idUKL3174965820080131> accessed 1 September 2011.

measures, commercial or trade disputes between private parties abound. These private disputes should thus be resolved in different forum, either domestic courts or through arbitration procedures.

As arbitration procedures, regardless of the judicial enforcement at a later stage, involve less sovereign concerns, they become more attractive to private parties. Besides, arbitration procedures seem to suit better the needs of private parties. Further, private parties may also refer to arbitration in jurisdiction other than Taiwan and Hong Kong and Macau through their acceptance of jurisdiction which becomes even more attractive to private parties, especially multi-national companies. Nonetheless, since this work focuses on the dispute resolution in the Greater China, arbitration done in other jurisdiction falls outside the scope of this work. This chapter thus limits itself to arbitration procedures located in these three Members, namely, Taiwan and Hong Kong and Macau. Arbitration done in other jurisdictions, including possible international arbitral tribunals, through the clause of acceptance of jurisdiction will be put aside. I will thus focus on judicial and arbitral procedures in Taiwan, Hong Kong and Macau. However, this relates to a persisting controversy, the recognition and enforceability of civil judgments and arbitral awards, given that 'the ultimate authority for arbitration procedures lies in the recognition and support of national legislative and judicial processes.'[33]

Since there is no intergovernmental agreement governing this issue, it is left to domestic law/regulation and judicial practice. It is thus essential to examine domestic legal framework and jurisprudence in relation to the recognition and enforceability of civil judgments and arbitral awards done in these three Members. Bearing this in mind, the following subsection will examine the complexities and diversities of their domestic law/regulation and judicial practice, and explore the relevance of Convention on the Recognition and Enforcement of Foreign Arbitral Awards (the New York Convention) on this issue.

C. *Domestic Legal Framework and Jurisprudence*

This subsection will investigate the domestic law/regulation and judicial practice in Taiwan, Hong Kong and Macau each by each. The analysis will begin with the legal framework, followed by the jurisprudence of the domestic courts. It will also explore the influence of China and the relevance of New York Convention in this regard.

---

[33] R Wai, 'Transnational Liftoff and Juridical Touchdown: the Regulatory Function of Private International Law in an Era of Globalization' (2002) 40 Columbia Journal of Transnational Law 209, 267.

1. *Taiwan's Domestic Legal Framework and Jurisprudence in Relation to Hong Kong and Macau*

a. *Taiwan's Law and Regulation in relation to Hong Kong and Macau*

Taiwan maintains a contradictory and ambiguous regulatory regime on affairs of Hong Kong and Macau.[34] Since their return to China, they have become part of China, regardless of the designation of SARs. The *Statute Governing Relations between People in Taiwan Area and Mainland Area* (the *Statute*) is nevertheless not applicable to Hong Kong and Macau. A different regulatory regime is laid down in the *Hong Kong and Macau Statute*. This *Hong Kong and Macau Statute* is aimed to regulate and promote trade, economic, cultural and other relations with Hong Kong and Macau.[35] In cases where this *Hong Kong and Macau Statute* does not regulate the relevant matters concerned, other relevant laws and regulations apply. However, provisions of the *Statute* are not applicable except where explicitly specified otherwise.[36] As a general principle, Taiwan views Hong Kong and Macau as different entities from China and provides a different regulatory regime in relation to these two SARs.

Apart from the transportation and shipment mentioned in Section II, the *Hong Kong and Macau Statute* also regulates differently in relation to economic and trade exchanges. Whereas restrictions may be imposed when major interests of Taiwan are threatened due to circumstantial changes, in general trade between Taiwan and Hong Kong and Macau can be directly conducted.[37] Goods imported or carried into Taiwan from Hong Kong and Macau are to be deemed as imported items, while goods exported to Hong Kong and Macau are also to be deemed as exported goods.[38] Customs matters, including inspection, quarantine, and taxation should be carried out with relevant import/export laws and regulations, such as *Foreign Trade Act* and *Customs Act*.[39]

Similar to its regulatory regime on trade and economic relations with Hong Kong and Macau, Taiwan maintains a different procedure governing the recognition of civil judgments and arbitral awards done by Hong Kong and Macau.

---

[34] This is also true for China's foreign trade regulatory regime. China's *Foreign Trade Law* is applies to *mutatis mutandis* to trade related to Taiwan and its SARs (Art. 69).

[35] The *Statute*, Art. 1(1).

[36] The *Statute*, Art. 1(2).

[37] The *Statute*, Art. 35(1).

[38] A resolution by the criminal tribunals of the Supreme Court further clarifies this issue. According to this resolution, as Hong Kong, being a separate customs territory is a Member of the WTO. The application of the *Statute* to Hong Kong is excluded even its return to China. Trade between Taiwan and Hong Kong and Macau can thus directly conducted as Hong Kong and Macau are deemed as third destinations other than China. *See* the 3rd Resolution of Criminal Tribunals of the Supreme Court (11 May 2004) <http://jirs.judicial.gov.tw/Index.htm> accessed 1 September 2011.

[39] The *Statute*, Art. 35(2), 35(3).

In Chapter III of the *Hong Kong and Macau Statute*, it lays downs the basic framework for civil matters between Taiwan and Hong Kong and Macau. In terms of private international law, the *Law Governing the Choice of Law in Civil Cases Involving Foreign Elements* should apply *mutatis mutandis* to those civil cases relating to Hong Kong and Macau.[40] In Article 42, the *Hong Kong and Macau Statute* specifies the procedures applicable in relation to civil judgments and arbitral awards made in Hong Kong and Macau. The general procedures governing the recognition and enforceability of foreign civil judgments and arbitral awards should *mutatis mutandis* apply. This article refers back to the Article 402 of *Code of Civil Procedure*[41] and Article 4 *bis* of *Civil Enforcement Act*[42] for the determination of validity, jurisdiction, and enforceability of civil judgments done in Hong Kong and Macau. It also refers to Articles 41-47 (Chapter VII foreign arbitral award) of the *Arbitration Act*.[43]

Article 402 of the *Code of Civil Procedure* dictates a final and binding judgment rendered by a foreign court to be recognised except in case of any of the following four circumstances:

1. Where the foreign court lacks jurisdiction pursuant to the ROC laws;
2. Where a default judgment is rendered against the losing defendant, except in the case where the notice or summons of the initiation of action had been legally served in a reasonable time in the foreign country or had been served through judicial assistance provided under the ROC laws;
3. Where the performance ordered by such judgment or its litigation procedure is contrary to R.O.C. public policy or morals;
4. Where there exists no mutual recognition between the foreign country and the ROC.[44]

Apart from the recognition aspect, the *Act on Civil Enforcement*,[45] in Article 4 *bis* provides that the enforceability of a foreign judgment may be granted only after the court declares it enforceable in the formality of a judgment. This article then refers to the conditions as provided in Article 402 of *Code of Civil Procedure* for the

---

[40] The *Statute*, Art. 38.

[41] An unofficial English version is available at <http://db.lawbank.com.tw/ENG/FLAW/FLAWDAT0201.asp> accessed 1 September 2011.

[42] The legal text provides 'Article 4, paragraph 1' of the Civil Enforcement Act. Nevertheless, due to the amendment and revision of this Act, the relevant provision should be Article 4 *bis* instead.

[43] The legal text provides 'Article 30 through 34 of the Commercial Arbitration Act.' For the same reason mentioned above, this Commercial Arbitration Act was revised and renamed as 'Arbitration Act' in 2002. The referred articles should thus be Article 47 to Article 51 of the *Arbitration Act*.

[44] The Code of Civil Procedure, Art. 4. Paragraph 2 of this Article then provides these four criteria apply mutatis mutandis to final and binding ruling, other than judgments, rendered by a foreign court.

[45] Available at <http://db.lawbank.com.tw/Eng/FLAW/FLAWDAT0202.asp> accessed 1 September 2011.

court to grant its enforceability.[46] As Article 42 of the *Hong Kong and Macau Statute* refers to Article 402 of the *Code of Civil Procedure* and Article 4 *bis* of the *Act on Civil Enforcement*, which regulate the determination of validity, jurisdiction and enforceability of foreign civil judgments, the *Hong Kong and Macau Statute* considers civil judgments done in Hong Kong and Macau more foreign civil judgments than Chinese civil judgments.[47]

The most relevant condition is the mutual recognition. In the case of Taiwan and Hong Kong and Macau, since there is no, and may never be agreement on the mutual recognition of civil judgments, controversies may arise thereby. Besides, it is not clear in relation to the formalities of the 'mutual recognition' referred to in this provision. In the absence of a formal agreement, is the court entitled to recognise a foreign ruling or judgment when the court believes, in so doing, to be in accordance with the spirit implicit reciprocity?

In respect of arbitration awards, Chapter VII of the *Arbitration Act*[48] outlines the framework for the recognition of a foreign arbitration award, including the definition of a foreign arbitral award and its enforceability after the recognition being granted by the court[49] and the procedures to be followed for the application of its recognition.[50] Article 49(1) then dictates the court to dismiss this application where the dispute is not arbitrable under the laws of Taiwan or where its recognition or enforcement is against the public order or good morals of Taiwan.[51] The second paragraph of the same article then follows the same practice of the *Code of Civil Procedure*, but takes a lenient approach. As provided, 'the court *may* issue a dismissal order with respect to an application for recognition of a foreign arbitral award if the country where the arbitral award is made or whose laws govern the arbitral award does not recognise arbitral awards of the Republic of China.'[52] According to this provision, regardless of the absence of recognition of Taiwan's arbitral award by foreign countries, the court may still approve the application and grant the recognition of the foreign arbitral award concerned. This designation is derived from the particular international situation of Taiwan where an agreement or arrangement on mutual recognition of arbitral awards is generally

[46] In terms of this reference, it is held by the Taiwan Higher Court that, as Article 42 of the *Statute*

[47] Taiwan Higher Court, Shang-Zhi No. 136 (1999) <http://jirs.judicial.gov.tw/Index.htm> accessed 1 September 2011, in Chinese. Cases of Taiwanese courts are generally available at the database referred to above by providing with year and case numbers. This article may not specify again except as necessary.

[48] An unofficial English version is available at <http://db.lawbank.com.tw/Eng/FLAW/FLAWDAT0201.asp> accessed 1 September 2011.

[49] The *Arbitration Act*, Art. 47(1).

[50] The *Arbitration Act*, Art. 48.

[51] The *Arbitration Act*, Art. 49(1).

[52] The *Arbitration Act*, Art. 49(2) (emphasis added).

not available. Nonetheless, a rigid approach is not feasible given the commercial needs of transaction between private parties. It is thus again left to the courts to decide whether or not to recognise a foreign arbitral award, including the arbitral awards made by Hong Kong and Macau.

b. *Jurisprudence in the Taiwan's Courts*

As regards the recognition and enforcement of the civil judgments and arbitration awards made in Hong Kong and Macau, Taiwan's courts have constantly taken a lenient position. Although the criterion of mutual recognition laid down by Article 402 of the *Code of Civil Procedure* may constitute an obstacle for Taiwan's courts to grant recognition to the civil judgments and arbitral awards concerned, nevertheless, existent jurisprudence has proved otherwise.

The general position of Taiwan's judiciary toward foreign civil judgments and arbitral awards dates back to 1980's. In an application for the recognition of an arbitral award made in the United Kingdom (the UK), the Higher Court in Taichung District rejected this application on the ground of the absence of British recognition of Taiwanese arbitral awards. According to the Higher Court, being a Contracting Party to Geneva Convention on Arbitral Awards and the New York Convention, the UK generally recognises arbitral awards made by Contracting Parties to these two Conventions. In respect of arbitral awards made by non-Contracting Parties, while recognition is likely to be granted in accordance with the spirit of reciprocity, the diplomatic recognition of the non-Contracting Party concerned is also relevant. The Higher Court further noted that, given the absence of mutual recognition agreement between Taiwan and the UK and British precedent on its recognition of Taiwanese arbitral awards, the application should thus be rejected.[53]

Nevertheless, this position was not supported by the Supreme Court. In repealing the ruling, the Supreme Court held that, as provided in Article 32(2) of the *Statute on Commercial Arbitration*. (the predecessor of *Arbitration Act*), wherever a country refuses to grant its recognition of arbitral awards made in Taiwan, courts in Taiwan may dismiss the application for the recognition of arbitral awards made in the country concerned. However, it does not necessarily suggest that, only when a foreign court grants its recognition to Taiwan's arbitral awards in the first place can a Taiwanese court grant its recognition to those made in the country

[53] Taiwan Higher Court, Taichung District, Guo-Mao-Kang-Zhi No. 1 (1986). The court also draws it conclusion from the fact that courts of the British Hong Kong does not recognise Taiwan's final and binding civil judgments, and thus concludes that the absence of the diplomatic recognition between Taiwan and the United Kingdom had prevented the British courts from recognising and enforcing the arbitral awards made in Taiwan. This issue, for Hong Kong's recognition of Taiwan's civil judgments and arbitral award will be further elaborated in the following subsection.

concerned. Otherwise, it would be inconsistent with the spirit of comity and undermine the international judicial cooperation. Moreover, the relevant provision instructs the court that an application for the recognition *may*, but not *shall* be dismissed.[54]

Later in an application relating to the recognition of an arbitral award made in British Hong Kong in 1992, the court took the same stance. The respondent argued that, while Taiwan's courts firstly recognised the arbitral awards made in Hong Kong in its earlier jurisprudence, the judiciary of British Hong Kong did not respond positively to this amicable attitude. The respondent then claimed that due to this development, Taiwan's judiciary should take a negative position in granting the recognition and enforceability of arbitral awards made in British Hong Kong. In addition, since its return to China, British rules governing the recognition of foreign arbitral awards were no long applicable in the HKSAR. According to the Article 269 of *Code of Civil Procedure of People's Republic of China*, arbitral awards made in a foreign country with which China does not maintain a mutual reciprocal agreement shall not be recognised. Taiwan's arbitral awards can thus not be recognised in Hong Kong according to either the British rules or China's *Code of Civil Procedure*. In responding to this argument, the court slightly noted that, in light of the trend of international commercial arbitration, it was feasible to grant its recognition to this arbitral award concerned.[55] In its appeal, the Higher Court firstly referred to the aforementioned holding of the Supreme Court and clarified that the arbitral award at dispute was done in 1992 when Hong Kong was still under the British rule. China's *Code of Civil Procedure* was thus irrelevant. However, the Higher Court still failed to provide a persuasive argument in relation to British refusal to recognise Taiwan's arbitral awards. The Supreme Court did not either express its view on this point as the appeal to the Supreme Court was dismissed on a procedural ground.[56] Nonetheless, this argument became irrelevant owing to change of the attitude of the judiciary of the HKSAR, as will be shown in the following case.

In a case regarding to a divorcement in 2004, the Supreme Court declared that the mutual recognition in terms of Article 402(4) of *Code of Civil Procedure* of Taiwan does not refer to diplomatic or governmental recognition under public international law. It refers to the mutual reciprocity between courts in different

[54] Taiwan Supreme Court, Tai-Kang-Zhi No. 335 (1986).

[55] Taiwan Taipei District Court, Zhong-Sheng-Zhi No. 4 (1998). Interestingly, in this case, the applicant emphasised on the nature of commercial arbitration, being a resolution mechanism between private entities without the intervention of sovereign powers. By contrast, the respondent focused on the refusal to grant recognition both by British Hong Kong and the HKSAR, and insisted on the national sovereignty.

[56] Taiwan Supreme Court, Tai-Kang-Zhi No. 186 (2002) <http://www.arbitration.org.tw/content/b8_65.htm#65-1> accessed 1 September 2011.

jurisdictions in relation to the recognition of civil judgments. Wherever the judiciary in a country or jurisdiction does not expressly refuse to recognise the civil judgments of Taiwan, Taiwanese courts should take an active and lenient approach on granting the recognition of civil judgments made by foreign courts. The Supreme Court then referred to *Chen Li Hung & others v. Ting Lei Miao & others* where the Court of Final Appeal (CFA) in the HKSAR, in 2000, explicitly recognised the validity of the civil rulings and judgments of Taiwan's courts. Based on these arguments, the Supreme Court then withheld the decision of the lower court to recognise the divorcement judgment concerned.[57]

2. *Hong Kong's Domestic Regulation in Relation to Taiwan*

a. *Hong Kong's Law and Regulation in Relation to Taiwan*

The recognition and enforcement of foreign judgments in Hong Kong is governed by the statutory *Foreign Judgments (Reciprocal Enforcement) Ordinance* (Cap. 319)[58] and common law rules; foreign arbitral awards are subject to the regulation of the *Arbitration Ordinance* (Cap. 341).[59] Given the absence of special arrangements on the recognition and enforcement of civil judgements and arbitral awards, these ordinances and common law rues may be applicable, as appropriate.

The *Foreign Judgments (Reciprocal Enforcement) Ordinance*, in Section 3 empowers the Governor of the Council (now the Chief Executive), by order, to extend the application of this Ordinance to judgments given in the superior courts of any foreign country. The condition for this extension relies upon the substantial reciprocity in respect of the recognition and enforcement of judgments given by superior courts in Hong Kong.[60] Once the Chief Executive extends the application of this Ordinance to that specific country, provisions provided in this Ordinance should be applicable to a judgment given by a superior court of that foreign country if the judgment is final and conclusive relating to a sum of money payable other than taxes or other charges of like nature or a fine or other penalty.[61] As instructed by this provision, a judgment shall not be registered if the judgment concerned, at the date of the application, has been wholly satisfied or unenforceable by execution in the original court.[62] Section 4 of the same Ordinance then

[57] Taiwan Supreme Court, Tai-Shang-Zhi No. 1943 (2004). *Chen Li Hung & others v. Ting Lei Miao & others* will be examined in greater detail in the following subsection, *infra*, text to (n 68)*et seq*.

[58] Available at <http://www.legislation.gov.hk/eng/home.htm> 1 September 2011.

[59] Available at <http://www.legislation.gov.hk/eng/home.htm> 1 September 2011.

[60] *Foreign Judgments (Reciprocal Enforcement) Ordinance*, S. 3.1

[61] *Foreign Judgments (Reciprocal Enforcement) Ordinance*, S. 3.2.

[62] Ibid. *See* also relevant provisions as embodied in *Foreign Judgments (Restriction on Recognition and Enforcement) Ordinance* (Cap. 46) <http://www.legislation.gov.hk/eng/home.htm> 1 September 2011.

provides the procedures for a judgment creditor to apply to the Court of First Instance (the CFI) for the judgment concerned to be registered.[63] That being said, there has so far been no order by the Governor of the Council or the Chief Executive to extend the application of this Ordinance to Taiwan's judgments. Consequently, a judgment creditor cannot apply to the CFI in the HKSAR for the registration of the judgment concerned. The recognition and enforcement of civil judgments made in Taiwan by virtue of the statutory regulation is not available.

In contrast to the judgments given by Taiwan's courts, arbitral awards made in Taiwan may be recognised and enforced in the *Arbitral Ordinance*. One of the major purposes of this revision is to adjust and rearrange the recognition and enforcement of arbitral awards made in China, which were previously governed by the New York Convention.[64] Since the HKSAR became a part of China, the New York Convention was no longer applicable. In addition to arbitral awards done in China, this revision also deals with arbitral awards made in non-Contracting Parties to the New York Convention. In this *Arbitration Ordinance*, arbitral awards not made in the HKSAR is defined as three main categories: Chinese awards,[65] Convention award,[66] and other awards. As Taiwan is not a Contracting Party to the New York Convention, arbitral awards made in Taiwan falls into the third category and should be governed by the general provision, namely, section 8 of the Ordnance. With the leave of the court or a judge of the court, an award, order or direction made or given, whether in or outside Hong Kong, in or in relation to arbitration proceedings is enforceable in the same way as a judgment, order or direction of the court that has the same effect.[67] The decisive point here is 'with the leave of the court or a judge of the court'. If the leave is given, the court can then enter into judgments in the form of an award, order or direction.[68] According to this provision, arbitral awards, orders or directions made in Taiwan may be enforceable with the leave of the court, and at the same time subject to the control of the court of the HKSAR.

[63] *Foreign Judgments (Reciprocal Enforcement) Ordinance*, S. 3.1.

[64] On 21 April 1977, the application of the New York Convention was extend to Hong Kong through a declaration of the United Kingdom. As a result, the recognition and enforcement of arbitral awards between China and the British Hong Kong was governed by the New York Convention. *See* AJ van den Berg, *The New York Arbitration Convention of 1958: Towards a Uniform Judicial Interpretation* (Kluwer Law and Taxation, Deventer ; Boston 1981) 411. After the handover, an Arrangement on the Mutual Enforcement of Arbitral Awards between Mainland and the Hong Kong Special Administrative Region was signed 21 June 1999. In response to this arrangement, the *Arbitration Ordinance* was subsequently revised. The whole text of this arrangement is available at <http://www.legislation.gov.hk/intracountry/eng/pdf/mainlandmutual2e.pdf> accessed 1 September 2011.

[65] The *Arbitration Ordinance*, Part III A.

[66] The *Arbitration Ordinance*, Part IV.

[67] The *Arbitration Ordinance*, S. 2GG.

[68] The *Arbitration Ordinance*, S. 2GG, paragraph 1, second sentence.

b. *Jurisprudence in the Courts of Hong Kong*

There were diverse views in relation to the recognition and enforcement of judgments and arbitral awards made in Taiwan. By virtue of Section 2GG of the *Arbitration Ordinance,* the enforcement of arbitral awards and other relevant orders and directions are currently enforceable in Hong Kong with the leave of the courts. By contrast, the application of *Foreign Judgments (Reciprocal Recognition) Ordinance* is not extended to Taiwan given the absence of an agreement on the mutual recognition and enforcement of civil judgments between Taiwan and the HKSAR. The statutory regime laid down by this Ordinance is thus not applicable to Taiwan's civil judgments. Besides, Taiwan's civil judgments were not recognised in the Colony during the era of British Hong Kong. It was thus unclear, at the point of handover, whether the courts in HKSAR, would recognise judgments made in Taiwan.

The CFA of the HKSAR clarified this point in 2000. In *Chen Li Hung & others v. Ting Lei Miao & others,*[69] the CFA explicitly recognises the validity and effect of Taiwan's civil judgments. The plaintiff Chen was adjudged bankrupt in one Taiwanese district court which also appointed the trustees in bankruptcy with a court order. The trustees, in the name of Chen sued before the CFI the defendants, the wife and son of Chen, for those assents registered under the name of the defendants and located in Hong Kong. The trustees of bankruptcy claimed that those assets registered under the name of the defendants constituted an act of trust and thus belonged to Chen. After serving his term of imprisonment in Taiwan and returning back to Hong Kong, Chen requested to be joined in the lawsuit and claimed that it was himself, instead of the trustees who should give instruction to the counsel.[70]

The CFI ruled against the plaintiffs, holding that a bankruptcy order delivered by a Taiwanese court should not be recognised in the courts of the HKSAR. Consequently, this order could not extend its legal extent to those assets located in Hong Kong.[71] The trustees appealed. The Court of Appeal reversed and ruled in favour of the trustees. This case then came to the CFA, where the appeal was dismissed. In the view of the CFA, two issues stood before them: whether a Taiwanese bankruptcy order was extended to Chen's assets located in Hong Kong; and, if so, whether the bankruptcy order concerned should be given effect by the courts of the HKSAR.

With regard to the first question, the CFA referred to Dicey and Morris in *Conflicts of Laws* and declared that the trustees are in capacity to sue in their own

[69] *Chen Li Hung & others v. Ting Lei Miao & others* [2000] 1 HKLRD 252 (CFA).
[70] Ibid 252.
[71] Ibid 256.

name to recover the debt in Hong Kong if they, under the law by which the bankruptcy order was delivered have such right. According to the CFA, it was not disputed that 'every step which they have taken in Hong Kong, is in conformity with directions obtained by them from the bankruptcy court in Taiwan.'[72]

The CFA then turned to the second question: whether the bankruptcy concerned should be given effects by courts of the HKSAR. The CFA answered this question affirmatively based on four arguments. Firstly, the CFA referred to the speech of Lord Wilberforce in *Carl Zeiss Stiftung v. Ratber & Keeler Ltd (No. 2)* in 1967, saying that 'non-recognition cannot be pressed to its ultimate logical limit'[73] and that 'where private rights, or acts of everyday occurrence, or perfunctory acts of administration are concerned[......], the courts may, in the interests of justice and common sense, where no consideration of public policy to the contrary has to prevail, give recognition to the actual facts or realities found to exist in the territory in question.'[74] The CFA then compared the 'rebellion' case with a bankruptcy order by a 'usurper' court. The CFA found that nothing prevented the court from recognising a bankruptcy order made by a Taiwanese court.

The CFA then referred to Grotius' statement in *De Jure Belli ac Pacis*, Book 1, Chapter IV, Section XV, discussing the power of a usurper. According to Grotius, the binding force of the acts of a usurper government lies in the fact that one, under the ruling of a usurper, would prefer that 'measures promulgated by [the usurper] should meanwhile have the force of law, in order to avoid the utter confusion which would result from the subversion of laws and suppression of the courts.'[75] Whereas the CFA regarded the bankruptcy order done in Taiwan was an order done by a usurper court, the found that the bankruptcy order should have binding force in order to avoid the utter confusion.

The CFA then continued on its argument that a sovereign should be more benevolent towards its people in usurped territories than those of other non-recognised foreign countries. Citing the *Rules of Supreme People's Court concerning the Recognition by the People's Court of Civil Judgments Delivered in Taiwan* as a proof, the CFA held that protection of rights and interests of litigants in civil proceedings by recognising civil judgments made in Taiwan is consistent with Taiwan's status as a part of People's Republic of China. The CFA further added that the validity of a judicial act should be recognised by other courts (courts in the HKSAR in the present case) in spite of the unlawfulness of the appointment of the judge or its authority stemming from an unlawful government.[76]

---

[72] Ibid 258.
[73] Ibid 259.
[74] Ibid.
[75] Ibid 260.
[76] Ibid 261.

Finally, the CFA turned to the 'public policy' argument. According to the CFA, whether the recognition of the validity and effect of a bankruptcy order delivered by a Taiwanese court is against public policy in the HKSAR could be rephrased as 'whether the recognition of the rights of the trustees in bankruptcy to sue in Hong Kong would be inimical to the interests of the sovereign power.'[77] The CFA then answered this question negatively and found the recognition of the present bankruptcy order not against the public policy.

The CFA summarily laid down its criteria to recognise the civil judgments of an 'unrecognised court', including the court 'under the control of a usurper government' as claimed:

(i) the rights covered by those orders are private rights;
(ii) giving effect to such orders accords with the interests of justice, the dictates of common sense and the needs of law and order; and;
(iii) giving them effect would not be inimical to the sovereign's interests or otherwise contrary to public policy.[78]

Applying these criteria to the present case, the CFA thus ruled the bankruptcy order concerned to be recognised in the courts of the HKSAR.

While one may argue that courts in the HKSAR takes a more lenient attitude on the recognition and enforcement of Taiwanese judgments, it should nevertheless be pointed to the importance of the arrangement between Taiwan and China on the recognition of civil judgments. This arrangement prompted the CFA of the HKSAR to recognise the effects and validity of Taiwanese courts. In addition, if one takes a closer look at the substantial content of the arguments, it would difficult to claim that the CFA actually takes a lenient attitude. While the decision to recognise civil judgments done in Taiwan should be applauded, those arguments based on political benevolence of the central government to civil judgments done by its usurper's courts are groundless and unfounded. The conclusion of the CFA that the recognition of Taiwanese civil judgments would not undermine the interests of sovereign power nevertheless reflects the importance of sovereign power in arriving at its decision.

3. *Macau's Domestic Regulation in Relation to Taiwan*

Several regulations lay down the regulatory regime on the recognition and enforcement of foreign civil judgments and arbitral awards. Firstly, the *Civil Code of Macau*[79] in its Book I (Parte Geral), Title I, Chapter III regulates the rights of

[77] Ibid 262.
[78] Ibid 263.
[79] Código Civil, Decreto-Lei n.° 39/99/M (3 August 1999), B.O. n.° 40/1999, I Série, 1.° Suplemento, 1794.

non-residents and the conflicts of laws. The essential element here is the differentiation based upon residence instead of nationality. This is aimed to suit the needs of 'One Country, Two Systems'.[80] Macau's *Civil Procedure Code*,[81] in Article 680, regulates the enforceability of civil judgments made outside the MASAR. In the first paragraph, civil judgments and arbitral awards done outside Macau may be enforced after reviewed and confirmed by the competent tribunals of the MASAR, except as applicable international conventions or agreements on judicial cooperation provide otherwise. In the meantime, there is no agreement on mutual recognition and enforcement of civil agreements or arbitral awards between Taiwan and Macau. Therefore, the enforceability of civil judgments and arbitral awards done in Taiwan is subject to the review and confirmation of competent tribunals of the MASAR.

The *Civil Procedure Code*, in Book V(Dos Processos Especiais), Title XIV, lays down procedure and criteria for this review and confirmation. Article 1199(1) firstly prescribes that, subject to the exception of international conventions or agreements on judicial cooperation, civil judgments and arbitral awards on privates rights done in any State or territory outside the MASAR may have legal binding effects after reviewed and confirmed by the competent tribunals. Article 1200(a) lays down the criteria for the competent tribunals to review and confirm those civil judgements concerned. These criteria are applicable to arbitral awards, as appropriate. The most relevant here is the requirement of public order. Namely, the civil judgment subject to review and confirmation bears no content that is manifestly incompatible with public order of the MASAR.

In respect of arbitral awards, by virtue of the Decree N.° 188/99,[82] the application of the New York Convention was extended to the Portuguese Macau. After China resumed its sovereignty on Macau, the Chief-Executive by Aviso do Chefe do Executivo n° 3/2007, extended the application of the New York Convention of the MASAR subject to those applicable to People's Republic of China. Domestically, the *Code on Approval of a Specific Regime on External Commercial Arbitration*,[83] in Article 35 and 36 also regulate the legal effects of arbitral awards done outside the MASAR. Article 35(1) provides that, without prejudice to the application of this

[80] R M M Ramos, 'The Private International Law of the New Special Administrative Region of Macau of the People's Republic of China' (2000) 60 Louisiana Law Review 1281, 1282.

[81] Código de Processo Civil, Decreto-Lei n.° 55/99/M (8 October 1999), B.O. n.° 40/1999, I Série, Suplemento, 3670.

[82] Decreto do Presidente da República n.° 188/99 (22 October 1999), BO N.° 49/1999, 6017. This decision was done after an affirmative resolution of Legislative Council of Macau, Resolution n.° 36/99 (26 July 1999), BO N.° 30/1999, 1779.

[83] Aprova um Regime Específico para a Arbitragem Comercial Externa, Decreto-Lei n.° 55/98/M (23/11/1998) B.O. n.° 47/1998, I Série, 1499.

article and Article 36, any arbitral award, irrespective of the State or *territory* where it is done, should be recognised and enforced. Article 36 then lays down the criteria for the competent tribunal to refuse to recognise or enforce the arbitral award concerned. The refusal to recognise or enforce an arbitral award can be made with the request and contention of any party to the pertinent arbitral award. The competent tribunal can also refuse to recognise or enforce an arbitral award if it finds that (i) the subject matter is not arbitrable according to the law of the MASAR; (ii) that it would be against the public order of the MASAR to recognise or enforce the arbitral award concerned; or (iii) that the State or territory where the arbitral award is made would refuse or enforce arbitral awards done in the MASAR. Again, the most relevant criterion here is the public order.

Then one would have to reflect whether to recognise or enforce a civil judgment or an arbitral award made in Taiwan, if using its official title of 'Republic of China' would be against the public order of the MASAR. The CFA of the HKSAR answers this negatively. It is still uncertain how courts of the MASAR define and perceive public order in this regard, since, to the best knowledge of the author, no request for review and confirmation of civil judgments and arbitral awards done in Taiwan has been reported so far.[84]

4. *Sovereign Interests, National Security and Public Order*

This section investigates the dispute settlement mechanisms between Taiwan and Hong Kong and Macau. It argues that that owing to the free-port status and zero-tariff policy maintained by Hong Kong and Macau, trade disputes between these three WTO Members are unlikely to occur in the WTO Dispute Settlement Mechanism. Besides, Taiwans reliance on Hong Kong and Macau for the transhipment of goods and passengers prior its direct transportation agreements with China also prevents Taiwan from going for the WTO forum. The attitude of China Central Authority also helps to curtail this possibility. It then argues that domestic courts and arbitration procedures turn out to be a good alternative for the settlement of disputes arising from commercial transactions. While private individuals and enterprises can choose to work with their governments in the WTO Dispute Settlement Mechanism, they may well opt for the domestic courts and arbitration

[84] One point deserves noting here is a case relating the refusal to grant the recognition of a civil judgment done in the HKSAR. This case relates to a decision for a mother by blood to adopt her daughter legally. The Court of Appeal in MASAR denies granting its recognition of this civil judgment done in the HKSAR since it is against the public order of the MASAR, since a mother by blood and a mother by adoption are two clearly differentiated concepts in legal system of the MASAR and should not be blurred. Case 102/2006 (25 May 2006) <http://www.court.gov.mo/decision/ctsuidetail.asp?seqno=1439&courtid=TSI> accessed 1 September 2011.

procedures. The reluctance of governments of these three WTO Members to go for the WTO forum induces/forces private individuals and enterprises to resort to a private international law approach.[85] They choose the domestic courts and arbitration procedures and seek recognition and enforcement in another jurisdiction. The private international law approach appears more appealing to private individuals and enterprises in these three memberships. This again points to the nature and limits of the intergovernmental WTO Dispute Settlement Mechanism. While international economic actors may request or press their governments to go for the WTO forum, a direct access is not possible for private individuals and enterprises. When the governments are determined not to opt for this approach, other forum must be made available for the absorption of economic and trade disputes arising from commercial transactions.

This section then examines the domestic regulation of Taiwan, Hong Kong and Macau in relation to the recognition and enforcement of civil judgments and arbitral awards. Jurisprudence of domestic courts is also dealt with. It then analyses how mutual recognition of civil judgments and arbitral awards are conducted by these three WTO Members. It finds that, in terms of the statutory designation, Taiwan and Hong Kong take a more lenient approach on arbitral awards than civil judgments. This is mainly because the nature of arbitration procedures, namely, to meet needs arising from commercial transactions. With regard to civil judgments, courts in Taiwan and the HKSAR come up with the conclusion to recognise civil judgments of each other based on different arguments. Taiwan's courts emphasise on the importance of 'comity' whereas courts on the HKSAR attach to the protection of private rights and interests of litigants. Relevant provisions of the MASAR then focus on public order. In terms of the relevance of the New York Convention, this section notes that this Convention is applicable to both the HKSAR and MASAR. Domestic legal framework explicitly regulates the recognition and enforcement of the Convention awards. Nevertheless, the Convention offers little help in dealing the recognition and enforcement of arbitral awards done in Taiwan, since Taiwan is not a Contracting Party to the New York Convention. The recognition of civil judgments and arbitral awards should be governed by the general rules where public policy and public order play a significant role.

[85] A pertinent issue in this private international law approach relates to domestic public policy. As argued, one of the characteristics of traditional private international law is that courts refuse to enforce any foreign law or judgment that is repugnant to domestic public policy. Wai (n 33) 243. *See* also, R Wai, 'Conflicts and Comity in Transnational Governance: Private International Law as Mechanism and Metaphor for Transnational Social Regulation through Plural Legal Regime' in C Joerges and E U Petersmann (eds), *Constitutionalism, Multilevel Trade Governance and Social Regulation* (Hart Publishing, Oxford and Portland, Oregon 2006) 229-262.

Lastly, one point needs further clarification. In deciding whether or not to recognise a civil judgment or arbitral award done in Taiwan, courts of the HKSAR should ascertain whether this recognition would be against the sovereign interests of People's Republic of China and thus against the public policy in the HKSAR. This argument to some degree resembles Taiwanese courts' argument on national security. Sovereign interests, national security and public policy/order are all an indeterminate concept subject to dispute. Thus, what these concepts denote relies mainly upon how the judge perceives them. One can easily refer to these ideas and thus refuse the recognition and enforcement of civil judgments and arbitral awards. This nevertheless neglects the needs arising from everyday economic activities and commercial transactions. While the author disagrees the wording of the CFA, by naming Taiwan as a usurper, its attachment to the protection of private interests bears its merit. Where one may not easily denounce national interests, national security, and public public/order as empty words, their importance should never be overestimated, especially in relation to the protection and enforcement of private rights. This reminds again importance of judicial protection of rights and interests of individual economic actors.

IV. Short Conclusion

This chapter has examined the trade dispute resolution mechanism between Taiwan, Hong Kong and Macau. It firstly uses the negotiation on traffic rights between Taiwan and Hong Kong to illustrate the role of China in this subject matter. It also clarifies that the economic interests of Hong Kong and China Central Authority, or of even of Macau may sometimes differ. Besides, whereas it is true that Hong Kong and Macau act as a intermediary between Taiwan and China, and help to ease potential political conflicts, the change of political climate between Taiwan and China would turn back to feed the economic ties between Taiwan and Hong Kong and Macau. This chapter then examines the relevance of WTO forum in dealing trade dispute between Taiwan and Hong Kong and Macau. It argues that, even though they enjoy full rights and obligations under the covered agreements, they would not go for the WTO Dispute Settlement Mechanism. Domestic courts or arbitral procedures may be an alternative for them. This chapter thus examines domestic regulation and jurisprudence relating to recognition and enforcement of civil judgments and arbitral awards. Comity, sovereign interests, public policy/order and private rights are the key elements which the courts have to balance when deciding whether or not to recognise a specific civil judgment or arbitral award. Since the concept of sovereign interests and public order bear no concrete elements, it is thus mainly dependent onthe judge's perception on his/her role and duty of being a judge and on the correct interpretation of these ideas.

CHAPTER TEN

CONCLUSION AND THE WAY FORWARD

This work has traced different roads for the four WTO Members of the Greater China to Geneva and explored their interaction within this multilateral trading system. Their coexistence in the WTO illustrates the diversity of the GATT/WTO system and evidences the constitutional journey from the GATT to the coming into being of the WTO. The constitutional feature of the GATT/WTO that allows a separate customs territory to accede to it was originally meant to meet the functional needs of a 'government' with less than complete sovereignty or newly-independent states in 1970's to participate in the international trading system. This constitutional feature then turns out to be an important device to safeguard the legal and economic autonomy of Hong Kong and Macau by virtue of their WTO membership and opens up the door for Taiwan to participate in the world trading system. WTO law and disciplines may contribute to the normalisation and constitutionalisation of trade relations between China and Taiwan, and enhance legal and economic integration in the Greater China.

This work stresses the importance of the WTO disciplines in regulating the integration processes and the role of dispute settlement mechanism in resolving trade disputes arising therefrom. This work argues that effective judicial review can help to ensure rational decision-making in foreign trade relations. It also helps to preserve the economic autonomy of Hong Kong and Macau. Besides, effective judicial review ensures the compliance to the WTO rules both in Taiwan and in China. In addition, an independent and impartial judicial review is an essential vehicle to protect the right to trade as prescribed in China's Accession Protocol. Above all, the WTO Dispute Settlement Mechanism is crucial in resolving trade disputes between the four WTO members of the Greater China. Judicial governance in the foreign trade relations is thus indispensible. A well-functioning dispute settlement mechanism is a central element for the economic integration in the Greater China that eventually contributes to their mutual understanding and mutual trust.

This work argues that the WTO constitutionalism may contribute to judicial settlement of trade disputes arising from these legal and economic integration processes. WTO membership may be perceived as a pre-commitment to the four WTO Members of the Greater China. The WTO accession is a pre-commitment to China for widening and deepening economic and legal reforms, and thus for promotion of rule of law in China. The right to trade and the obligation to provide an independent and impartial judicial review prescribed in China's Accession

Protocol would gradually sustain a constitutionalism in its minimum form. The WTO accession is a pre-commitment to Taiwan for the progressive liberalisation of cross-Taiwan strait trade in order to enhance economic and legal integration, to contribute to mutual understanding, and therefore, to ensure peace and security across the Taiwan Strait. The WTO memberships of Hong Kong, China and Macau, China are also pre-commitments of these two separate-customs-territory for them to observe free trade rules/policies and thus to maintain their economic autonomy. Their memberships are also China's pre-commitments to these two SARs in relation to their legal and economic autonomy to participate in the international trading system.

After examining various provision in the WTO agreements governing domestic judicial review, this work analyses the scope and nature of China's WTO obligation to 'provide an independent and impartial judicial review' and its implication to China's judicial reform. Compared to existent provisions in the WTO agreements pertaining judicial review, this work finds that China's Accession Protocol lays down a more stringent requirement concerning the 'prompt review' of administrative actions. The scope is also wider than existent provisions in the WTO agreements. This work argues that a complaint relating to China's obligation to provide 'an independent and impartial judicial review' is not hypothetic but highly possible. It thus investigates the existent WTO jurisprudence in order to clarify the criteria of 'independence' and 'impartiality' and finds that no sufficient and clear guidance is available. As informed by Article 3.2 of DSU, this works argues that it is indispensable to examine international standards as well as jurisprudence concerned. Therefore, it discusses various global and regional standards in relation of independence and impartiality and explores the jurisprudence laid down by the ECtHR. After examining the efforts and progresses that China has so far made for the implementation of this WTO obligation, this work finds that the administration of justice, the practices of legislative interpretation, adjudicative committees and case guidance system cannot pass the scrutiny of the WTO panel/Appellate Body in light of these global or regional instruments as well as the jurisprudence of the ECtHR.

This work also proposes a better approach for Taiwan's courts to deal with cases relating cross-Taiwan-strait trade relations. It firstly examines the legal status of treaties and international agreements in Taiwan's national legal system. Based on this, it then explores the role of the WTO Agreement in Taiwan, focusing on the legal hierarchy, self-executing, and relevant jurisprudence. It then examines the WTO-incompatibilities as contained in Taiwan's regulatory regime on its trade relations with China. It argues that Taiwanese courts should refrain from being tempted to refer to Article 11 of the Amendment to the Constitution and national security arguments. On the contrary, they are under their constitutional obligation to ensure both the WTO Treaty constitution and national constitution to be equally respected. In so doing, judicial governance in foreign trade relations with

China can thus not only contribute to Taiwan's faithful implementation of international obligations under the WTO treaty constitution, but also guarantee the right to work, freedom of profession and equal rights protection as enshrined in Taiwan's constitution.

This work then examines dispute resolution among the four WTO Members of the Great China: between China and Taiwan; between China and Hong Kong and Macau; between Taiwan and Hong Kong and Macau.

Through the lens of third party participation, this work finds that Taiwan tends to participate as a third party in complaints brought about by/against China. Taiwan may stand in line with China; it may argue against China; it may also act as a passive observer without making clear its position. China has also participated in the complaint brought about by Taiwan, namely, the *EC – IT Products*, where China takes the same position as Taiwan does as China has the same trade interests on information technology products into the EU's market. This work also explores the dispute settlement mechanisms provided by the ECFA and other bilateral agreements concluded between Taiwan and China. This work finds that the dispute settlement mechanisms are rather primitive and diplomatic in nature, which is insufficient to safeguard the rights and obligations of both Parties and to provide security and predictability for individual economic actors therein. This work also analyses trade defence measures imposed by Taiwan and China against each other and explores the effectiveness of domestic judicial review on these trade defence measures. It finds that only limited affected parties resort to domestic judicial review which offers little protection.

Regarding dispute resolution between China and Hong Kong and Macau, this work approaches this issue under two frameworks: the constitutional/national law framework and the WTO/CEPA framework. Under the constitutional/national law framework, this work examines vertical and horizontal interaction between China and its two SARs. Emphasis is actually placed on the interaction between the NPCSC and the CFI of the HKSAR. This work sees a danger of undermining the legal and economic autonomy of the two SARs by the NPCSC through the interpretation of the two Basic Laws. Under the WTO/CEPA framework, this work briefly recalls the trade policy and practice of Hong Kong and Macau in the GATT and WTO. It then explores the nature of the CEPA under the WTO rules and examines existent trade dispute mechanisms in both the WTO and the CEPAs. This work argues that it is unlikely that China, Hong Kong or Macau to refer to the WTO Dispute Settlement Mechanism. At the same time, the dispute settlement mechanism as set out for in the two CEPAs does not offer adequate judicial protection as well. Whereas the preference of China, Hong Kong and Macau not to internationalise or judicialise their trade disputes, such approach may prejudice the rights and interests of individual economic actors.

With respect to dispute resolution between Taiwan and Hong Kong and Macau, this work finds the same tendency not to refer to the WTO Dispute Settlement

Mechanism. It also illustrates how China may affect policy making or trade negotiation between Taiwan and Hong Kong and Macau. It argues that private parties prefer to refer to domestic courts and arbitral procedures to resolve their disputes given the attitude of their governments to avoid intergovernmental confrontation. After examining domestic legal framework and jurisprudence in relation to the mutual recognition of arbitration awards and civil judgments, this work finds that the ideas of 'sovereign interests', 'national security' and 'public order' play a key role in granting their recognition and enforcement.

The way ahead of the four WTO Members of the Greater China would be closer economic interdependence. But the persisting question remains: can the institution sustain such interdependence? So far, Taiwan and China has concluded the ECFA and a number of bilateral agreements. China has also concluded the CEPAs and seven supplements with Hong Kong and Macau. Spurred by the ECFA, Hong Kong and Macau may soon conclude a bilateral agreement with Taiwan. These bilateral agreements would contribute to legal and economic integration in the Greater China, but at the same time bring about numerous disputes. The WTO discipline and the scrutiny of the Committee on Regional Trade Agreements should come into play with a view to ensure these bilateral agreements WTO-compatible. Dispute settlement mechanisms provided in these bilateral agreements need to evolve so as to provide effective judicial protection both for the Parties and for the individual economic actors in the Greater China. Domestic courts are strongly encouraged to review external trade measures and protect rights and interests of private parties. They should also ensure the faithful implementation of WTO rules in the Greater China. Above all, the WTO Dispute Settlement Mechanism has to remain intact should the four WTO Members of the Greater China decide to avail of this mechanism.

BIBLIOGRAPHY

Books, Journal Articles, and Books Chapters

Alexandroff A S (1998), Concluding China's Accession to the WTO: The U.S. Congress and Permanent Most Favored Nation Status for China, 3 UCLA International Law & Foreign Affairs, 23–42.

Alexandroff A S and et al. (eds) (2002), China and the Long March to Global Trade: The Accession of China to the World Trade Organization, London; New York: Routledge.

Algieri F (2002), EU Economic Relations with China: An Institutionalist Perspective, in Edmonds R L (ed), China and Europe since 1978: A European Perspective, 64–77, Cambridge: Cambridge University Press.

Almstedt K W and Norton P M (2000), China's Antidumping Laws and the WTO Antidumping Agreement, 34 Journal of World Trade, 75–114.

Alston P (2002), Resisting the Merger and Acquisition of Human Rights by Trade Law: A Reply to Petersmann, 13 European Journal of International Law, 815–844.

Arrowsmith S (2003), Government Procurement in the WTO, Dordrecht, The Netherlands: Kluwer Law International.

Balme S (2005), The Judicialsation of Politics and the Politicisation of Judiciary in China (1978–2005), 5 Global Jurist <http://www.bepress.com/gj/frontiers/vol5/iss1/art1>.

Bhala R (2002), Enter the Dragon: An Essay on China's WTO Accession Saga, 15 American University International Law Review, 1469–1538.

Bhattasali D and et al. (eds) (2004), Impacts and Policy Implications of WTO Accession for China, China and the WTO: Accession, Policy Reform, and Poverty Reduction Strategies, 1–18, Washington, D.C.: World Bank.

Brown R C (1997), Understanding Chinese Courts and Legal Process: Law with Chinese Characteristics, The Hague; Boston: Kluwer Law International.

Burbank S B and Friedman B (eds) (2002), Judicial Independence at the Crossroads: An Interdisciplinary Approach, Thousand Oaks, California; London; New Delhi: Sage Publications.

Busch M L and Reinhardt E (2006), Three's a Crowd: Third Party and WTO Dispute Settlement, 58 World Politics, 446–477.

Cao J (2002), WTO and the Rule of Law in China, 16 Temple International and Comparative Law Journal, 379–390.

Cass D Z (2005), The Constitutionalization of the World Trade Organization, International Economic Law Series, Oxford: Oxford University Press.

Chan M K (2003), Different Roads to Home: the Retrocession of Hong Kong and Macau to Chinese Sovereignty, 12 Journal of Contemporary China, 493–518.

Chan S (1994), Taiwan's Application to the GATT: A New Urgency with the Conclusion of the Uruguay Round, 2 Indiana Journal of Global Legal Studies, 275–299.

Charnovitz S (2001), The WTO and the Rights of the Individual, 36 Intereconomics 98, reprinted in Trade Law and Global Governance, London: Cameron May,377–96

Charnovitz S (2006), Taiwan's WTO Membership and its International Implication, 1 Asian Journal of WTO and International Health Law and Policy, 401–431.

Chen A H (2000), The Interpretation of the Basic Law – Common Law and Mainland Chinese Perspectives, 30 Hong Kong Law Journal, 380–431.

Chen A H (1993), The Basic Law and the Protection of Property Rights, 23 Hong Kong Law Journal, 31–78.

Chen A H (2002), Interaction of Legal Systems in Hong Kong and Mainland (Huigui hou Hong Kong yu neidi fazhi de hudong), in Chen A H (ed), The World of Legal Theory (Fa lixue de shijie), Beijing: China University of Politics Scienceand Law Press, in Chinese.

Chen L and Gu Y (2001–2002), China's Safeguard Measures Under the New WTO Framework, 25 Fordham International Law Journal, 1169–1186.

Chen L and Zhao Y (2006), A Study on the Dispute Resolution Mechanism in Region Trade Agreements: Article 19 of CEPA (Quyu maoyi xieding zhong de zhengduan jiejue jizhi yanjiu—— jian xi CEPA di 19 tiao), in Wang G (ed), A Research on the Economic Arrangement among the Cross-Strait Four Areas (Liang an si di jingmao anpai yanjiu), 242–253, Beijing: Beijing University Press, in Chinese.

Correa C M (2007), Trade Related Aspects of Intellectual Property Rights: A Commentary, Oxford: Oxford University Press.

Cottier T (2000), Reforming the Swiss Federal Constitution: An International Lawyer's Perspective, in Butler M, et al. (eds), The Making of Modern Switzerland: 1848 – 1998, 75–96, New York: St. Martin's Press.

Cottier T (2000), Limits to the International Trade: the Constitutional Challenge, American Society of International Law Proceedings, 220–224.

Cottier T and Oesch M (2003), The Paradox of Judicial Review in International Trade Regulation: Towards a Comprehensive Framework, in Cottier T and Mavroidis P C (eds), The Role of the Judge in International Trade Regulation, 287–306, Ann Arbor, Mich: The University of Michigan Press.

Covelli N (2003), Member Intervention in World Trade Organization Dispute Settlement Proceedings After EC-Sardines: The Rules, Jurisprudence, and Controversy, 37 Journal of World Trade, 673–690.

Dam K W (2005), Cordell Hull, the Reciprocal Trade Agreement Act, and the WTO, in Petersmann E U (ed), Reforming the World Trading System: Legitimacy, Efficiency and Democratic Governance, 83–96, Oxford: Oxford University Press.

Eeckhout P (2002), The Judicial Enforcement of WTO Law in European Union: Some Further Reflections, 5 Journal of International Economic Law, 91–110.

Estanislao M L E (2000), Right of Final Adjudication in Hong Kong: Establishing Procedures of Constitutional Interpretation, 1 Asian – Pacific Law & Policy Journal 10.

Feng H (2006), The Politics of China's Accession to the World Trade Organization, London, New York: Routledge.

Francioni F (ed) (2007), The Rights of Access to Justice under Customary International Law, Access to Justice as a Human Right, 21–94, Oxford; New York: Oxford University Press.

Francois J and Wooton I (2005), Market Structure in Services and Market Access in Goods, CEPR Discussion Paper No. 5135 <http://ssrn.com/abstract=784687>.

Gao H S (2004), The Closer Economic Partnership Arrangement (CEPA) between Mainland China and Hong Kong? Legal and Economic Analyses, in Davidson P J (ed), Trading Arrangements in the Pacific Rim: ASEAN and APEC, New York: Oxford University Press <http://ssrn.com/paper=752785>.

GATT (1995), Guide to GATT Law and Practice: Analytical Index, 6th edn, Geneva: WTO.

Gertler J L (2002), Negotiating China's Protocol of Accession, in Alexandroff A S and et al. (eds), China and the Long March to Global Trade: the Accession of China to the World Trade Organization, 22–29, London; New York: Routledge.

Gervais D (2003), The TRIPS Agreements: Drafting History and Analysis, 2nd edn, London: Sweet & Maxwell.

Griller S (2000), Judicial Enforceability of WTO Agreement in European Union: Annotation to Case C–149/96 Portugal v. Council, 3 Journal of International Economic Law, 441–472.

Halverson K (2004), China's WTO Accession: Economic, Legal and Political Implications, 27 Boston College International and Comparative Law Review, 319–370.

He W (1997), Two Problems of the Administration of Justice in China (Zhongguo sifa guanli zhidu de liang ge wentí), 6 China Social Science (Zhongguo shehui kexue), 117–130, in Chinese.

He W (1999), Some Comments on the Adjudicative Committees (Guanyu shenpan weiyuanhui de ji dian pinglun), 1 Beijing University Law Review (Beida falu pinglun), 365–374, in Chinese.

Hilf M (1997), The Role of National Courts in International Trade Relations, in Petersmann E U (ed), International Trade Law and the GATT/WTO Dispute Settlement System, 559–585, London; The Hague; Boston: Kluwer Law International.

Hills M (1994), The Rule of Law and Democracy in Hong Kong – Comparative analysis of British Liberalism and Chinese Socialism, 1 E Law <http://www.murdoch.edu.au/elaw/indices/title/mhills_abstract.html>.

Howse R (2002), Human Rights in the WTO: Whose Rights, What Humanity? Comment on Petersmann, 13 European Journal of International Law, 651–659.

Howse R and Nicolaidis K (2003), Legitimacy through "Higher Law"? Why Constitutionalizing the WTO Is a Step Too Far?, in Cottier T and Mavroidis P C (eds), The Role of the Judge in International Trade Regulation, 307–348, Ann Arbor, Mich.: The University of Michigan Press.

Huang D and Wang Z (2004), Understanding Foreign Trade Law of PRC and Related International Rules (Zhonghua renmin gongheguo duiwai maoyi fa: Tiaowen jing shi ji guoji guize), Beijing: Law Press, in Chinese.

Huang D (2006), Legal Interpretation of Paragraph 242 of the Report of the Working Party on the Accession of China under the World Trade Organization Legal Framework, 40 Journal of World Trade, 137–152.

Huang T W (2002), Taiwan's Protocol 16 Special Safeguard and Anti-dumping Enforcement on Imports from China, 41 Journal of World Trade, 371–409.

Huang T W (2002), The Gathering Storm of Antidumping Enforcement in China, 36 Journal of World Trade, 255–283.

Huang T W (2003), China Launches its Safeguard Enforcement: A Critical Assessment, 37 Journal of World Trade, 329–357.

Huang T W (2007), Taiwan's Protocol 16 Special Safeguard and Anti-dumping Enforcement on Imports from China, 41 Journal of World Trade, 371–409.

Hudec R E (1993), The Role of Judicial Review in Preserving Liberal Trade Policies, in Hilf M and Petersmann E U (eds), National Constitutions and International Economic Law, 347–370, Deventer; Boston: Kluwer Law and Taxation Publishers.

Hung V M (2004), China's WTO Commitment on Independent Judicial Review: Impact on Legal and Political Reform, 52 American Journal of Contemporary Law, 77–132.

Hsieh P L (2005), Facing China: Taiwan's Status as a Separate Customs Territory in the World Trade Organization, 39 Journal of World Trade, 1195–1221.

Hsu T-L and et al. (eds) (2000), The Special State-to-State Discourse and Taiwan's National Identity (Liang guo lun yu Taiwan guojia dingwei), Taipei: Xunlin Press, in Chinese.

International Commission of Jurists (ed) (2004), International Principles on the Independence and Accountability of Judges, Lawyers and Prosecutors: A Practitioners' Guide, Geneva: International Commission of Jurists.

Jackson J H (1989), The World Trading System: Law and Policy of International Economic Relations, Cambridge, Massachusetts: The MIT Press.

Jackson J H (1998), The World Trading Organisation: Constitution and Jurisprudence, London: Royal Institute of International Affairs.

Jackson J H (2002), Sovereignty, Subsidiarity, and Separation of Powers, in Kennedy D L M and Southwick J D (eds), The Political Economy of international Trade Law: Essays in Honor of Robert E Hudec, 13–31, Cambridge: Cambridge University Press.

Jackson J H and et al.(2002), Legal Problems of International Economic Relation: Case, Materials and Texts on the National and International Regulation of Transnational Economic Regulations, 4th edn West Group, Minn: St. Paul.

Jackson J H (2003), The Impacts of China's Accession to the WTO, in Cass D Z and et al. (eds), China and the World Trading System: Entering the New Millennium, 19–30, Cambridge; New York: Cambridge University Pres.

Jackson J H (2006), Sovereignty, the WTO, and Changing Fundamentals of International Law, Cambridge: Cambridge University Press.

Jensen E G and Heller T C (eds) (2003), Beyond Common Knowledge: Empirical Approaches to the Rule of Law, Stanford: Stanford University Press.

Jordan A D (1997), Lost in the Translation: Two Legal Cultures, the Common Law Judiciary and the Basic Law of the Hong Kong Special Administrative Region, 30 Cornell International Law Journal, 335–380.

Killion M U (2003–2004), Quest for Legal Safeguards for Foreign Exporters Under China's Anti-Dumping Regime, 29 North Carolina Journal of Law & Commercial Regulation, 417–456.

Killion M U (2005), China's Amended Constitution: Quest for Liberty and Independent Judicial Review, 4 Washington University Global Studies Law Review, 43–80.

Kong Q (2002), Can the WTO Dispute Settlement Mechanism Resolve the Trade Disputes Between China and Taiwan?, 5 Journal of International Economic Law, 747–758.

Krebs J R (2000), One Country, Three Systems? Judicial Review in Macau after Ng Ka Ling, 10 Pacific Rim Law and Policy Journal, 111–146.

Lee J (2007), Socialist Rule of Law with Chinese Characteristics, 43 Issues & Studies, 115–157.
Leebron D W (1997), Implementation of the Uruguay Round Results in the United States, in Jackson J H and Sykes A O (eds), Implementing the Uruguay Round, 209–221, Oxford: Oxford University Press.
Liebman B L (2007), China's Courts: Restricted Reform, 21 Columbia Journal Asian Law, 1–44.
Lin F (2000), The Constitutional Crisis in Hong Kong – Is it Over?, 9 Pacific Rim Law and Policy Journal, 281–315.
Liu N (1989), An Ignored Source of Chinese Law: the Gazette of the Supreme People's Court, 5 Connecticut Journal of International Law, 271–316.
Liu N (1991), Legal Precedents with Chinese Characteristics: Published Cases in the Gazette of Supreme People's Court, 5 Journal of Chinese Law, 107–140.
Liu N (1997), Opinions of the Supreme People's Court: Judicial Interpretation in China, Sweet & Maxwell, Hong Kong; London: Sweet & Maxwell Asia.
Lo C-F (2010), Can There Be an Interim Agreement for Economic Integration in GATS, presented in Conference on Trade Remedy, Financial Crisis and the Challenge to the WTO, Taipei, 17–21.
Luke F M (2000), The Imminent Threat of China's Intervention in Macau's Autonomy: Using Hong Kong's Past to Secure Macau's Future, 15 American University International Law Review, 717–756.
Maduro M P (1998), We the Court. The European Court of Justice and the European Economic Constitution: A Critical Reading of Article 30 of EC Treaty, Oxford; Portland, Oregon: Hart Publishing.
Maduro M P (2002), The Constitution of the Global Market, in Snyder F (ed), Regional and Global Regulation of International Trade, 49–70, Oxford and Portland, Oregon: Hart Publishing.
Marceau G (2005), Consultations and the Panel Process in the WTO Dispute Settlement System, in Yerxa R and Wilson B (eds), Key Issues in WTO Dispute Settlement: The First Ten Years, 29–45, Cambridge: Cambridge University Press.
Mavroidis P C (2005), The General Agreement on Tariffs and Trade: A Commentary, Oxford: Oxford University Press.
Mo J S (2003), Settlement of Disputes between Mainland China and the Separate Territory of Taiwan within the WTO, 2 Chinese Journal of International Law, 145–174.
Open Society Institute (2001), Monitoring the EU Accession Process: Judicial Independence, Budapest; New York: Open Society Institute.
Ortino F and Petersmann E U (eds) (2004), The WTO Dispute Settlement System 1995–2003, London; The Hague; Boston: Kluwer Law International.
Pearsall J and et al. (eds) (2002), Concise Oxford English Dictionary, USA: Oxford University Press.
Petersmann E U (1991), Strengthening the Domestic Legal Framework of the GATT Multilateral Trade System: Possibilities and Problems of Making GATT Rules Effective in Domestic Legal System, in Petersmann E U and Hilf M (eds), The New GATT Round of Multilateral Trade Negotiations: Legal and Economic Problems, 33–113, Deventer: Kluwer Law and Taxation Publishers.
Petersmann E U (1997), The GATT/WTO Dispute Settlement System: International Law, International Organizations, and Dispute Settlement, London; The Hague; Boston: Kluwer Law International.
Petersmann E U (2006), Multi-level Judicial Trade Governance without Justice? On the Role of Domestic Courts in the WTO Legal and Dispute Settlement System, EUI Working Paper 2006/44, Italy: European University Institute.
Petersmann E U (2006), Multilevel Trade Governance in the WTO Requires Multilevel Constitutionalism, in Joerges C and Petersmann E U (eds), Constitutionalism, Multilevel Trade Governance and Social Regulation, 5–58, Oxford; Portland, Oregon: Hart Publishing.
Petersmann E U (2006), State Sovereignty, Popular Sovereignty and Individual Sovereignty: From Constitutional Nationalism to Multilevel Constitutionalism in International Economic Law?, in Shan W and et al. (eds), Redefining Sovereignty in International Economic Law, 27–60, Oxford; Portland, Oregon: Hart Publishing.
Petersmann E U, Dispute Prevention, Dispute Settlement and Justice in International Economic Law (Forthcoming).
Peng S-Y (1998), Economic Relations between Taiwan and Southeast Asia: A Review of Taiwan's "Go South" Policy, 16 Wisconsin International Law Journal, 639–660.
Pierola F (2007), Third-party Participation in WTO Dispute Settlement Proceedings for Training Purposes, 2 Global Trade and Customs Journal, 367–368.

Qiang B and et al. (2006), China: New Franchising and Direct Selling Regulations, 40 The International Lawyer: International Legal Developments in Review 2005, 547–556.
Qin J Y (2003), "WTO-plus" Obligations and Their Implications for the World Trade Organization Legal System – An Appraisal of the China Accession Protocol, 37 Journal of World Trade, 483–522.
Qin Y (1992), GATT Membership for Taiwan: An Analysis in International Law, 7 New York University Journal of International Law and Politics, 1059–1106.
Qiu B-S (2003), A Study on the Negotiation of Freedom of the Air between Taiwan and Hong Kong (Tai gang hang quan tanpan zhi yanjiu) (National Chung Hsing University, Taipei 2003), Taipei: National Chung Hsing University.
Ramos R M M (2000), The Private International Law of the New Special Administrative Region of Macau of the People's Republic of China, 60 Louisiana Law Review, 1281–1295.
Reich A (2005), The Threat of the Politicization of the WTO, 26 University of Pennsylvania Journal of International Economic Law, 779–814.
Rhode S A and Jackson J H (1999), United States law and China's WTO accession process, 2 Journal of International Economic Law, 497–510.
Sajo A (ed) (2004), Judicial Integrity, Leiden: Martinus Nijhoff Publishers.
Shaffer G (2003), Defending Interests: Public-Private Partnerships in WTO Litigation, Washington, D.C.: Brookings Institution Press.
Shaffer G (2007), "Public-Private Partnership" in WTO Dispute Settlement: the US and EU Experience, in Taniguchi Y and et al. (eds), The WTO in the Twenty-first Century: Dispute Settlement, Negotiations, and Regionalism in Asia,148–184, Cambridge: Cambridge University Press.
Slaughter A M and et al. (1998), The European Court and National Courts – Doctrine and Jurisprudence: Legal Change in its Social Context, Oxford: Hart Publishing.
Stone Sweet A (2000), Governing with Judges: Constitutional Politics in Europe, Oxford: Oxford University Press.
Strait Exchange Foundation (ed) (2001), Talks and Meeting between Koo and Wang (Gu wang huitan yu gu wang huiwu), Taipei: Strait Exchange Foundation, 441–472, in Chinese.
Sung Y-W (2005), The Emergence of Greater China: The Economic Integration of Mainland China, Taiwan and Hong Kong, New York: Palgrave Macmillan.
Sung Y-W (2006), The Evolving Role of Hong Kong as China's Middleman, in Ho L S and Ash R (eds), China, Hong Kong and the World Economy: Studies on Globalization, 152–169, New York: Palgrave Macmillan.
Tai B (2002), Is "Final" Really Final?, 32 Hong Kong Law Journal, 25–34.
Tiefer C (2001), Sino 301: How Congress can effectively review relations with China after WTO accession, 34 Cornell International Law Journal, 55–93.
Van den Berg A J (1981), The New York Arbitration Convention of 1958: Towards a Uniform Judicial Interpretation, Deventer; Boston: Kluwer Law and Taxation.
Van den Bossche P L H (1997), The European Community and the Uruguay Round Agreements, in Jackson J H and Alan O. Sykes (ed), Implementing the Uruguay Round, 23–102, Oxford: Oxford University Press.
Vermulst E (2006), The WTO Anti-Dumping Agreement: A Commentary, Oxford: Oxford University Press.
Volcansek M L (2002), Courts and Regionalism, in Snyder F (ed), Regional and Global Regulation of International Trade, 165–180, Oxford; Portland, Oregon: Hart Publishing.
Wai R (2002), Transnational Liftoff and Juridical Touchdown: the Regulatory Function of Private International Law in an Era of Globalization, 40 Columbia Journal of Transnational Law, 209–274.
Wai R (2006), Conflicts and Comity in Transnational Governance: Private International Law as Mechanism and Metaphor for Transnational Social Regulation through Plural Legal Regime, in Joerges C and Petersmann E U (eds), Constitutionalism, Multilevel Trade Governance and Social Regulation, 229–262, Oxford; Portland, Orego: Hart Publishing.
Wang Y (2005), An Analysis on the Act of State and Political Question in the Basic Law of Hong Kong and Macau (Lun gang ao jibenfa zhong de guojia xingwei he zhengzhi wenti), 30 Journal of Macau Studies (Aomrn yanjiu), 7–27.

Wang Z (2002), The Relationship between Central Authority and the Special Administrative Regions: An Analysis of Legal Structure (Zhongyang yu tebie xingzhengqu guanxi: yi zhong fazhi jiegou de jiexi), Beijing: Tsinghua University Press, in Chinese.

Wang Z (2004), Constitutional Review in China (Zhongguo weixian shencha zhidu), Beijing: China University of Politic Science and Law Press, in Chinese.

Wang Z and Yu M (2006), China Foreign Trade Law (Zhongguo waimao fa), Wuchang: Wuhan University Press, in Chinese.

Wang W (2004), Regional Integration: Comparative Experiences: A Lawful Free Trade Agreement under "One Country, Two Customs Territories, 10 Law and Business Review of the America, 647–666.

Winkler A and Zagel J (1995), The Independence of Judges, 46 Mercer Law Review, 795–834.

WTO (2003), Guide to WTO Law and Practice: Analytical Index,1st edn, Geneva: WTO Publications.

WTO (2003), Protocol on the Accession of the Separate Customs Territory of Taiwan, Penghu, Kinmen and Matsu, Cambridge: Cambridge University Press.

Wu C-H (2008), How Does TRIPS Transform Chinese Administrative Law?, 8 Global Jurist, Article 6 <http://www.bepress.com/gj/vol8/iss1/art6>.

Yang G and Cheng J (2001), The Process of China's Accession to the WTO, 4 Journal of International Economic Law 297–328.

Yang L (2004), Some Issues on China's Judicial Review, Justice in China (Zhongguo sifa shencha zhidu xu guanzhu de ji ge wenti), 68–70. <http://www.moj.gov.cn/zgsfzz/2004-07/07/content_1 14771.htm>, in Chinese.

Yenkong N H (2004), Third Party Rights and the Concept of Legal Interest in World Trade Organization Dispute Settlement: Extending Participatory Rights to Enforcement Rights, 38 Journal of World Trade, 757–772.

Zhou L (2003), WTO Rules and Theoretical Innovation of Chinese Economic Law (WTO guize yu zhongguo jingji fa lilun chuangxin), Beijing: China University of Political Science and Law Press, in Chinese.

Zhu S (1999), Examination and Reflection on the Adjudicative Committee in Chinese Local Courts (Jiceng shenpan weiyuanhui zhidu de kaocha ji sikao), 1 Beijing University Law Review, 320–344, in Chinese.

Zou K (2006), China's Legal Reform, Leiden, Boston: Martinus Nijhoff Publishers.

Official Documents and Reports

GATT (15 September 1947), Second Session of the Preparatory Committee of the United Nations Conference on Trade and Employment – Report of the Ad Hoc Sub-Committee of the Tariff Agreement Committee on Paragraph 3 of Article XXIV, E/PC/T198 <http://www.wto.org/gatt _docs/English/ SULPDF/92290253.pdf>.

United States Congress House (2001), US-China Bilateral Trade Agreement and the Accession of China to the WTO: Hearing before the Committee on Ways and Means, House of Representatives, One Hundred Sixth Congress, Second Session, 16 February 2000, Washington: US GPO.

WTO (12 August 2008), Trade Policy Review Report on People's Republic of China, Secretariat Report, WT/TPR/S/199/rev.1.

Speeches, News, Press Release, Electronic Resource

AFP (19 July 2008), Hong Kong, Taiwan Leaders Agree to Strengthen Economic Ties <http://ph.news .yahoo.com/afp/20080718/tbs-hongkong-taiwan-politics-economy-710a28b.html>.

Xue J (2002), 'The Application of the WTO Agreement in China (WTO xieding zai zhongguo guonei de shiyong)'<http://www.wtolaw.gov.cn/display/displayInfo.asp?IID=200207071511263073> in Chinese.

China Post News Staff (10 January 2009), China Asked to Boost direct Flights for Lunar New Year Holiday', Taipei: China Post <http://www.chinapost.com.tw/taiwan/china-taiwan-relations/ 2009/01/10/191357/China-asked.htm>.

General Chamber of Commerce of Hong Kong, Chamber's Question on CEPA: A Preliminary Update <http://www.chamber.org.hk/wto/content/cepa_papers_rta_main.asp>, in Chinese.

Kuo S-L (19 January 2009), Gravel Shippers to Stage Protest' Taipei News, Taipei <http://www.taipeitimes.com/News/taiwan/archives/2009/01/19/ 2003434117>.

Reuters (31 January 2008), UPDATE 1-Antigua Seeks WTO Arbitration in US Gambling Dispute <http://uk.reuters.com/article/mediaNews/idUKL3174965820080 131>.

Tseng and Wu (17 July 2010), ECFA Should Benefit Human Rights, Taipei: Taipei Times <http://www.taipeitimes.com/News/editorials/archives/2010/07/17/2003478124>.

WTO (2001), China's accession to the WTO and its relationship to the Chinese Taipei's accession and to Hong Kong, China and Macau, China <http://www.wto.org/english/thewto_e/acc_e/chinabknot_feb01.doc>.

INDEX

www.ingramcontent.com/pod-product-compliance
Lightning Source LLC
LaVergne TN
LVHW020651300926
849161LV00004B/896
* 9 7 8 9 0 0 4 2 0 8 9 8 8 *